The Life and Times of Francis Cabot Lowell, 1775–1817

The Life and Times of
Francis Cabot Lowell,
1775–1817

Chaim M. Rosenberg

LEXINGTON BOOKS

A division of
ROWMAN & LITTLEFIELD PUBLISHERS, INC.
Lanham • Boulder • New York • Toronto • Plymouth, UK

Published by Lexington Books
A division of Rowman & Littlefield Publishers, Inc.
A wholly owned subsidiary of The Rowman & Littlefield Publishing Group, Inc.
4501 Forbes Boulevard, Suite 200, Lanham, Maryland 20706
www.lexingtonbooks.com

Estover Road, Plymouth PL6 7PY, United Kingdom

British Library Cataloguing in Publication Information Available

Library of Congress Cataloging-in-Publication Data

Rosenberg, Chaim M.
  The life and times of Francis Cabot Lowell, 1775–1817 / Chaim M. Rosenberg.
    p. cm.
  Includes bibliographical references and index.
  ISBN 978-0-7391-4683-5 (cloth : alk. paper) — ISBN 978-0-7391-4685-9
(electronic)
  1. Lowell, Francis Cabot, 1775–1817. 2. Industrialists—Massachusetts—
Biography. 3. Textile industry—Massachusetts—History. 4. Industrial
Revolution—United States. I. Title.
  HD9730.L69R67 2011
  338.7'67721092—dc22
  [B]   2010037466

Printed in the United States of America

Contents

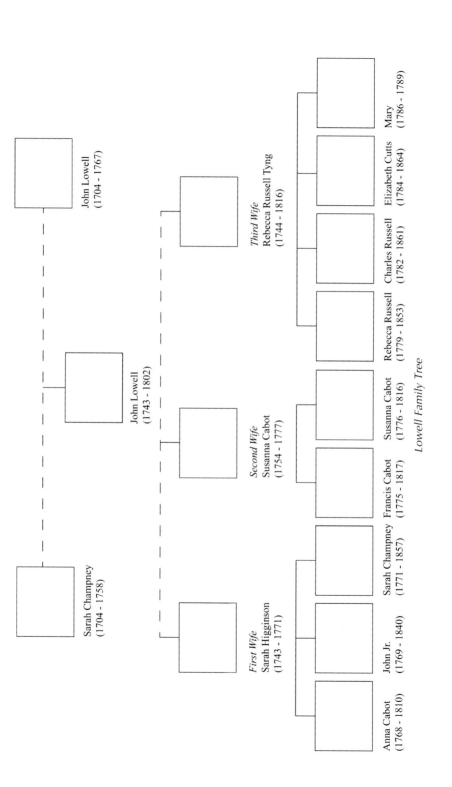

John Lowell
(1704 - 1767)

Sarah Champney
(1704 - 1758)

John Lowell
(1743 - 1802)

First Wife
Sarah Higginson
(1743 - 1771)

Second Wife
Susanna Cabot
(1754 - 1777)

Third Wife
Rebecca Russell Tyng
(1744 - 1816)

Anna Cabot
(1768 - 1810)

John Jr.
(1769 - 1840)

Sarah Champney
(1771 - 1857)

Francis Cabot
(1775 - 1817)

Susanna Cabot
(1776 - 1816)

Rebecca Russell
(1779 - 1853)

Charles Russell
(1782 - 1861)

Elizabeth Cutts
(1784 - 1864)

Mary
(1786 - 1789)

Lowell Family Tree

Notable Lowell Descendants

John Amory Lowell (1798–1881), son of John Lowell Jr., industrialist

John Lowell Jr. (1798–1836), son of Francis Cabot Lowell, founder Lowell Institute

James Russell Lowell (1819–1891), son of Charles Russell Lowell, poet

Charles Russell Lowell (1835–1864), Union general, killed at Battle of Cedar Creek

Edward Jackson Lowell (1845–1894), historian

Abbott Lawrence Lowell (1856–1943), president of Harvard University

Percival Lowell (1855–1916), astronomer, founder of Lowell Observatory

John Lowell V (1824–1897), judge, U.S. Court of Appeals

Amy Lowell (1874–1925), writer

Francis Cabot Lowell (1855–1911), judge, U.S. Court of Appeals; author

Guy Lowell (1870–1927), architect of the Museum of Fine Arts, Boston

John Lowell Gardner (1837–1898), married to Isabella Stewart Gardner

Ralph Lowell (1890–1973), banker, founder of WGBH-FM and TV

Acknowledgments

The Commonwealth of Massachusetts into the twenty-first century is full of the skeletons of its great industrial age. Along the banks of the Charles River at Waltham still stands the Boston Manufacturing Company founded by Francis Cabot Lowell. Along the Merrimack River are the mighty mills of Lowell and Lawrence. Close to the centers of towns are the remains of the shoe, spade, kitchen range, loom, gun, bicycle and piano factories, so sited to be near the railroads that brought in the coal to generate steam power. Almost every town and city in Massachusetts was once home to large factories. The first of these factories was built at the beginning of the nineteenth century as the United States shifted from rural to urban and from farming to manufacturing. The growth of the factories attracted millions of immigrants hoping for their piece of the American dream. By the middle of the twentieth century the Massachusetts industrial revolution was played out.

My interest in the industrialization of New England began years ago when working as a physician in a number of the old industrial towns. No smoke came forth from the smokestacks. The large redbrick buildings were silent where once machines clanked and motors spun. I looked to the beginnings of all this effort and all roads led to one man—Francis Cabot Lowell. He had the vision to start a cotton textile factory. His timing was impeccable, but he died at age forty-two before he could see the full flower of his creation. He chose good men and they carried forward his dream, first by creating the great industrial city of Lowell, named in his honor, and then carrying the idea to all parts of the nation.

Francis Cabot Lowell died nearly two hundred years ago. His is a well-known name and stories about his life are often written, filled with inaccuracies. For whatever reason, no biography on his life has ever been published. I took it upon myself to research the man and his times, read his letters and breathe life into his tomb. Apart from two years touring Great Britain and short trips to France, Washington, DC, New York and Philadelphia, Francis Cabot Lowell, like a good Yankee, lived his whole life in and around Boston. He was born in Newburyport, raised in Boston and educated at Phillips Academy, Andover, and Harvard College. He lived, worked and was buried in Boston.

Reading his spider-like script, written with quill on rag paper, has been tiring to my fading eyes. Otherwise it has been a pleasure to read his papers at the Massachusetts Historical Society. I spent many hours in the reading room at the Society reading the correspondence of Francis Cabot Lowell, his wife Hannah and his brothers John Jr. and Charles, as well as other relatives and business contacts. Hanging on a wall of the reading room is the portrait of James Sullivan (1744–1808), the first president of the Society and the lead prosecutor of the Jason Fairbanks trial. On another wall is a portrait of the Reverend Charles Lowell, a secretary of the Society and brother to Francis. The "presence" of these worthy gentlemen encouraged me to be careful and accurate in reading and preserving the two-centuries-old correspondence. I read sections of his father's papers kept at the Houghton Library, Harvard University, visited his gravesite, toured the Longfellow House where his sister Sarah lived, read his brother's diaries at the Harvard Divinity School, walked along the harbor front where his India Wharf once stood and toured the Boston Manufacturing Company in Waltham. Every one of these sites is less than an hour's drive from my home.

My research has taken me to the Massachusetts Historical Society, Boston Public Library, the libraries of Newton, Brookline and Wellesley, Harvard Divinity School, and the Longfellow House. The assistance I received from curators and librarians was been simply wonderful. Also, I would like to thank members of my fall 2009 class at Bolli, Brandeis University, who read the manuscript and offered me many useful suggestions. The readers were Steve Baron, Judy Cohen, Marilyn Stein, Sheila Lesnick, Irving Lessing, Muriel Kanoff, Nathan Rome, Bonnie Albert and Bonnie Newman. I would like to record by gratitude to members of my spring 2010 class at the University of Massachusetts, Boston, who read sections of the manuscript. They are Kathleen McGovern, Barbara Trusello, Jay Landers, Helaine Simmonds, Eileen Kiley, Susan Gilmore, Paula Sindone, Mary Turley, Tom Fitzgibbon, Ann Walsh and Allen Scherr.

Dan Yaeger, director of the Charles River Museum of Industry and Innovation, housed in Waltham in the very building of Francis Cabot Lowell's 1814 cotton mill, honored me by reading and correcting my chapter on the Boston Manufacturing Company.

It has been a privilege to read the letters of Francis Cabot Lowell, his wife, children and other members of the Lowell family. Even though the Lowells only talk to the Cabots, I have had the temerity to examine their lives, particularly that of Francis Cabot, the man who brought the Industrial Revolution to the United States and helped move the nation from farming, fishing and trading to manufacturing.

Glynis Swanepoel's assistance was invaluable, as she formatted the first draft of the manuscript. My daughter Linda Reed spent many hours editing and formatting the final draft.

Above all, I thank my wife Dawn, who has been my great support and has, for too long a time, allowed Francis Cabot Lowell and his family to enter our home. Dawn read and reread every word I wrote.

Introduction:
The New
Industrial System

The center of interest in Massachusetts shifts from wharf to waterfall, by 1840 she becomes predominantly a manufacturing state.

Samuel Eliot Morison, 1921

Mr. Lowell is unquestionably entitled to the credit of being the first person who arranged all the processes of the conversion of cotton to cloth, within the walls of the same building. It was Mr. Lowell who was the informing soul, which gave direction and form to the whole proceeding.

A tribute by Nathan Appleton to the memory of Francis Cabot Lowell

[The mill built at Waltham in 1814] was the only mill, not simply in the United States, but in the world, where the cotton was taken in at one end and turned out finished cloth at the other. The whole of that idea was Mr. Lowell's.

From the address by John Amory Lowell
on the semi-centennial celebration of
the city of Lowell, 1876

[Francis Cabot Lowell and his partners in the Boston Manufacturing Company] were men of vision [and] the fathers of American big business.

Caroline F. Ware, 1966

In 1810, Francis Cabot Lowell and his family spent several months in Edinburgh at the start of their two-year tour of Great Britain. During that time he reflected on his career as a merchant sending his cargoes from Boston laden with lumber, dried fish, rum, flour and grains in return for

1

Francis Cabot Lowell (1775–1817): This black-and-white silhouette of Francis Cabot Lowell is his only known likeness to have survived, circa 1798, when Francis and Hannah were married. (Francis C. Lowell, "From a Silhouette loaned by Francis C. Lowell, Esq., of Boston," page 175, The Bay State Monthly *article "The Cotton Industry in New England," by George Rich, New England Magazine Corporation, Typography by* New England Magazine, *Boston. Massachusetts. Presswork by Potter & Potter, Boston, Massachusetts.* The New England Magazine. *Volume III. September 1890–February 1891.)*

Hannah Jackson Lowell: Black-and-white silhouette of Hannah Jackson Lowell, circa 1798, around the time of her marriage to Francis Cabot Lowell. (Hannah Jackson [Mrs. Francis C. Lowell], "From a silhouette in possession of Mrs. S. T. Morse," A Memoir of Dr. James Jackson, *by James Jackson Putnam [Boston and New York: Houghton Mifflin, The Riverside Press, Cambridge, 1906], 78.)*

tea, silks and chinaware from Canton, textiles from Calcutta and wines from Bordeaux. To enlarge his fortune he bought a rum distillery, dabbled in real estate, constructed the India Wharf and speculated in forestlands. His business survived the Embargo Act of 1807 that forced many other merchants into bankruptcy. His brothers, John Jr. and Charles, had toured Europe a few years earlier and enthralled Francis with their descriptions of the places and the people they had seen. Now it was his turn to enjoy at his leisure the delights of Europe. On his return to Boston, he planned to buy a country estate and become, like John Jr., a gentleman farmer. His three sons, would, of course, follow his path and enter Harvard College.

But Francis lacked an eye for the British traditions and history, the beauties of the countryside, the elegance of the city parks or the delights of the theater and the opera. Instead, what caught his attention were the textile factories that were generating great wealth for Great Britain. Locked in a titanic battle against France, Great Britain commanded the seas while Napoleon ruled the lands of the Continent. Britain was able to support the great cost of the war through its wealth acquired from the Industrial Revolution. The tasks that for centuries were done at home and by hand were now mass-produced by machines in factories.

Great Britain's industrial might began with the textile industry using ingenious machinery for spinning cotton invented by James Hargreaves, Richard Arkwright and Samuel Crompton. The most remarkable of the new textile machines was the power loom patented in 1785 by Edmund Cartwright. The general introduction of the Cartwright loom, however, was delayed by some twenty years following the hostility of the workers who smashed his machines and burned down the factory. By the time Francis Cabot Lowell was visiting Great Britain, the Cartwright power loom, much modified and improved, was finally entering the mills to replace weaving by hand.

Moving from leisurely tourist to visionary entrepreneur, Francis Cabot Lowell fashioned in his mind the bold idea of bringing the industrial revolution to America, starting with the manufacture of textiles. Visiting cotton mills in Scotland and England, he questioned the managers and examined the machines. Because Britain forbade the export of even drawings of its textile machinery, he kept secret the true motives of his curiosity. Lowell committed to memory the details of his industrial espionage, especially the workings of the power loom. Using his excellent mathematical skills and deep experience in business, he calculated the cost of setting up a large factory in America, designing and constructing the machines, hiring the workers to produce textiles, buying Southern cotton and using the power of American rivers. He concluded that in America he could make cloth as good as, and cheaper than, British imports.

Nathan Appleton visited Francis Cabot Lowell in Edinburgh in 1811. They were both Boston merchants whose fortunes were built on overseas trade. Lowell shared with Appleton his plan to create a cotton textile industry in America. "Whilst in Edinburgh," Appleton recalled, "I saw a good deal of Francis C. Lowell Esq., who was there with his family. We had a good deal of conversation upon the subject of cotton manufacture; he told me that he had determined before he returned to make himself fully acquainted with the subject, with the view of the introduction of it at home. I urged him to do so, with the understanding that I would be ready to co-operate with him in such an undertaking."

Upon his return to America, Lowell prepared drawings of the machinery, developed a business plan for his great venture and gained the support of his brothers-in-law, Charles, James and Patrick Tracy Jackson. Having incorporated the Boston Manufacturing Company, Francis Cabot Lowell together with Patrick Tracy Jackson, in 1813, visited Nathan Appleton at the Boston Exchange to tell him they were ready to build their textile factory. Jackson agreed to give up all other business commitments and devote himself fully to the success of the mill. Francis Cabot Lowell and his brothers-in-law agreed to put up most of the money and asked Appleton to buy stock worth $10,000. Appleton was skeptical that the plan could work but agreed to put up $5,000 "in order to see the experiment fairly tried."

With Appleton on board, Lowell and Jackson set about interesting other merchants in investing in the venture. They soon raised $100,000 of the $400,000 needed to buy land, build a factory and prepare a constant water flow by building a storage dam upriver. Lowell hired Paul Moody, a gifted mechanic, to construct and install the machines in the factory at a site along the Charles River at Waltham, Massachusetts. What machines they could not find to buy, they made themselves. Lowell spent weeks refining his power loom and was reluctant to show it off until he and Moody were certain that it was working properly. At length they invited Nathan Appleton to see the loom in operation. "I well recollect the state of admiration and satisfaction," recalled Appleton, "with which we sat by the hour, watching the beautiful movement of this new and wonderful machine."

Francis Cabot Lowell possessed the mind of a scientist. More than a decade earlier he spent months experimenting with ways to improve the process of distilling rum. He showed the same determination and persistence developing his loom. Lowell did not merely copy the power loom he saw in Great Britain but designed, built and patented an improved version. The power loom designed by Lowell used a crank motion in the spinning process with a novel double speeder that required the most careful mathematical calculations to make it work.

Lowell and Moody traveled to Taunton, Massachusetts, to buy the winding machines invented by Silas Shepherd. After agreeing on the cost per item, Lowell asked for a price reduction for a bulk order. The haughty Mr. Shepherd insisted on the full price, saying, "You must have them. You cannot do without them." Moody, who had already seen a way to improve on Mr. Shepherd's design, said, "I am just thinking that I can spin the cops direct upon the bobbin." "You be hanged," said Mr. Shepherd. "Well, I accept your offer." "No," responded Mr. Lowell. "It is too late."

Francis Cabot Lowell had witnessed the social upheaval in Great Britain caused by the Industrial Revolution and the Luddite rebellion during which workers smashed the machines that had degraded their work and their worth as human beings. He was determined to avoid such chaos in his Waltham factory where he "was especially devoted to arrangements for the moral character of the operatives employed." Lowell recruited young women from farming families, well educated, physically healthy and eager to earn money. The women, who worked long hours, were fed and housed at the company's expense in boarding houses "under the charge of respectable women, with every provision for religious worship. Under these circumstances, the daughters of respectable farmers were readily induced to come into these mills for a temporary period." Known as the Waltham mill girls, they worked hard, saved their money and after a few years left the mill to marry or return to the farm.

Francis Cabot Lowell was by no means the only or even the first American merchant-capitalist fired up by the idea of manufacturing cotton textiles on home soil. The Beverly Cotton Manufactory, financed by the Cabot brothers, and the Pawtucket mills, run by Samuel Slater, were the pioneers, followed by other small cotton mills from Massachusetts to Maryland, producing cotton thread and yarn for home weaving. Other inventors filed patents for their power looms. But it was Francis Cabot Lowell, with his Boston Manufacturing Company, who developed the system of processing raw cotton into finished textiles, all under one roof, and introduced the modern factory to the United States. The Waltham-Lowell system, comprising a well-capitalized company with gifted management, a thorough business plan, a modern plant using efficient machinery, a healthy and productive workforce housed and fed at the company's expense, a reliable source of cheap power and an effective sales network, was the necessary ingredient for its success.

During 1817, the president of the United States, James Monroe, embarked on a triumphal tour of the eastern and northern states. Enthusiastic crowds, marching bands and interminable speeches greeted him at every stop. Arriving at the beginning of July 1817, Monroe spent several days in Boston and its environs. During his stay the president "visited the most important manufactories in the town and in the neighborhoods." Monroe told the people that his first concern was the defense of the nation "but his next was devoted to the various manufacturing establishments. On this subject he had expressed not only his delight, but his surprize at their extent and improvement. He mentioned at Waltham that a few such establishments as he there saw, would be sufficient to supply the United States with cotton fabric."[1] It is not known whether Francis Cabot Lowell was on hand to meet the fifth president of the United States and show him the workings of the Boston Manufacturing Company. At that time, Lowell was ill and about to set out for a vacation to the Niagara Falls.

Henry Clay represented Kentucky in the House of Representatives and later in the U.S. Senate and was, with Daniel Webster and John C. Calhoun, a member of the "Immortal Trio." In 1820, Clay visited Waltham to see firsthand the achievements of the Boston Manufacturing Company, where he met with Patrick Tracy Jackson and Paul Moody. In a speech before the House of Representatives, April 26, 1820, Henry Clay defended the use of tariffs to protect home industry and presented Waltham as a shining example of American entrepreneurship. The Boston Manufacturing Company, he told the House, "has the advantage of a fine water situation, a manager of excellent information, enthusiastically devoted to its success, a machinist of the most inventive genius, who is constantly making some new improvement and who has carried the water loom to a degree of perfection which it has not attained in England—to such perfection as to reduce the cost of weaving a yard of cloth adapting to shirting to less than a cent—while it is abundantly supplied with capital by several capitalists in Boston. These gentlemen have the most extensive correspondence with all parts of the United States. Owing to this extraordinary combination of favorable circumstances the Waltham establishment is doing pretty well."[2]

Francis Cabot Lowell died in 1817. His close associates kept his vision alive and founded America's first industrial city, named Lowell in his honor. During their early years, the Lowell mills had high profits and the shares were selling 40 percent over par. But the "commercial Utopia" described by Anthony Trollope was not to last. After 1840, the proud, healthy and educated Yankee mill girls were fast being replaced by waves of impoverished immigrants from Ireland, England, French-speaking Canada and Central Europe. By 1850, the city of Lowell had had thirty-four large mills engaged in the production of cotton and woolen goods, employing 7,524 females and 2,427 males. Together the factories had 305,004 spindles and 19,369 power looms. A half-century after the death of Francis Cabot Lowell, the city that bears his name was home to 38,376 people, with forty-five school buildings and twenty-two churches. Most of the people of Lowell of working age were employed in the textile mills, using eight hundred thousand pounds of cotton and one hundred thousand pounds of wool each week. The Boston & Lowell Railroad carried in the raw cotton, wool and the coal from the port of Boston and took back thousands of yards of finished textiles. Called the City of Spindles or the Manchester of America, Lowell grew to be the largest city in Massachusetts after Boston. The one hundred acres of farmland on which the town of Lowell was established were bought in 1819–1822 at $15 an acre. Within a few years, the success of the enterprise raised the value of the land to $15,000 an acre—a one-thousand-fold increase.

The year 1876 was the centennial of the United States of America and the semi-centennial of the incorporation of Lowell, America's first industrial city. March 1 was a day of celebration for the proud city with John Amory Lowell invited to speak. The city could not have chosen a more fitting man for the occasion. The seventy-eight-year-old gentleman was nephew and son-in-law to the late Francis Cabot Lowell and, in his youth, his best friend was John Lowell Jr., son of Francis Cabot Lowell. John Amory Lowell knew the town of Lowell from its infancy and saw it grow into an industrial powerhouse, based on cotton textiles.

Speaking in the Huntington Hall, which was packed with town dignitaries and prominent guests, John Amory Lowell paid tribute to his uncle, dead nearly sixty years. Francis Cabot Lowell was among the first to realize that the future of the United States of America lay in manufacturing. During his visits to the textile factories of Great Britain, Francis understood the importance of the power loom but was not able to procure a set of the detailed plans for its construction. John Amory Lowell explained that even though Francis Cabot Lowell "could not get any description of it [he] determined that the thing could be done, and said it should be done. That was the nature of the man. It was necessary, therefore to re-invent it. It was necessary, in fact, to re-invent a great part of the machinery, because they conceived the bold idea of carrying on every process from the first coming in of the cotton to the going out of the finished cloth in one mill—a thing which had never been done before. It was therefore necessary that all the machinery should be adapted to that purpose."

While Francis Cabot Lowell was perfecting his power loom, continued John Amory Lowell, "Mr. Paul Moody had been at work upon the rest of the machinery: the throstle-spindle; the double-speeder; the drawing-frame—all these machines were re-invented by Mr. Moody. In inventing the double-speeder, which was quite a different machine from the English fly-frame, he was obliged to introduce some motion, which required accurate mathematical calculations. The double-cone of that instrument affected the winding of the spools directly, without the intervention of any machine, it became necessary that it should be an exactly calculated motion. The calculations for this motion were made by Mr. Lowell entirely."[3]

Francis Cabot Lowell came from one of the leading families of Massachusetts and was educated at Harvard. Unlike his father-in-law, who commissioned several portraits of himself by leading artists, Francis Cabot Lowell was not a vain man. There exists today no known likeness of him other than a single silhouette of his profile in black, done probably in his twenties. Francis had a full head of hair, a sharp nose and thin lips. He was described as sickly, somewhat nervous, but kind, honest, willing to help others and a man of his word. From his youth he was accustomed to wealth but determined to make his own way in life. Despite his elevated social position and wealth he married Hannah Jackson, who lacked a fortune of her own. Lowell was eager to leave his mark in the annals of progress. His older brother John had strong political views, while his younger brother Charles found expression through religion. Francis Cabot Lowell, by contrast, rarely expressed political or religious opinions. Rather, he was a practical man of business who carefully weighed the risks and the potential benefits before taking action. He had a narrow range of interests but focused intently on those issues that captured his attention. In his late thirties, Francis Cabot Lowell decided against the life of a country gentleman and instead chose to devote the remaining years of his short life to his experiments and to the success of his factory. His family and fellow merchants discouraged his efforts to set up a cotton mill and strongly opposed his advocacy of tariffs to protect the young industries of America.

Francis Cabot Lowell is unfairly remembered as the man who stole the design of the British power loom and copied the machine when he returned to America. Edmund Cartwright patented his loom in 1785, only to see his device destroyed by angry workers. Greatly discouraged and nearly bankrupt, Cartwright gave up textile manufacturing. The beginning of the nineteenth century proved a more favorable time for the introduction of power machinery in weaving cotton thread. British manufacturers adapted Cartwright's invention to their own purposes, making great modifications and improvements.[4] Francis Cabot Lowell carried the power loom to the next stage of development. After months of calculations, designing and building, Francis Cabot Lowell was ready to test his power loom in the Waltham factory, and it worked.

Francis Cabot Lowell was fortunate in his timing. He was born at the start of the Revolutionary War and grew up during a time of peace. He began his career as a merchant just as American trade with the outside world was expanding. He visited Great Britain when the power loom was being widely introduced into the mills. He started manufacturing textiles at home when imports from Great Britain and India were sharply reduced. His Boston Manufacturing Company, founded in 1814, was the start of the American industrial revolution and became the model for the nineteenth-century American factory. This shift, from farm to factory, from manpower to waterpower, and from craftsman-ship to mass production, was an event in American history as profound as the automobile age in the early twentieth century and the digital age of our times.

1

✝

Occasionem Cognosce (Know the Opportunity): Motto of the Lowell Family

The family probably began in Normandy as Lowle and settled in the west of England in the eleventh century during the reign of William the Conqueror. The family bore heraldic arms showing a stag's head above three arrows pointing down and gripped by the right hand. Percival Lowle, born in 1571, hailed from Somersetshire before moving as a young man to the town of Bristol, before it become a major port of call in the slave trade. Percival "engaged in merchandising, at wholesale, chiefly of imported wares, carrying the firm name of Percival Lowle & Co." In the year 1639, and in his sixty-eighth year of life, Percival, a man of substantial means, elected to leave England for good and immigrate to the New World. Accompanying him on the nine-week voyage on the *Jonathan* to Boston were his wife Rebecca; son John, married to Mary Gooch, and their four children; son Richard, married to Margaret, with two children; and daughter Joanna, married to John Oliver. Included in Percival Lowle's party to the New World were Richard Dale, apprentice; William Gerrish, merchant; and Anthony Somerby, clerk. There were seventeen people in all.[1]

Arriving in June, Percival Lowle and his party presented themselves to his friend John Winthrop, governor of the Massachusetts Bay Colony, who urged them to settle in the village of Newberry near the mouth of the Merrimack River, where Winthrop was sending solid families as a bulwark against French expansion. Newberry (later known as Newbury) was first settled and incorporated in the year 1635 when the Reverend Thomas Parker and others originally from Wiltshire, England, moved from Ipswich to occupy the land where once Pawtucket Indians fished, hunted and farmed. Cattle were brought by ship from England. Two hundred acres were given to each man who paid £50, and fifty acres to the settlers who paid their own way from England. The governor encouraged wealthy folk to settle in Newbury, allowing Richard Dummer to acquire 1,080 acres, Henry Sewell 630 acres, and others to acquire farms of four hundred to six hundred acres.

Fearing an attack by Indians, the men folk of Newbury were divided into four equal companies and encouraged to carry their arms, even on Sunday to church. Farmers and their indentured servants were engaged in clearing trees and getting the land ready for plowing and planting. Francis Plummer opened his tavern in 1635; the first mill for grinding corn started in 1636, and the first store opened its doors soon after. Nicholas Easton was the first tanner in the village, but was soon banished from Massachusetts and moved to Rhode Island, where he became the governor of the colony. The tradition of fine silverwork began. The town voted to construct the first meeting house and the first schoolhouse. Boat building, weaving, tanning and shoemaking were the early cottage industries. Mary Brown, daughter of Thomas Brown, was the first child born in Newbury. By the time Percival Lowle and his party arrived, the community of Newbury already had a settled feel and was home to one hundred families.

Percival Lowle's eldest son John served briefly as town clerk, followed by Anthony Somerby, who served next as the town's schoolmaster. The first of the American Lowles was Joseph, born in Newbury on November 28, 1639. After him came Benjamin (1642), Thomas (1644), Elizabeth (1646) and many others. Each of Percival's children spawned numerous descendants. Percival Lowle lived another twenty-five years and died in Newbury in the year 1664, aged ninety-three.

In the study of the life of Francis Cabot Lowell, we will follow the progeny of Percival Lowle's eldest son, John Lowle. John lost his wife Mary after childbirth the year they came to Newbury, leaving him to care for five children. He married Elizabeth Goodale, who gave him five more children, but in 1647 John, too, was dead, aged fifty-two. In his last will and testament he bequeathed half his property and £20 in cash to his wife, and the other half he divided equally among his children. John Lowle II (1629–1694) married Naomi Torrey, who bore him eleven children, among them Ebenezer (1675–1717). Ebenezer married Elizabeth Shailer, who bore him six children, among them John, who was the first in his family to attend college.

Newbury town records show the spelling of the family name as Lovell, Loel, Louel and even Lowhill. It was the Reverend John Lowell, grandfather to Francis Cabot Lowell, who finally fixed the spelling of the family name "that most appealed to his taste and fancy, and we must say that this selection speaks well of his taste."

THE GRANDFATHER OF
FRANCIS CABOT LOWELL

John Lowell was born on March 10, 1704, in Boston, where his father was a merchant. He was a serious and precocious child, who entered Harvard College as "a mere boy" of thirteen, and he was the first of many Lowells to attend Harvard. At Harvard in 1721 young John, together with his close friends Isaac Greenwood and Ebenezer Pemberton, issued a weekly periodical called *Telltale*, a critical and sometimes sarcastic view of student life, but "decidedly dry reading." One article, published on September 9, 1721, bore the elevated title "Criticism on the Conversation & Behaviour of Schollars to Promote the Right Reasoning & Good Manner." The earliest student periodical in America, *Telltale* was given to sermonizing and improving behavior, as well as a sophomoric delight in showing off knowledge of Greek and Latin. Most of the fourteen students involved with John Lowell in the writing of the journal and in joining the Spy Club became ministers upon graduating from Harvard, including Ebenezer Pemberton, who was one of the founders of New Jersey College, later called Princeton University. A notable exception to the donning of ecclesiastical robes was the brilliant Isaac Greenwood, chosen in his mid-twenties as the first Hollis Professor of Mathematics at Harvard.[2]

John Lowell was awarded a bachelor of arts degree from Harvard at the tender age of seventeen years. His Harvard graduating class of 1721 comprised thirty-seven men, among them John Adams, Nathaniel Hancock, Oliver Peabody and Joseph Champney, brother of Sarah Champney, John's future wife. John Lowell placed last in his class at Harvard. After obtaining his degree, John continued his religious studies at Harvard, was granted a master of arts degree at age twenty-one, and was ordained a minister the following year. In 1725, he married Sarah, who bore him two children, of whom one died in infancy.

In 1726, John was appointed minister to the Third Church of Newbury and returned to the town of his American forebears. The Reverend John Lowell remained with the church until his death forty-two years later. He was a "very scholarly man" who read widely in English, as well as Greek, Latin and French. He was awarded the salary of £130 a year and given £200 to buy and furnish a home. John Lowell bought a house on Temple Street, with an entrance from State Street. He was careful with his money and invested in property in Newbury.

Tolerant and liberal during his college years, the Reverend Lowell became a "very decided Congregationalist" who grew alarmed by "the advances, which Episcopany was making within the bounds of his own parish." In his forties he took up the cause of the Great Awakening, a revivalist movement aimed at bringing "into the Kingdom of God vast numbers of careless and sinful souls," but pulled back from the frenzy that gripped his flock at the height of the Awakening. He was an intellectual man whose sermons were "earnest but never vehement or excited [and] rather polished than pungent." His wife Sarah died in 1756 and two years later, the Reverend Lowell married the elderly Elizabeth Whipple, the widow of the Reverend Joseph Whipple.

THE TOWN OF NEWBURY

The town expanded steadily along the Merrimack River during the forty-two years that John Lowell served his congregation. Many of the wealthy in the town owned slaves; a census taken in 1755 listed fifty slaves, "negroes and Indians," of whom thirty-four were male and sixteen female. In 1764 the commercial heart of Newbury split off to form the town of Newburyport, and the Reverend John Lowell's Third Church was renamed the First Church of Newburyport. Occupied by merchants, traders, lawyers, doctors and apothecaries, Newburyport, comprising only 647 acres "on the water side," was the smallest town in size in Massachusetts. Still, it had 357 dwellings, including grand houses along High Street, many shops (including three selling English goods), three shipyards, a cordage factory and a comb factory. Fishing boats daily returned with their catch. Ships from Newburyport sailed to Barbados and Jamaica as well as to the French sugar islands laden with dried fish, farm products and lumber. The ships returned with sugar and molasses for the rum distilleries in the town. A potash works was established, and around 1770 the town acquired an insurance company for the shipping trade. Rural Newbury, in contrast to the bustle of urban Newburyport, depended on farming and fishing. The towns together had a population of 2,882 men, women and children.[3] Nineteen Lowell (or Lowle) children were born in Newbury and Newburyport during the eighteenth century.[4]

By the 1750s, outside events impinged on the towns along the Merrimack River. The goal of Great Britain in the French and Indian War (1754–1760) was to drive out the French from America. On May 12, 1755, Colonel Moses Titcomb and his men assembled at the Third Church of Newbury where the Reverend John Lowell prayed for their safety. Titcomb and his Newbury men formed part of the force of three thousand colonists and three hundred Indians who met the French at the Battle of Lake George, Monday, September 8. At four o'clock in the afternoon, Colonel Titcomb was shot dead. On hearing the sad news, the Reverend John Lowell gathered together his congregation to bid farewell to the town's fallen hero. Using the theme "Moses my servant is dead," from the first chapter of Joshua, the Reverend Lowell eulogized the bravery of Colonel Titcomb, who had died for his king.

The British conquest of New France was greeted with delight and relief throughout the thirteen colonies. The Treaty of Paris, concluded on February 10, 1763, gave Britain all the lands to the east of the Mississippi River, save for the city of New Orleans, which was ceded to Spain. The royal governor of Massachusetts, Sir Francis Bernard, gleefully declared that France "who hath so long stuck like a thorn in the sides of our colonies is removed: and North America is now become entirely British."

The Seven-Year War, together with the French and Indian War, severely burdened Great Britain, which looked to shore up its finances by imposing fresh taxes at home and in its colonies. The Sugar Tax of 1764, the Stamp Tax of 1765 and the Townshend measures of 1767 fell heavily on the North American colonists, leading to a dramatic shift from reverence of king and mother country to a deepening hatred of England and its institutions. On August 26, 1765, a mob ransacked the home of the Massachusetts Lieutenant Governor Thomas Hutchinson, taking £900 in cash, stealing his silver and destroying his collection of rare Massachusetts manuscripts and books. John Malcom, a Boston customs officer, was tarred and feathered and "carried through the streets in derision." In Newburyport, an effigy of the local tax collector was strung up in a tree. With the battle cry "No taxation without representation," the mood shifted away from the monarchy and toward independence and self-rule.

Soon after the town split into Newbury and Newburyport, the Reverend John Lowell died on June 28, 1767, in his sixty-fourth year, and was laid to rest on Burying Hill. His monument stone salutes his piety, virtue and his vast scholarship. By his first wife he left only one son, another John Lowell. His surviving second wife, Elizabeth Cutts Whipple of Kittery, Maine, remained "a loyalist to her death and whenever Independence Day came around, instead of joining in the general rejoicing, she would dress in deep black, fast all day and loudly lament over our late unhappy differences with his most gracious Majesty."

Through Elizabeth Cutts Whipple the Lowells formed a distant kinship with one of the leading families of Virginia. Her relative, Richard Cutts of Kittery, attended Phillips Academy and entered Harvard University. He served in the Congress of the United States, representing Massachusetts. Richard Cutts married Anna Payne, younger sister of Dolley Payne Madison, wife of President James Madison. In Washington, DC, Richard Cutts built for his bride an elegant townhouse overlooking Lafayette Square. Their son was named James Madison Cutts.

THE FATHER OF FRANCIS CABOT LOWELL

John Lowell was born in Newbury on June 17, 1743. He was thirteen years old when his mother died. Like his father, he attended Harvard, entering the college at age fourteen. Among his classmates was William Hooper, who, after graduating with honors, moved to the South to establish a law practice. Hooper was a passionate supporter of American independence and attended the first and second Continental Congresses, representing North Carolina. Hooper missed the vote on July 4, 1776, approving the Declaration of Independence but added his name to the document on August 2. The British regiment stationed in Wilmington hounded Hooper and destroyed his property, forcing his family to flee and hide. At war's end Hooper made a tidy living selling the confiscated properties of the banished Loyalists.

Four members of John Lowell's Harvard class, all from old Massachusetts families, remained loyal to the British king. Thomas Brattle went to England for the duration of the Revolutionary War. Brattle Street in Cambridge is named for the family. Daniel Leonard came from a wealthy Taunton family, and he practiced law there. For his outspoken support of the king and Parliament, Leonard's house was ransacked, forcing him to flee. With his name on the list of the Banishment Act of 1778 and the Conspiracy Act of 1779, Leonard lost his property and citizenship. After living some years in London, Leonard was appointed chief justice of Bermuda. William Bradford was a direct descendant of the Mayflower Pilgrim William Bradford, who served as governor of the Plymouth colony. His wife Dorothy survived the harrowing journey from England only to fall overboard and drown while the *Mayflower* was at anchor off the tip of Cape Cod. Daniel Bliss came to Harvard on a scholarship. After his admission to the bar, he practiced law in his hometown of Concord, Massachusetts. He was an early and open supporter of the king. In 1775, Bliss passed on to British spies information about the arms caches, including twelve cannon, hidden in the town, precipitating the British raid on April 19. Branded as "the enemy within," Bliss fled to Quebec, survived the American attack on December 31 and settled in New Brunswick, where he served as a judge. The Bliss home in Concord was confiscated.[5] Sixty of the three hundred Tories who were banished from Massachusetts in 1778 were Harvard graduates.

Another member of the remarkable Harvard graduating class of 1760 was James Baker. After training for the ministry, he decided instead to set up in Boston as a physician. A chance meeting in 1764 with a chocolate maker convinced Dr. Baker once again to change careers. Baker rented a small sawmill on the Neponset River near his home and set about making chocolate with cocoa beans imported from the West Indies, using the mill-stones to grind the beans. Years later, James Baker bequeathed his factory to his son Edmund, who in turn gave it to his son Walter. The enterprise became Walter Baker & Company, America's oldest chocolate company, and a name that continues to our day.

Harvard College when John Lowell attended had strict rules of con-duct, issuing heavy fines "for playing cards, profaning the Lord's name, frequenting taverns and displaying foul behavior at public worship." In 1759, the prohibition on drinking on campus was eased by allowing that "it shall be no offence if any scholar shall, at Commencement, make and entertain guests in his chamber with punch." The rule was further amended to allow scholars to entertain guests and serve them punch at other times, provided that it was done in "a sober manner."

At Harvard, John Lowell met Jonathan Jackson of Boston, graduating class of 1761, and formed the deepest love of his life. Both John Lowell and Jonathan Jackson were born in the month of June 1743. James Jack-son Putnam, a descendant of Jonathan Jackson, wrote in 1906 that "the relationship that stood nearest to Jonathan Jackson's heart and counted as much for his children's welfare as for his own was that which began in college days in the form of a romantic attachment between himself and John Lowell." John James Currier wrote in 1896 that the facile and vain Jackson became "intimately acquainted" with the intellectual Lowell, who was already inclined to corpulence and ruddiness of face. Jackson graduated from Harvard "without reproach, though without special honors" and was less of a scholar than his friend. The most compelling evidence of a deep homosexual attraction between the young men comes from Jackson's son, James Jackson, MD. Writing in 1866, Dr. Jackson details the "very close relationship, which began in college and bore the character which seems to have been almost romantic. It was certainly very strong and continued to be so, as long as they lived." Dr. Jackson writes that he "once saw a few letters which had been passed between them, written under fancy names, when they were very young, full of tender, warm and romantic feelings."[6]

In their letters and to each other, John Lowell was Philocles and Jona-than Jackson went by the name of Philander. Philocles and Philander are characters from *The Triumphs of Love and Honour*, by the Elizabethan dra-matist Robert Greene (c. 1558–1592).[7] In the play, General Philander has defeated the enemies of Cyprus and, for his reward, asks permission to marry Urania, the daughter of the king. But the king has already prom-ised her to Philocles, the prince of Rhodes. Urania secretly loves Philander and runs away disguised as a shepherdess. The gallant Philocles yields his claim, allowing her to marry Philander. In 1731, the English novelist Thomas Cooke issued his own work, titled *The Triumphs of Love and Honour*, and it is probable this was the version Lowell and Jackson read together. The play celebrates the triumph of love and honor in the face of lust and insult, a telling theme that signified the passions and hopes of these innocent young male lovers at Harvard College in the middle of the eighteenth century.

The word *philander* comes from the Greek *philandros*, meaning loving of man. A *philanderer* is one who carries on illicit or extramarital sexual affairs. The letters between the two young men "full of tender, warm and romantic feelings" suggests a homosexual love that was regarded in colonial Massachusetts as contrary to natural affection and an abomination, severely punishable by law. When John Lowell and Jonathan Jackson were alive, marriage and raising a family were the strong expectations. In eighteenth-century Massachusetts, few cases involving sodomy were heard by the courts and no case is recorded of consensual sexual relations among men. Same-sex love was viewed as a grave moral sin that, if made public, would forever damn the reputations of the participants.[8] The flow of letters between the two youngsters at Harvard was not restricted to declarations of love. John Lowell and Jonathan Jackson were intelligent youngsters who also discussed such issues as the nature of mankind. "The differences among men are not very great," opined John Lowell. "Men are influenced by external or accidental circumstances." Not so, responded Jonathan Jackson. The differences between men are "the result of an original bent or native tendency."

At graduation in 1760, John Lowell placed seventh in a class of twenty-seven. That year saw the death of George II and the ascent to the British throne of his grandson as George III, America's last king. Lowell returned to his father's home in Newbury. When Jackson graduated the following year, having lost both his parents, he followed John Lowell to Newbury. In 1762, Lowell was admitted to the practice of the law and took as his clients the town's leading merchants, Patrick Tracy and Tristram Dalton. Jackson, with his Harvard education and an inheritance of twenty thousand guineas, went to work as a clerk for Patrick Tracy.

Born in Wexford, Ireland, and of humble birth, Tracy came to Newbury as a poor boy but worked his way up to become a ship owner and dealer in goods from the West Indies, and one of the town's richest men. At the peak of his success, Patrick Tracy, a stocky rough-hewn man with little formal education, owned 110 merchant ships with a gross tonnage of 15,600 tons and a combined value of $2,738,000. Tracy married Hannah Carter in 1742, with the Reverend John Lowell officiating. Hannah died four years later and Tracy married Hannah Gookin, who mothered his children. After Hannah Gookin died, Patrick Tracy married for the third time. He died in 1780, aged seventy-eight years.

For several years John Lowell and Jonathan Jackson "lived together as bachelors, Lowell engaged in the practice of law and Jackson in commercial pursuits. They both professed to prefer single to married life and avowed their intention to continue permanently in a state of single blissfulness." The two young men were so contented "with each other's company that they vowed eternal celibacy." No doubt, tongues wagged in puritanical Newbury concerning two men in their twenties who shared "a love without a name" and lived together, especially when one was the son of the very proper Reverend John Lowell. The two decided to live apart, yet they continued their deep bond. In 1764, when Newburyport became a separate town, John Lowell moved to Boston to read law under the tutelage of Oxenbridge Thacher. Jonathan Jackson frequently traveled to Boston to visit his great friend. While in Boston, John Lowell was inoculated against smallpox and was given permission to visit his family and friends in Newburyport.

Oxenbridge Thacher descended from one of the oldest families of Massachusetts Bay. His ancestor Thomas Thacher arrived in Boston in 1635 and served as the pastor of the Old South Church. Over the years, various members of the Thacher family achieved distinction in the life of the colony. Oxenbridge Thacher was born in 1717 and at age twenty-one graduated third in his class at Harvard College and went on to became one of the leading lawyers, serving as counsel to merchants in Boston and Salem. John Adams regarded Thacher as one of the first to awaken the principles and feelings that led to American independence. Thacher saw himself as a loyal subject of the crown but protested against the Sugar Tax of 1764. In his pamphlet *The Sentiments of a British American,* Thacher argued that the colonists had "reason to expect that their rights should be preserved to them. The Colonists are not the property of the mother state; they have the same rights as other British subjects. It is esteemed an essential British right that no person shall be subject to any tax but what in person or by his representation he hath a voice in saying." Thacher insisted that the Sugar Tax was a tax on the colonists "without the consent of their representatives." Oxenbridge Thacher, who died in 1765, trained a number of the brightest lawyers in Massachusetts.

Much influenced by his mentor, John Lowell joined a debating club in Boston, together with other young students of the law on the path to becoming attorneys. Among them was his Harvard classmate Elisha Hutchinson, the younger brother of the future royal governor of Massachusetts. Frank Dana, America's future first minister to Russia, and the man who took young John Quincy Adams to St. Petersburg, joined the group, as did Josiah Quincy Jr., who later assisted John Adams in the defense of the British troops in the aftermath of the Boston Massacre. In the January 20, 1766, entry to his diary, John Adams, the future president of the United States, wrote that he learned from Daniel Leonard that the members of the little club were vexed over the Stamp Act and discussed "arguments for and against the Right of Parliament to tax the Colonies" and whether a British subject could be taxed without his consent and whether "we Americans are represented in Parliament or not." John Adams already had the measure of John Lowell, whom he judged to be "very warm, sudden, quick and impetuous, and all such people are unsteady, Too much Fire."

Having learned the import-export business, Jonathan Jackson joined with Patrick Tracy's sons, Nathaniel and John, to form the firm Jackson, Tracy & Tracy, engaged in shipping flax grown in the Merrimack Valley to dealers in Philadelphia and transporting linen to the West Indies. From the Caribbean their ships carried sugar and molasses to England in return for finished textiles to be sold in the thirteen colonies. Jackson, Tracy & Tracy saw their advantage after the merchants of Boston voted to boycott British goods in response to the Townshend Act of 1767. John Lowell, now a fully trained attorney, returned to Newburyport to practice law and became legal advisor to Jackson, Tracy & Tracy, an arrangement that made the friends rich. Boston sought the support of Newburyport and other Massachusetts towns to widen the Non-Importation Agreement. On December 17, 1767, Newburyport established a committee to decide whether to support the stand of the Boston merchants. The members of this committee were John Lowell, his friend Jonathan Jackson, Patrick Tracy, Tristram Dalton and Nathaniel Carter.

John Lowell wrote the response to the Boston request that was accepted by the town of Newburyport on March 10, 1768. Lowell noted that for many years Newburyport was supported "by the building of ships which have been purchased mostly by the Inhabitants & for the use of Great Britain. The manner in which we have been paid for our ships has been mainly by British manufactures so that the importation & purchase of these & our staple Business have been almost inseparably mixed." For reasons of trade and loyalty, Newburyport declined to join the boycott but instead continued to trade with Britain. The people of Newburyport, stated John Lowell, regard "Great Britain with all the respectful affection of a child to the parent" and hope that "a mutual confidence" be maintained since "we think it is necessary to be watchful against any Encroachment on our Rights as Englishmen."[9] The situation for the Newburyport merchants changed after September 4, 1769, when the town voted to support Boston by banning British imports and declaring that "every Person who shall buy of an importer contrary to the spirit of said agreement shall be deemed an Enemy to the Liberties of this country."

Perhaps to hide their love under a cloak of respectability and to preserve the family names, the two young men, both only sons, decided to marry. Jonathan Jackson married Sarah Barnard, the daughter of Reverend Thomas Barnard of Salem, and twenty-four-year-old John Lowell married Sarah Higginson, two years his junior, the daughter of the ship owner Stephen Higginson and his wife Elizabeth, also of Salem. The Higginson family descended from the Reverend Francis Higginson, one of the earliest Puritans to settle in the Massachusetts Bay Colony. His grandson, the Reverend John Higginson, was a leading prosecutor in the infamous Salem witch trials of 1692–1693. On the evening of January 3, 1767, John Lowell, Jonathan Jackson and their brides were joined in a double wedding, performed in Salem by the Reverend Thomas Barnard. The Reverend John Lowell did not officiate at the marriage of his only son.

John Lowell was kept busy doing the legal work for Newburyport's leading merchants as well as making a name for himself as a criminal lawyer. In his book *The Lowells and Their Seven Worlds*, Ferris Greenslet records that while practicing law in Newburyport, Lowell was counsel for the defense in no less than fifteen cases of murder. These included a case of a mother-in-law accused of poisoning her son's wife (*Rex vs. Ames*), and a son accused of killing his father (*Rex vs. Wilkins*). In June 1767, after the Reverend John Lowell died and his widow moved to Portsmouth, the lawyer John Lowell and his wife Sarah took over the house in Greenleaf Lane, where their children Anna Cabot, John Jr. and Sarah Champney were born.

In Newburyport and elsewhere in Massachusetts the mood shifted to open rebellion against the British. In 1768, the British government sent troops to Boston, but the presence of the Redcoats and Hessian mercenaries only inflamed the anger against the mother country. The British troops were abused and sometimes beaten up by townspeople. On a cold and snowy March 5, 1770, Edward Gerrish, a wig-maker's apprentice, hurled insults at a British officer along King's Street, Boston. Seeing Gerrish clubbed for his insolence, a mob of three hundred Bostonians gathered to taunt the Redcoats, throwing snowballs, pieces of ice, stones and even lobster shells. On the orders of their officers, the Redcoats lined up in columns to confront the mob. Shots were fired and people fell dead. News of the Boston Massacre, in which five colonists were shot dead and eleven others wounded, spread quickly through the colonies.

In March 1771, John Lowell and Jonathan Jackson together bought a five-acre property on High Street, Newburyport, from the widow Elizabeth Stickney. After dividing the property in two equal parts, Lowell and Jackson built almost identical three-story wooden houses side by side at 201 and 203, so that they "should pass their lives in close proximity." Writing to his wife Abigail on June 28, 1774, John Adams bemoaned his

lack of financial success compared to other Massachusetts lawyers such
as David Sewell and Theophilus Bradbury. Adam wrote enviously that
John Lowell "has built himself a house like the palace of a nobleman and
lives in great splendor. His business is very profitable."[10] The two houses
on High Street were among the most handsome residences in all of Newburyport. Each house had a stately hall from which "ascends one of the
noble staircases of the place and period." Upstairs were large bedrooms,
"each with its capacious fireplace and ornate overmantel." Seen from the
rear of the houses was a splendid view of meadows and woods. Into his
new home Lowell took his second wife, Susanna Cabot of Salem. With
their fine houses, servants, extensive libraries, liberal education, elegantly
dressed women and polite society, the close friends John Lowell and
Jonathan Jackson had decidedly entered the New England ideal of the
gentleman's life. John Lowell served from 1771 to 1776 as a selectman
of Newburyport, together with Tristram Dalton, Matthew Perkins, John
Stickney and David Moody.

Both John Lowell and Jonathan Jackson were sexually potent with
women. Sarah Higginson Lowell died on May 5, 1772, aged twenty-seven,
leaving three children all under four years of age. She was buried in the
Old Burying Ground off High Street, Newburyport. Sarah Jackson died in
1770 without any offspring. In 1772, Jonathan Jackson married eighteen-
year-old Hannah Tracy, the daughter of his mentor (by his second wife),
and sister to his partners Nathaniel and John Tracy. This marriage was
blessed with nine children born in ten years, including Hannah, Charles,
James and Patrick Tracy Jackson, who will feature significantly in the
pages ahead.

SLAVERY IN NEWBURYPORT

In October 1773, Caesar Hendrick, "a colored man," sued Richard Greenleaf of Newburyport for holding him in bondage as a slave. Represented
by attorney John Lowell, the plaintiff was awarded £18 and his freedom.
The case "excited much interest as it was the first, if not the only one of
its kind, that ever occurred in the country." After the verdict, abolitionist pressures in Massachusetts intensified with Lowell at the forefront of
the efforts to end slavery in the colony. Jonathan Jackson owned several
black slaves to take care of his grand home, and enjoyed the formality of
a black slave, named Pomp, properly attired, standing behind his chair, to
serve his meals. After Mr. Hendrick received his freedom, Jackson agreed
to release Pomp for the nominal sum of five shillings. With his newfound
conviction that "holding a person in constant bondage, more specially at
a time when my own country was so warmly contending for the liberty

which every man ought to enjoy," was morally wrong, Jackson notified the Suffolk Probate Court on June 19, 1776, that he would set Pomp free. "Having sometimes since promised my negro man Pomp that I would give him his freedom," wrote Jackson, "and in further consideration of five shillings paid to me by said Pomp, I hereby set him free." Pomp joined the Continental Army and proved himself a good soldier. After receiving an honorable discharge from the army, Pomp settled in Andover near a pond, known to this day at Pomps Pond. Others in Newburyport followed the example set by Jonathon Jackson. Old Patrick Tracy set "free a negro and his wife, well known in Newburyport, who had lived long as trusted servants in his household, and making provisions in his will securing to them a home and maintenance for the remainder of their days."

THE COMING WAR OF INDEPENDENCE

In November 1773, the cargo ships *Dartmouth*, *Beaver* and *Eleanor* berthed at Griffin's Wharf, Boston, loaded with forty-five tons of Chinese tea. The angry citizens of Boston gathered at the Old South Meeting Hall to declare a boycott on the tea. For two weeks the tea remained on the ships, until the night of December 16, when Boston men dressed as Mohawk Indians went aboard, systematically opened the 342 cases and dumped the tea overboard. The British response to what later became known as the Boston Tea Party was harsh. On March 31, 1774, Parliament passed the Boston Port Act, barring any goods and ships from entering or leaving the port, until full restitution for the tea was paid to the British East India Company. The charter of Massachusetts was annulled, the royal governor recalled and replaced by a military governor, General Thomas Gage, backed up by four thousand British troops, sent to achieve "full and absolute submission."

With British ships in the harbor and British troops in Boston, the mood of rebellion spread throughout New England and the other colonies. Hundreds of men in Newbury and Newburyport joined thousands of others to form local militia to drill and practice their shooting. Some were called minutemen, who pledged to be "ready to march or fight at a minute's notice." During the French and Indian War their fathers fought for the king; now these men were preparing to fight against the king. On February 9, 1775, the British Parliament declared Massachusetts in rebellion.

In this combustible atmosphere, General Gage learned that Samuel Adams and John Hancock, two leaders of the rebellion, had left Boston and were housed in the town of Lexington, and that the rebels were secretly storing arms in the village of Concord. Gage ordered Lieutenant Colonel Francis Smith with seven hundred men to capture the rebel leaders and destroy the caches of arms. Warned by Paul Revere and others that the British were coming, the Lexington militiamen lay in wait and on April 19, 1775, fired the first shots of the American Revolutionary War. Before they dispersed, eight of their number, including John Brown, Samuel Hadley and Caleb Harrington, lay dead and ten more wounded.

From Lexington, the British marched on to Concord to destroy the stores of munitions. The alarm was sounded and thousands of militiamen from surrounding towns lay in wait for the British on their way back to Boston. Seventy-three Redcoats were killed, 174 injured and five missing, with American casualties numbering forty-nine dead, thirty-nine injured and twenty-six missing. The entrance by land into the town of Boston was by way of a narrow stretch of land called the Boston Neck. After the British troops crossed back into Boston members of the twenty-thousand-strong militia shut the Neck tight. The siege of Boston had begun, leaving the British to escape only by sea. John Hancock left Lexington for Philadelphia to attend the Second Continental Congress, May 10, where he was elected president.

To tighten the noose around the British, the Massachusetts Committee ordered troops to occupy Bunker Hill, the highest point in Charlestown facing Boston. On the night of June 16, the Reverend Samuel Langdon, president of Harvard College, prayed with Colonel William Prescott and his force of 1,500 men before they set out on their mission. In the dark of night the American force crossed from Cambridge into Charlestown, occupied the hills and began to dig in. Before dawn the *Lively* and other British ships saw the Americans and opened fire. General Gage sent 2,600 troops to dislodge the Americans from their formidable positions. The Battle of Bunker Hill began on a clear and sunny day of June 17, and after three hours of bloody warfare, the British finally succeeded in driving the Americans off the hills of Charlestown. In the battle, the Americans lost 140 men, with 271 wounded and thirty captured. British losses were far higher, with 226 killed and 828 wounded. The Americans showed they could stand and fight "the flower of English soldiery."

The siege of Boston—from April 20, 1775, to March 17, 1776—took its toll on the British. There were shortages of flour, eggs and vegetables. For lack of grazing on the Boston Common, the cattle were slaughtered for the meat. The men injured in the Battle of Bunker Hill were weakened by infection and malnutrition, leading to many deaths. The American prisoners taken at the battle were especially vulnerable and some starved to death.

During the winter, the British cut down the trees of Boston and demolished homes and church halls for firewood. To prevent a collapse of order, General Howe warned that "on pain of death no man should be guilty of the shameful and infamous practice of pillaging and pilfering in the deserted houses." The food supply into Boston improved during the winter of 1775–1776, when British ships brought cattle, vegetables, wheat, flour, beer, rum and fodder, as well as coal and warm clothing—although not enough to sustain twenty thousand people, including the residents, fleeing Loyalists and the British army.

After the sun set on March 4, 1776, several thousand of General Washington's men hauled the cannon recently retrieved from Fort Ticonderoga up the Dorchester Heights. The British woke the following morning to a heavy bombardment of the city and the harbor. Howe realized that the British presence in Boston was no longer tenable. In negotiations with Washington he promised not to destroy the city in return for permission to evacuate without hindrance. On March 17 (celebrated in Boston as Evacuation Day) eight thousand British troops and officers and fifteen hundred frightened Loyalist supporters crowded into the 130 ships gathered together in Boston Harbor, and sailed for Halifax.

NEWBURYPORT AT THE BEGINNING
OF THE REVOLUTION

By 1776, the population of Newburyport had grown to 3,681 people. The town was home to John Lowell and several other distinguished lawyers. Theophilus Parsons opened his law office in the town in 1777. He attracted a number of distinguished students-in-training, including Rufus King, Robert Treat Paine and John Quincy Adams. Rufus King graduated from Harvard in 1777. After completing his legal training, he moved to New York and was elected a U.S. senator, and later was appointed minister plenipotentiary to the Court of St. James. Rufus King was the Federalist vice presidential candidate in 1804 and 1808, and presidential candidate in 1816, all unsuccessful. John Quincy Adams, the son of John Adams, returned from Europe to study at Harvard. In 1788 John Quincy, the future president of the United States, studied law with Parsons, and boarded with the widow Martha Leathers in her home off Market Square. In a December 23, 1787, letter to his mother, Abigail Adams, John Quincy wrote, "In the beginning of September I came to this town and began to study the law with Mr. Parsons. I could not possibly have an instructor more agreeable than this gentleman. His talents are great, his application has been indefatigable, and his professional knowledge is surpassed by no gentleman in the Commonwealth." The John Quincy Adams diaries for the years 1787 and 1788 contain many references to Newburyport and its people.[11] At the urging of his father, John Quincy Adams moved to Boston, and rented an office from John Lowell to start his law practice. Theophilus Parsons also left Newburyport for Boston, where in 1808 he was appointed chief justice of the Supreme Court of Massachusetts.

Jonathan Jackson lived an opulent life, financed by his inheritance and by revenue from Jackson, Tracy & Tracy. With his "refined and polished manners" the prim and proper Jackson cultivated good taste and was especially particular about his appearance. He commissioned five portraits of himself by the famous painter John Singleton Copley. One portrait captures his steely blue eyes, straight nose, erect posture and shows him "dressed in a loose green morning gown, trimmed with pink, a ruffled shirt and has powdered hair." Another painting shows Jackson wearing a "coat of deep blue color with gilt buttons, and the handsome waistcoat with broad stripes." One of the Copley paintings was inherited by his descendant, the Supreme Court Justice Oliver Wendell Holmes. Copley also did portraits of Jackson's second wife and several of their children.[12]

Influenced by Oxenbridge Thacher and by his family's loyalist traditions, John Lowell still supported the king and Parliament even after the Boston Massacre and the Boston Tea Party. On May 30, 1774, he and twenty-one other prominent Massachusetts attorneys-at-law and barristers sent a farewell letter to the last royal governor of the colony, Thomas Hutchinson, noting their "sincere respect and esteem" and thanking him for his "inviolable attachment to the real interest of this your native country." The decision to remove the governor "we view as a fresh instance of the paternal goodness of our most gracious sovereign."[13] When General Thomas Gage, the British military governor of Massachusetts, visited Salem on June 11, 1774, he was greeted with a letter of support from the "merchants and others, inhabitants of the ancient town of Salem," signed by, among others, Lowell's brother-in-law, William Cabot, and his father-in-law, Francis Cabot, as well as Henry Gardner, Henry and Stephen Higginson, Timothy Orne and others related by marriage. By December 1774, however, John Lowell was cautiously moving from being a "king's man" toward "serving the interests of my country," and advocating for the liberties of Americans. The events at Lexington, Concord and Bunker Hill brought him to denounce the British and favor American independence. In a letter to the people of Newburyport, published early January 1775 in the *Essex Journal and Merrimack Packet*, John Lowell noted that his earlier support of governor Hutchinson had left an "ill impression of me . . . I was serving the interests of my country [and] never wished any of your liberties abridged, of any unconstitutional power submitted to but, on the contrary, I am ever ready to join in preventing such mischief." His explanation was well received in the town and John Lowell was again voted in as a selectman. When Newburyport responded to the threat of a British attack, Jonathan Jackson was elected chairman of the Committee of Safety, with John Lowell serving as a member of the committee. Jonathan Jackson was appointed lieutenant colonel and John Lowell a major in the town militia.

In 1774, John Lowell married his second wife, Susanna, the daughter of the merchant Francis Cabot of Salem and his wife Mary. The Reverend Thomas Barnard again officiated in a Lowell wedding. On April 7, 1775, a mere twelve days before the momentous events in Lexington and Concord and seventy-two days before the Battle of Bunker Hill, Francis Cabot Lowell, the son of John and Susanna, named for his maternal grandfather, was born in Newburyport, Massachusetts. After a century and a half of relative obscurity in the New World, the Lowell family was now ready to take its place at the very lead of the Brahmin stakes. The birth of Francis Cabot Lowell strengthened the union of the Lowell and Cabot families, a linkage popularized by the poet John Collins Bossidy, who in 1910 wrote the following:

> And this is good old Boston,
> The home of the bean and the cod,
> Where the Lowells talk only to Cabots,
> And the Cabots talk only to God.[14]

On December 28, 1776, a daughter, Susanna, was born and on March 30, 1777, her mother Susanna Lowell, only twenty-three years of age, was dead, leaving John Lowell as a widower for the second time, with five children all under the age of nine years. Susanna Lowell's funeral was held in Salem on April 2.

The news of the battle of Lexington and Concord reached every hamlet and town in the thirteen colonies. All hopes for a peace with Britain were now dashed and the American War of Independence began. The port town of Newburyport, some forty miles north of Boston at the mouth of the Merrimack River, increased in importance after the British closed the port of Boston on March 31, 1774. False rumors spread that British regulars were killing people in the nearby towns of Ipswich and Haverhill and were now "close behind cutting and slashing all before them." A rider galloped through the streets shouting, "The regulars are coming. Flee for your lives."[15] Panic set in, with people hiding their valuables and fleeing Newburyport. Others swore to stay and protect their properties to the death. At an emergency town meeting Ezra Lunt came forward to form a militia of sixty men to guard the town against a British attack. On April 19, Captain Moses Norwell led his force of 130 men from Newburyport to do battle against the British. Benjamin Perkins rallied a force of eighty men, among them Joseph Whittemore, John Coffin, Zebulon Titcomb, Moses Pidgeon and Joseph Stickney, who set out for Cambridge to join the nascent Continental Army.

In Newburyport, the people prepared for a possible British attack.[16] Forsaking his Loyalist tendencies, John Lowell committed himself to the cause of independence. At a meeting on October 24, 1775, the town was divided into four districts "and the able-bodied men in each district were enrolled and organized for military duty" under the command of Captains Charles Cook, Joseph Huse, Richard Titcomb and Ralph Cross Jr. Colonel Jonathan Titcomb, Lieutenant Colonel Jonathan Jackson, and his close friend thirty-two-year-old Major John Lowell assumed overall command of the Newburyport militia, using Timothy Pickering's training manual, *An Easy Plan for Discipline of Militia.* In January 1776, the citizens of the town voted £4,000 to buy heavy guns and ammunition and build a fort on Plum Island for their protection. Pressure on Newburyport eased substantially after March 17, 1776, when the British evacuated all their troops from Boston and sailed for Halifax. Still alert to danger, in April the shipbuilders of Newburyport completed work on the twenty-four-gun *Boston* and the thirty-two-gun *Hancock.*

Another way to help the new nation was to convert merchant ships into armed privateers. The firm of Jackson, Tracy & Tracy commissioned the 120-ton *Yankee Hero* with six swivel guns, and manned by twenty-six sailors under Captain James Tracy. While on a trip from Newburyport to Boston, *Yankee Hero* was attacked by the British frigate *Milford* firing from its twenty-eight guns. Captain Tracy was wounded in the thigh; he was captured but later exchanged for a British officer. After Captain Tracy's return home, the firm of Jackson, Tracy & Tracy built for him a second *Hero*, this one with twenty guns. On its maiden voyage on July 23, 1777, *Hero* and her crew sailed from the harbor and were never heard from again. In addition to *Hero*, Jackson, Tracy & Tracy spent $160,000 of its own money to outfit the *Pilgrim, Minerva, Vengeance, Essex, Hannibal* and nineteen other ships, with 2,800 men into privateers to pick off British vessels. During the course of the war the Newburyport ships captured 120 enemy vessels, with 2,225 men, and cargoes worth together $4 million.[17] But Newburyport lost twenty-two vessels and one thousand men, many of whom where never heard from again, while others languished for the duration of the war in the Old Mill Prison at Plymouth, England. Jackson, Tracy & Tracy lost several of its ships and many lives. With commerce suspended, the cost of these acts of patriotism bankrupted the company, which collapsed in 1778.

On May 2, 1776, the General Court of Massachusetts, in an act of independence, removed all references to the British crown from the 1691 charter that governed the Massachusetts Bay Colony. John Lowell represented Newburyport in the deliberations of the General Court. On June 7 at the Second Continental Congress, held in the State House in Philadelphia, Richard Henry Lee of Virginia offered a motion that "these United Colonies are, and of a right ought to be, free and independent states." John Adams rose to second the motion, starting a vigorous debate on the future of the

American nation. During those momentous days, John Adams found time on June 12, 1776, to write from Philadelphia to John Lowell to express his delight on learning that Lowell, together with other "wise and prudent men," had been elected to lead Massachusetts. The great task now was to protect an independent American nation from military defeat. It was urgent, wrote Adams, for Massachusetts to set the example to arm the new nation and require that every man "who can work about any part of a gun or bayonet" be put to the task of making weapons and gun powder. "The other colonies," Adams told Lowell, "are too lazy and shiftless to do anything until you set them the example." Reflecting on the mighty struggle of giving birth to a nation, John Adams wrote, "You and I know very well the fatigues of practice at the bar, but I assure you this incessant round of thinking and speaking upon the greatest subjects that ever employed the mind of men, and the most perplexing difficulties that ever puzzled it, is beyond all comparison more exhausting and consuming. We have no resources left, my friend, but our own fortitude and the favor of heaven."

On that same day, June 12, John Adams wrote to Francis Dana, the future American ambassador to Russia: "We are drudging on as usual. Sometimes it is seven o'clock before we rise. Prepare yourself for vexation enough, for my tour of duty is almost out; and when it is, you or Lowell, or both, must come here and toil a little, while we take a little rest."

Delighted by the letter from John Adams, John Lowell responded in a patriotic rush on August 14 that he was "bound, in this Crisis, to afford my Country the little Assistance that I may be able to. I wish to see the Liberties of America fixed on a firm, immovable Basis, and to effect it I know they must be constructed on a broad and liberal Scale." Although his own skills lay in the law, John Lowell assured John Adams that the General Court of Massachusetts was encouraging the manufacture of small arms and had already erected four mills to make gunpowder, and "some successful Method of making Cannon." Massachusetts would fight the enemy by cutting off the supply of fish to the British islands in the West Indies, and soon ships from Boston, Salem and Newburyport would be armed and ready to take on "the Cruisers of the Enemy."

John Adams and John Lowell—Harvard-educated, Boston lawyers and members of the Suffolk Law Association—were now comrades-in-arms in the mighty battle to throw off British rule and establish an American nation in which liberty was guaranteed by law. "I have no Doubt," continued John Lowell, showing Adams that he too had answered the call of history, "that this is the critical Year, and I have not more Doubt that the Crisis will be favourable; but our Fortitude and unremitting Endeavours must not abate, for it is these that are to insure Success."[18]

On July 3, 1775, George Washington arrived in Cambridge to take command of the Continental Army assembled on the common. Among his eager officers was thirty-four-year-old Benedict Arnold, who with Ethan Allen had gained fame leading a band of eighty-three men, known as the Green Mountain Boys of Vermont, on May 10 to capture Fort Ticonderoga. The munitions and cannons taken from the fort would prove vital in keeping the British besieged in Boston until they were forced the following March to evacuate the city. On September 14, Washington wrote Arnold that he was entrusting him "with a command of the utmost consequence to the interests and the liberties of America," the capture of Quebec from British rule.[19] Arnold and his 1,150 men, "the very flower of the colonial youth," departed Cambridge early the following day, marched to Salem in time for dinner and reached Newburyport at 10 o'clock that night.

The town of Newburyport welcomed Colonel Benedict Arnold and his men with great enthusiasm. The colonel and his senior officers "were entertained here by Messrs. Nathaniel Tracy and Tristan Dalton, whose mansions were well accustomed to the presence of distinguished guests." On September 17, hundreds of townsfolk lined the streets to cheer "so many brave fellows going to be sacrificed for their country." On September 19, eleven transport ships arrived at Newburyport to carry Arnold and his army on the eighty-five-mile sea journey to the mouth of the Kennebec River. After traveling upriver, the men slogged north through three hundred miles of uncharted wilderness where they were beset by disease, low rations and floods. By the time he reached the outskirts of Quebec City, Arnold had lost over five hundred of his men through desertion or death, leaving him with six hundred starving survivors. Arnold waited for his troops to recover and, with the aid of General Richard Montgomery, who had captured Montreal, attacked Quebec City during a severe snowstorm on the last day of 1775. After hours of fierce street-by-street fighting, the Americans were defeated in the Battle of Quebec. Arnold and his men tried to besiege the city into surrender but gave up after months of severe cold, starvation and disease. Benedict Arnold gained infamy when he moved from patriot to traitor by conspiring with the British and switching sides.

In the meantime, the Newburyport selectmen, brimming with patriotic fervor, voted on November 28, 1776, to raise and equip an army comprising of one-sixth of the town's able-bodied men, to be paid £9 a month to join the Continental Army. These Newburyport men formed part of the army that defeated Burgoyne's forces during October 1777 at the Battle of Saratoga.[20] With the Revolutionary War moving south, the citizens of Massachusetts felt relatively safe until June 1779, when a British force invaded Penobscot Bay in the district of Maine to set up a royalist enclave called New Ireland. The British remained in Castine until the end of the war.

The siege had left Boston in a sorry state; the docks were quiet and merchants and shopkeepers ruined from a lack of business. Boston Commons was trampled by thousands of troops living in tents. The Old South Church had been occupied by the cavalry and used as a riding school. A smallpox epidemic killed many. Over ten thousand residents fled the town. The town "spiralled further into economic decline [and was] a very gloomy place."[21]

Among the Loyalists who left with the British army were descendants of a number of the earliest settlers of the Massachusetts Bay Colony. The wealthy among them left behind mansions, farms, livestock, furniture and silver. Thomas Hutchinson, the last colonial governor of Massachusetts, came from a family that arrived in the New World in 1634. The ancestors of Judge Samuel Curwen settled in Salem in 1638. Richard Saltonstall's ancestors arrived in Salem with Governor Winthrop on the *Arabella* on June 12, 1630. Since 1640, generations of the Brattle family lived in or near Boston. At the start of the Revolution, Harris Brattle abandoned his Cambridge house and property and moved to Boston, where he was "on terms of friendship with many of the regular army officers." Robert Winthrop was a descendant of Governor John Winthrop, one of the most illustrious figures in the annals of the settlement of the Massachusetts colony. John Singleton Copley, one of the most distinguished artists born in America, settled in England. The family of Jonathan Sewall arrived in the New World in 1634. A graduate of Harvard, Sewall was a close friend of John Adams, and as young and poor lawyers they lived together. Sewell rose to become the attorney general for Massachusetts and married John Hancock's sister-in-law. The Sewall home in Cambridge was attacked by a mob, forcing the family to flee to British-controlled Boston. Among the other Loyalists who left Boston were the parents of Lucy Flucker, married to Henry Knox, who served as the nation's first secretary of war (1785–1794). The ancestors of the Gore family arrived in Boston in 1635. John Gore was a merchant who fled Boston with the British in 1776 for Halifax, leaving behind several members of his family including his youngest son Christopher. John Gore was banished from Massachusetts in 1778 but was pardoned in 1787. Despite social and financial burdens, young Christopher completed Harvard and went on to a distinguished career in the law. From 1809 to 1810, Christopher Gore was governor of Massachusetts.

The Loyalists who went into exile included senior government officials, clergymen, shopkeepers, merchants, doctors, several prominent lawyers, and also carpenters, sailors and humble laborers. The names of four hundred Loyalists were affixed to the Banishment Act of Massachusetts, September 1778, preventing "the return to this state of certain persons who have left this state or the United States, and joined the enemies thereof," allowing Massachusetts to confiscate their money and properties.

JOHN LOWELL MOVES FROM
NEWBURYPORT TO BOSTON

James H. Stark, author of *The Loyalists of Massachusetts and the Other Side of the American Revolution* (1910), writes, "The Loyalists, to a great extent sprung from and represented the old gentry of the country." After they left, their properties were seized and "new men exercised the social influence of the old families, and they naturally dreaded the restoration of those whom they had dispossessed." Within weeks of the British departure from Boston, King Street was renamed State Street and Queen Street became Court Street. Several of the leading barristers of Boston fled with the British, and others, like John Adams, left the city to take their place in building the American nation. John Lowell was one of those new men who took charge of the affairs of the Commonwealth after the loyalists departed. Boston offered him greater opportunities and early in 1777, John Lowell left Newburyport to open a law office in Boston, temporarily leaving his family with his wife's parents, the Cabots, in Salem. Lowell sold his grand house in Newburyport for $10,000 to Patrick Tracy, who gave it to his son John. Soon after Susanna Lowell's death on March 20, 1777, the thirty-four-year-old twice-widowed man moved his five young children into the spacious house in Boston at the corner of Tremont and Beacon streets, previously occupied by the Loyalist John Amory, paying an annual rent of £40. His oldest son, John Lowell Jr., entered Boston Latin School on March 25.

The British departure from Boston opened great opportunities for the Essex County merchants and lawyers, now eager to fill the high positions abruptly vacated by the exiled Loyalists. John Lowell was appointed legal advisor to the committee dealing with properties confiscated by the state of Massachusetts from exiled Loyalists, earning him thirty shillings for each deed of sale. To further boost his income, he dealt with the owners' claims for compensation over the loss of their ships and men in the fight against the British. According to Ferris Greenslet, John Lowell processed seven hundred war claims, earning him at least $200,000. After the war, Lowell served as advisor to the families of prominent exiles such as Thomas Hutchinson, John Amory and William Vassall, helping them to recover their properties and wealth, and even permission to return to Massachusetts.

On April 24, 1777, Jonathan Sewall, the last British attorney general of Massachusetts, sent from his exile in London a stern letter of rebuke to his former friend John Lowell. Sewall accused Lowell of opportunism and unprincipled ambition. Sewall told Lowell that he "wished and endeavoured to keep you steady in the path of honour and Loyalty: so I now wish to save you from certain perdition. The fire of your ambition, the unhappy fluctuations of your judgment . . . were circumstances which always rendered your future character and conduct problematical." Sewall hinted that it was "a romantic friendship" (perhaps the influence of the patriotic Jonathan Jackson?) that moved Lowell to the side of the rebels. It was not yet too late, argued Sewall, for John Lowell to influence his "deluded countrymen [and] bring them back to the Loyalty from which you and they have foolishly and wantonly departed."

On January 27, 1778, John Lowell married for the third time. His new bride was Rebecca Tyng, the thirty-year-old widow of James Tyng of Dunstable (1731–1775), and daughter of the Honorable Justice James and Katharine Russell of Charlestown. Rebecca, one of eleven children, was "charming, wise and sympathetic [and her marriage to John Lowell] was the happiest of his alliances."[22] During the Revolutionary War, the Russell family of Charlestown was caught along the Loyalist-Patriot divide. Rebecca's brother Dr. Charles Russell was a Loyalist who fled with the British troops in 1776 and settled in Antigua, where he died in 1780. Her brother James, also a Loyalist, left America and settled in Bristol. Rebecca's brother Thomas Russell remained and was a prominent Boston merchant.

The children of Judge John Lowell and Rebecca Russell Tyng were Rebecca Russell (born 1779), Charles (born August 15, 1782), Elizabeth Cutts (born May 31, 1784) and Mary (who was born in 1786 and died three years later). To her stepchildren and her own alike, Rebecca Lowell was "an angel," who treated them all as one family. Francis Cabot Lowell regularly wrote to her while still a schoolboy and continued to write to her well into his adult life, calling her his "Honored Mamma."

John Lowell's increasing eminence in Boston brought him eager students wishing to study the law. Among them was Harrison Gray Otis, a 1783 graduate of Harvard who originally planned to study the law in London but was prevented by the bankruptcy of his father. "Nevertheless, young Otis had the best legal education afforded by the time and place, through the generosity of the eminent lawyer and patriot John Lowell, who took him as a pupil into his office without charge."[23] Otis described his mentor as a man about five feet ten inches in height and "inclined to corpulence." John Lowell spoke rapidly and was given to "impassioned eloquence and vehement gestures, taking the jury in his balloon and landing them where he pleased. [Lowell was the] most amiable, pure and honorable of men, and his honesty and moderation were proverbial." After three years of study Otis was admitted to the Suffolk Bar Association.

John Lowell sent clients his way and Otis soon had a highly successful law practice in Boston. Harrison Gray Otis later served as mayor of Boston, a U.S. senator, and was a leader of the Federalist Party.

From 1778 until 1802 at least sixteen other law students sought Lowell's tutelage, including John Tucker, Edward Clarke, John Brown Cotting, John Lathrop, Edward Wendell, Thomas Russell and Benjamin Lincoln. His oldest son, John Lowell Jr., studied under him, as did the youngest, Charles, who was not suited to the law. John Lowell maintained close ties with many who were loyal to Great Britain and its sovereign, George III. He accepted as his law students Christopher Gore and Rufus G. Amory, both sons of Loyalist exiles. The able and ambitious Christopher Gore, future governor of Massachusetts, paid £100 to apprentice under John Lowell. Lowell's son, John Lowell Jr., married Rebecca Amory, daughter of the once-banished John Amory. In the early years of the American Republic, the sins of the Loyalists were not visited upon their children, some of whom, like Christopher Gore and Rufus G. Amory, went on to play prominent roles in the body politic.

In October 1779 John Adams was selected by Congress to serve as minister plenipotentiary to France, with a salary of £2,500 sterling. John Lowell congratulated Adams on his appointment, telling him, on October 12, "You must accept the Appointment which Congress has lately made you. Your choice was unanimous, save one Vote." While Adams was occupied with the good of the nation, Lowell concentrated on local affairs. "The Interest of America requires, blind as some people are to it," Lowell continued in his letter to Adams, "that a New England Man should negotiate a peace." Lowell assured Adams that if the salary Congress offered him was too meager for his needs, "Our Friends in N.E. ought, and will, if the Provision is not adequate, make it so." John Adams accepted the great mandate issued by Congress and, accompanied by his twelve-year-old son John Quincy Adams, left Boston Harbor on November 15 on board the French ship *Sensible*.

Two weeks later, Abigail Adams wrote from Braintree to John Lowell, "Sir, Before Mr. Adams left me he mentioned 2 or 3 gentlemen to me to whom he would have me apply for advice and assistance during his absence. You Sir was one of those Friends upon whom he directed me to reply who would consider my Situation and render me any little services I stood in need of." Abigail was concerned about the "rate of exchange of hard Money into paper. There are so many persons disposed to take advantage of me, in this respect that unless I can find a Friend or two upon whom I can rely, I shall be imposed upon as I have heretofore been, and I have need enough I am sure of making the best exchange in my power. It has been my Lot in Life to be called repeatedly to the painful task of separating from the dearest connection in Life, Honour and Fame."

Abigail told John Lowell that she was able to accept these separations in the "hope of rendering Essential service to a distressed and Bleeding Country."

John Lowell replied to Abigail Adams on December 15 that "I have every Motive to wish to be serviceable to Mr. Adams and his Connections, to Mrs. Adams in a peculiar Manner, and I hope you will without the least Hesitation give me every Opportunity of so doing as the Pleasure and Obligation will be entirely mine." Making inquiries into the rate of exchange between hard money and paper, Lowell learned that it fluctuates "from thirty to thirty five to one," and assured Abigail that he would be willing to arrange any exchange of currencies for her.[24]

It fell to John Lowell's generation to fight the battle for independence as well as begin to establish the laws and institutions of the new nation. In 1779, the General Court of Massachusetts invited the towns to send delegates to prepare a state constitution. Although a newcomer, John Lowell was selected to represent Boston along with Samuel Adams, John Hancock, Oliver Wendell and seven other prominent men. John Lowell, Theophilus Parsons, Robert Treat Paine and John Adams were the leading figures involved in drafting the constitution. The Massachusetts constitution, the oldest functioning constitution in the world, was completed in September 1, 1779, and went into effect October 25, 1780. Lowell is credited as the author of a key phrase in the Bill of Rights, stating, "All men are born equal, and have certain natural, essential and inalienable rights, among which may be reckoned the right of enjoying and defending their lives and liberties." After March 1788 these words inscribed in the constitution brought an end to slavery in Massachusetts. Anyone found guilty of trading in people would be liable to a fine of £200 sterling. The Massachusetts constitution also guaranteed freedom of religion and provided checks on power, arguing that "power without any restraint is tyranny." John Lowell was so pleased with the addition of the equality clause that he exclaimed, "Now there is no longer any slavery in Massachusetts, it is abolished and I will render my services as a lawyer gratis to any slave suing for his freedom, if it is withheld from him."[25]

In 1782, John Lowell moved his wife and eight children to a large house at 41 Tremont Street, close by the King's Chapel burying ground. During that year, Jonathan Jackson and John Lowell represented Massachusetts at the Constitutional Congress in Philadelphia, helping to settle the boundary disputes between New York and Massachusetts. In 1783, Lowell was appointed, with William Paca, Cyrus Griffin and George Read, "all men of the highest caliber," as judges of the U.S. Admiralty Court of Appeals. The court heard sixty cases before it was closed in 1787.[26] John Lowell joined the historic Brattle Street Church, erected in 1699 by Thomas Brattle. Lowell was attracted to the liberal leanings of this Congregational church that counted among its parishioners such eminent figures as John Hancock, Samuel Adams and John and Abigail Adams.

With peace established and trade resumed, a bevy of successful merchants and lawyers, forming a Boston elite, was eager to display their wealth, with a house in the city and an estate in the country. The merchant Theodore Lyman built a fine house on his thirty-acre farm, named the Vale, in Waltham. The lawyer Christopher Gore built his imposing Gore Place nearby, and Harrison Gray Otis enjoyed his country home, Oakley, also in Waltham. Josiah Quincy bought a 170-acre farm in Braintree. Following the fashion of the British aristocracy, members of the old families, often educated at Harvard, aspired to be country gentlemen while still keeping their occupations and political connections.

On March 10, 1785, Judge John Lowell bought from Thomas Gunter a thirty-acre estate in Roxbury, just outside the limits of the town of Boston. The property, called Bromley Vale, after a London park, "lay between the south side of old Heath and Centre streets, extending northerly to a point nearly opposite the Heath mansion, and on Centre street, where it had a frontage of five hundred feet." On the land was an "attractive house, furnished without ostentation." The house had two parlors, a large living room and six bedrooms; it was large enough to accommodate the Lowell family of two adults and eight children. The library held nine hundred books. In his free time, Judge Lowell enjoyed his garden with its five greenhouses, and visited the barn, which housed three milk cows, three horses and a carriage. Two servants did the housework and several more were employed to care for the plants and animals. Lowell collected plant specimens from all over the world, including cuttings from fruit trees grown by the Agricultural Society in London. For a number of years, he served as president of the Massachusetts Society for Promoting Agriculture. Lowell traveled regularly across Boston Neck to his office in the city, but as he grew older he increasingly conducted his law practice from his home. Still amiable, astute and eloquent, he lived at Bromley Vale for the remainder of his life. After his death, his oldest son, John Jr., inherited the estate; he enlarged the greenhouses and added a windmill.[27]

One of the best-known clients of the lawyer John Lowell was William Vassall, born in Jamaica in 1715. Owners of large sugar plantations with thousands of slaves, the Vassalls sent some of their children to be educated in Massachusetts. William attended Harvard College and graduated in 1733. His brother John built the Vassall House on Tory Row in Cambridge. Until the Revolutionary War, William Vassall enlarged on his Jamaica resources to amass a fortune, owning one of the finest homes in Boston and a grand estate near Bristol, Rhode Island, among other properties. His appointment by the king as sheriff of Middlesex County provoked the people to turn against him. Vassall and his family went into exile soon after the Battle of Bunker Hill and settled near London. Despite his claims that he was friendly to Massachusetts, Vassall was declared a Loyalist and his properties were confiscated. After peace between the United States and Great Britain was declared in 1783, William Vassall hired John Lowell in an effort to regain ownership of his Massachusetts properties.

William Vassall decided to sue the Commonwealth of Massachusetts in the United States Court. His plan met an obstacle when on September 26, 1789, John Lowell was appointed a U.S. judge for the district of Massachusetts. Lowell gave his law practice to his twenty-year-old son John Lowell Jr., who became the lead attorney to William Vassall. "I think it would be indelicate," wrote Vassall to John Lowell Jr. on August 3, 1790, "to bring an action before the District Court of which your father is a judge, as he has been council for me." Against the advice of John Lowell Jr., the determined Mr. Vassall petitioned the Supreme Court of the United States, which agreed on February 11, 1793, to hear the case of *Vassall vs. Massachusetts*. The Vassall case ended in 1795 with the passage of the Eleventh Amendment to the Constitution, putting an end to the efforts of citizens of foreign nations to test the validity of the laws of the states. The Supreme Court never heard *Vassall vs. Massachusetts*. Although William Vassall lost at least £5,000, in confiscated properties, he still had means enough from his Jamaica plantations to live out his life in relative comfort.[28]

John Lowell also acted as agent to Martin Gay, a member of an old Massachusetts family, who chose to go into exile in 1776. Gay worked as a coppersmith and became wealthy enough to own a house on Union Street and another on Winter Street. John Lowell helped Martin Gay to regain ownership of some of his confiscated properties and to return to Boston. Gay set up in his old profession as a coppersmith.

FEDERAL COURT JUSTICE

From 1784 to 1786 John Lowell served as a justice on the Massachusetts Court of Appeals. The first bill introduced to the U.S. Senate was the Judiciary Act of 1789, calling for a Supreme Court, headed by a chief justice and supported by five associate justices. The act divided the nation into thirteen judicial districts and gave the president the power to recommend justices for the approval of the Senate.

The Judiciary Act set off a torrent of lobbying among the states and leading lights across the young nation to advance their favorite candidates. William Cushing and John Lowell were the leading candidates from New England. John Adams recommended that "only the best and ablest men may be brought into the public service, such as have the clearest and fairest reputations." Benjamin Lincoln wrote from Boston on July 18, 1789, to Henry Knox, a Massachusetts man and secretary of war, "The eyes of people here are much fixed on Mr. Lowell for one of the judges of the Supreme Court." Lincoln asked Knox, who had "very much the ear" of President George Washington, to put forward Lowell's name. That same day, Benjamin Lincoln wrote directly to the president, stating that "Mr. Lowell is a gentleman well qualified to fill one of the seats upon the bench of the Supreme Court. The purity of his mind, and strength and promptitude of his judgement and his knowledge of the law" make him a worthy choice. On August 7, John Lowell wrote to John Adams, stating, "if I should be thought capable of doing Service to my Country," he would accept the appointment of "the important & honorable office of an Associate Justice" of the Supreme Court.[29] Jonathan Jackson, in New York, and with his ear close to the political ground, wrote to Lowell on August 8, "I think at least a district appointment will be offered you—perhaps more—perhaps not." To comfort his great friend against disappointment, Jackson added, "As a general rule it may be laid down perhaps that the most deserving are least apt to push themselves in view."

President Washington chose John Jay from New York as the chief justice and as associate justices James Wilson of Pennsylvania, John Blair of Virginia, James Iredell of North Carolina and William Cushing of Massachusetts. Like Lowell, William Cushing came from an old Massachusetts family and was educated at Harvard College. On September 24, 1789, Washington sent the Senate a list of his nominations for Federal district judges, attorneys and marshals. Instead of the Supreme Court, John Lowell was appointed on September 26 as the U.S. justice for the district of Massachusetts, Christopher Gore was chosen as attorney and Jonathan Jackson as marshal. Jonathan Jackson had hoped for the post of collector of revenue for Massachusetts. When he heard that Benjamin Lincoln coveted the same position, Jackson urged the appointment of Lincoln. Washington learned of Jackson's noble sacrifice, and compensated him with the job of marshal of the federal court for the district of Massachusetts.[30]

One of the most remarkable cases to come before Judge John Lowell was *Bingham v. Cabot*. The case involved the privateer *Pilgrim*, owned by the Cabot brothers and their associates. In 1779, while the United States and Great Britain were at war, *Pilgrim* attacked the *Hope of Arundel* off the Portuguese coast, believing that she was a British ship carrying British cargo. The *Pilgrim* escorted the *Hope* to the French Caribbean island of Martinique only to learn that the ship was Danish and the cargo Portuguese. The case came before the agent of the Continental Congress in Martinique, Mr. Bingham, who decreed that the *Pilgrim* had erred in capturing a ship from a neutral country. The cargo of one thousand barrels of flour worth $35,000 was sold and the proceeds sent to the Continental Congress until the matter was finally settled.

The Cabot brothers took the case before the U.S. Court for the District of Massachusetts, where it was heard by district judge John Lowell (even though Lowell and the Cabot brothers were related by marriage). The jury decided for the Cabot brothers but the case was appealed to the Supreme Court where it was heard twice: in 1795 and again in 1798. After going back and forth between the Supreme Court and the Massachusetts Supreme Judicial Court, the case finally ended in 1804, after twenty-four years, only after Bingham died at age fifty-two, and the executors of his estate were willing to settle for just under $35,000.

SPECULATION IN LAND

In John Lowell's time, Maine was part of Massachusetts. On the morning of June 12, 1779, a British fleet coming from Halifax occupied the village of Castine in Penobscot Bay. At the Battle of Penobscot Bay the following month, the British decimated an American force coming from the port of Boston to retake the territory. The British planned to gather Loyalists and establish a crown territory to be called New Ireland. The British force remained until October 1783, taking with them hundreds of residents who chose to remain loyal to the king, and settling them in Nova Scotia. After this experience, the Commonwealth of Massachusetts was determined to settle northeastern Maine with patriotic soldiers, veterans of the War of Independence. Land speculators from Boston and elsewhere bought huge sections of Maine forestlands at prices as low as fifty cents an acre.

Judge John Lowell, his brother-in-law Thomas Russell and Benjamin Lincoln formed a partnership to buy land in Maine. Their first venture was at Perry on Passamaquoddy Bay, where they were granted a large tract of land "on the condition that the proprietors should place here twenty settlers within a given time, and give to each 100 acres of land." The settlers did well, selling the timber for ship building and housing rather than clearing the land for farming. Over the course of the next fifteen years, Judge Lowell and his partners bought vast tracts of Maine land, mainly in Washington County. The towns of Pembroke, Dennysville, Dover and Charleston all lie on the land once owned by Judge John Lowell. The three-man partnership acquired 24,040 acres of Maine land, including fifteen islands on the St. Croix River. By granting these lands to Lincoln, Lowell and Russell, the Commonwealth of Massachusetts had effectively dispossessed the Passamaquoddy Indian tribe. After his death, the rights to Judge John Lowell's lands passed on to his sons. In later years, much of the territory was returned to its original inhabitants.[31]

In the 1780s Judge John Lowell formed part of a syndicate buying eighty thousand acres of land at two dollars an acre near the Rocky River in Mecklenburg County, North Carolina. This land was once part of the vast holdings of the Royal Governor of North Carolina, Arthur Dobbs. In this land speculation John Lowell was joined by his brothers-in-law Stephen Higginson and Thomas Russell and his great friend Jonathan Jackson, as well as Andrew Cabot and Nathaniel Tracy. The property was bought from Alexander Ross who assured the Massachusetts speculators that the land was "well situated and very good" and that the title to the land was "clear and good." Despite the fact that the North Carolina property was "a very great distance from here," Lowell and his partners went ahead with the purchase, each owning ten thousand acres.[32]

THE BANK OF MASSACHUSETTS

In 1783, the Commonwealth of Massachusetts noted that well-regulated banks offered a safe place to store money, helped in the performance of contracts, assisted in the collection of taxes and provided the capital to stimulate trade. On February 7, 1784, the Bank of Massachusetts was officially chartered and, with a capital of $300,000, was the third bank in the United States after the Bank of North America, Philadelphia, and the Bank of New York. The Bank of Massachusetts was the first federally chartered bank in the United States. The founding board of directors of the bank included James Bowdoin, William Phillips, Isaac Smith, Jonathan Mason, Stephen Higginson, George Cabot and Judge John Lowell, who was the only one who was not primarily a capitalist or a merchant. The bank, situated on the corner of Park and Tremont Streets, opened its doors to the public on July 5, 1784. Among its customers were Nathaniel Tracy, Benjamin Gorham and Thomas Russell. The bank gave credit to the China and East India trade and helped open markets to South America. George Cabot soon left the Bank of Massachusetts to take up the presidency of the Boston office of the Bank of the United States. For many years, the Bank of Massachusetts was the largest bank in New England.

Judge John Lowell was one of the most respected men in Massachusetts. His calling was on the local stage, leaving the national platform to men like John Adams and Timothy Pickering. Lowell was one of the original trustees of Phillips Andover Academy, serving from 1777 until his death. He was called upon to lend his good name to give respectability to a number of the leading institutions of the young republic. Judge Lowell was one of the founding members in 1792 of the Massachusetts Society for Promoting Agriculture, serving as president from 1796 until 1800. For eighteen years he served as a member of the Harvard Corporation, helping to establish the professorship in Natural Philosophy. Harvard rewarded him with an honorary L.L.D. degree. On May 4, 1780, with John Adams, Samuel Adams, John Hancock and Jonathan Jackson, he became a founding member of the American Academy of Arts and Sciences. In November 1790, John Lowell gave the eulogy for James Bowdoin, late governor of Massachusetts, for whom Bowdoin College in Maine is named. Lowell also found time to be a founding trustee of the Bank of Massachusetts. In 1801, at the close of his term of office, President John Adams elevated John Lowell to chief justice of the U.S. Circuit Court for the First Circuit, comprising Massachusetts, Maine, New Hampshire and Rhode Island, with a salary of $666 a quarter.

SECRET ALLEGATIONS AGAINST JOHN LOWELL

In 1784 at a town meeting in Boston, Benjamin Hichborn was selected to deliver the Fourth of July oration at the Old South Meeting house. Born in Boston in 1746, Hichborn was a cousin of Paul Revere. Although of an artisan background, he showed intellectual promise and entered Harvard, from which he graduated in 1768, and then trained in the law. Benjamin Hichborn showed patriotic zeal and in 1775 was captured by the British. For two months he was held on a prison ship before he managed to escape. Now free, he was appointed a colonel in the Independent Cadets, the second-oldest military order in Massachusetts.

Hichborn was proud of his military exploits and his military rank acquired during the Revolutionary War. It would seem that Hichborn did not much like Judge John Lowell, perhaps resenting his coming to Boston from Newburyport and meeting great success. In December 1800, Hichborn, in private conversations with Thomas Jefferson, described the characters of certain prominent men in Massachusetts, in particular Judge John Lowell. In his diary entries of December 25 and 26, 1800, Thomas Jefferson, then vice president of the United States, recorded the gist of his talks with Hichborn: "Speaking of Lowell, he said he was in the beginning of the Revolution a timid whig, but as soon as he found we were likely to prevail he became a great office hunter. And in the breath of speaking of Lowell, he stopped: says he, I will give you a piece of information, which I do not venture to speak of to others. There is a Mr. Hale in Massachusetts, a respectable worthy man, who becoming a little embarrassed in his affairs, went to Canada on some business. The Governor there took great notice of him."

Benjamin Hichborn went on to tell Jefferson that sometime in the recent past the governor of Canada gave Hale a bag full of money to take back to Massachusetts with instructions "to give from three to five thousand guineas each to himself and others, to induce them, not to do anything to the injury of their country, but to befriend a good connection between England and it." Hichborn intimated to Jefferson that four Massachusetts men had accepted the bribe and "from that moment [began] to espouse the interests of England in every point and on every occasion." When Jefferson pressed for the names of the four men alleged to have accepted the bribes, Hichborn said that two of them had since died. According to Jefferson's account, Hichborn went on to say "that there were no persons he thought more strongly to suspect than [Stephen] Higginson and Lowell. Higginson is employed in an important business about our navy."

The election of 1800 chose Thomas Jefferson and Aaron Burr over John Adams. On March 4, 1801, Thomas Jefferson entered office as the third president of the United States, with Aaron Burr as vice president. The capital moved to Washington and, in the words of Edward Channing, "the South was in the saddle" with the Congress dominated by the slave-owning states. David Hackett Fischer wrote (1965) that the victory of Thomas Jefferson signaled the expansion of the ideas of liberty and equality at the expense of "old-fashioned elitism, the orders and distinctions, the postures of deference and subordination which had prevailed in eighteenth-century America." Jefferson moved to abolish the Judiciary Act of 1801 (also known as the Midnight Judges Act), costing John Lowell his position as chief justice of the Circuit Court for the First Circuit. Stephen Higginson, brother-in-law to John Lowell, was serving in a senior position in the American navy. In 1802, he was dismissed "to accommodate one of Mr. Jefferson's partisans." The accusations of bribe taking and disloyalty against Lowell and Higginson only became public a half-century later. There exists no evidence that either John Lowell or Stephen Higginson, Federalists both, accepted British bribes or were disloyal to their country. It is unlikely that either Lowell or Higginson were aware of the grave accusations made against them. Rather, it appears that Benjamin Hichborn, a Boston lawyer and a member of Jefferson's political party, was engaged in false and malicious gossip-mongering to harm his political rivals.[33]

THE DEATH OF JUDGE JOHN LOWELL

Judge and Mrs. John Lowell joined the First Church of Roxbury, founded in 1630. The judge entered the spirit of country life and was elected the first president of the Roxbury Charitable Society, the oldest charity in the parish. There are several portraits of John Lowell. Around 1795, Edward Savage painted the portraits of the judge and his wife Rebecca. The Massachusetts-born Savage is best known for his portrait of George

John Lowell (1743–1802), father to Francis Cabot, was known as "the judge." His first wife died and left him with three children: Anna Cabot, John Jr. and Sarah Champney. His second wife also died young, leaving him with Francis Cabot and Susanna Cabot. The portrait was done at the same time as that of his wife, Rebecca Russell, shown on the next page. Portrait by Edward Savage, circa 1795, when the judge was in his early fifties. (Reproduced with permission from the Mead Art Museum, Amherst College, Amherst, Massachusetts. Bequest of Herbert L. Pratt [Class of 1895].)

Washington and his family, now at the National Gallery of Art, Washington, DC. Joseph Blackburn's portrait of Judge John Lowell was given to Harvard University. The finest of the portraits of Judge John Lowell, wearing a white wig and adorned in a blue silk robe, was a miniature done by John Singleton Copley. Judge Lowell suffered cruelly from gout.

He died on May 6, 1802, at his home in Roxbury, aged fifty-nine years. Born in 1743, he was for the first half his life a loyal subject of the King of England, and for the second a proud American patriot. His elitist views lived comfortably within the Federalist Party that remained dominant until 1800. Patriot, judge, landowner, banker, merchant, a Harvard man and a loving father, John Lowell left a legacy his sons deeply admired and struggled all their lives to emulate. Judge John Lowell died as the walls of

Rebecca Russell Lowell, third wife of Judge John Lowell. Rebecca Russell Lowell was the mother of Rebecca, Charles and Elizabeth. Portrait by Edward Savage, circa 1795. (Reproduced with permission from the Mead Art Museum, Amherst College, Amherst, Massachusetts. Bequest of Herbert L. Pratt [Class of 1895].)

Mrs. James Russell (Katherine Graves) 1717–1778, circa 1770. Katherine Graves was married to Judge James Russell of Charlestown, Massachusetts, and was the mother of Rebecca Russell Tyng Lowell. Rebecca was the third wife of Judge John Lowell; she raised all his children, including John Jr. and Francis Cabot Lowell. (Artist John Singleton Copley [American, 1738–1815, active in Britain from 1774.] Reproduced with permission from North Carolina Museum of Art, Raleigh, purchased with funds from the North Carolina Art Society [Robert F. Phifer Bequest] and the State of North Carolina, by exchange.)

his Federalist world were tumbling to the ground. His son John Lowell Jr. would try in vain to hold back the clock and retain the Federalist structure of elitism and privilege.

Judge John Lowell left an estate worth $67,902.13, which included the Bromley Vale house and land, valued at $10,000, property in Maine and North Carolina, and part ownership of the vessel *Adventure of the Sea* worth $22,000. In addition he owned eleven shares in the West Boston Bridge project worth $2,569.33 and $1,446.82 cash in his account at the Bank of North America. Most of the property was sold and converted to cash. The judge's widow, Rebecca Lowell, was left $18,608.47, and each of his children received $5,902.10. The oldest son, John Jr., elected to take Bromley Vale and paid to the estate the sum of $4,331.99. Francis Cabot Lowell received a one-twelfth share of the furniture (worth $234.09), a sixth share of the ship (worth $3,637.20) and the remainder of his inheritance in cash. Francis Cabot Lowell was entrusted to manage the inheritance given to Rebecca Lowell and her daughter Elizabeth.

JONATHAN JACKSON AND HIS FAMILY

To more fully understand the life of Francis Cabot Lowell, it is necessary, even essential, to examine the lives of Jonathan Jackson and his offspring. Jackson's ancestor Christopher Jackson arrived in the New World in 1643. The Jacksons were merchants who ran a store in Boston selling goods imported from England. Jonathan Jackson was born in Boston, June 4, 1743, the only son of Edward Jackson. His sister Mary married Oliver Wendell, a prominent Bostonian. The Jackson family was also related to John Hancock and Edmund and Josiah Quincy. After Harvard, Jonathan Jackson moved to Newburyport to be close to John Lowell. He spent the next five years learning the merchant's trade under Patrick Tracy, after which Jonathan formed a partnership with John Bromfield importing goods from Britain for sale in America. After the death of his first wife, Jonathan Jackson cast his gaze on sixteen-year-old Hannah Tracy, whom he married two years later on June 1, 1772. Young Hannah was "very much restrained early in life." In 1774, Jackson formed a partnership with Hannah's brothers, Nathaniel and John. The firm of Jackson, Tracy & Tracy distilled molasses into rum for sale in Africa as part of the slave trade. Their ships carried grain to Spain and returned with manufactured goods.

At the start of the Revolutionary War the newly declared United States had no navy able to take on the immense power of the Royal Navy or to prevent British transport ships supplying the army. By a brilliant stroke of imagination, Congress authorized the conversion of private mercantile ships into men-of-war, with the promise that ship owners, captains and crews could share in the booty. During the course of the war some two thousand American ships were converted into privateers by cutting gun ports and adding the extra crewmen needed to board enemy ships. The ship conversions were done both as acts of patriotism and with the expectation of profit. The merchants of Newburyport fitted seventy-five of their commercial ships into armed privateers to attack the enemies of the United States and disrupt communications between the government in London and the British army and navy fighting in North America. Jonathan Jackson and his partners owned some thirty of these privateers, including *Yankee Hero*, *Hawk*, *Pilgrim* and *Game Cock.* These ships harassed British supply vessels, hoping to capture the cargoes of clothing, food and war materials.[34] The deeply patriotic Jonathan Jackson loaned his ships and his fortune to the national government. He lost several of his vessels but was not repaid. Nearly bankrupted by the war, Jackson dissolved his partnership with the Tracy brothers.

In May 1782, John Lowell and Jonathan Jackson traveled together from Boston to Philadelphia to serve as the Massachusetts delegates at the Continental Congress. Lowell was appointed to several committees, including a finance committee headed by James Madison; a committee on the exchange of prisoners; foreign affairs; and a committee looking into the loss of the French frigate *La Fayette.* On June 20, the Congress selected the bald eagle as the emblem of the United States and later that year declared Thursday, November 28, as a day of Thanksgiving. John Lowell was the first of the pair to return home. To his brother-in-law Oliver Wendell, Jackson wrote, on August 3, "Brother Lowell is the Bearer of this & is much better informed than I shall be. The French fleet arrived off Chesapeake, there are various Reports that they are bound to the Southward, some to the Northward for Repairs. Don't Affairs look approaching towards a Peace? It appears to me they do. As Mr. Lowell is the Bearer of this, to him I refer for everything you can ask."[35]

In 1783, Jonathan Jackson tried to restore his wealth through a partnership with Stephen Higginson. From an old Salem family, Stephen Higginson Jr. was born in 1743, the son of Stephen Higginson Sr. and Elizabeth Cabot. His sister Sarah was the first of the three wives of Judge John Lowell. It is likely that Lowell introduced his dear friend to his brother-in-law, Stephen Higginson, who had made a profit of $70,000 from his privateers during the Revolutionary War. Jonathan Jackson traveled to Britain, Ireland and France to buy goods for Jackson & Higginson. Because there were few buyers in war-exhausted America for these goods, the firm was dissolved in 1786, leaving Jackson almost penniless. Jonathan and Hannah moved from their splendid home in Newburyport to rented rooms with a family on Federal Street, Boston, still attended by their faithful servant Molly Knapp. Jonathan Jackson borrowed heavily to educate his sons Robert, Charles and James, who attended the Boston Latin School. In 1787, Jonathan Jackson, now "a poor man," returned to Newburyport and for several years was obliged to take paid employment and live frugally. He had his moment of glory on October 31, 1789, when, as marshal, he dined with President George Washington, who was in Boston as part of a celebratory tour of New England. Governor John Hancock arrived late for the dinner swaddled in bandages, complaining of a severe attack of gout. One report alleges that "Washington shed tears when he saw the servants bringing the helpless man into his presence."

Hannah Tracy Jackson, exhausted by nine births in ten years and the shame of poverty, died April 28, 1797. Despite his losses, Jackson made every effort to recover his status. As a loyal supporter of the Federalist Party, Jackson received a patronage appointment (1792–1801) by Alexander Hamilton, as an inspector in the internal revenue. By 1805, Jonathan Jackson was well on the way to restoring his position in Boston society as well as his finances. With his former partner Stephen Higginson, John Lowell Jr. and Andrew Cabot, he speculated in land, buying thousands of acres in North Carolina at $2 per acre. Jackson was appointed president of the Boston Bank, which, with a capital of $1,800,000, was then the largest bank in New England. He also was appointed treasurer of Harvard College and treasurer of the Commonwealth of Massachusetts, with an office at the State House.

During the last years of his life, Jonathan Jackson accumulated some wealth in the form of stock in the Boston Bank, the Massachusetts Bank and Boston Marine Insurance Company, and also in property. He died in 1810, and after all obligations were settled his estate was worth $26,245.60, most of which he left in equal shares to his four surviving daughters. The share to his youngest daughter, Mary Jackson Lee, was especially timely as her husband was bankrupt and sailed for India in the hope of a financial recovery. Jonathan Jackson left to his son Charles his writing table and three mahogany chests, to James a wardrobe and "a gold top'd cane & buttons marked with his initials and mine," and to Patrick Tracy he left his "gold stock buckle & broach,—my best gun & bayonet—my pistols and sword [and] wearing apparel of all kinds." To his son-in-law Francis Cabot Lowell he left "the portable writing desk which was formerly my son Robert's."[36] Jonathan Jackson outlived his beloved friend Judge John Lowell by eight years. He was laid to rest in the Granary Burying Ground, Boston.[37]

All nine of the Jackson children were born in Newburyport. According to James Jackson Putnam, writing in 1906, the Jackson family was "remarkably united. Spirited, affectionate, unselfish, helpful in all relations in life, [and had] a fine tradition of public service." The sons Henry and Robert became sea captains and died young. The clever Charles Jackson gained admission to Harvard, where he and Francis Cabot Lowell were founding members of the Porcellian Club.[38] Charles Jackson served as a judge on the Massachusetts Supreme Judicial Court. His brother James, born in 1777, graduated from Harvard and went on to a distinguished career in medicine. The youngest son was Patrick Tracy, named for his maternal grandfather. Because of family financial difficulties, Patrick did not attend Harvard but went to sea. On his return to Boston, Patrick Tracy Jackson went to work for Francis Cabot Lowell and became his closest ally.

In a letter to Anne MacVicar Grant (January 6, 1813), Hannah Jackson Lowell skillfully summarized the attributes of her three surviving brothers. Charles, "my eldest brother, the lawyer, is thought to have more than common talents; these talents are exclusively devoted to the Law and Politics." Her brother, James, however, was "without uncommon talents," but had pleasing manners and was a good physician. Lastly, her youngest brother Patrick Tracy was "a man of plain good sense, excellent feelings [and was] a respected merchant."

Because of Jonathan Jackson's financial difficulties his older daughters, Hannah and Sally, "were at lodgings in some pleasant residence in the country," probably as tutors to the children there. The two younger Jackson daughters were placed in a home in Hingham. Despite the widening gap in wealth and social class, the Lowell and Jackson children continued the close friendship of their fathers.

Financial woes stiffened the resolve of the Jackson children. As adults the sons were "social and lively people, inclined to make acquaintances and mingle with the world pleasantly. But they got some Cabot wives, who shut them up. The fact is that the Cabots had been the 'best people' in Beverly; but were a little doubtful whether they would be properly received in the larger city [Boston], so they kept in seclusion; the Jacksons had no such anxieties but were ruled by their wives." The Lee, Cabot, Lowell, Jackson and Higginson clans, linked by marriage and all from Essex County, "had the satisfying belief that New England morally and intellectually had produced nothing better than they were; so they very contentedly made a little clique by themselves, and intermarried very much, with a sincere and cheerful faith that in such alliances there could be no blunder."[39]

Jonathan Jackson, father-in-law of Francis Cabot Lowell. Portrait made by John Singleton Copley, circa 1766, when Jackson was in his early twenties. The elegant Jackson is dressed in a damask morning gown. The portrait was given to his dear friend John Lowell. Jonathan Jackson commissioned several more portraits of himself from Copley and other artists. (John Singleton Copley [American, 1738–1815], Jonathan Jackson, the late 1760s, Pastel on paper mounted on canvas 60.32 x 45.08 cm [23 3/4 x 17 3/4 inches]. Museum of Fine Arts, Boston. Gift of Mr. Francis W. Peabody in memory of George C. and Virginia C. Shattuck and Henry H. and Zoe Oliver Sherman Fund, 1987.295. Photograph © 2010 Museum of Fine Arts, Boston.)

Hannah Tracy Jackson (1756–1797), daughter of Patrick Tracy, was eighteen years old when she became the second wife of Jonathan Jackson. She had nine children, including sons Charles, James, Patrick Tracy, and daughter Hannah, who married Francis Cabot Lowell. (Hannah Tracy [Mrs. Jonathan Jackson] [Photogravure], "From Copley's portrait, in possession of Mrs. James Jackson of Boston," A Memoir of Dr. James Jackson, by James Jackson Putnam [Boston and New York: Houghton Mifflin, The Riverside Press, Cambridge, 1906], 54.)

Charles Jackson (1775–1855) attended Harvard with Francis Cabot Lowell, where they became the best of friends. Charles opened a law practice in Newburyport, but later moved to Boston. In 1813, he was appointed judge of the Massachusetts Supreme Judicial Court. Grandfather to Oliver Wendell Holmes Jr., associate justice of the U.S. Supreme Court. (Judge Charles Jackson [Photogravure], "From Healy's portrait, in possession of the Misses Paine of Boston," A Memoir of Dr. James Jackson, *by James Jackson Putnam [Boston and New York: Houghton Mifflin, The Riverside Press, Cambridge, 1906], 96.)*

Dr. James Jackson (1777–1867) was cofounder of the Massachusetts General Hospital and professor of the theory and practice of physic at Harvard Medical School. (Dr. James Jackson [Photogravure], "From the portrait by Chester Harding, now in possession of Dr. Charles P. Putnam of Boston," A Memoir of Dr. James Jackson, by James Jackson Putnam [Boston and New York: Houghton Mifflin, The Riverside Press, Cambridge, 1906], frontispiece.)

Patrick Tracy Jackson (1780–1847) went to sea at age fifteen. In 1812, he joined with Francis Cabot Lowell to establish the Boston Manufacturing Company in Waltham, Massachusetts. He was one of the founders of the textile city of Lowell on the Merrimack River. (Patrick Tracy Jackson [Photogravure], "From Healy's portrait, in possession of Dr. Francis P. Sprague of Boston," A Memoir of Dr. James Jackson, by James Jackson Putnam [Boston and New York: Houghton Mifflin, The Riverside Press, Cambridge, 1906], 128.)

2

A Privileged Education

Aim to be the first *in everything you undertake. Nothing can be accomplished without great industry, activity and perseverance. Avoid the tavern, wine, idle companions and bad women.*

From a letter written by John Lowell Jr.
to his brother Francis dated March 3, 1793,
after Francis was suspended from Harvard College

Francis Cabot Lowell and his brothers John Jr. and Charles enjoyed the finest education offered at that time in the United States. Each of the boys attended Phillips Academy, Andover, followed by Harvard, America's oldest and most prestigious college. With each class size around thirty scholars the privilege was indeed rare. Their attendance at Phillips and Harvard was testimony to Judge John Lowell's ambition and wealth as well as the intelligence and application of his sons.

On April 30, 1778, Samuel Phillips, Harvard class of 1771, with the help of his wealthy family, opened a boarding school for boys in his hometown of Andover, Massachusetts. Phillips Academy, the oldest boarding school in the nation, then strictly Calvinist, aimed at "instructing youth not only in English and Latin grammar, writing, arithmetic and those sciences wherein they are commonly taught but more especially to learn them the great end and real business of living."[1] Twelve trustees were selected to guide the school, including four from the Phillips family, as well as Nehemiah Abbot, Oliver Wendell and John Lowell. The first headmaster of the school was twenty-six-year-old Eliphalet Pearson, a 1773 graduate from Harvard, who received a house, wood for heat and £80 a year. After leaving Phillips Andover in 1786, Pearson became professor of Hebrew at Harvard College.[2]

Phillips was soon established as the school of choice for the sons of the leading families of Massachusetts and served as a preparatory school mainly to Harvard University. During its early years the student population hovered around fifty. Discipline was strict and the academy did not tolerate "profanities or any other scandalous immorality." The headmaster and the trustees "did not hesitate to reprimand boys, and frequently took occasion to address them in the school hall on the odiousness of vice and the beauty of virtue." From its beginning Phillips Andover wished to admit poor children alongside its wealthy fee-paying scholars but "no feasible method of accomplishing this had yet been discovered." In 1789, the academy received a grant of $20,000 to admit "poor children of genius." Despite the poor roads and communications, the reputation of the school spread. George Washington was a great enthusiast of Phillips Academy and persuaded his relatives to send their children there. In 1785, fifteen-year-old Howell Lewis, son of Washington's favorite sister, Elizabeth, arrived at Andover. Ten years later Colonel William Augustine Washington sent his sons Augustine and Bushrod. Washington's grandnephews Cassius and Francis Lightfoot Lee arrived the same year, followed by more Washington descendants over the course of the nineteenth century.

A typical day at the academy began at eight o'clock in the morning with a religious service, followed by classes in Greek, Latin and English grammar, mathematics and translations from classical authors. In the afternoons, the boys studied mathematics, practiced their penmanship, and repeated the morning lessons. The school day ended with evening prayers.

The first Phillips Academy class of 1778 was comprised of fifty boys and included seven-year-old John Phillips, later the first mayor of the city of Boston. Six-year-old Josiah Quincy was miserable at the academy as his mother did "her duty" by sending the little fellow away to school. Young Josiah Quincy and John Thornton Kirkland, both future presidents of Harvard College, were selected to deliver the Exhibition of 1786, taking the roles of Brutus and Cassius from Shakespeare's *Julius Caesar*. These experiences stiffened Quincy's resolve. He served as the second mayor of Boston (1823–1828), during which time he built the famous Quincy marketplace adjacent to Faneuil Hall. William King went on to become the first governor of Maine, and John Abbot was the first professor appointed to Bowdoin College. Others admitted to the first class of the academy ranged in age from seven to twenty-one. Eight-year-old John Lowell Jr., oldest son of the lawyer John Lowell, transferred from the Boston Latin School to become a member of the Phillips Academy class of 1778. His mother, Sarah Higginson Lowell, had died when he was only three years old, and his father, by this time living in Boston, had recently entered into his third marriage. The dutiful and clever John Jr. excelled at Latin and Greek.

Francis Cabot Lowell, at age eleven years, was one of the twenty-seven students in the 1786 entering class at Phillips Academy, Andover. Among his fellow scholars were William Tudor, aged seven, and John Locke, aged twenty-two years. Most of the boys and young men came from Massachusetts towns, but Gardner Green was from New Hampshire, Nathaniel Marston from New York and John March, the son of a plantation owner, hailed from the island of Jamaica.

The Tudor family came from Devon, England to Boston in 1715. Their descendants became merchants and led privileged lives. William Tudor Sr. graduated from Harvard before studying law in the office of John Adams. His son, William Jr., attended Phillips Academy, and his younger son Frederic went to the Boston Latin School. The Tudor boys resided in the family's Boston townhouse and spent their holidays on the family farm at Rockwood. After Phillips Academy, William attended Harvard College and entered the law. In 1805, William and Frederic devised a plan to cut blocks of ice from Boston ponds in the winter, insulate the ice with burlap and sawdust, and ship it to the Caribbean, Europe and as far away as India. It was Boston ice that cooled the gin and tonic of the British army officers stationed in Bombay, Madras and Calcutta. Having become wealthy in his own right, William Tudor chose the intellectual life and became one of Boston's leading literary figures, a founder of the *North American Review* and the Boston Athenaeum. It was William Tudor, in 1819, who christened Boston the Athens of America. His younger brother Frederic remained with the business. He was known as the Boston Ice King, and earned a fortune shipping ice around the world.[3]

On September 27, 1788, Francis Cabot Lowell, as a thirteen-year-old Phillips Academy schoolboy, wrote a heartfelt letter to his "Honored mamma" in his round schoolboy script, telling his stepmother that he wished "to answer all your letters as soon as I receive them that I may receive more. Please do come to the Trustees meeting at the end of the term, which will be a fortnight from next Tuesday

I am,

Honored mamma,

Your most dutiful son

Francis Cabot Lowell."[4]

On November 19 came another plea for her attention: "Please tell me whether you are going to any place to spend the winter: if you are not, please come and see me: but do not forget to ask papa to come with you; if he cannot come please to come without him. I thank you for the bundle you sent to me: please do send me some stockings, those which I bought are so small." Francis (also known as Frank) asked his mother for a new coat and a toothbrush, "my other toothbrush I have lost. I have found my old great coat and I will send it by the next opportunity."

On March 15 the following year, a homesick Francis showed his eagerness to go home for the vacations. He wrote to his "honorable mamma [that] the vacation will be on the eighth of April, please tell me how I am to come down." Mr. Blanchard from Andover was offering a service to accompany scholars to their Boston homes for the vacations. Francis established that Mr. Blanchard "will carry me if I want to go, he asks a dollar" for the service. "I hope you will not think I am tired of study because I write so soon to come home. Please to give my duty to Papa & love to all my brothers and sisters." Francis did well at Phillips Academy, graduated in 1789 and successfully passed the entrance examination for Harvard University. Ten other scholars in his class at Andover were accepted to Harvard. Nathaniel Seaver, however, went to sea but in 1792, a lad of sixteen years, was drowned off the coast of Arabia.

HARVARD UNIVERSITY

On August 12, 1789, the fourteen-year-old Francis Cabot Lowell received his letter of acceptance to Harvard, signed by the college president, Joseph Willard. The letter advised his parents that "those who had been accepted on examination should pay three pound in advance towards defraying college charges." Also, the family was required to post a bond to the college "in the form of two hundred ounces of silver" and to pay dues quarterly.

Harvard was a small college during the years Francis Cabot Lowell and his brothers were in residence. Classes were comprised of twenty to thirty students, taught by three professors in divinity, mathematics and Oriental languages. Each professor received an annual salary of £150 together with a housing allowance worth another £100. The president of Harvard was paid £320 a year. In 1787, the Harvard corporation owned the "sum of £11,078, 3s 4d in solid specie, at the disposal of the college." According to Josiah Quincy, the prosperity of the college depended on three people: Ebenezer Storer, James Bowdoin and John Lowell.

The position of treasurer traditionally went to a clergyman but in 1784 John Lowell, "then one of the most distinguished lawyers in Massachusetts," was elected treasurer. John Lowell "united high powers of intellect and professional talent with practiced skills and acquaintance with men and affairs. His zeal in the service of the college, the soundness of his judgement, and his characteristic integrity gave great weight to his influence." John Lowell remained treasurer until the year of his death, after which the post went to his dear friend Jonathan Jackson. Harvard began to expand during the time Francis Cabot Lowell was a student. A professorship in anatomy was funded in 1790 and in chemistry the following year.[5]

One of the brightest students in his class at Phillips Academy, John Lowell Jr. entered Harvard in March 1783 at thirteen years of age, following his grandfather and father into the college. Among the forty-five scholars who graduated with John Jr. in 1786 was Alden Bradford, a descendant of two of the passengers on the *Mayflower*. The class included Christopher Grant Champlin, who served as U.S senator from Rhode Island, and Thomas Weston Thompson, who served as U.S. senator from New Hampshire. Isaac Parker became the chief justice of the Massachusetts Supreme Court and in 1815 was appointed the first professor of law at Harvard College. Another illustrious classmate of John Lowell Jr. was William Harris, who later served as the sixth president of Columbia College. John Jr. excelled in the classics and in mathematics and graduated from Harvard before his seventeenth birthday.

John Quincy Adams, future president of the United States, graduated from Harvard in 1787. President George Washington visited Harvard in 1790, at the start of Francis Lowell's college career. Francis' closest friend at Harvard was Charles Jackson, repeating the strong bond that started between their fathers at Harvard over thirty years earlier. Francis Cabot Lowell and Charles Jackson were born in Newburyport within days of each other. According to James Jackson Putnam, "While in college, Charles Jackson was the chum of Francis Cabot Lowell. This was a natural and most fortunate friendship. Mr. F. C. Lowell's character and talents were of the finest." Where Francis excelled at mathematics, Charles had literary interests and was chosen to deliver the English oration at the Commencement of 1793.

Francis and two other close Harvard friends, John Avery and John Curtis Chamberlain, resurrected a quasi-military group called the Marti-Mercurial Band from its motto *Tam Marti quam Mercurio* (As much for Mars as for Mercury). The Marti-Mercurial Band was founded at Harvard in 1769 by William Peabody Whetmore, graduating class of 1770, and was the first military company in North America founded by students. The band enjoyed its own uniform of a "blue coat, the skirts trimmed with white, nankeen breeches, white stockings, top-boots and a three-cornered cocked hat." As clerk of the band, Francis Lowell prepared a detailed set of rules and regulations for membership: The captain of the band must come from the senior class, the sergeants and clerk from the junior class, and the corporals from the sophomore class. All officers were to be chosen by secret ballot. Freshmen would only be accepted after the spring vacation. Himself 5 feet, 10 inches, Francis stipulated, "No person shall be admitted under the height of 5 feet & 6 inches." Francis went so far as to write to John Hancock, governor and commander-in-chief of the Commonwealth of Massachusetts, that "the students of Harvard University desire to gain a knowledge of the military art while in literary pursuits, have with the consent of the Corporation, formed a military company. Their inability to equip themselves in a suitable manner obliges them to request your Excellency to furnish them with arms. The promptness with which your Excellency has ever patronized institutions of this kind allows your petitioners to hope their request will meet with your approbation."

In the heyday of the Ivy League clubs, the Porcellian Club at Harvard ranked as one of the oldest and most exclusive. Known as the Pig Club, with a pig as its emblem, the Porcellian was founded in 1792 by a group of students who enjoyed eating well and having fun. The motto of the club is *Dum vivimus vivamus* (While we live, let's live). Robert Treat Paine Jr., whose father was one of the signers of the Declaration of Independence, was among the first members of the club. He was joined in the club by John Curtis Chamberlain, Charles Cutler, William Jones, Francis Gardner and Francis Cabot Lowell. Francis' younger brother Charles Lowell, and Charles Jackson, James Jackson and Benjamin Gorham, all three future brothers-in-law of Francis Cabot, were also members of the Porcellian Club. His son Francis Cabot Lowell Jr. became a member in 1821. Over the generations the Porcellian Club at Harvard built on its mystique and counted among its members Theodore Roosevelt, Henry Cabot Lodge, Edward Everett, Oliver Wendell Holmes Jr., and the architect H. H. Richardson.[6]

Francis was a conscientious student who wrote poetry and prepared many papers for his tutors to read and assess. With his fellow students, Francis pursued the Harvard curriculum for the degree of bachelor of arts, studying classical Greek, Hebrew and Latin, English grammar, mathematics and history. On October 30, 1792, Francis Cabot Lowell submitted his senior thesis titled *Problems in Algebra*. His academic career was almost derailed the day after Christmas 1792 when Lowell and others lit a "bonfire in the play yard." Meeting on December 31 the president Joseph Willard and the professors and tutors at Harvard met to punish the perpetrators and voted that "Lowell be suspended untill [sic] the fifth day of May next and that he be put under the care of the Revd. Mr. Sanger of Bridgewater and that during his suspension he pursues his collegiate studies in all respects confirming with the law in the case of suspension provides." The president set out that Lowell was obliged to study projections of the space, spherical trigonometry, nature, political law and modern history.

The banishment from Harvard was a severe blow to the seventeen-year-old Francis Cabot Lowell, son of Judge John Lowell, a prominent member of the Harvard Corporation, trustee of the Bank of Massachusetts and a justice of the United States District Court. Feeling shame and embarrassment, Francis wrote from Bridgewater on January 23, 1793, to his "Honored Mamma" that his spirits were low as he found himself "among entire strangers in a strange place." He begged his mother to have his siblings write to him because "everything that comes from home will be comforting to me." Letters soon came from his sisters, mother and even his ten-year-old brother Charles, a scholar at Phillips Academy. His friend Thomas Wigglesworth assured him that Harvard social meetings floundered "on the reflection that Francis cannot be one of our members." A less empathic John Curtis Chamberlain wrote to Francis about the entertainments he enjoyed, including "two very excellent balls." After Harvard, Wigglesworth went on to prosper as an East India merchant, and Chamberlain settled in New Hampshire to represent his state in the U.S. Congress.

Francis Lowell's older brother John Jr. viewed the suspension from Harvard as an opportunity for chastising others and praising himself, a style of behavior he would carry into his political life. John Jr. graduated from Harvard at age eighteen without a blemish to his reputation. Writing to Francis on March 3, 1793, he began by criticizing the president of Harvard, and then berated Francis for giving way to self-pity and seeking sympathy. "Aim to be *the first* in everything you undertake," John Jr. admonished. "Nothing can be accomplished without great industry, activity and perseverance. Avoid the tavern, wine, idle companions and bad women. Boston is the sink of vice. It is the Babylon of profligacy. I have never spent a shilling at a tavern. I have avoided idle companionship—all drinking clubs— and I have never defiled myself with a connection with one woman of abandoned character." John Jr. prided himself in his "good constitution and clear heart." He told Francis of his marriage to "an amiable woman with whom I pray I may spend the residue of my days in happiness, sincerity and virtue." The twenty-four-year-old priggish John Lowell Jr. ended his long letter by directing Francis to "pursue the paths of virtue."

On March 12, 1793, came a cold "Dear Frank" letter from his father Judge John Lowell, who told his son that he has taken care "of your Cambridge debts" and sent along £5 for his current needs. Judge John Lowell expressed the hope that Francis "would receive as much or more advantage from the performance of your studies with Mr. Sanger as at Cambridge."

Zedekiah Sanger, born in the village of Sherborn in 1748, was a descendant of the blacksmith Richard Sanger. Zedekiah, an excellent student, entered Harvard in 1767 and graduated in 1771 with high honors. In July 1776 he was ordained as pastor to the congregation in Duxbury. Handicapped by eyesight grown weak by excessive study, after a number of stressful years, he asked to be allowed to step down and move to the village of Bridgewater to take up a position as junior pastor. The Reverend Zedekiah Sanger earned extra money by "fitting boys for college." He was a good tutor and sensitive to the emotions of his students. He wrote to Judge John Lowell on April 29, 1793, "I have the pleasure to acquaint you with your son's very good behavior while with me. He has been as studious as I could wish. My only fear is that he would injure himself by his too close application. He is a happy genius for mathematics. I presume that few if any of his class equaled him in mathematical and astrological attainments. He is very accurate in calculating projecting eclipses."

After five months' banishment in Bridgewater a more serious Francis Lowell returned to Harvard and in July 17, 1793, at the tender age of eighteen years, graduated with his class from Harvard with honors in mathematics, and in the presence of John Hancock and Samuel Adams. His suspension from Harvard and the criticism from the college president, his father and his brother left Francis Cabot emotionally brittle. He was educated to be ambitious and acquire personal wealth. Still, he had a deep sense of duty and the desire to serve his fellow man. His wish to please his father, the demands of his conscience and his obsessive need for order conspired to make him anxious and earnest, with little room for frivolity and spontaneity. All the rest of his life he could not be idle but needed to be busy and productive. On a long sea voyage a few years later, Francis complained of "ennui beyond sufferance. Without books a sea life would be intolerable. Each day is a month and a month a year."

The year 1793, when Francis Cabot Lowell graduated from Harvard, was a momentous year in the affairs of the world. In Paris on January 21, a carriage bearing Louis XVI passed slowly through the streets and came to a stop at the Place de Louis XV. The king alighted from the carriage, took off his coat, untied his neck cloth and loosened his shirt. In a short statement in front of the vast multitude, the king claimed he was innocent of all the crimes of which he had been charged. The executioners dragged him to the guillotine and placed his head under the blade. With one stroke the head of Louis XVI was severed from his body. A young soldier raised the head to display it to the crowd. Shouts of "Vive la Republique" filled the air. On February 1, revolutionary France declared war on Great Britain, the Netherlands and Spain. On September 1, the Reign of Terror began its attack on counterrevolutionary forces and on October 16, Marie Antoinette was beheaded. The wars in Europe would continue until Napoleon's exile on St. Helena in 1815. These events deeply influenced the political landscape for Francis Cabot Lowell and his generation of Americans.

THE LOWELLS AT HARVARD UNIVERSITY

In the year 1636, only sixteen years after the Pilgrims landed at Plymouth, the Great and General Court of the Massachusetts Bay Colony voted to establish a school of higher learning in the village of Cambridge. The following year, a young minister arrived from England to take up a post in Charlestown. John Harvard died of consumption in 1638, barely thirty years old, leaving half his estate worth £779 and his library of 360 books to the new college. In gratitude to its first benefactor the college was named in his memory. Harvard University offered a classical education in the model of the English universities. The first class, in 1642, had nine students. For the century and a half under British rule, classes remained small, numbering fewer than fifty students a year, with many of the graduates becoming ministers in Puritan congregations throughout New England. Harvard is the nation's oldest institution of higher learning.

The Reverend John Lowell, class of 1721, was the first of many Lowells to attend Harvard. His class of 1721 had thirty-seven graduates. His son, known as Judge John Lowell, graduated in 1760 with twenty-six others. John Lowell Jr. graduated in 1786 with forty-four others and Francis Cabot Lowell in 1793 with thirty-seven others. Judge John Lowell and his sons continued to support their alma mater for the rest of their lives. Judge John Lowell, "a solid man of Boston," helped Harvard toward solvency, and was awarded in 1792 the honorary degree of doctor of laws. His son John Jr. also served the college as fellow and overseer, and in 1814 was awarded an honorary L.L.D. The Reverend Charles Lowell had a difficult time as a student at Harvard but later served as fellow and overseer.

Judge John Lowell in 1784 was the first of the Lowell family to serve as a fellow of Harvard College. In 1810, his oldest son John was appointed a fellow of Harvard and, in 1818, so was his youngest son Charles. John Amory Lowell was appointed a fellow in 1837, as well as Justice Francis Cabot Lowell in 1895.

The Lowell dynasty at Harvard continued through the nineteenth century into the twentieth. Most of the sons of John Jr., Francis and Charles attended the university. James Russell Lowell, class of 1838, was a leading poet and professor of modern languages. Charles Russell Lowell Jr., class of 1854 valedictorian, served as a general in the Union Army during the Civil War and was killed at the Battle of Cedar Creek. His brother-in-law, Colonel Robert Gould Shaw, was another Civil War hero. Percival Lawrence Lowell, class of 1876, was an astronomer and founder of the Lowell Observatory at Flagstaff, Arizona. Francis Cabot Lowell, class of 1876, was a judge in the U.S. Court of Appeals for the First Circuit. Abbott Lawrence Lowell, Harvard class of 1877, served from 1909 to 1930 as president of his alma mater. Staunchly conservative, he expelled students for homosexuality, imposed a Jewish quota and opposed the nomination of Justice Louis Brandeis to the Supreme Court. Another artistic Lowell, Robert Trail Spence Lowell IV (1917–1977), remained only two years at Harvard, and was the sixth poet laureate of the United States. Lowell House, one of the twelve residential student houses at Harvard, was completed in 1930, during the presidency of Abbott Lawrence Lowell.[7]

3

The Young Merchant: 1793–1802

India was a new region, and only Salem knew the way thither.

From *The Scarlet Letter*, 1851,
by Nathaniel Hawthorne, the Salem-born novelist

One need look no further than to events in Europe to account for almost every twist and turn in the fortunes of the American economy. The years 1793–1808 were years of unparalleled prosperity.

Douglass Cecil North, from his 1961 book
The Economic Growth of the United States; 1790–1860

Upon graduation from Harvard, Francis Cabot Lowell remained close to Charles Jackson, but most of his forty classmates went their various ways. For a while, Francis kept in touch with John Curtis Chamberlain, Francis Gardner and a few others. Writing on January 12, 1794, Chamberlain shared his anxieties about making the transition from student to adult: "I must confess, Frank, that my present situation is rather awkward, feeling so mightily elated with my emancipation from college, I expected to shift immediately to the life of a man, and take part in the theater of the world. But, still, I have not finished the years of childhood. I still am helpless and unfit for usefulness. This requires more patience than I can command. I am your friend in a hurry, John C. Chamberlain."

Francis Gardner adopted a different tone when writing on March 24, 1794: "Since we left old Cambridge I have seen no classmates except [John] Pierce and [William] Jones. We have a number of hearty lads in our neighborhood with whom I am spending time agreeably. [Charles] Cutler talks highly about his gallantry, his knowledge of the French language, his industry and the quality of his employment. He means to surpass me in gallantry and industry but his efforts will be in vain. God bless and protect all your undertakings, Francis Gardner."

Not one of these new Harvard graduates, all of them members of the Porcellian Club, needed to be anxious about his future. Francis Gardner was admitted to the bar and practiced law. He represented New Hampshire in the 10th Congress (1807–1809). John Curtis Chamberlain followed a similar path and was the representative from New Hampshire in the 11th Congress. Charles Cutler taught at the Boston Latin School before turning to a career in the law. He was highly gifted but became ill and died at age thirty-two years. William Jones was another who followed the law and became a judge of the Probate Court in Maine. John Pierce became a Unitarian minister and served at the First Church, Brookline from 1797 until his death in 1849. Another Harvard classmate was Charles Coffin, who went on to become the president of Greenville College, the oldest college in Tennessee. Coffin sought donors in his hometown of Newburyport and elsewhere in Massachusetts and took with him to Greenville a library of six thousand books. In 1848, Greenville College joined Tusculum College.

By choosing to become a merchant, trading goods to and from the New World, the eighteen-year-old Francis Cabot Lowell was following a long-established New England tradition. As early as 1655, over three hundred New England ships were trading as far away as Barbados, Madeira and Europe. In addition, thirteen hundred smaller fishing boats brought their catch into local ports. By 1675, there were reports that Boston merchants were becoming rich and furnishing their large homes in the manner of London.[1] Trade expanded during the eighteenth century, attracting many educated young men to the life of the merchant. With the restoration of peace after the Revolutionary War, ships from Boston again sailed the high seas carrying mainly dried fish, rum and grains. The trade between Boston and the West Indies expanded despite British restrictions. The Orient was the new region for trade. In the year 1789, Boston sent out forty-four ships to China and India, which returned with tea, coffee, spices, silks and cotton textiles. By 1790, Boston and Salem were among the busiest ports in the United States. That year a total of 455 foreign ships entered the port of Boston; in 1793, 404 vessels came to Boston, and in 1794, the number rose to 464. In those years, the trade links of Massachusetts extended more to Canada, the Caribbean, Europe and the Orient, than to the American states to the south.

Shipyards in Boston and elsewhere were kept busy building larger ships for the journeys to the four corners of the world. In 1793, Simeon Lowell opened the Lowell Boat Yard in Amesbury, close to Newburyport.

The *George* astonished the seafaring world by sailing from Salem to Calcutta in only ninety-five days. In addition to commercial vessels, ships of war were built in Boston shipyards. The most famous was the U.S.S. *Constitution*, one of the original six frigates authorized by the Naval Act of 1794. Constructed at the Edmund Hartt shipyard, the 2,200-ton *Constitution*, carrying fifty-two guns, was launched on October 21, 1797. The sailcloth for the vessel was handwoven at the Boston Sailcloth Factory at the corner of Tremont and Boylston Streets, Boston. Two years later, the Edmund Hartt shipyard launched the four-hundred-ton U.S.S. *Boston*.

For two centuries the people of New England remained homogeneous and almost all of English stock. In the summer of 1794, Henry Wansey, a clothier from Wiltshire, England, made *An Excursion to the United States of North America* (1798). He found Boston, a town of eighteen thousand inhabitants, "a very flourishing place, full of business and activity. The merchants and tradesmen meet every day, from twelve till two o'clock, in State Street, as in an exchange." State Street and Cornhill were the principal streets, but "the foot ways are not yet paved with flat stones. The buildings likewise are but indifferent." The new part of town, called West Boston, where the wealthy merchants settled, "is an exception for the houses there are all neat and elegant (of brick) with handsome entrances and door cases, and a flight of steps." To Wansey's eye, Boston resembled a prosperous English town. In Cambridge, across the Charles River, Wansey much admired Harvard College, "an excellent institution, well endowed, and supports three hundred students; two large handsome brick buildings separate from each other." The new bridge joining Boston to Cambridge was "a most prodigious work for so infant a country, above one thousand eight-hundred feet long, and about thirty feet wide, well lighted all the way and into Boston. This bridge is built entirely of wood, and costs about twenty-four thousand pounds, and marks the genius and spirit of the town of Boston. At the center was the machinery to open the drawbridge to vessels on the river. Boston had forty hackney coaches, charging a quarter-dollar to travel to any part of the town. On one side Boston Common was a pleasant tree-lined promenade, called the Mall." Apart from a lace factory employing one hundred workers, Boston lacked large manufactories. There was no need, Henry Wansey noted, for England to "fear a rivalship here."[2]

A merchant's career was a precarious one. Buying goods too high, misjudging the market or a ship lost at sea spelled disaster. Dealing in goods from many countries, a merchant needed to be an expert on the buying and selling prices of commodities, the costs of shipping and the value of currencies, including the American silver dollar, introduced in 1792 by the U.S. Mint. Other currencies then used in Massachusetts included Spanish and Portuguese silver and gold coins and British sterling.

Those merchants who knew the relative values of the currencies and understood the marketplace could make a comfortable living, and a few of them grew very rich. The knowledge of foreign languages and a trained mind helped, but even in New England, a university education was not a prerequisite for success as a merchant. Thomas H. Perkins, John and Benjamin Crowninshield, George Cabot, Nathan and Samuel Appleton, and Amos and Abbott Lawrence did famously well without acquiring a Harvard degree.

Percival Lowle, the first of the Lowells in America, was a merchant. His descendant Francis Cabot Lowell began his mercantile career at age eighteen years, working as an agent for his father. Each month, Francis received from his father Judge John Lowell the sum of £20 in British currency and in his small account book meticulously recorded all his expenses. These included the purchase of stockings at six shillings; shoe repairs, nine shillings; six handkerchiefs, £1.16 shillings; postage of letters, six shillings; bridge tolls, eight shillings; and a dinner at Mores', six shillings. His father indulged young Francis with a new chaise to ride around town, costing $106.67. His horse and chaise were stabled with Mr. P. Connor, who charged Francis twelve shillings every two weeks for the service. During the winter months Francis kept his horse and sleigh at the firm of Wheelock & Simmons.

The Middlesex Canal linking the Merrimack River with Boston was one of America's engineering wonders of the eighteenth century, and John Lowell bought Francis shares in the canal worth $80. Francis valued the monthly allowance he received from his father and throughout his life he kept exact records of his expenses, offset by the assets he was rapidly accumulating.

THE UNITED STATES AND THE FRENCH REVOLUTION

Americans were grateful to the French for their help during the Revolutionary War in defeating the power of Great Britain. American enthusiasm for France was heightened in 1789 after the fall of the Bastille, the Declaration of the Rights of Man and the abolition of the monarchy. America and France seemed to be following the same path toward the liberty and equality of all men. Bastille Day was joyously celebrated in Philadelphia, Baltimore and New York. The news that the French revolutionary army stopped the invading Russians at Valmy on September 20, 1792, was greeted by parades across America as a great victory for freedom. Americans took to greeting each other in the French manner as "Citizen So-and-so," rather than "Mr." or "Mrs." The largest and most spectacular of the American parades in support of the French revolution took place in the Federalist stronghold of Boston on the cold winter day of January 24, 1793: The excitement began with a notice in the *Boston Gazette* of January 21, announcing a civic feast. "A number of Citizens, anxious to celebrate the success of our allies, the French, in their present glorious struggles for Liberty and Equality, and that every member of the community should partake in the general joy, have agreed to provide an Ox, with suitable Liquors, on Thursday, the 24th inst., being the day appointed for the Civic Feast."

The celebration began at eleven o'clock with a salute of cannon fire from the fort in Boston Harbor. Two men on horseback waving civic flags led the procession. Behind them came Citizen Waters, the marshal of the parade, followed by a marching band. Next came twelve citizens dressed in white aprons carrying cleavers, knives and other carving utensils. A wagon carrying the roasted ox adorned with ribbons was the peace offering to liberty and equality. Next was a cart drawn by six horses laden with eight hundred loaves of bread, followed by two carts each carrying a hogshead of punch. The procession passed in front of the homes of the Governor John Hancock and Lieutenant Governor Samuel Adams before coming to a halt at State Street in front of a sixty-foot liberty flag pole. As French and American flags fluttered in the cold wind, the one-thousand-pound ox was carved up, the bread divided and the punch poured, much to the delight of the assembled thousands from "all classes and persons without distinction" gathered together to support "the glorious cause of freedom." Half of all the people in town took part in the festivities. At two o'clock in the afternoon the procession continued the short distance to Faneuil Hall for a great banquet. So infectious was the celebration that the prison gates were thrown open and the inmates invited to share in the spirit of liberty. That evening fireworks and bonfires completed the celebration that lingered long in the memory of Bostonians. The section of town where the celebration took place was renamed Liberty Square.[3]

The Revolutionary Wars on the Continent began in 1793 the year Francis Cabot Lowell started his career in business, presenting great trade opportunities for merchants from neutral America. Britain's naval supremacy prevented France and its allies from trading directly with their colonies in the East and West Indies. Instead, goods were shipped to American ports, offering "opportunities to trade as neutrals in foreign goods which were landed at U.S. ports and then reloaded for export."[4] With Britain and France locked in battle, the small American commercial ships regularly visited St. Petersburg in Russia, the Baltic and the Mediterranean as well as ports in India and China.

In France, the Reign of Terror started on September 5, 1793, some fifty months after the onset of the Revolution. The *Comite de Salut Public* (Committee of Public Safety), through its Revolutionary Tribunal, had broad powers to destroy the enemies of the Revolution. Upward of forty thousand Frenchmen were put to death on the orders of the Revolutionary Tribunal. The Terror burnt itself out with the execution of Robespierre on July 28, 1794. The bloody wars between the European powers would continue until June 18, 1815, when Napoleon was defeated at the Battle of Waterloo.

The French Revolution was a dominant theme in the American body politic, serving as a template for arguments on monarchy versus republic, the rule of the elite versus the equality of all men, and the place of religion in a free society. The Federalists were the first party to turn against the French while the Republicans, led by Thomas Jefferson, continued to admire the revolution and its reformist agenda. In 1800, Thomas Jefferson defeated the Federalist John Adams and was elected president of the United States. Pro-French sentiments served those who harbored animosity toward Great Britain and its king, George III. The American enthusiasm for revolutionary France began to cool with news of the beheading of Louis XVI and his wife Marie Antoinette, the Reign of Terror and the repression of the church.

FRANCIS CABOT LOWELL GOES TO FRANCE

In July 1795, barely a year after the worst excesses of the Reign of Terror, twenty-year-old Francis Cabot Lowell arrived in Bilbao, in the Basque Country of northern Spain, on an American ship carrying a cargo of rice and flour. The ship was owned by Thomas Russell, whose sister Rebecca was the third wife of Judge John Lowell. As supercargo of the vessel, Francis Lowell traveled abroad to learn about ships, crews and cargoes, as well as to visit the ports to which the goods were shipped. His responsibility was to sell at a good profit the rice and flour owned by his father, Thomas Russell, and other Boston merchants, and to buy as cheaply as possible cases of wine, sherry and brandy to take back to the United States. From Bilbao, the ship made its way some 120 miles northeast to the French port city of Bordeaux on the Garonne River. En route Lowell's ship was stopped by His Majesty's fifty-gun ship *Jupiter*. The British captain examined the American ship very closely "but not finding any evidence of our going to France, he dismissed us." Having fooled the British, the vessel continued to the port of Bordeaux, where Francis sold the rice and flour at a good profit.

Francis Lowell was excited by his visit to beautiful Bordeaux, surrounded by vineyards and chateaux producing some of the world's finest wines. His trip to France was less an opportunity for business than a chance to study the country and learn its language, especially at so momentous a time. His father kept him supplied with money and in France he had his relatives John and George Higginson, born in Salem, and Edward Bromfield from Newburyport.[5] In Bordeaux he chanced to meet John Higginson and readily agreed to travel to Paris, where Higginson owned "a very handsome place." In Paris, Higginson wined and dined his young relative, even taking him to the opera and reminding him, "Do not forget the opera glasses."

Francis was amused by the disquiet in Boston over the French Revolution. He wrote to his father from the relative safety of Bordeaux, on July 26, "The ideas you have of France in America are quite erroneous. We have as much safety here as in America. We walk about the streets without any trouble; a pickpocket or thief have not been heard of for a long time. A duel yesterday was fought between two gentlemen at the riverside. . . . One of them shot the other's pistol out of his hand but he returned the shot and killed his adversary."

Much of the Paris that Francis saw was destroyed, especially the properties associated with the *ancien regime*. The Church of St. Sulpicia was "stripped of everything" and the statues smashed. The citizens of the city were issued ration cards and were allowed "as much bread as the municipals consider sufficient for him and his family." People stood in long queues waiting to buy wood or coal for fuel. The Luxemburg Gardens "have been converted into vast cannon foundries. The noise is great; all the refuse from the works is falling pell-mell into the Seine."[6]

The French Revolution fascinated Francis, who wrote that on July 20, six men went on trial for starting an insurrection and "when found guilty one of them took a knife and stabbed himself and handed it to the next. He did the same and so on the whole six. Three had life enough left to be dragged to the guillotine, as they went along, one of them laughed." In his letters home, Francis shifted easily from the profound to the mundane. After describing the horrible death of the six men, Francis blithely told his father that in France "everything is cheap. The crops of wheat are said to be more abundant than ever." However, if the chaos of the war continued, Francis was certain there would be good markets in France for American farm products.

In Revolutionary Paris, Francis acted the tourist. With the help of John Higginson he found comfortable rooms at No. 5, Rue de la Michodiere, two blocks from the Opera House. From there, as he wrote to his father on September 21, 1795, he visited "several of the principal places in Paris. The actors in the theatres are much superior to anything I ever saw. Though I do not understand a word of their language, I enter purposefully into the story. There is scarcely a sentence to which I do not affix an idea, whether right or not I cannot say." Francis planned to visit the palace at Versailles, hoping to see its famous gardens.

John and George Higginson were the sons of the merchant Stephen Higginson, uncle to John Lowell Jr., whose late mother was Sarah Higginson. The young men chose to settle in France, where they served as agents for American merchants. In 1796, the eccentric John failed to show up for his marriage to Josephine de la Porte of Paris. His anxious friends rushed to his lodgings and "found him with his feet on the mantle-piece. He had forgotten all about it." John married his Josephine and had two French daughters: Jeanette, who died young, and Simplice, who married the Viscount de Rouille.

In France, Lowell was addressed as Citoyen Francois Cabot Louell. Francis was determined to become proficient in French and planned to stay in the country over the winter. He accepted an invitation from George Higginson to move to the town of Tours, where he could immerse himself fully in the French language. Writing to Citoyen Francois Lowell on October 5, George admitted that he was "much enraged by my Boston friends" who faulted the French Revolution. George was "not surprised at your disliking Paris. I do not like it myself." His Paris-based brother John Higginson, however, "was prejudiced in favor of Paris and its sights." In Tours, Citoyen Lowell found comfortable accommodations at chez le Citoyen Fay. Having a family who supported and protected him, and supplied him with ample cash, Francis set out from Paris to Tours. He carried with him a special right of passage that, translated into the English language, reads, "Citizen James Monroe, minister plenipotentiary of the United States of America to the French Republic has issued this passport. The Masters of the Post are ordered to furnish the citizens François Cabot Louell, merchant, and Simon Tisdale, merchant, with the horses needed to journey from Paris to Tours, in return for a fee as prescribed by the law." The right of passage was issued in Paris by *Le Comite de Salut Public* on 23 Vendemiare on the fourth year (equivalent to September 23, 1795) of the French Republic, one and indivisible, and signed by T. Berlier.

James Monroe resigned his seat as a U.S. senator in 1794 to take up the appointment of ambassador to France. Despite America's declared neutrality, Monroe's own sympathies lay strongly with the French in their epic battle against Great Britain. So open was his support for the French that Monroe was recalled to the United States in 1796. Seven years later, Monroe returned to Paris as ambassador and successfully negotiated the Louisiana Purchase, doubling the landmass of the United States.

With his special passport, wealthy friends and family in France to welcome him, young Francois Cabot Louell traveled unhindered from Paris to the ancient town of Tours, with its magnificent fifteenth-century Gothic cathedral, situated along the Loire River. To his father, Francis wrote, "I am universally told that I ought neither to speak or write, not think English if I wish to obtain the French. You must not therefore expect to hear from me much more these three months." In the same letter, Francis told his father about the Paris tribunals that executed hundreds of opponents a day. These mass executions no longer excited the mob: "One of our training days [with the Marti-Mercurial Band at Harvard] made a great deal more noise than the killing of four or five hundred men here."

His cousin Edward Bromfield amused him by writing long letters entirely in the French language. Dating one such letter 4 Brumaire, the second month of the calendar of the French republic, corresponding to late October to late November 1795, Edward Bromfield wrote in earthy French to his "dear former neighbor" to ask how Francis was enjoying his travels.

> Do you find, [asked Bromfield] that Paris has more attractions than Tours? I believe it does. I am sure you had fun with quite a few little French mistresses; how can one do without? It takes a lot of self-control to resist them. Instead you could have a nice bourgeois lady to give you secret lessons. She will soon have you stammering in French, then you will be easier understood, and soon you will be speaking freely like a trueborn Frenchman. Everyone is astonished by the rapid progress made by our compatriot [George] Higginson who is succeeding as brilliantly in commerce as he has in learning French. Is your traveling companion in good health? He is so charming that others, including myself, are eager to help him. I don't take part in politics and will not tell you my views. It is sufficient for me to say that the general public will come around to support the revolutionary government. From the time you arrived in Paris, I tried my best to put myself at your disposal, in recognition of the strong bond that exists between our families. Before you arrived in France, I only knew of you by name, but now I regard you as a friend and value you and your interests. The more chances I have to assist you the happier I will be. Write to me often in French. I embrace you with my heart and my friendship.

The Bromfield family of Newburyport was indeed indebted to the Lowells. After suffering financial setbacks, the Bromfield family left Newburyport in 1782 and moved to Boston with the help of Judge John Lowell, who rented them a house at a low rent. The boys Edward and John could not afford a university education. Edward became a merchant and moved to Paris, where he lavished attention on young Francis in gratitude for the kindnesses Judge Lowell had shown his family.[7]

Footloose and fancy-free and absorbed in the pleasures of France, young Francis neglected his obligations to family and friends. His father and mother wrote anxiously to inquire if he were safe and pleaded with him to return home. As usual, the most blunt and strident remarks came from his older brother, John Lowell Jr. From Boston, on February 10, 1796, John Jr. wrote, "I am to scold you for your abominable neglect of your friends in not giving them any information whatsoever relative to yourself—not a line has been received since sixteen days after your arrival in France. This has not only made us uneasy as we expected some little attention from you [but we are also] apprehensive for your safety. It has never been decided whether you intend to return this winter or not." To indicate that his scolding was done out of love, John Jr. told Francis that a bill of exchange worth £140 sterling was on its way to him, together with a money order for £40. John Jr. ended his letter wishing Francis "health & happiness & a speedy return to Boston."

In a follow-up letter, John Lowell Jr. demanded that Francis leave France and return to Boston before the summer of 1796. It was time to give up the freedoms of youth and assume the responsibilities of manhood: "The sooner you get settled in business, in my opinion, the better for your future interest and certainly better for your happiness. No man can, in my opinion, duly appreciate the advantages of being early in business and being settled at an early period of life. The habits which are formed in the younger parts of life seldom forsake us and they always sit with more care upon us—Like old friends they understand us in our good or ill fortune. If indolence takes possession of our character in vain do we attempt to extricate the unwelcome intruder. You may think me a moralizer if I persevere in these remarks but I perhaps will conclude that I think you are wanting in reflection."

Francis absorbed the language and culture of France at a time when thousands were under arrest and many beheaded. The French armies occupied Holland and Belgium, and defeated the Italians and Austrians. Francis Cabot Lowell gave little thought to the high-minded values of the Revolution: Liberty, Equality and Fraternity. Seemingly unaware of the hunger and civil unrest all around him, Francis Cabot Lowell lived pleasantly in Tours, studying his French grammar and practicing his spoken French, until June 1796, when he finally heeded his brother and returned to Boston to the bosom of his welcoming family.

FRANCIS BEGINS HIS CAREER AS A MERCHANT

Having served his apprenticeship and accompanied a cargo to a foreign port, young Francis Cabot was ready for the life of a Boston merchant. Within weeks of his return from France, the merchant Francis Cabot Lowell opened a store (warehouse) at No. 60 Long Wharf, Boston, and, with the aid of a clerk to record letters and transactions in large ledger books, was open for business. Although Francis lived in Boston from an early age, his business and social contacts were largely restricted to the old Essex County families, the Jacksons of Newburyport, and the Cabots, Lees and Thorndikes of Salem and Beverly. He wrote to his uncle William Cabot of Salem on July 22, 1796, restating "my offer if you have any business to employ me I will come to Salem at any time when I am not very much occupied here. But I cannot consent to stay here without doing anything."

William Cabot, a bachelor and brother to Francis' late mother, lived in a grand house in Salem that he inherited from his father. To test his nephew's abilities, William suggested that Francis buy rice under twenty-five shillings a ton. Francis responded that "I could not get rice under 36 shillings instead of the 25 shillings, the price you told me to buy it at." Next Francis tried to sell tea, but William, a seasoned merchant, was not buying. "From the price this is at in London," responded William Cabot, "I think it must fall. I would therefore rather wait, especially as my purchase is to be so large." William asked Francis to buy a gross of cork from London together with two dozen bottles of excellent claret wine. But William was not satisfied with the claret and Francis had to take the order back. However, wrote Francis, "Several vessels have arrived from Bordeaux. I have therefore no doubt to find you the claret you want."

William was impressed by the efforts Francis was making to satisfy his customers. "At present," wrote William on July 28, "I am much pleased with your mode of doing business for me, as it gives me pleasing hopes of your transacting business for yourself in a profitable way."

Francis Cabot Lowell started his career as a merchant at a fortunate time. The wars in Europe created a great demand for American tobacco, lumber, flour and rice, as well as for re-exports of sugar, coffee, cocoa and pepper. Eli Whitney's cotton gin created a vast expansion of cotton production, most of which went to feed the insatiable demand of the textile mills of the English Midlands. Ships and crews from the Northeast sailed to Charleston carrying foodstuffs, clothing and shoes for the slaves and picking up cargoes of cotton, rice and flour destined for Europe. Ships arrived in Boston, New York and Philadelphia carrying silks, cotton textiles and chinaware from the Orient. Merchants like Francis Cabot Lowell were fast developing domestic markets by trading between Boston, New York, Baltimore, Philadelphia and other ports along the eastern seaboard. Nearly all this trade was carried on American-made ships with Yankee skippers and sailors.

Still learning his trade, Francis bought part of a shipment of salt from Cadiz, "which I am told is very good for fisherman, especially for dry fish." He wrote to his uncle William on August 21, hoping to sell the salt at a profit, "If any of your friends want any I will thank you to recommend me to them." The domestic market for goods was still small, as the vast bulk of the American population was made up of self-sufficient farmers or impoverished slaves. When Francis began as a merchant the urban market was beginning to grow. As his confidence in business grew,

Francis bought a range of goods from China, India and Europe for sale on the American market, the West Indies, South America or wherever he could find buyers.

Throughout his mercantile career, Francis received regular listings of current prices of goods sent to him by his agents in Amsterdam, Rotterdam, Bordeaux, Calcutta and other port cities. The "Current Prices" bulletins listed the latest prices obtained for over one hundred commodities including various teas, coffee, sugar, tobacco, cotton, cocoa, rice, whale oil, hides, potash, flour, lumber and indigo. Alongside each price were comments such as "little demand," "dull sale," "slow sale," "without demand" and the hoped-for "in demand." Also listed were the current values of the competing currencies. Sent by ship, these price lists were always weeks old by the time they reached the merchant's office. Calculating the price he paid, where his goods were most likely to be in demand and checking the values of currencies, Francis would decide where best to send his cargoes. He also needed to know the availability of shipping and to choose a captain and crew he could trust.

UNCLE WILLIAM CABOT

The relationship between Francis and his demanding uncle changed after William Cabot retired from his business and passed the management of his financial affairs on to his nephew. Checking the regular business statements Francis sent him, William objected to the management fees charged. Francis respectfully responded on January 23, 1802:

Dear Uncle,

I hope you will do me the justice to remove from your mind any ill feelings my account has occasioned you. I cannot let this opportunity pass without saying that I am certain my conduct towards you has always been the result of a proper affection for you and that wherein I have neglected it has not been proceeded from any want of Regard and affection but from a natural negligence which I have not the power of overcoming. Providence has so far smiled on my honest exertions as that I have been enabled to obtain for myself a competent living & have increased my property as fast as my wishes could suggest.

I hope you will not suffer your feelings to be wounded by any improper suggestions you have made against me. And I am sure your own good judgement & affection uninfluenced will do justice to my affection to you.

Yours,
Francis C. Lowell

William Cabot—aging, ill and cantankerous—continued to pester his nephew, demanding that Francis come to visit him and correct alleged errors in his accounts. Francis sent an exasperated response on March 23, 1803: "I am certain I have paid as much attention to your affairs than to any other human being whatever. If you consider my situation, it has been impossible for the past six months [to visit you as] my wife has been in such a situation for that time that she could not leave her house for any distance, and you know too well the duties of a husband to wish me to come at such a time without her." Francis paid as much attention to William's finances as "to my own affairs which I consider very important, believing as I do I have but a few years to remain here, and think I shall leave behind a very young family who must depend on charity unless I am able to accumulate sufficient for their support before I leave them."

Francis visited William and arranged for Ezra Shipley to look out for him. Shipley reported to Francis that William had difficulty walking and the doctor expected his spasms to continue "but not with violence." Most of all, the old fellow was lonely and Francis' "visits are very gratifying to him." As William's attitude shifted from petulance to gratitude, the old bachelor uncle became a regular visitor to the Lowell home.

BEST FRIENDS

Charles, one of the sons of Jonathan Jackson, was born in Newburyport within months of the birth of Francis Cabot Lowell. Like Francis, he was admitted to Harvard at age fourteen, where the two became fast "college chums" and enjoyed the same degree of closeness shared when their fathers attended Harvard. Charles Jackson was a brilliant scholar. After graduation he apprenticed to Theophilus Parsons in Newburyport, where he later opened his own law practice. Charles Jackson in Newburyport and Francis C. Lowell in Boston kept up a weekly correspondence. These were letters of close friends who trusted each another with their deepest thoughts, anxieties and hopes. But unlike the romantic letters of their fathers, there is no hint of a sexual attraction between Charles and Francis. Charles shared his excitement, but also the difficulties in starting a law practice in a small town. "I have been most miserably dull," wrote Charles Jackson to Francis on August 23, 1797, "for almost a total want of business. I feel in the worst ill-humor with the law, of everything related to it." While waiting for legal work, Jackson occupied himself reading Edward Gibbon's six-volume work, *The History of the Decline and Fall of the Roman Empire.* "I am devouring historical anecdotes with a most gluttonous appetite. [I have] sold aunt Tracy's farm for 4000 pounds, 1000 pounds paid down." He planned to invest the proceeds from the sale

wisely as "the interest of the money is all her family will have to live on."
Charles planned to place the money "in different parcels with private
people," including Francis Cabot Lowell.

An optimistic letter from Charles (March 31, 1798) told Francis that he
had "in fact been very much occupied. I have done more business in my
office in the last three or four weeks than I have ever done before in three
months." Charles proudly reported that during those few weeks he had
submitted fifty-three writs, compared with an average of only seventeen
before, and as many as submitted by the illustrious Theophilus Parsons,
Newburyport's star attorney. With so erratic an income, Charles Jackson
regularly turned to Francis to borrow money to pay his personal expenses
as well as the cost of keeping open his law practice. Charles confessed
(May 25, 1798), "I am not pleased with drawing so much money out of
your hands." Charles wrote Francis about the welfare of the rest of his
family, including his father Jonathan Jackson, who was experiencing hard
times and was feeling unwell.

Another concern was how to pay for the medical education of his
brother James Jackson. Born a year later than Charles, James graduated
from Harvard in 1796 "with some of the lower marks of distinction in
his class." James set his heart on the practice of medicine and served his
apprenticeship under Dr. Edward Augustus Holyoke of Salem. Lacking
the $400 a year he needed to complete his studies he turned to his brother
Charles, who, in turn, asked Francis Cabot Lowell for the money. With
this support, James journeyed to London to study at St. Thomas' and
Guy's Hospitals. In August 1800, Dr. James Jackson boarded the *Superb*
for his return to Boston, where he established a fashionable and lucrative
practice, counting Francis Cabot Lowell and family among his patients.

Francis Cabot Lowell provided regular advice to the Jackson family,
and lent them thousands of dollars. By 1799, Charles Jackson's loan account with Francis Cabot Lowell stood at $7,592.49, made up of regular
monthly borrowings of $100 to $300. Charles was mortified to learn that
his impoverished but self-indulgent father was also asking Francis for
money. Charles wrote to Francis (May 11, 1801), "I understand you have
lately advanced him money. I hope you will not repeat it. It will deal a
loss to yourself and do him no good." Unable to make a decent living in
Newburyport, Charles Jackson saw his future in Boston and moved to the
town in 1803, living at 1 Hamilton Place and establishing a lucrative law
practice at 7 State Street.

In 1796, Boston experienced an outbreak of yellow fever, a viral infection transmitted by the mosquito. Before reaching Boston, the epidemic
ravaged Philadelphia, at that time the nation's capital and largest city,
killing 3,645 people—nearly one in ten of the population—and in New
York killing 1,310 more. The usual symptoms of the infection include

high fever, coughing and vomiting. One case in six is more virulent, with coughing up blood (hence the name "black vomit") and jaundice (hence "yellow fever"). Compared with Philadelphia and New York, Boston got off lightly with only two hundred deaths. Writing (October 6) to his sister Susanna, Francis told her that a mutual friend "has left town in a fright on account of the Yellow Fever. I hope she has not given it to the whole town of Portsmouth. The people who occasioned this alarm by their deaths lived some of them in the house next to my store, and others right behind it. Still, I live to glorify God, I shall continue to live if no worse fever rages."

In March 1750, Puritan Massachusetts had passed a law "to prevent Stage plays and other Theatrical entertainments" on the grounds that the theatrical plays lead "to great and unnecessary expenses, and discourage industry and frugality, but likewise intended generally to increase immorality, impiety and a contempt for religion." On December 2, 1792, an acting troop on a visit to Boston staged Richard Brinsley Sheridan's hilarious farce *The School for Scandal*. A sheriff suddenly appeared on the stage and arrested one of the actors. The struggling young lawyer John Quincy Adams wrote a series of articles in the *Columbian Centinel*, December 19–22, 1792, supporting stage shows in Boston. The arrested actor was defended in court by Harrison Gray Otis, the up-and-coming lawyer and a disciple of Judge John Lowell. Otis won the case and afterward "Boston was permitted to enjoy the theatre." In 1793, this law was officially repealed and in February 1794, the Boston Theatre at the corner of Federal and Franklin streets was open to performances. Charles Bulfinch designed the opulent brick theater. The range of plays included Shakespeare, Sheridan and Goldsmith. In September 1796, the theater staged a production of Shakespeare's *Romeo and Juliet.* The Boston Theatre was followed two years later by the building of the Haymarket Theatre at the corner of Tremont and Boylston Streets. The Haymarket opened with *The Comedy of the Belle's Stratagem* and Maxamilien Gardel's 1779 ballet *Mizra and Lindor*, performed by a visiting French corps de ballet. By the time Francis Lowell entered his adult years, the theater, and even ballet, were established parts of the fabric of life of Boston's well-to-do.[8]

Charles Bulfinch was Boston's leading architect. His design for the Massachusetts State House (1795–1798) built on Beacon Hill was based on Somerset House in London, completed some twenty years earlier. Close by his Boston Theatre was the elegant Tontine Crescent. Here, the Bulfinch plan called for two curving rows of town houses surrounding an oval shaped tree-lined park, with each row comprising sixteen townhouses. Because of financial constraints, only one of the rows of townhouses was actually built. The first of three houses Bulfinch designed for Harrison Gray Otis was completed on Cambridge Street in 1796. At the start of the nineteenth century, other architects in Boston followed the style of Charles Bulfinch to give elegance to sections of the fast-growing town.

HANNAH JACKSON

Yellow fever or not, Francis attended the newly opened twelve-hundred-seat Haymarket Theatre in the company of Sally Wendle, his sister Sarah Champney Lowell and Hannah Jackson, paying $1 per ticket to see *Know Your Own Mind*, by the Irish-born Arthur Murphy. The playwright Murphy changed his story, which was based on Philippe Destouches' 1713 French play *L'Irresolu*, into a comedy of English manners and intrigue. In 1777 the play had opened to mixed reviews at London's Drury Lane Theatre. Francis Lowell enjoyed the Boston performance, admired some of the actors and considered, "The players were not so wretched as they were represented."

In 1797, Charles Jackson wrote to his brother that "my old & good friend Frank Lowell has made himself very agreeable to Hannah—the lady did not think it fit to reject his suit & he found no difficulty in obtaining my father's consent." Their father, Jonathan Jackson, was twenty-nine when he married eighteen-year-old Hannah Tracy. Her namesake Hannah was the oldest of the Jackson girls. While on his trip to England in 1785, Jonathan Jackson addressed a delightful letter to nine-year-old Hannah: "To Miss Jackson. And did my sweet little Hannah write part of the letter herself, which her Mamma was so kind as to enclose me? I am glad to find that she has learned to write and hope she will write still better by the time that I get home. I long for the time to come when I shall take her and her sweet little sisters into my arms and squeeze and hug them so that I shall almost take their breath away. Sister Sally has not forgotten me, I hope and Harriet has, I suppose; and as for little Mary, she never knew much about me. Give my love to 'em all—and learn to work as fast as you can to make Shirts etc. and assist your mother. I shall bring you home a guitar to play upon—and at all times be assured of the love of your affectionate father. J. Jackson." When Jonathan Jackson returned home he found poverty and privation and too few buyers for the fancy goods he acquired in England.

The year 1797 was a low point in the lives of Jonathan and Hannah Jackson. Their money was gone and they were obliged to live in rented rooms in Charlestown. Exhausted from giving birth to nine children in ten years, Hannah Tracey Jackson died on April 28 in an attack of apoplexy.

Because of Jonathan Jackson's financial difficulties the closely knit and loving family was forced to separate. Daughter Hannah Jackson wrote to her brother Henry about "all the changes that have taken place in our family—we shall never be again collected as we have been." Her older brothers were at sea, Charles was in Newburyport, "everyday increasing his reputation as a lawyer there," James was due "shortly to begin his studies of physic," Patrick "remains as clever a fellow as ever, Harriet and Mary are at boarding-school in Hingham, and Sally and myself are out at board in the same town." Hannah attempted to keep the family together through the frequent exchange of letters. When a young cousin failed to respond to her letter, Hannah sarcastically commented to her brother Henry, "I will acknowledge that it would be the height of presumption to suppose that a man of business would have the time to write to a woman."

The sweet and thoughtful Hannah Jackson was increasingly entering into Francis Lowell's thoughts. Francis had known the Jackson family all of his life and regarded Charles Jackson as his closest friend. In May Hannah, now twenty-one years old, accompanied the Reverend Edward Bass to Philadelphia. Bass was the rector of St. Paul's of Newburyport, founded in 1711 and the oldest continually functioning Episcopal Church in Massachusetts. In Christ Church, Philadelphia, Bass was consecrated bishop of the Diocese of Massachusetts, which included New Hampshire and Rhode Island.[9] Francis Cabot Lowell did not allow the differences in economic status of the Lowell and Jackson families to deter him from wanting to marry Hannah.

On November 2, 1798, in the town of Boston, the twenty-three-year-old Francis Cabot Lowell married Hannah Jackson, born February 2, 1776, and aged twenty-two. Francis's oldest sister, Anna Cabot Lowell recorded the joy of the wedding: "Everything looked as cheerful as the smiling countenance of our Hannah. Charles pronounced it the pleasantest evening he had had in many years. There is nothing like having one's feelings attuned to happiness." The love that began at Harvard between their fathers—Philander and Philocles—also burned bright among their children. The Harvard College chums, Francis Cabot Lowell and Charles Jackson, were now brothers-in-law.

MERCANTILE CAREER ADVANCES

Francis began small by supplying goods to grocery shops around Boston. In July 1797, for example, he filled an order for raisins, rum, chocolate, molasses, rice, cinnamon and sugar for the grocer Benjamin Hammatt at Southack's Court. With his business progressing, a more serious Francis Lowell was emerging. He observed that people respond differently to friends than to business contacts. "I know my talents too well," he wrote to his sister Susanna (October 6, 1798). "I have often wondered how those we call our friends are distinguished in our own minds from the common run of people. We are willing to run all over town to serve an indifferent man. I do no other business till he is attended to. But if a friend charges us with a message we neglect it and say any time will do as it only regards my friend." All his adult life, Francis Lowell was driven to attend promptly to his business commitments but was equally prompt in meeting obligations to family and friends.

A sudden lack of goods in Boston sent Francis Lowell scurrying to Philadelphia, where he arrived on June 18, 1798. Representing his father, he came in search of gin, tea and duck (a heavy, plain woven cotton fabric). There, too, "I find I shall not accomplish anything," as prices were too high and available quantities too limited to take much back to Boston. In search of goods, Francis contacted Captain Robert Jackson (Hannah's brother), who responded (July 17), "I have no India goods whatsoever myself." Soon, though, ships from the Orient were arriving at Boston, offering Francis good opportunities for trade. From September 20, 1798, to September 3, 1799, he was the chief broker for consignments totaling 9,399 gallons of gin, valued at $9,927.33, then ostensibly used for medicinal purposes in the treatment of gout, arthritis, kidney stones and consumption. Francis bought a shipment of 8,000 nankins (china porcelain with blue ornamentation on a white background) valued at $7,613.50. The nankins were resold in lots of five hundred to one thousand on terms of 90 to 120 to various Boston merchants, including the firms of John Salter, Daniel Weld, Forbes & Keith, Sawyer & Wigglesworth, Louis & Cutler and Stevens & Henry. The brokers attempted to sell their lots for a quick profit to pay Francis Lowell before the due date of the loan. Francis exported flour, dried fish and timber. He received in Boston shipments of brandy and handwoven Indian bandannas (large colored kerchiefs with white spots and figures on a red or blue background). The bandannas were especially popular for sale as head coverings on the Caribbean islands.[10]

As his reputation grew Francis Lowell was filling larger orders, such as thirty cases of claret wine, sold to William Orne for $375. Francis bought peppers, figs, sugar, raisins, and coffee on consignment for the large Beverly merchants Joseph Jr. and Nathaniel Lee and Israel Thorndike, who would long continue to play important roles in his life. He imported rum from Tobago and Antigua, wines from France and brandy from Naples. Francis established trade links with merchants from Maine to South Carolina as well as Bordeaux, London and Barcelona. From the start of his career as a merchant Francis Cabot Lowell, backed by his father's money, set about to establish trusting relationships with his suppliers and customers. He soon learned, however, that the values of integrity, honesty, timeliness and keeping promises did not easily transfer into the rough world of business.

For example, Oliver Phelps took a loan of $1,000 from Judge John Lowell at 6 percent compound interest. Phelps paid off part of the loan, only to borrow more and soon owed the Lowells the sum of $2,538.67. Phelps wrote to Francis asking for more time to pay down the loan. After consulting his father, Francis responded (July 25, 1797), "I hope you will pay much earlier than the time you mentioned as you possibly can—as you must be sensible the interest is no compensation for the use of the money to a young man." Born in 1749, Oliver Phelps joined the Continental Army and served as superintendent of purchases of army supplies. At war's end, Phelps borrowed money to speculate in land in Massachusetts, New York, the Western Reserve, Georgia and West Virginia. Once the largest landowner in the United States, Phelps was pursued by his creditors, lost all his property and was thrown into debtor's prison, where he died in 1809. His tombstone reads, "Enterprise, Industry and Temperance cannot always ensure success, but the fruit of these virtues will be felt by society."

In 1797, Francis Cabot Lowell sold $450 worth of Russian Duck (white linen canvas) and Raven's Duck (sailcloth) "of a very superior quality" to the son of William Martin of North Yarmouth, Maine. The English-born William Martin immigrated with his family to the United States in 1783 after suffering losses as a wholesale merchant in London. He set himself up in Boston as a bookseller but soon moved to Maine, where he opened a store. Martin became involved in politics and played an important role in the establishment of Bowdoin College. He seemed the right sort of man for Francis Cabot Lowell to trust and do business with. Despite repeated promises to settle the debt, the money did not arrive. "I was contented & am still, to make every reasonable allowance for the difficulty you have in raising money to pay your son's debts," wrote Francis Cabot to William Martin Sr. (October 3, 1797), "as I think it is extremely wrong for any son to put his father in such a situation." Martin sent small sums in an attempt to placate Francis, who responded (February 19, 1798), "I request you to be particular when I may depend on the money you owe me. You have so often promised me & so often disappointed me." The matter dragged on month after month. "I find you have paid debts to other people," wrote Francis (March 7), "while mine has been neglected." Martin replied that he was in the process of selling property to raise the money owed to Lowell. "This sir," responded Francis in anger, "is your own promise. I wish to know what has prevented your complying with it." The exasperated Francis wrote (December 19), "I assure you I have never been kept so long out of my money since I have been in business. I had very good reason to expect it punctually paid. I am very much in want of money at present as it is extremely scarce and I have large obligations which I am obliged to be punctual to the hour." Francis had reached the end of his patience with William Martin, who had repeatedly broken his promises. On April 21, Francis wrote to the lawyer Benjamin Whitwell of Augusta, Maine, instructing him seek redress from Martin and "attach any property you can find so as to make him pay."

Born in Boston in 1772, Benjamin Whitwell attended the Latin School and graduated from Harvard College in 1790. Finding Boston crowded with lawyers—even John Quincy Adams had difficulty establishing a law practice in the town—Whitwell moved to Augusta, Maine, a village of one thousand people. There he made a good living managing the vast tracts of land owned by absentee proprietors. Refined in manner and elegant in dress, Whitwell was decidedly out of place in the rough frontier of Maine. "More fond of poetry than of pleading," Whitwell later returned to Boston. Francis Cabot Lowell had other occasions to use the services of Benjamin Whitwell. Francis asked Whitwell to call on Ruben Tabor from the nearby village of Vassallborough in the hope of recovering money from him. "I will readily pay you for your expenses & attention. I believe you will find him [Tabor] an honest man but eccentric & foolish. His father resides in Portland & is a man of some property. I should be perfectly satisfied with his father's guarantee." Whitwell suggested that Lowell sue the Tabors, but Francis (May 17, 1797) was "very much averse to getting into law-suits in your eastern country unless it is absolutely necessary." The Tabors repeatedly promised but did not deliver the money. Matters dragged on into the year 1800, when Francis asked his lawyer to sue the Tabors and attach their properties.

Another problem that Francis Cabot Lowell had to manage was his dealings with John Balfour of Tobago. Columbus sighted Tobago in 1498, and over the years the West Indian island changed hands many times. In 1793, the British took the island from France. With an economy based on sugar cane, Tobago had a population of fifteen thousand, nearly all African slaves ruled over by a small military force, five hundred British settlers, some three hundred freed slaves, and a few of the French who remained. One of the leaders of the English establishment was John Balfour, who served as chief magistrate and acting governor. Balfour also had a lucrative business exporting Tobago rum. "Rum from your island is at present rather dull," wrote Francis to John Balfour (March 17, 1798), "occasioned by the great quantity of brandy, which has been brought from France. But the importation of brandy has in a great measure ceased, arising from the present situation with France." Francis Cabot Lowell ordered rum from Balfour, believing that the demand would grow. The transaction, alas, did not go smoothly after Balfour accused Francis Cabot Lowell of charging him higher fees than he charged other rum suppliers. "This is the first time," responded Lowell indignantly (April 10). "I ever had my honesty called into question by those I am doing business with.

If you take the trouble of enquiring of any merchant in this place you will find I am not in want of business & that I have more character than to merit the language you have seen pleased to give to me." Lowell and Balfour did not do business again.[11]

HELPING BUILD A NATIONAL ECONOMY

On August 19, 1797, Francis wrote to his agents in Bordeaux to let them know that a shipment of seventy-five boxes of brown sugar, valued at $4,180.77 on the brig *Enterprize* was en route from the West Indies. In return he asked for a shipment of wine and olive oil to be sent to John Stille & Company in Philadelphia. The passage of goods was much influenced by world events. Francis informed a customer (August 23) that "the news we have this day received from Ireland that the prospect of an accommodation between the sister republics would render it very imprudent for any person to procure salt petre at the present time at a price near its nominal one." Francis was referring to French efforts to drive out the Protestant Establishment from Ireland and set up a pro-French republic. The Irish rebellion was severely repressed by British troops under Charles Cornwallis, the newly appointed chief-of-staff and governor-general of Ireland.

Over the years, Francis Cabot Lowell nurtured a strong and trusting business relationship with John Stille & Company of Philadelphia. Located at the corner of Chestnut and Water streets, John Stille & Company was a long-established Philadelphia commission house connected with Massachusetts shipping interests. "I should recommend to my father or any of my friends," Francis wrote (August 27), "to employ you in any business they might have in your city. It is a justice I owe them & you that I should recommend them where I know they would be best served." Employing his brothers-in-law, Captains Robert and Henry Jackson, Francis shipped to Philadelphia nankins from Canton, muslins from Calcutta, and rum distilled in the West Indies and in New England. In addition, Souchong tea left his Boston warehouse bound for John Stille & Company in Philadelphia. "The post arrives here every day at noon," wrote Francis to John Stille (May 20, 1799). "Your letter of 15th inst. arrived this noon. The letter I am now writing will leave tomorrow morning. The mail closes every morning for Philadelphia at 8 o'clock. It would be a little hazardous to wait till the last day because the mail from Philadelphia is often a day or two late." Letters between Boston and Philadelphia in 1799 took only five to seven days from sending to arrival.

Francis Lowell found new customers in New York and Baltimore. He sold French wines and brandy to Moses Hayman Levy, merchant of Newport,

Rhode Island, and New York. Levy was one of the original benefactors of
the Truro Synagogue in Newport, the oldest synagogue in the United States.
In New York he was involved with the Shearith Israel Congregation of the
Spanish and Portuguese Jewish community established in 1654.

To Benjamin Williams, commission agent, 126 Lombard Street, Baltimore, Francis wrote (December 4, 1799), "I have a good quantity of fine
Indian muslins. I wish to know if they would sell well at your market &
what price. I mean fine muslins and not cotton which I believe are called
muslins with you. I have about three thousand dollars worth. They commonly sell for one dollar. I am willing to sell them at 80 cents." Williams
was born in Roxbury, Massachusetts and moved to Baltimore. In the
1820s, the sons of Benjamin Williams followed Lowell's lead into manufacturing and established the Savage Cotton Mill.

THE CABOT FAMILY AND THE EAST INDIA TRADE

The Cabot family played only a small role during his childhood, but now
the links with his uncle William Cabot and other merchants of Salem allowed Francis to become one of the first merchants in Boston to specialize
in the East India trade.

The story of the Cabot family in America started in the year 1700 when
the twenty-year-old John Cabot, accompanied by his two older brothers,
left the channel isle of Jersey, close to the Normandy coast, to settle in
Salem, Massachusetts. In 1702, John made a good match with Anna Orne,
from a prominent Essex County family. The couple had six daughters
and three sons. Four of John Cabot's children married into the Higginson
family, whose ancestor, the Reverend John Higginson, in 1692 served as a
prosecutor in the Salem witch trials. The middle son, Francis Cabot, was
born in 1706, and was married on June 20, 1745, to Mary Fitch of Ipswich,
who bore two sons and four daughters. Francis Cabot became a successful merchant in Salem. One of his two sons, William Cabot, born April 27,
1752, remained a bachelor all his days; his company was a source of delight to his friends and family. William was hospitable and served excellent dinners, with venison as the main course. Among the four daughters
of Francis Cabot was Susanna, born 1753. Susanna became the second
wife of John Lowell of Newburyport. She was the only one of Francis
Cabot's six children to raise a family, but even Susanna did not long enjoy her children. She died age twenty-three, leaving behind two-year-old
Francis Cabot, named for his grandfather, and three-month-old Susanna.

John Cabot's third son, Joseph, married Elizabeth Higginson, who bore
him a large family of two daughters and nine sons, including Samuel,
John, George and Andrew. George Cabot (1751–1823), the seventh child,

was especially gifted. The Cabot brothers engaged in the Baltic and East India trade, as well as trading in slaves from Africa and opium from Turkey. Samuel Cabot opened an office in Canton to sell opium and buy Chinese tea, pottery and silks. The three Cabot brothers, John, George and Andrew, were the leading shareholders in the Beverly Cotton Manufactory.

Members of the Cabot family married with the Lee, Jackson, Lowell, Higginson, Winthrop, Lodge and other leading families north of Boston. Marriages between first cousins were common and a means to keep the money in the family. These families had a head for figures and paid attention to detail. Practicality, however, was combined with eccentricity and a touch of madness. Mental disorders followed the Lowell family down the generations. Though educated and widely traveled, the Essex County families preferred their own company and were suspicious of outsiders. They were linked in business and were prominent members of the Essex Junto, a group of merchants and lawyers that supported Alexander Hamilton and opposed the policies of Thomas Jefferson. The Essex County elite families scorned John Adams and his illustrious son John Quincy Adams from Norfolk County to the south.

Anna Cabot Lowell, the oldest of the children of Judge John Lowell, left an account in her letters of the joys and tribulations of "the family." She loved company and wrote (August 1797), "There is no luxury to me half so great as happy faces." Anna enjoyed meeting people but believed that "true friendship must be found in virtue." She described the family festival occasioned by the marriage of George Higginson (February 3, 1799). The wedding "caused much festivity in our family, balls, parties and dinners. A ball and supper was given in honor of the bridal suite, including most of the agreeable people in town and consisting upwards of eighty. A genteel, respectable company, a great deal of dancing, animating music and universal good humor could not fail in making us all happy. The supper was elegant, well arranged, the tables so judiciously disposed in two rooms that all the company supped at once."

Among the wedding guests was John Thornton Kirkland, soon to be president of Harvard University. Kirkland was stiff and formal at first but soon entered into the fun. Anna "danced six dances with him, and have seldom had so lively a partner." The highlight of the festivities occurred when Henry Higginson invited the youngsters on to the dance floor. "I never witnessed a more beautiful scene," wrote Anna Cabot, "thirty young girls from fourteen to eighteen, in the very season of their bloom, innocence and gaiety, and young men from seventeen to twenty-one, formed a lovely set of dances. Sallie Russell was the belle of the evening and Susan Higginson was much admired by the young men."[12] With a family so close it is little wonder that the marriage of first cousins was so common.

Anna captured the understated goodness of her brother Francis Cabot Lowell, describing him as "a most signal example of the elevated rectitude of the justice which embraces benevolence, and leads to the exercise of benevolence as simple justice, so as not to furnish a claim of merit."

INDIA CLOTH

Until the Industrial Revolution, Bengal in India was the chief source of hand-spun and handwoven textiles imported into Europe. The efforts of the merchants of Salem, Newburyport, New York and Philadelphia to enter the East India trade were long hampered by the imperialistic designs of the European powers. The Dutch East India Company was established in 1602. The long journey from Holland to India so severely affected the health of the sailors that in 1652 the Dutch settled the tip of the African continent and used the Cape of Good Hope as a halfway station to supply fresh food for the crews of its vessels. After the Dutch came the French, Portuguese and British, all exploiting the wealth of India. The rapacious British East India Company, established by the Virgin Queen, opened the ports of Bombay and Calcutta and infiltrated along the Ganges River to occupy large parts of the subcontinent. The Battle of Plessey in 1757 firmly established British hegemony over Indian soil. After the loss of its American colonies, India became the brightest jewel of the British crown.

During the last decades of the eighteenth century much of the American trade with China and India was carried on ships owned by Salem merchants and sailed by Salem sea captains. In the year 1784, Elias Hasket Derby sent his ship *Grand Turk*, under Captain Jonathan Ingersoll, around the Cape of Good Hope to Canton, with a cargo of rum, flour, sugar, salt and butter. When the *Grand Turk* returned many months later, carrying silks and tea, half the town of Salem turned out to greet her: "Crowds of people thronged her decks listening to the crew's accounts of the strange Chinese manners and customs or examining the curios brought from the distant and almost mythical East by these Eighteenth Century Marco Polos." Starting in 1788, Salem ships called on Bombay and Calcutta, where the Governor General Lord Cornwallis—who only six years earlier as General Charles Cornwallis was defeated in the Battle of Yorktown— welcomed the Americans "as the most favored foreigners."[13]

The government in London was of two minds whether to maintain hegemony over India or allow in the ships of other nations. American private ships proved useful carrying Indian goods to the Continent. Sir Francis Baring welcomed the rapid growth of American trade with India, arguing that the industry-poor United States would use its new wealth to buy British manufactured goods. "Whoever will bring silver," Baring opined, "to pay for production industry of a country, should be received with open arms and on equal terms whether a Briton or a foreigner." Others argued for an extra tax on American vessels in India.[14]

The China and East India trade brought great wealth to Salem. William Gray was born poor but grew immensely rich and privately owned sixty sailing ships, mostly engaged in trading with the Orient. Elias Hasketh Derby, Joseph Felt and Simon Forrester built grand homes along Chestnut and Derby Streets. In 1799, the Salem East-India Marine Society was established with members who had "actually navigated the seas beyond the Cape of Good Hope or Cape Horn, as masters or supercargoes of vessels belonging to Salem." The aims of the society were to help the widows and children of members lost at sea and to collect and share information for "the improvement and security of navigators."[15] Through the efforts of the Salem merchants and sea captains indigo, sugar and especially cotton and silk textiles from India began to appear in American shops. The quality of the Indian textiles ranged from cheap plain cloth for the plantation slaves of the American South and the West Indies to elegant Kashmir shawls sold in the finer shops of Boston, New York and Philadelphia. In 1797, the Salem merchant Jacob Crowninshield transported a live Indian elephant, which he promptly sold for $10,000. The new owners took their elephant on tour, charging twenty-five cents a look. Among the most successful of the China and India trade merchants were Elias Hasket Derby and William Gray of Salem and Israel Thorndike of Beverly, whose fortunes ran into the millions of dollars.

Shrewd Indian merchants such as Ram Dololl Dey of Calcutta found ways to bypass the British East India Company and establish direct trade links with American merchants like Francis Cabot Lowell, the Cabot brothers and the Lee brothers of Massachusetts.[16] Ram Dololl Dey sent Francis Cabot Lowell on April 29, 1800, a fascinating account of the Yankee shipping in and out of Calcutta. "The markets for piece goods," he wrote, "were very high during the months of January, February and March on account of the number of American and Portuguese ships that are purchasing at that time, but this has now become very reasonable. There is now about to sail for America three ships—the *Recovery*—Captain Philips—the *Ulysses*, Captain Menkford and the *Winthrop & Mary*, Captain Colling. The *Delaware* out of Philadelphia, the brig *Washington* of Boston and the *William Penn* of Philadelphia have arrived. The *Elizabeth*, belonging to Mr. [William] Gray of Salem was run on shore on her passage down the river and was entirely lost, the greater part of her cargo was saved. Mr. Gray's supercargo of the ship *Ulysses* was so unfortunate as to fall out of the window and was so wounded that he expired in three or four days."

AARON BURR

Francis Cabot Lowell was little involved in the world of politics, so it is surprising to find amongst his papers a letter of July 21, 1797, from Aaron Burr responding to Lowell's offer to sell him a number of books. Burr thanked him "for your obliging attention and offer of service," adding that he was willing to pay for the books and the cost of postage. Lowell replied (August 4), "I have shipped your books by ship *Harwich*, Jeremiah Stimpson master, bound to New York. I have directed the captain to call on you & inform you when he arrives which he has promised to do." The cost of the books with duties paid to the custom house was $50.95; trucking from Lowell's warehouse to the ship, $2; freight from Boston to New York, $19.69; and cost of postage on letter sent to Burr, 20 cents, for a total of $74.34. Francis probably met the illustrious Senator Aaron Burr at a dinner party earlier that year at his father's home on School Street, Boston.

Aaron Burr achieved fame in the Revolutionary War during the attempt by Colonel Benedict Arnold to take Quebec from the British. Burr rose to the rank of colonel before retiring from the army. He entered the U.S. Senate in 1791 as a Democratic-Republican, where, despite party differences, he struck up a friendship with the Massachusetts Federalist George Cabot, a worldly, polished and skillful politician. When Cabot "arose to speak, all were attentive." Cabot in turn was full of praise for his political opponent from New York. Aaron Burr and George Cabot "were not estranged by political differences, but often met each other at the social level."[17] George Cabot, strongly opposed to the French-leaning Thomas Jefferson, proposed Aaron Burr as president of the United States. In the presidential election of 1800, Jefferson and Burr each received seventy-three votes. It took thirty-six ballots in the House of Representatives before Jefferson was finally declared president and Burr vice president.

It is not known whether George Cabot was linked with Francis Cabot Lowell in the sale of books to Aaron Burr and whether this was part of a move by New Englanders to get him to commit to the Federalist agenda. The nature of the books sent to Aaron Burr is also unknown.

FRANCIS AND THE LEE FAMILY

In July 1798, Francis Cabot Lowell formed a loose partnership with his cousins Joseph Jr., Nathaniel and Henry Lee, yet another link between the old families of Essex County, many of whom moved to Boston. Francis Cabot Lowell and Nathaniel Cabot Lee shared a warehouse at 25 Long Wharf, while Joseph Lee Jr. was at 22 Long Wharf. Nathaniel and Joseph Jr. lived together on Alden's Lane, joining Cambridge Street to Sudbury Street. Francis Cabot Lowell lived with his family nearby on Cambridge Street.

Nathaniel Cabot Lee was born on May 30, 1772, and attended Phillips Academy before entering Harvard. His Harvard graduating class of 1791 comprised just twenty-seven students. Like his brothers, Nathaniel moved to Boston where he set up as a sedentary merchant, handling cargoes for his father and brothers. On March 26, 1799, Francis Lowell and Nathaniel Lee received a shipment of Batavia coffee worth $8,935.35. On December 3, the firm sent out from Boston the *Caroline* carrying $12,909.02 worth of dried codfish. On December 15, Lowell and Lee took delivery of 6,666 gallons of sherry wine, valued at $7,332.50 arrived from Cadiz on the *Advent*, under Captain A. H. Smith. Early in 1800, the *Caroline* returned to Boston carrying $11,131.53 worth of wine and sherry from Malaga, in Andalusia, Spain. In September 1800, the *Caroline* arrived from Italy, carrying a large quantity of silks, 1,600 boxes of soap, 988 cases of Lucia olive oil and 55 cases of marble for chimney places. Lowell and Lee, who dealt in large shipments, faced financial disaster if they lost their ships and cargo or even if they miscalculated the price of their goods.

RISKS OF INTERNATIONAL TRADE

During the prolonged war between Britain and France the unarmed American commercial ships were at the mercy both of French privateers and the Royal Navy. To lessen the risks, merchants were willing to buy insurance. Marine insurance in the United States was first offered in 1793. In New England, the Fire & Marine Insurance Company of 16 State Street, Boston, the Boston Marine Insurance Company, the Salem Marine Insurance Company and others offered insurance against loss due to "seas, men of war, fires, enemies, jettisons, rovers, thieves, taking at sea, arrests, restraints, detachment of kings, princes or peoples of what nations, condition or quality soever, or mariners." The cost of insurance between Boston and other American ports was 1.5–2 percent of the amount ensured; to European ports, 2.5–3 percent; to Mediterranean ports, 3– 3.5 percent, and to China and India, 10–12 percent or even higher.

Over the years, Francis Cabot Lowell took out many insurance policies on his cargoes and ships, significantly adding to the cost of doing business with the Orient. One $5,000 policy cost him 18 percent plus the cost of the stamps, for a total of $902.50. Another ship and cargo was insured for $5,000 at a cost of $850 for a period of eighteen months. In time competition between the marine insurance companies brought the costs down. In 1803, Francis insured a $15,000 cargo on the brig *Washington* for a premium of only $375. By 1805, the insurance on a $5,000 cargo cost $197 and for a cargo of $10,000 the insurance had fallen to $251.

FRANCIS LOWELL'S RUM DISTILL HOUSE

In 1493, on his second voyage, Columbus carried fifteen hundred sugar cane shoots from the Canary Islands to plant in the West Indies. The shoots grew luxuriantly on Caribbean soil and in the Caribbean heat. To feed the rapacious European appetite for sugar, great numbers of Africans were enslaved and sent to the West Indies to grow the cane. When ripe, the cane was cut, the husks burned off, and then cooled, leaving the sugar juice to crystallize in vast clay pots. At the bottom of the pots were holes to allow the thick syrupy residue, called molasses, to escape. Although first regarded as a waste product, the settlers in seventeenth-century Barbados discovered that molasses changed into alcohol by the process of fermentation. After distillation to increase the alcohol content, the liquid was aged in oaken caskets. They called it "kill devil," better known as rum.

The New England rum industry developed in the eighteenth century through contacts with the West Indies sugar islands. New England merchants sent lumber, farm products and horses in return for sugar and molasses. By 1750, there were fifty-three rum distill houses in Massachusetts alone, using fifteen hundred hogshead of molasses a year. Each distill house employed its own methods to make rum in the effort to get the best price. Rum was a major Massachusetts export and was sold in taverns throughout the thirteen colonies and used as barter in the slave trade.

In colonial times the sale of rum was a major source of revenue. Samuel Adams Drake in his book *Old Boston Taverns and Tavern Clubs* lists over forty other taverns in Boston in 1800, as well as many inns and clubs that served alcohol.[18] Taverns serving alcohol dotted the roads from Boston leading north, south and west. Public drunkenness in Boston and other towns became a noticeable problem.

By the year 1800, the twenty-five-year-old Francis Cabot Lowell was an established Boston merchant. From his office and warehouse on Long Wharf, he imported teas and silks from China, handwoven textiles from India, wines and brandy from France, and sugar and molasses from the West Indies. He employed agents in Calcutta, Bordeaux, Barcelona and Rotterdam and had credit with a bank in London. His brothers-in-law Robert and Henry Jackson were trustworthy captains of merchant ships collecting goods from far-off ports for delivery to dealers from Maine to the Carolinas. Francis Cabot Lowell now added rum produced in his own distill house to the list of goods he offered for sale.

On July 14, 1801, Francis Cabot Lowell bought for $6,666.67 the rum distill house located at the corner of George and Belknap Streets in West Boston. The distillery, which dated from before the American Revolution, was once the property of Richard Lechmere, son of Thomas Lechmere, surveyor general of His Majesty's Customs for the Northern District of America. The Loyalist Lechmere family fled to Halifax in 1776 and then sailed for England. The Lechmere family was banished from Massachusetts, their property confiscated.

Francis Cabot Lowell saw big profits from his Boston-made rum and redoubled his efforts to sell it to his customers. To John Stille he wrote (April 27, 1802), "The price of rum has kept up beyond my expectations owing to shipments to the North of Europe. We have not been able to make rum as fast as we have sold it. West Indies rum is as cheap as New England or nearly so." Francis was not content to stay with the traditional methods of rum distillation but sought to develop a new and more efficient technique. However, his early experiments in fermenting and distilling molasses did not succeed. Showing his customary determination when a big idea preoccupied him, he wrote on May 12 in great detail to Alexander Anderson, an established rum manufacturer in Philadelphia, seeking to employ Anderson's latest methods of rum production. Francis experimented with Anderson's equipment and related that he

fixed a still to distill molasses agreeably to your patent improvements. The first still I fixed was one of about four hundred gallons. It was an old still & attempting to use the liquor it burst out in such quantities as to occasion a very large waste. I then got a still of about three hundred gallons, made uncommonly thick and strong. The condensing tub I made of pine, about two inches thick to contain about 600 gallons, the copper half-globe contains about 80 gallons. The distance of the bottom of the tub from the head of the still is about 40 inches. The tub which leads from the copper half-globe is 6 inches in diameter and that which leads to the warm from the globe is 5 inches in diameter. We were able to run this still about as fast again as in the old construction besides the savings of time in heating the liquors. When we attempted to run it any faster, it ran foul. On distilling the charges that were heated on the condensing tub we found it did not produce as much spent by 25 per cent as in the common method. When the charge was about half distilled the liquor in the tub would be so hot as to force out considerable steam notwithstanding our utmost exertions to fasten the cover down. I should think from the quantity that escaped that the liquid in the tub must have actually boiled. We gave the experiment a fair trial by trying it six times on two successive days, during which in addition to the screws to screw the cover tight, we put braces from the top of the wall on to the cover of the tub but it did not diminish the quantity of steam that escaped by the hole in the top which contains the spout which let the liquor in, altho' it was corked up at each operation. The only way we are now able to use the still is by putting water in the condensing tub, which is a lengthy and tedious operation. I will thank you to inform me what is the fault in the construction of the works that I may have it remedied if possible. It appears to me that the wash, which is made with the molasses, is considerable thinner than your melt wash & therefore boils much easier & exits the vapor at a less heat than yours. It answered my expectations in the quantities with which it boiled, for after we had distilled a charge and let a heated one down, it began immediately to boil & distill over. When we had put the fire out at night it would distill 10 or 12 gallons without any fire. The vent hole which you directed to be left open while the still was filling appeared to discharge a great deal of vapor which if it was the spent of the liquor must be a considerable loss. Is there any occasion to leave that open when the tube which leads to the warm is so long?

Despite weeks of experimentation, Francis could not get the results he desired. "I mean still to persevere," he wrote to Alexander Anderson on June 25, "in endeavoring to fix the still as much from Pride as from any sanguine expectation of success. If I do succeed I should be happy to render you any assistance." Still eager to improve his distillery in Boston, Francis in 1803 wrote to his brother Charles, a student at the Divinity School, and his older brother John, then visiting Edinburgh, to discover the secrets of the Scottish methods of distillation. Neither John nor Charles, however, was adept at industrial espionage. Instead of visiting the distilleries and relaying their secrets, John simply bought a book on the subject and sent it on to Francis in Boston. This, John replied, was "the Scotch mode of distilling as far as I could obtain information." Francis sought the help of relatives closer to home. Anne Bromfield of Newburyport responded with delight on July 16, 1805, to the query on the development of "some machine to improve your distillation. I consider you as somewhat of an original." Even though Francis was "occupied by active exertions in your own business and so encumbered by the additional cares which your friends bestowed upon you," Anne thanked him profusely "for the attention you so kindly give my affairs." In ending her letter, Anne Bromfield sent her "love to your wife & all the children. I send them a kiss if they are good."

Determined to further improve his rum making technology Francis wrote to John Ducas of Liverpool, a maker of scientific instruments. In 1780, Ducas obtained the United Kingdom patent #1,259 for his hydrometer with a slide rule to measure the strength of alcoholic spirits. So successful was the Ducas hydrometer that it was selected in 1790 by the U.S. government as the standard to measure the proof of alcohol. Francis wrote to the company on August 20, 1802, to buy "one of your patent hydrometers. I wish you would be careful to send me one that is accurately made. I wish also a thermometer that accompanies its use to be true and accurate so as to be easily affected by change of temperature."

Another letter to Alexander Anderson (February 4, 1804) shows that Francis Cabot Lowell was still doggedly seeking a better method to turn molasses into rum. "After several attempts to fix your still," Lowell wrote, "we have at last a method, which after a fatiguing trial seems likely to answer the purpose." Lowell concluded that Anderson's patented method was better suited to grain distilling than to rum. After conducting many experiments in rum distillation Francis Cabot Lowell concluded that he had come up with a new technique, and was willing to enter a business relationship with Anderson to share the patent rights. After two years of effort, the distilling process in the Lowell rum house was at last working efficiently and profitably. Writing to merchants in New York, Philadelphia, Baltimore and abroad Francis let them know that he had New England rum for sale, cheaper in price but as good as that imported from Jamaica, St. Croix and Tobago. To the merchants Benjamin and George Williams of London, he sent, on August 20, 1802, fifty-two hogshead of New England rum; to John Stille in Philadelphia on September 15, he sent forty-five barrels; and to Peter Remsen in New York, thirty hogshead of rum. To John Stille he wrote (January 15, 1803), "Rum is in good demand here at 40 or 50 cents & I have no doubt it will rise with you from 50 to 60 cents. We will be able to supply you with any quantity of rum you can sell this year."

The demand for rum was so brisk that Francis wrote to John Peabody, a leading merchant in Newburyport, to hire a cooper smith. "We want you to get for us an excellent cooper well acquainted with making rum casks," Francis wrote on April 18, "and that will be very industrious & active. We expect to pay good wages. We want a young man, unmarried, that loves work better than women. He must be used particularly to making rum hogsheads. We shall be willing to pay $400 a year for such a man and to pay his boards, which in this town will be three dollars a week. We should like to have him on trial before we engage him for a year. This work will not be confined to making hogsheads, but to shape molasses hogsheads made bad into hogsheads right & when not otherwise employed to do anything that he is wanted for."

Francis Cabot Lowell misjudged the liquor market. Rum was associated with the British occupation, and its use in America declined after the Revolution. By 1800, the production of rum in America was less than half what it had been a decade earlier. When Francis Cabot Lowell bought his rum distill house there were thirty competitors in Boston alone. Spanish and French wines, sherry, brandy and gin were gaining in popularity as the rum distill houses in New England were shutting down.[19] At heart a scientist, Francis entered the rum business to make money but also to invent better technology. Francis Cabot Lowell "was always studying out some scheme of development to benefit his fellow man."[20]

The sale of local rum and imported brandy, whiskey, wine and gin, together with the opening of ever more rum shops and grog shops, led to an increase in public drunkenness. In 1812, the Massachusetts Society for the Suppression of Intemperance was formed to control the "excessive use of ardent spirits in our country." The first president of the society was Samuel Dexter, former U.S. secretary of the treasury. A member of the society from its origin was Francis' brother, the Reverend Charles Lowell. The society warned that "many thousands sink annually to poverty, were stimulated to crime, were affected by the most loathsome diseases, and were prematurely falling the victims of death. We are about to be a nation of drunkards." Responding to these warnings the governor of the state signed into law an "Act regarding the sale of spirituous liquors" in an effort to limit "the great evils to individuals" from the excessive use of alcohol.

4

The Brothers Lowell

The three brothers were the seventh generation of the Lowell family in America after the arrival of their ancestor Percival Lowle. John Lowell Jr., the eldest of the three sons of Judge John Lowell, graduated from Harvard in 1786, to start his legal training under the supervision of his proud father. On July 21, 1788, at only nineteen years of age, he was admitted to the Suffolk County Law Association. John Jr. took over his father's accounts and for the next twelve years had a flourishing law practice. The law association was an exclusive club, preferring men educated at Harvard University. Other students applying for admission were required to study one year longer than those educated at Harvard. Among the distinguished members of the association in John Lowell's time were Francis Dana, Harrison Gray Otis, Theophilus Parsons, Christopher Gore, Samuel Sewall and Daniel Webster, as well as his own father, John Lowell Sr.

After completing his legal education in Newburyport, John Quincy Adams followed the advice of his father, Vice President John Adams, with some reluctance and moved to Boston to open his law practice on August 9, 1790. He lost his first case to Harrison Gray Otis. In letters to his parents John Quincy contrasted his own poor beginning at the law with the success of Otis and other young lawyers in the town. Writing to his father on September 21, 1790, John Quincy Adams offered a perceptive assessment of the character of John Lowell Jr., two years his junior. John Lowell Jr., wrote Adams, "was just sworn into court and his father John Lowell Sr. has conveniently left all his unfinished business to him. The young gentleman has talents, activity and application, with a great deal of self-confidence in himself; a quality which is not amiable, but which perhaps is very serviceable to him, in helping him forward. His peculiar advantages have given him an unusual share of business, for a person of so lately admitted. He is rather disposed to attribute the circumstances to his superior abilities, and expresses some contempt for persons less successful than himself." John Quincy Adams was impressed by the intelligence of John Lowell Jr. but not by his character. After hearing a talk delivered by young Lowell "which included a number of very good observations," John Quincy added that Lowell's "delivery was not without a share of that affectation which, if I may so express myself, is natural to him."[1]

In 1793, John Lowell Jr. married Rebecca Amory. Their marriage showed the complex interplay between Patriots and Loyalists after the Revolutionary War. Rebecca's father, John Amory, was a Boston merchant of long standing. In 1774, he traveled with his wife to London to settle a business matter, leaving his six children in the care of his brother Jonathan (his similarly named sibling). The outbreak of the Revolutionary War left him stranded in England, where his wife died in 1777. Determined to show that he was not a Loyalist, he left England to live in Brussels, writing urgent letters to his brother Jonathan, seeking a way back to his family in Massachusetts. In turn, Jonathan Amory sought legal advice from Judge John Lowell. Banished from Massachusetts, John Amory had to wait until 1783 to make his way to New York, which was at that time still held by the British. To make matters worse for him, in New York he swore an oath of allegiance to the British king. John Amory waited impatiently in Providence, Rhode Island, while his brother Jonathan petitioned the Massachusetts legislature to restore John's citizenship and property. In June 1783, Jonathan, accompanied by John's six children, traveled the forty miles from Boston to Providence to visit their father. Overwhelmed by the emotion of the meeting, John Amory saw that his children had "grown entirely out of my knowledge" and he could only recognize the oldest of them. With the help of lawyers all his rights and property were restored to him in 1784 and John Amory returned to his family in Boston, where he died in 1805, leaving a large fortune. Another of John Amory's daughters married John McLean, the benefactor of the asylum for the insane, still known as the McLean Hospital. His son Rufus Amory was a law student under Judge John Lowell, and went on to a distinguished legal career. In 1794 Rufus Amory married Nancy Geyer, whose own father Frederick William Geyer had been banished as a Loyalist. Like John Amory, the merchant Geyer eventually recovered his Massachusetts citizenship and property. The marriage of their children was "a very gay and brilliant affair" held in the middle of a heavy snowstorm and in the presence of a special guest, Prince Edward, the future Duke of York, and father of Victoria, the future queen of Great Britain.

With his law practice and his family expanded, John Lowell Jr. decided to buy a bigger house. On Monday, May 25, 1795, an advertisement appeared in the *Independent Chronicle and Daily Advertiser*, announcing the sale by auction of a "Convenient and Handsome House, at the head of Williams Court, now occupied by Mr. John Lowell Jun. Said house has three lower rooms and six chambers in excellent repair."

THE AMERICAN AND THE FRENCH REVOLUTIONS

In 1797, John Lowell Jr., under the title *Antigallican, or, The Lover of His Own Country*, wrote a feisty denunciation of the French Revolution and its influence on the United States of America. Over the course of ninety-two pages John Jr. wrote that the American Constitution is "founded on the genuine unadulterated principles of liberty, an administration seeking the public good, freely and frequently elected." By contrast, revolutionary France "exhibited to the world a painful example, and had taught us in letters of blood, that no common interest, no national danger, no general zeal can stifle the efforts of misguided ambition or arrest the hydra of faction in his ruinous career." America, he argued, would be ill served by following the French example. John Lowell Jr. would continue his anti-French crusade for years to come.

After serving George Washington as vice president, John Adams won the election to become president of the United States for the term 1797 to 1801. The presidency of the man from Quincy, Massachusetts, was marred by continuous conflict with Revolutionary France, which began seizing American merchant ships suspected of trading with the British. Tensions heightened after the French refused to receive American envoys sent to settle the conflict. The United States feared a French invasion and the use of saboteurs sent to undermine civil order. Between June and July 1798, the Federalist-controlled government passed the Naturalization Act, Alien Act, Alien Enemies Act and the Sedition Act to muzzle the opposition and to deport opponents of the government. The passage of these acts deeply divided the nation, already in fear of a possible war against France.

Across the nation there were isolated protests against these oppressive acts. In early November 1798, a freedom pole was erected in the town of Dedham, some eight miles southwest of Boston. The inscription on the pole read, "Liberty and Equality—No Stamp Tax—No Sedition—No Aliens Bill—No Land Tax—Downfall of the tyrants of America—Peace and Retirement to the President—Long Live Vice President and the minority—May moral virtue be the basis for civil government." Secretary of State Timothy Pickering judged the writings on the pole as criticism of President John

Adams and in support of Vice President Thomas Jefferson, and the rallying cry for insurrection and civil war. Federal Marshall Samuel Bradford was instructed to round up those who had erected the liberty pole and escort them to the Federal Circuit Court of Boston for a hearing.

One of those caught in the government's web was Benjamin Fairbanks of Dedham, who was charged with sedition. Fairbanks, a wealthy farmer, property owner and town selectman, appeared before U.S. District Court Judge John Lowell, who ordered him to post bail of $4,000—a veritable fortune—and to attend for trial in June the following year. At his trial, before Justice Samuel Chase, Mr. Benjamin Fairbanks admitted his guilt, and was sentenced to six hours of imprisonment and a fine of $5. His conviction kept him silent thereafter. Others convicted of sedition received harsher sentences. To one observer, John Adams' laws were "a pompous array of tyrant power" used to stifle dissent. During the same month Benjamin Fairbanks was on trial for sedition, President John Adams came home to Massachusetts to attend commencement at Harvard and participate in the Fourth of July celebrations at Faneuil Hall.

For some years, the citizens of Boston had celebrated Independence Day by inviting a prominent person to deliver an oration. In the midst of the political turmoil gripping the nation, John Lowell Jr., thirty years of age, was chosen to deliver the Fourth of July 1799 oration at Faneuil Hall. President John Adams "honoured the assembly with his presence." The confident John Lowell Jr. chose as his topic the contrast of the American Revolution of 1776 with the French Revolution of 1789. The principles of the American Revolution he said "were an ardent Love of Liberty—an unconquerable Spirit of Independence—a hatred of foreign domination—a detestation of domestic oppression." The French Revolution, John Lowell Jr. argued, was very different. "We have the misfortune to live in an age of violent Revolution." Gallic intrigue, he said, threatened "to destroy the repose of the whole Civilized World." Under the cloak of liberty and equality, the French set about to destroy both the monarchies and the "happy and peaceable Republics." The French were "plundering their neighbors" and destroying religion. While "professing to secure the rights of man, [the French Revolution] had thrown down all the barriers which had hitherto protected them. It had let loose on Society the most ferocious passions of the worst of men. Virtue is persecuted—Vice is patronized and rewarded." The true purpose of the French Revolution, Lowell said, was "to make and keep men Slaves [and strip] them of those virtues and of those principles which alone fit them to be free." The French Revolution destroyed the monarchy, confiscated private property, defiled the clergy and the church, reduced other nations to servitude and spawned the likes of Robespierre to take away the liberties of the people. The goal of the French Revolution, John Lowell argued, was to establish "the government of the sword [and] to reduce mankind to two simple classes of Soldiers and Serfs."

The United States, by contrast, argued John Lowell Jr., "exhibited no marks of a wild and fanatic Revolution." America freed itself of a foreign power but kept the rule of law, its colleges, respect for religion, and the inviolability of private property: "From the moment we assumed the attitude and character of a nation, obedience, peaceable submission to the constituted authorities, have been the standing creed of Americans." After expelling the foreign power, America established "a mild government of Laws and Manners, founded on the solid and sacred basis of Rational Liberty and Revealed Religion." To preserve its stability, America must stand firm against an atheistic France, this "insatiable Monster" hiding under the cloak of liberty and equality. Before the French Revolution, the emperor and the aristocracy grabbed for themselves the lion's share of the nation's wealth, leaving the people mired in poverty and helplessness. Not so, emphasized John Lowell; inequality is the natural order of things. "There will always be the lazy and the industrious, the drones and the working bees; of necessity the poor and the rich, the ignorant and the well-informed."

John Lowell Jr. supported the efforts of Alexander Hamilton to set up the Bank of the United States and the national mint to issue American currency. The task of ruling the nation during its formative years belonged to men like him coming from the old families, with the necessary integrity, education and devotion to hard work.

Because of the influence of the French Revolution, America was "enveloped with dangers, domestic and foreign," stated John Lowell Jr. "We have enemies without and traitors within. We must repel the one, and restrain the other." The Sedition Act gave the government the means to control the "Gallic faction," which sung the praises of the French while "degrading their own country." America should not be so naïve as to believe that the French are honorable. To comprehend the evils of the French Republic John Lowell suggested that one ask "my mercantile friends whose ships and whole cargoes the French have taken," or ask the seamen who have been captured, starved and beaten by the French. Lowell complimented President John Adams, who was not deceived by the French olive branch of peace, since he saw "under the leaves of which was concealed a Dagger." To preserve the American way of life it may be necessary to go to war. "Let us treat with Frenchmen, only at the points of our bayonets."

George Cabot, a leading Federalist, was in the audience at Faneuil Hall and was delighted with the oration delivered by his nephew John Lowell Jr. On July 8, he wrote to Timothy Pickering, the U.S. secretary of state, that the oration "gave great pleasure to the auditory on Thursday. The President was particularly grateful with it, and declared his approbation of every sentiment, except those which were complimentary to himself."[2] Since the exuberant pro-French parade of January 1793, the mood of Boston had decidedly shifted in the opposite direction. The leaders of the Federal Party in Massachusetts on July 4, 1799, applauded John Lowell Jr. for revealing the dangers of the French and illustrating the superiority of the American Revolution.

During his rousing oration hailing the American Revolution, the American way of life and the rule of law, John Lowell Jr. failed to mention the confiscation of the property of the exiled Loyalists during the Revolutionary War, the attack on civil liberties under the Sedition Act of 1798, the trial of Benjamin Fairbanks, the displacement and decimation of the Native Americans, or the fact that one million of the five million people then living in the United States were black slaves, the property of their masters.

As part of the expansion of the American navy, President John Adams, while in Boston, launched the 400-ton, 28-gun *Boston*, and on July 23, watched the beautiful and noble sight as the 2,200-ton, 44-gun *Constitution* left the harbor in a light breeze. The frigate *Boston* sailed the high seas protecting American merchant ships. On October 12, 1800, the ship proudly returned to Boston with the captured French *Le Berceau* in tow. Built at the Edmund Hartt boatyard in Boston, and launched in 1797, the *Constitution*, now known as *Old Ironsides*, is still in service with the U.S. navy.

THE TRIAL OF JASON FAIRBANKS

The beginning of the nineteenth century saw profound changes in the Lowell family. The venerable Judge John Lowell was brought low by gout and restricted his activities to his estate in Roxbury. On May 6, 1802, aged fifty-eight years, he died, leaving Bromley Vale to his oldest son, John Jr. The "short, slender, frail and fiery" John Lowell Jr., after a brilliant academic career, was well on his way to be one of Boston's leading men.[3] His role as head of the Lowell family, however, was cut short after the conclusion of the sensational trial of Jason Fairbanks.

Both Benjamin Fairbanks (convicted of sedition in 1799) and Jason Fairbanks were members of the prominent Fairbanks family of Dedham, Massachusetts, a town of two thousand people, eight miles west of Boston. The twenty-year-old Jason was accused of the May 18, 1801, brutal murder of the sweet and beautiful eighteen-year-old Elizabeth Fales, known to her family as Betsy. Jason claimed that the two, who were sweethearts from childhood, secretly planned to meet at Mason's pasture, an isolated place, to share their love and decide on the date of their marriage. Before the rendezvous Elizabeth had been reading the romantic novel *The History of Lady Julia Mandeville*, written in 1763 by Frances Brooke. Jason, known for his temper, had "already possessed her person and received the pledge of her most tender attachment." Betsy demanded to know whether Jason "had ever told any one of our [sexual] connection." He replied that he had shared this secret with two of his best friends. "Oh, you are a monster," exclaimed Betsy as she grabbed the whittling knife out of Jason's hand and began wildly stabbing herself. Elizabeth's throat was cut and she had multiple stab wounds to the breasts, arms and back. Seeing his beloved lying dead on the ground, Jason claimed that he took the knife and stabbed himself, intending to die beside her, in the style of Romeo and Juliet, but despite his injuries, was able to stagger to her house to raise the alarm.

The Commonwealth of Massachusetts did not believe Jason's account and elected to prosecute him on the charge of murdering Elizabeth Fales. At considerable expense, the Fairbanks family hired two prominent Boston lawyers, Harrison Gray Otis and John Lowell Jr., to lead the defense of their son. In their six-hour summation, Otis and Lowell claimed that Elizabeth was "a young lady, of eighteen, with her head filled with melancholy and romantic tales, passionately in love, a passion which adverse circumstances forbade the gratification of, with every gleam of hope extinct, had in a moment of frenzy, put a period to her own existence. Has despair never induced Suicide? Has the softer sex been peculiarly exempt from these feelings and these results?" Otis and Lowell argued that the distraught Betsy grabbed the knife from Jason, cut her own throat and "had attempted to find her heart, and destroy the vital principle, by attempts upon her breast, and finding that she could not reach it on that side, is it extraordinary, that unacquainted with the anatomy of the human frame, she should attempt a shorter route to it, through the back?"

The prosecutor, James Sullivan, who was the attorney general of the Commonwealth of Massachusetts, argued that Elizabeth Fales could not have stabbed herself in the back but Jason, out of sexual frustration and rage, had repeatedly stabbed her and caused her death. The trial started in Dedham on August 6, 1801, before the chief justice of Massachusetts, Francis Dana, assisted by the justices Robert Trent Paine, Thomas Dawes and Simeon Strong. The three-day trial, watched by hundreds of curious spectators, ended when Jason Fairbanks was found guilty of the murder of his sweetheart and sentenced to "be carried from hence to the gaol from whence you came, and from thence to the place of execution, and there be hanged by the neck, until you are dead, and may God Almighty have mercy on your soul."

Jason was taken in shackles to the Dedham jail, from which, aided by his brother and friends, he escaped, but later was captured just south of the Canadian border. On September 10, 1801, Jason Fairbanks was hanged on the Dedham Town Common with ten thousand people, five times the town's population, gawking at the spectacle.[4]

The Fairbanks family of Dedham suffered a social and economic collapse after the trial of their son Jason. One branch of the family moved to St. Johnsbury, Vermont, where two brothers, Erastus and Thaddeus Fairbanks, built a foundry to make stoves and cast iron plows. E & T Fairbanks Company became the world's leader in weighing machines.

The Jason Fairbanks trial had far-reaching consequences. James Sullivan (1744–1808), the first president of the Massachusetts Historical Society, used his success in convicting Jason Fairbanks to vault himself into the position of governor of Massachusetts (1807–1808), but he died before completing his term of office. John Lowell Jr. had described Boston as the "sink of vice [and] the Babylon of profligacy" and warned against "the tavern, wine, idle companions and bad women." The Dedham tale of frustrated love, death by stabbing, the defeat to James Sullivan and the public hanging of his client Jason Fairbanks proved too much for the repressed and sensitive John Lowell Jr.

If the hanging of Jason Fairbanks took John Lowell Jr. to the proverbial edge, it was the death of his father, on May 6, 1802, that tipped him over it. The symptoms of his emotional turmoil included anxiety, depression, flashbacks of the trial and a lack of confidence and bouts of anger, fitting the modern diagnostic category of post-traumatic stress disorder. John told a friend on May 17 that "my mind was so agitated by the unexpected death of my excellent father. To love a parent is always a severe trial of the human feelings, but to be deprived of so much excellence and with a father so affectionate and so attentive to our happiness is almost insupportable." John Jr. was concerned about his mother, who was in "feeble health and the frail structure and exquisite sensibility of some of my sisters, and the orphanage of my youngest brother, deprived of his best at the most interesting moment of his life—all troublesome diversions continue to agitate and depress me. [But it is] my duty to comfort, protect, solace and support those whom Providence has thus by an afflicting dispensation thrown upon me."

Despite his intention, as the new head of the family, to do his duty and protect others, John Lowell was hardly able to control his own emotions. In late September he traveled to New Hampshire to distract his mind and calm himself. "I am on the whole as much better as I could expect in so short a time," he explained to Francis Cabot on September 30, but "my nerves are yet irritable but much more quiet than they were." John was planning to visit Newburyport and then "take some agreeable ride tomorrow morning, lodge at Ipswich and reach home on Saturday noon, so as to dine at my mother's."

These distractions did not calm him and for months to come his nerves were "still troublesome." Being in crowded places "increased my nervousness and I am now scarcely able to write," he told his wife on July 15, 1803. His doctor recommended taking the waters of the natural springs at Ballston Spa and Saratoga Springs, north of Albany, New York. Traveling by carriage and accompanied by servants John left Boston for the recuperative waters of Ballston. Every mile of the long journey from Boston was a torment to him. "If my health had been good," wrote John to his wife on July 23, "I would have enjoyed the fine country through which we had passed. Unhappily, I have grown weaker and more unwell for 3 days past, and I dread least I should relapse into my old wretched, miserable state. I wish I could be more happy."

Lebanon Spring, High Rock Spring and other mineral springs north of Albany, New York, were known since colonial times. After the Revolutionary War, Philip Schuyler and members of the van Rensselaer family developed the spa patterned after the fashionable English spa towns of Bath and Cheltenham they had visited on their tours abroad. But it was Nicholas Low who best succeeded with his spa at Ballston Springs. In 1803, his grand San Souci Hotel opened with one hundred guest rooms and a large dining room, serving wholesome meals. The hotel was fashioned on the palace of Frederick the Great of Prussia, complete with grand chandeliers and a smoking room. The cost for room and board was $2 a day or $10 a week.[5] At the hotel John Lowell Jr.'s anxieties intensified with the din of the hotel dining room, filled with unfamiliar faces. Lowell attempted to disguise his nervousness with his intellect, and "attracted the attention of all by his high conversational powers."

JOHN AND REBECCA LOWELL LEAVE FOR EUROPE

The mineral waters of the Ballston Spa did not benefit John Lowell Jr. The invalid, aged thirty-two, returned to Boston and closed his law practice. In September 1803, on the advice of his physician, John Lowell Jr., accompanied by his wife Rebecca, left Boston on the *John Adams* bound for an extended tour of Great Britain and the Continent. On route their ship was stopped and searched by the fifty-gun British frigate *Leander*. The *John Adams* arrived in Liverpool without further mishap on November 13, 1803. The war between France and Great Britain raged from 1793 until the Peace of Amiens was signed on March 25, 1802. Despite the treaty, the British remained in Malta and Napoleon began amassing eighty thousand troops for an invasion of England. To counter a French invasion, the British strengthened their defenses along the southeast coast. John and Rebecca Lowell arrived in England six months after the war between Britain and France had commenced anew.

Far away from the stresses of Boston, John was soon his enthusiastic self as he visited the theater, the botanical gardens and the literary institutions. Using Liverpool as their base, the Lowells took excursions to nearby Manchester, Chester, Derby, Leicester and Northampton before journeying to London. Refreshed John Lowell wrote rhapsodic letters home of the places he visited. In addition, John sent Francis regular instructions on what bonds, notes and properties in Massachusetts to sell to finance his luxurious and leisurely three-year trip abroad. Francis assumed the responsibility for John's financial affairs while his older brother was abroad, including the heavy burdens of supervising the building of the addition to John's house on his estate at Bromley Vale and watching over John's children, who remained in Boston. John Lowell instructed Francis "to sell any house or other property I own" in order to meet the estimated cost of $5,000 for the home construction. Francis was asked to talk to their stepmother Rebecca to learn when she planned to vacate the Roxbury house in order to allow the construction to begin. Over several letters, John provided the exact specifications for the two-story addition. The new parlor would measure twenty by twenty-three feet with eleven-foot-high ceilings and French doors leading out to the garden. Upstairs would be two bedchambers. John wanted the addition completed in time for his return to Boston. "Please let me know," John inquired, "what my mother's expenses are compared to her income. I feel anxious to know on every account but especially as she said she would direct her surplus income to Charles even during her life—a resolution I approve highly if her expenses fall considerably short of her income." John believed that the family should help those in need, but preferred the funds to come from another pocket. Francis was also assuming responsibilities for the rest of the family. After Judge John Lowell died, eighteen-year-old Elizabeth Cutts Lowell chose Francis as her "guardian with the full power and authority for me in my name."

The many letters sent from 1803 to 1806 by John Lowell Jr. to his mother and sisters in Boston were full of endearments as well as charming observations of the places and people he visited. The letters between John and his brother Francis Cabot were more serious and revealed the very private world of their personalities, values, opinions, finances and aspirations.

John and Rebecca Lowell left behind in Boston their children: Rebecca Amory, aged nine; John Amory, aged five; and Anna Cabot, aged two. (Their fourth child, Sarah Champney Higginson, was born in 1810.) John, who had amassed a fortune by inheritance and his legal practice, was now focused on the pursuit of pleasure and building loving relationships. By contrast, the younger Francis Cabot Lowell was still driven by the desire to enlarge his mercantile empire, acquire more wealth and property, and build his reputation. Although their goals were far apart, the brothers respected their differences and helped each other with little hesitation.

On December 3, 1803, John Lowell Jr. penned from London a letter to Francis about the manifold pleasures of the life of the English gentleman-about-town. The thirty-three-year-old John Jr. met regularly with his cousins George Higginson and Edward Bromfield, and with Thomas Palmer, "my father's and Mr. [Jonathan] Jackson's early friend." London offered John Lowell "a fund of amusements and entertainments." He regularly attended the theater at Drury Lane and Covent Gardens and enjoyed both comedy and drama. "The evening we were at Drury Lane," wrote John Lowell Jr., "we had the gratification to see the Royal Family. I say gratification, for to me it was really such and I should not believe the severest Republican that ever lived if he should deny that he had any curiosity to see individuals, whom birth, accident or the folly of mankind, had elevated so much above their fellow mortals. I saw in their King, a monarch exemplary in his morals, who had inherited the scepter of the greatest Kingdom in the world for above 40 years and who would now proudly consider himself as the greatest bulwark against unlimited despotism. The queen is very good looking, sort of an old-fashioned lady, [but] Princess Elizabeth is too short and corpulent to be lady-like."

The object of veneration was none other than George III, the last British monarch to rule over the thirteen colonies in America. The American Declaration of Independence is harsh to George III: "The history of the present King of Great Britain is a history of repeated injuries and usurpations, all having a direct object the establishment of an absolute Tyranny over these states." Less than thirty years later, John Lowell Jr., born in the epicenter of the American Revolution, still approved the displays of loyalty and affection for King George III, his wife Sophia Charlotte and his daughter Princess Elizabeth, one of the fifteen royal children. Like his father before him, John Lowell Jr. carried within himself the contradiction of an abiding love for Old England as "the greatest Kingdom in the world" together with the American faith in democracy, the rule of the people and the equality of all men before the law.

John Lowell Jr.'s ambivalence of being an American in England is reflected in his preoccupation with the high cost of living in London. "They told me I could live like a gentleman on 1,200 pounds or guineas per annum," he wrote to Francis from London on December 14. "Double that would not support me as I thought. Higginson in 13 months spent 1900 pounds sterling." The luxurious Adelphi hotel in the Royal Borough of Kensington and Chelsea cost five guineas a week, living expenses £20 a week, renting a fashionable coach with horses cost £25 a month, the coachman fifty guineas a year and the footman forty guineas a year.

John's travel money had run out and he was already £227 in debt. He instructed Francis Cabot urgently to sell bonds and notes from his share of their father's estate and sell "the Dedham shares, and the mortgage in Cold Lane and the other in Roxbury, rather than borrow on my account or advance your own funds. I fear there will be a deficit & you will really offend me if in addition to trouble, you make advances for me."

"We are all well, except myself," John Lowell explained on December 14. "I still have many of my old feelings about me occasionally, but I hope I should wear them away." John was convinced that his leisurely and expensive trip abroad was essential to restore his health and he was determined to continue the tour despite the high cost and the need to sell so many of his assets. The necessity to economize would have to wait until he returned to Boston, unless "I can bring my means up to the level of my wishes."

John Lowell told Francis on March 29, 1804, of his visit to the Houses of Parliament, where he heard speeches by the former prime minister, Pitt the Younger, and the sitting prime minister, Henry Addington, whom he described as "dull, drowsy and verbose." From London, John Lowell and his wife traveled to Bath to take the waters. Despite a state of war between France and Great Britain, John and Rebecca with brother Charles coming along, crossed to Holland and made their way to Paris, where John was invited to attend the Fourth of July celebrations at the American Embassy. After a sumptuous dinner, the minister plenipotentiary Robert R. Livingston toasted the president of the United States, the government and people of the United States, and Napoleon Bonaparte. John Lowell, the future "Boston Rebel," was already sharpening his literary quill to attack Thomas Jefferson and James Madison. It was Robert Livingston, on behalf of President Jefferson, who on April 30, 1803, successfully concluded negotiations for the Louisiana Purchase, giving the United States an additional 828,800 square miles in return for the payment of sixty million francs (about $11,250,000). As he stated in a letter (July 5), John Lowell was particularly vexed over "the Louisiana treaty, which has no merit in it whatsoever." In John Lowell's opinion, the great expansion of the American nation to the west and south increased the power of the slave-owning states and diminished the authority of New England.

Responding to John's urgent requests to sell more property to raise money needed for his expensive overseas trip, Francis sold four thousand acres of Passamaquoddy land for the sum of $4,500. The Passamaquoddy nation had for centuries occupied a large swath of land in northeastern America, now made up of Maine and New Brunswick. The First Nation people hunted in the winter and grew crops in the summer. At the end of the Revolutionary War the Passamaquoddy tribe was driven off its forestlands as speculators from Boston and elsewhere moved in to make huge purchases at pennies to the acre. Among the leading land specula-tors, as early as 1784, were General Benjamin Lincoln of Hingham and John Lowell of Boston. After Judge John Lowell died, the lands in Maine passed down largely to his oldest son John Jr., who sold most of it to sus-tain his affluent life style. A small part of the twenty-four thousand acres was kept in the hope of encouraging settlers to move north and start a township. In 1809, John Lowell Jr. together with his brother Francis Cabot Lowell and their brother-in-law Warren Dutton deposited bonds with the General Court of Massachusetts as surety for the proposed township. On February 9, 1813, John Lowell petitioned the General Court for an exten-sion of his plan to attract forty settler families to his township.

Charles Lowell, the divinity student, spent several months touring Europe in the company of his older brother John Jr. In Paris, Charles bade farewell to John and traveled to Rotterdam on his way back to the University of Edinburgh. He wrote to Francis on September 25, 1804, on his way back to Edinburgh, saying that he was "satisfied with my visit to France but long most heavily to see Old England again." Charles noted that "Bonaparte is firmly in control. Frenchmen are delighted with the idea of a splendid coronation." How right he was. The French Republic was coming to an end and on December 2, 1804, in a three-hour ceremony in the Cathedral of Notre Dame, the "Little Corporal" was crowned em-peror of the French.

Charles remained in Edinburgh over the winter of 1804–1805 and came under the spell of the philosopher Dugald Stewart. Later, in London, Charles met William Wilberforce, the one man in England above all oth-ers who brought an end to the British trade in slaves. The meeting with Wilberforce strengthened Charles Lowell's life-long abhorrence of slav-ery. From London, Charles traveled to Bristol, the ancestral home of the Lowell family, before returning to Boston.

A MAN OF PROPERTY

While John Lowell Jr. was selling property, his brother Francis Cabot was buying. From 1802 to 1810, Francis Cabot Lowell bought more than twenty Boston properties on India Wharf, Long Wharf, and in the North End and West End, as well as property in Maine. His relentless drive for success and to expand his property came at a high emotional price. John Lowell Jr. responded on July 5, 1804, with sympathy to Francis' complaints of the burdens of his many businesses and family obligations: "I am unhappy at hearing of your indisposition. Your constitution even more than mine requires indulgence but never receives it. Believe me, for I speak those words of sober experience, no pecuniary reward can compensate for the loss of health. Be indulgent to yourself, if not for your own sake, at least for your family. Recollect that to a young and growing family, your life and your health are indivisible, and even if you undervalue your own comfort, think about their wants. No man is so heedless of this first of obligations as you are. Let the Distillery and the Wharf perish rather than hazard that, without which the profits of both will be of no avail to you. I have suffered by the errors of which I now warn you to beware, and I am now profiting by the example which I recommend you to follow. Many an active, vigorous young man has sacrificed his health to the attainment of property, and because he has not the resolution to quit his golden pursuits has fallen victim to his thirst for acquisition."

The difference in attitude between John Lowell Jr., the arrogant young lawyer of 1793, and the hesitant John Lowell of 1804 is striking. When Francis was sent down from Harvard, his brother lectured him to "Aim to be first in everything you undertake. Nothing can be accomplished without great industry, activity and perseverance." When the carefree Francis was enjoying his tour of France in 1795 he was severely reprimanded by John to "give up the freedoms of youth and assume the responsibilities of manhood." John now realized that the single-minded drive for success and the "thirst for acquisition" brought him misery and led to his mental breakdown. Through leisurely travel, the study of history and culture, and the support of family and friends, John hoped to achieve peace of mind. He wanted to protect Francis from a similar fate. "I do not think my health fully established," John explained September 22. "I believe however that another year will establish it, if Heaven should please to preserve the health and happiness of my friends upon which mine in a great measure depends." Francis was not ready to take his brother's advice but tried another tactic to gain John's approval. Rather than complaining about the burdens of success, he began to boast of his business achievements. John wrote it off in a single sentence on April 19, 1805: "I am happy to hear of your prosperity and success."

REBECCA AND JOHN LOWELL JR.
CONTINUE THEIR TRAVELS

From Paris, John and Rebecca Lowell moved south to the wine country of Bordeaux. Their leisurely journey carried them to the town of Orleans, along the Loire River to Tours "beautifully situated," to La Rochelle "a charming place," to Rochefort "a fine port but the most unhealthy spot in France," on to Saintes "1 or 2 interesting antiquities," and then Bordeaux. By John's calculations the journey from Paris to Bordeaux covered 395 kilometers. "No description can give an adequate idea of the beauty of a wine country when the grapes are gathering," wrote John Lowell on September 22. "It is the richest & most noble exhibition in nature. It is the most striking example of the goodness of Heaven. The country from Paris to Bordeaux is a perfect garden. The banks of the Loire, especially from Orleans to Tours, are remarkably beautiful." John loved the sweet Muscat *vin ordinaire* of the region, "which we have been taught to think excellent, is here deemed poor."

At the time of his visit, Bordeaux was the principal French port for the arrival of American vessels carrying flour and grain. At the port of Bordeaux, John Lowell saw how much American merchant shipping gained from its neutral status in trade with France. "The American ships usually moor together," he wrote to Francis on September 22, 1804, "so that 30 or 40 of them display their flags on Sundays. I assure you that nothing is pleasanter than seeing your countrymen or even inanimate objects [flags] which belong to them. It is extremely interesting to me. My heart swells with pleasure and palpitates with anxiety, when I take a view of these ships displaying our National Flag. The love of my country is a much more ardent passion than I ever thought it."

Despite the wars on the Continent, John Lowell and his wife set off from Nice to enjoy the pleasures of Italy. From Naples John sent to Francis with a letter of January 16, 1805, "a small box of lava from Mount Vesuvius which cost 2 dollars," together with eleven paintings of Rome, in oil, showing different subjects, that cost £22; two wax profiles of Bonaparte, £2; several prints and maps, £5; and a copy of *Ancient History* by Charles Rollin and published in 1738, £2 and 5 shillings. "Remember me tenderly to your excellent wife," John wrote at the end of his letter, "whom I love as much as she deserves. Will say no more."

Tiptoeing around the great conflicts on the Continent, John and Rebecca visited Florence, Leghorn, Venice and Bologna. After Italy, came classical Greece and then, by ship, to Marseilles. Placing the responsibility on his wife, John Lowell wrote to Francis on March 17, 1805, that "Mrs. Lowell has felt a strong inclination to stay in Europe another winter for John Amory's benefit, and since I have been prevented from going into Germany I feel the same inclination, but I cannot and will not stay without my son. If John could be sent out to France or England by some person or family in whom you have confidence, I should be glad." John and Rebecca gave Francis several reasons to extend their tour: "One motive is to enable you to finish the proposed addition to my home, another is to give [son] John the foundations of the French language." John Amory Lowell, born on November 11, 1798, was four years old when his parents left for Europe. Now a boy of five and a half years, his father wanted him sent across the ocean "to France or England." Fortunately, the emotional needs of his father did not harm the boy. John Amory learned the French language, delighted in its culture and led an exemplary life. He was best friends with his first cousin John Lowell Jr. and married his first cousin Susanna Cabot Lowell, both of them children of Francis Cabot Lowell. During his eighty-three years, John Amory Lowell excelled as a scholar, merchant, businessman and director of the Lowell Institute.

From Marseilles, John and Rebecca Lowell traveled back to Paris. "This enticing city," he explained in a letter to Francis on May 19, "has stolen away so much of my money for books and furniture that I perceive I shall need a speedy rescue." He asked Francis to send him £300 sterling as soon as possible as "this will give me time to look around & see how much more I shall want." During the previous twelve months John and Rebecca had spent £2,470 sterling, worth "above 11,000 dollars" in American currency. From Paris, the Lowells traveled to Holland to discover that, due to the war, "all intercourse rigidly prohibited by ordinary packets & I was obliged to ship in an American ship." By June 10, 1805, on board the American ship *Samson*, John was "safely on my way to the U. States." But John still hesitated to return to Boston and instead traveled to England for more entertainment and to buy more books and furniture.

Comfortably settled again in London, John in his letters to Francis returned to his favorite topics: money, his properties and the delights of travel. "As to my houses," he wrote on July 4, "you will do as I wrote you before; that is, to build two houses but not upon your plan, which I do not like." John wanted his primary home built, as he explained in a letter on August 23, "exactly according to the plan I sent you." John emphatically rejected Francis' suggestion to raise money by selling some of his land at Bromley Vale to wealthy Bostonians. "I will not let any stranger into my premises," responded John, "however fashionable or preferable it may be in the opinion of others to squeeze themselves in such a manner." He now wanted to build a second home on the property "where my mother and [unmarried] sisters may be permanent for their lives at a moderate & reasonable rent." Such a rent was worth $700 to $900 a year, but from his family he would accept $500. Francis tried to temper his brother's extravagance, telling him on April 12, 1805, that "the expenses of building your house are greater than you expected." While still complaining about costs, John Jr. insisted that the building project move ahead, according to his specifications.

The journey to Paris cost the Lowells £300 sterling, and the tour through Europe a further £1,000. Measured in U.S. dollars, John Lowell had already spent over $20,000. The sale of John's bonds, shares and property yielded only $13,200, leaving a deficit of $6,800. In London, John Lowell borrowed £1,300 from the banker Samuel Williams in return for the deeds on his Framingham farm. He instructed Francis Cabot to sell the property in Framingham, worth $4,000: "You must sell it and all the woodland for as much cash and as little credit as you can, without sacrifice and remit to Williams the money. I am distressed to trouble you so much but I pay you in gratitude & affection as you well know. The 500 pounds you credited me is already exhausted. Borrow on my bank shares. You must supply me with cash as I am exhausted wholly." On no account was Francis to write to Rebecca about their heavy spending and indebtedness. "My wife does not yet know of it."

Despite his heavy debts, John continued to spend lavishly. On a single shopping spree to a bookshop, he bought Wilkinson's *Modern Atlas*, three volumes of Shakespeare, John Pinkerton's *Geography*, and twenty-seven volumes of poetry. Using the port of Rotterdam, John shipped to Francis his purchases of silk curtains, looking glasses, books and crockery to adorn the enlarged house. He obsessed about the safety of the goods he shipped from Naples and Leghorn. "I feel an anxiety to know if they arrived safe," he wrote to Francis on September 23, "particularly the marble chimney pieces." He instructed Francis to break open the locks on the cases to inspect the goods. If the goods were in good order Francis should repack them and apply new locks. If anything was broken Francis should let John know as soon as possible. "I shall replace them in case they have suffered."

Skilled in the art of rationalization, John explained that when he returned to Boston, "I will be able once more to live within my income. As it has been I shall not have expended a farthing of my capital, except for furniture which is worth the money I pay for it."

The weekly letters sent to Francis were largely filled with urgent requests about money and his houses, but from time to time John focused on events in Massachusetts, family affairs and international events. From his Boston sources, John learned "that a very great degree of distress prevails among the commercial part of the community in consequence as it is said of the multiplication of banks. It is even stated that good banks of exchange, for cash, will settle at 4 per cent higher than at 90 days credit. Good men will pay 16 per cent premium for money." During such times, he warned Francis it is best "to pause & look to one's safety. I know of your habitual vigilance and even distrust of credit, but it is not enough to be careful of the persons you trust, but you must also [be careful] of the quantity of your credit." Wars and economic turmoil "would affect the ability of the best of men in the community, and if you extend your concerns so far as to be involved excessively in the fate of others, you must suffer in such times. Let me then entreat of you not to extend yourself too far at a time when distress for money threatens some commercial convulsions." John offered this advice "not because I doubt your judgement but because I have a high opinion of it, but because I know that persons in the vortex are not so apt to see the motives of those around them." In other words, there is a limit to generosity; do not trust people and take care of your own interests first and foremost.

In September 1805, John and Rebecca Lowell left England for Rotterdam and then journeyed by coach to Paris. On the day Napoleon in triumph entered Vienna, John Lowell was in a comfortable hotel in Paris where he sat down to respond to his brother in a long letter about money, property and success. "So you have bought Isaac Davis' house for $20,000," John began. "I think the purchase an excellent one. But, how my good brother, can I put any reliance in your assessment of your own situation? Thirty days before you wrote me that you cannot afford to retain one of your Somerset Street houses, which cost I suppose 7000 dollars, and in five weeks you buy a house at $20,000. So we preach & so we practice!" Tallying up the cost all the houses, properties, stores and wharves that Francis had previously written about, it was clear to John that his brother Francis was engaged in speculation in an inflationary market. "I therefore considered that you had encumbered the amount of at least $100,000," wrote John on December 12. "I know also your extensive speculations in rum and molasses." John knew that the British had cut off supplies of sugar to France, thus opening new opportunities for the neutral American vessels. He recommended this market to Francis, "if you should happen to be shipping sugar to Europe."

The Isaac Davis house purchased by Francis Cabot Lowell was a four story Georgian dwelling at No. 2 Park Street. Isaac P. Davis sold the house before it was completely built. Francis Lowell finished the house and sold it at a profit to the merchant Jonathan Mason, who gave it to his daughter, the wife of Dr. John C. Warren (1753–1815), professor of anatomy at the Harvard Medical School. The eminent Dr. Warren was the younger brother of the physician Joseph Warren, who was killed on June 17, 1775, in the Battle of Bunker Hill.

Park Street is one of Boston's most elegant streets, running the short distance from Tremont Street up Beacon Hill to the State House, and facing the trees and open spaces of the historic Boston Common. During the first half of the nineteenth century the street was home to some of the most prominent families of Boston. No. 1 Park Street, at the bottom of the hill, belonged to the East India merchant Thomas Wigglesworth. No. 3 was the home of George Cabot, relative of Francis Cabot Lowell, a U.S. senator and leader of the Federalist Party. No. 5 was the home of Josiah Quincy, mayor of Boston (1823–1829) and then president of Harvard University (1829–1841). No. 7 was owned by the merchant Thomas Handasyd Perkins, benefactor of the Massachusetts School for the Blind, known as the Perkins Institute. No. 9 Park Street, at the top of the hill, was a four-story Georgian-style home built for the merchant Thomas Amory. In 1830, the house was bought by George Ticknor, professor of modern languages and literature at Harvard University and one of the founders of the Boston Public Library.[6]

John Lowell showed little interest in his brother's single-minded quest to buy properties and enlarge his fortune. John was selling his property in order to prolong his stay abroad. "Sell my mortgage in the Ruggles estate," John instructed Francis (November 17), before telling him that "France is perfectly victorious. A perfect peace will ensure in 3 or 4 months. Perhaps the naval success of England will balance the Continental victories of France." The British naval success was the Battle of Trafalgar, off the southwest coast of Spain, on October 21, 1805. In that momentous battle, Viscount Lord Nelson on board the HMS *Victory*, along with twenty-one other ships of the Royal Navy, battled thirty-three French and Spanish men-of-war. Twenty-two French and Spanish ships were destroyed with no loss of British vessels. With Nelson's victory, Great Britain was the undisputed mistress of the seas. John Lowell believed that the peace would come soon but on terms dictated by France, which planned to keep the whole of Austria and the Tyrol. "The Conqueror will dictate his own terms."

On December 2, the French army defeated the army of the Third Coalition at the Battle of Austerlitz. That same day, John Lowell penned a long letter to *Mon cheri frere*, written entirely in French. Two days later he sent Francis another letter, this one written in English, saying that he was practicing his French. "I wrote it as fast as English and it has few corrections in it. I do not speak the language well. I come too old and I have too many English friends about me but I know the language well in reading it and taste the beauties as well as most natives. This is quite pleasurable to me."

Before leaving Paris, John summarized his feelings toward France and its people. The French, he wrote to Francis, are "a frivolous people. They are a gay, lively people possessing a sensibility, which renders them alive to everything. They are easily elated or as easily depressed. They are men who love their country ardently, who are ready to quit all their pleasures and amusements to endure the hardships of the [battle]field. The French are very industrious [but] love pleasure more ardently than others."

In his July 4, 1799, oration delivered in the historic Faneuil Hall, Boston, in the presence of President John Adams, the ardent Federalist John Lowell Jr. hurled abuse at Revolutionary France as the "insatiable monster that reduced its citizens to soldiers or serfs, and terrorized them into docile drones." Now, six years later, and in their midst, he found the French fun-loving yet willing to sacrifice their lives out of love of country. John Lowell passionately upheld American independence from foreign domination, but in London was awed by the presence of George III. In many ways John Lowell Jr. the political analyst was a different person from John Lowell Jr. the tourist.

Traveling home after three years abroad, John Jr. took with him many of the refinements of the upper-class English and French life. He stayed in fine hotels, hired a butler, rented a carriage and driver, and purchased many expensive books, furnishings, paintings and a piano. He spent over £6,000 sterling on his grand tour of Europe, equivalent then to $20,000 in American currency, and well over $400,000 in today's money.

In April 1806, John and Rebecca Lowell returned to Bromley Vale, their Roxbury estate. John Lowell remained emotionally brittle and was unable to return to the practice of law, but instead settled into the life of the wealthy country gentleman. Despite the great cost of his European tour and the fact that he was no longer employed, John Lowell still had plenty of money to live in affluence for the rest of his days. Using his contacts with the eminent horticulturists he met during his tour of Europe, John filled his greenhouses with the seeds and cuttings of exotic plants. He employed gardeners and farm workers to raise his crops and delighted in sharing his knowledge with the members of the Massachusetts Society for Promoting Agriculture. He enlarged the greenhouses at Bromley Vale and grew flowers and vegetables using the latest scientific principles. He graced many a dinner party, showing off his conversational skills and political opinions. John Lowell became a respected member of his village, paying $307 to the First Church of Roxbury, his late father's church, for ownership of pew 101, on the lower floor.

John Lowell became politically active at the time of the Embargo of 1807 and the threat of war against Great Britain. An ardent Federalist, John identified with the Essex Junto, described by Samuel Eliot Morison as "the ultra-conservative and ultra-sectional wing of the party, refused all compromise with democracy, distrusted the French Revolution from the very start, failed entirely to sympathise with the South and the West and, in short, was blind to the fact that the world had moved forward since 1775 and 1789."[7]

John Lowell Jr. joined the Federalists while the party enjoyed power. After 1800, both he and the Federalists were in the opposition. Resenting the shift of authority from New England to the South and West, John Lowell, as the mouthpiece for the Essex Junto, advanced his conservative views in a series of pamphlets signed as "The Boston Rebel" or "A Roxbury Farmer." His close friends and political allies were Christopher Gore, Timothy Pickering and George Cabot. Although he no longer practiced at the bar, he kept abreast of the laws of the land. He wrote dozens of pamphlets and magazine articles on topics ranging from politics, religion, animal breeding, agriculture, religion, to the rights and privileges of professors at Harvard University. Cocksure and fearless, John Lowell reprimanded his opponents even if they happened to be past or present presidents of the United States. John Lowell criticized

John Adams, accusing the former president of being overpaid for his services to the nation. Writing to Dr. Benjamin Rush on August 15, 1811, from his home in Quincy, the seventy-five-year-old John Adams had his quiet revenge on the Lowells, both father and oldest son. Adams told Rush that in 1774 he gave up his law practice in Boston to aid his country. For ten years he served as America's ambassador abroad, followed by eight years as vice president and four years as president. The Lowells, by contrast, made no sacrifices for their country. Instead, John Lowell Sr. moved to Boston, and "stepped into my shoes, undertook my business, engaged in the employment of my Clients; and died lately worth several hundred thousand Dollars; left a very handsome fortune to all his sons and daughters; and that very Spartacus, that leader of the Rebel Slaves, that very 'Rebel' [John Lowell Jr.], who lately reproached me with being overpaid, has a magnificent seat in Boston, a splendid Villa in the country and large sums of Funds, Banks, and Insurance all derived from his father, for he never earned much of anything himself. After travelling over a large part of Europe with his Family, this very Spartacus tells the world I have been overpaid. I might safely offer him all I am worth, as I believe, for One Quarter part of his."[8] Both John Adams and his son John Quincy Adams, who served their country so well, spoke of John Lowell Jr., the rich armchair politician, with a mixture of contempt and envy.

John Lowell served as president of the Massachusetts Agricultural Society, benefactor of the Massachusetts General Hospital, the prime mover of the Boston Athenaeum, and founder of the Provident Bank for Savings. From 1810 to 1822, he was overseer of the Harvard Corporation and in 1814 the university awarded him the degree of L.L.D. In 1815, John Lowell urged the appointment of a professorship in law at the university. Through his efforts and those of his brother Francis Cabot Lowell, the sum of $7,500 was raised to endow the law professorship. The position was offered to John Lowell but he declined and at his recommendation, it went to Isaac Parker, the sitting chief justice of the Massachusetts Supreme Court. With this appointment the study of law in Massachusetts shifted from clerkships in the offices of established lawyers to a specialized university degree. An ardent supporter of elitist institutions, John Lowell was less concerned with uplifting the poor. In 1818 he opposed the efforts to establish in Boston a network of public primary schools for children aged four to seven, financed by the town. John Lowell Jr. was an old-fashioned Boston gentleman: educated and intelligent, elegant in dress, an elitist, a moralizer and a conservative. Lawyer, country squire, Harvard overseer, anglophile and political theorist, John Jr. followed in his father's footsteps. He died on March 12, 1840, outliving his brother Francis by twenty-three years.

CHARLES LOWELL

Born on August 11, 1782, in Boston in his father's house on Tremont Street, corner of Beacon, Charles was the youngest of the sons of Judge John Lowell. He was fourteen years younger than John Jr. and seven years younger than Francis Cabot; too young, too timid and too spiritual to want to compete with his brothers in the quest for worldly success. Charles was ten years old when he arrived at Phillips Academy, Andover, to share a class with twenty-six other boys. Among them was Stephen Longfellow, who became a prominent lawyer in Maine, served in the 18th Congress of the United States (1823–1825) and was the father of the poet Henry Wadsworth Longfellow. Young Charles studied only three years at Phillips Academy before his father removed him to Bridgewater to be privately tutored by the self-same Reverend Zedekiah Sanger who had helped Francis. Charles recalled later that Zedekiah Sanger was "entrusted with the care of many lads in their preparatory education for college. [Sanger was] a man of much simplicity of character of great sensibility, of an ardent temperament, perhaps somewhat excitable but habitually gentle and kind. He had nothing austere about him but his eyebrows, which were abnormally long."

Charles graduated from Harvard in 1800 and briefly studied law under the tutelage of his brother John Jr. But the law was not for him and in 1802, after his father died, the twenty-year-old Charles sailed for Scotland to start his studies at the prestigious Divinity School of the University of Edinburgh, living off £120 a year.

In Charles Lowell's time Edinburgh was at the center of Scottish Enlightenment. The city of one hundred thousand was home to Adam Smith, who published in 1776 his seminal work *An Inquiry into the Nature and Causes of the Wealth of Nations*, and to David Hume, author of the multi-volume *The History of England* and *A Treatise of Human Nature*. Charles found cheap accommodation in the home of Anne MacVicar Grant, a Scottish writer, who as a child had traveled with her father to America, where he served as a British officer during the French and Indian War. Anne MacVicar Grant wrote of her experiences in her *Memoirs of an American Lady*. Charles studied under the esteemed Dugald Stewart, who taught moral philosophy and counted the novelist Sir Walter Scott among his protégés. Charles' fellow student at the Divinity School of the University of Edinburgh was David Brewster. A child prodigy, Brewster chose instead a career in the sciences and achieved great fame for his research in the laws of the polarization of light.

In Edinburgh, Charles Lowell met his older brother John Jr. at the start of his three-year tour of Europe. Charles introduced his brother to a number of the intellectual leading lights of Edinburgh society, including Francis Jeffrey, editor of the *Edinburgh Review*, and Henry Brougham, later lord chancellor of Great Britain. Armed with powerful letters of introduction the brothers traveled to London and visited the House of Commons and heard a rousing speech by William Pitt the Younger. From London, John and Charles journeyed to Paris and glimpsed Napoleon Bonaparte before he was proclaimed emperor. The contacts and impressions John Jr. and brother Charles made in Great Britain were passed on to their middle brother Francis Cabot when he began his European tour six years later.

On New Year's Day 1806 the Reverend Charles Lowell was inducted into the West Boston Church, where he "nobly sustained the traditions of liberty and spiritual freedom." His brother John wished that Charles "will continue his industry & I know he will be successful." His congregation of three hundred members included many from the leading families of Boston. The Reverend Charles Lowell started a Sunday school, with Louisa May Alcott as one of the students. Charles married Harriet Bracket Spence of Portsmouth, New Hampshire, on October 2, 1806. Harriet was the daughter of Keith Spence, who immigrated from the Orkneys to New England shortly before the Revolutionary War. Proud of her heritage, Harriet had "a great memory, an extraordinary aptitude for language and a passionate fondness for ancient songs and ballads." The Reverend Charles Lowell was "a man of unusual culture and refinement and possessed a pure and gentle spiritual nature." Not only did he minister to his own wealthy church but ventured into the rough sections of Boston to assist the poor. Charles preached passionately against slavery. He was an active member of the Massachusetts Society for the Suppression of Intemperance, a member of the Massachusetts Bible Society and the Society for the Propagation of the Gospel among the Indians. Charles must have felt distress that his brother Francis traded in slave-grown sugarcane and cotton, supplied wines and brandy, and imported Caribbean molasses to make rum in his Boston distillery. The brothers, however, were able to separate business from piety and principle. In 1823, Harvard honored Charles Lowell with a doctor of divinity degree.

The Harvard- and Edinburgh-educated Reverend Charles Lowell was much in demand. On June 4, 1810, he addressed the Ancient and Honourable Artillery Company on the characteristics of a good soldier. "The love of life," he told the company, "is one of the most vigorous principles of our nature." Yet nations call their men to fight, and fight they must. The qualities of a good soldier include courage, love of country and piety. The demands of his congregation and his many other commitments soon undermined Charles Lowell's "health so much that the congregation advised him to live in the country a few miles from his church." Charles in 1818 bought the restful Elmwood mansion surrounded by ten acres in Cambridge.

In 1825, the Reverend Charles Lowell gave a sermon on the "Duty and Responsibility of a Christian Minister." He may well have spoken about

The Reverend Charles Lowell (1782–1861), younger half-brother to Francis Cabot Lowell and father of the poet James Russell Lowell. The reverend served for many years as pastor of the West Congregational Church, Boston. (Old West Church—United Methodist, 131 Cambridge Street, Boston, MA 02114. www.oldwestchurch.org/Historic_Images/ Charles_Lowell.)

himself, or his idealized self. "In the first place," Charles Lowell said, "a minister must be a Good Man" and imbued with piety. But goodness is not enough. "His mind must be informed with knowledge, to reading, meditation and prayer [and develop] a candid, unprejudiced, unbiased mind. He must study his own heart and make himself acquainted with human nature. He must study man, [display] fidelity, diligence, and zeal in the performance of his ministerial duties, [and] he must be easy of access to his people, and free to communicate."[9] Goodness of heart, without bias, accessibility, sincerity and understanding were the qualities Charles Lowell strove to bring to his ministry. He was an eloquent speaker. His son James Russell Lowell later wrote that "nothing could shake my beloved and honored father's trust in God and his sincere piety."

The Elmwood estate has played an important role in American history. Built in 1767, Elmwood was originally the ninety-acre estate of Andrew Oliver, the son of a wealthy West Indian merchant who was appointed by George III as the royal lieutenant governor of Massachusetts. The house received its name from the row of English elm trees that stood in front of it. Elmwood was one of the eighteenth-century country estates—known as Tory Row—built along the banks of the Charles River and occupied by officers of the crown or loyalist merchants who went into exile at the start of the Revolutionary War. On September 2, 1774, the house was surrounded by an angry mob demanding that Oliver resign his office. That day, the last royal lieutenant governor of Massachusetts left his estate, never to return.

With the American army stationed in Cambridge at the start of the Revolutionary War, the grand Elmwood home was used as a hospital. Later it was sold to Andrew Cabot of Salem and then bought by Elbridge Gerry, one of the signers of the Declaration of Independence, governor of Massachusetts (1810–1812) and vice president of the United States under Madison (from 1813 until his unexpected death the following year). At his Elmwood estate, the Reverend Charles Lowell combined his piety with grand living.

The sermons of the Reverend Charles Lowell were passionate but his inner life was austere. His diaries contain only brief notes about the people he met, where he preached and how he spent his time. He was often "at home all day" without any description of his thoughts and activities. In the diaries, there is no mention of his brother Francis Cabot Lowell, even on the day he died. Charles Lowell, however, kept a careful record of his expenses and he was especially diligent recording the daily temperatures and the force of the winds.

The last years of the life of Charles Lowell were marred by "sickness and infirmity and pain from which sleep affords scarcely a temporary refuge." His increasing deafness made conversation difficult. Furthermore, he suffered "disastrous losses to his moderate inheritance."[10] Having entrusted his fortune of some $400,000 to his oldest son, Charles Jr., he lost it all in the Panic of 1837, and was reduced to living off the meager wages of a clergyman. In a sermon "Making Haste to Be Rich," Charles Lowell warns that the headlong pursuit of money can lead to "ruin and distress. Compassion will and should be felt for one who has lived in affluence and become bankrupt." A debtor can never be free of his debts, but is morally obligated "to repay all his creditors to the utmost farthing, when it is in the power of his hand to do it."[11] Charles Lowell remained at the West Church for fifty-five years until he died in 1861, aged seventy-nine. Charles Lowell was born at the end of the War of Independence and died at the beginning of the Civil War. Charles outlived his brother Francis by forty-four years, and outlived all his other siblings save for Elizabeth Cutts Dutton. In 1854, the Reverend Charles Lowell dedicated his book *Sermons Chiefly Practical* to his sister Elizabeth. They were children of the same parents and lived all their lives in harmony "without the recollection of one unkind action, or word, or thought towards each other; and are the last survivors of our father's household. Your loving and only brother."

In 1819, the youngest of Charles Lowell's five children, the future poet James Russell Lowell was born at Elmwood. Here he heard the birdsong, watched the flowers bloom and the colors change with the seasons. So endearing was the house and grounds to James Russell Lowell that he declared, "I have but one home in America, and that is the house where I was born. I shouldn't be happy anywhere else." The poet and first editor of the *Atlantic Monthly* died at Elmwood in 1891.[12] The beautiful house and grounds remained the possession of the Lowell family for almost a century. Since 1971, Elmwood has served as the residence of the president of Harvard University.

Their father, Judge John Lowell, had played his part in the war for American independence. Blessed with wealth, high social class and an elite education John, Francis and Charles Lowell were well equipped to seek their places in a society that admired success and achievement. John excelled in politics, Francis in business and industry and Charles in matters of the spirit. The brothers Lowell were taught that success came to those who were able, intelligent, confident, and prepared to work hard. Conversely, failure came from laziness, foolishness, and the want of application. Having graduated from Harvard while still in their teens, John, Francis and Charles Lowell all possessed the determination to excel and all three had a dread of failure. Beneath the Lowell façade of strength, however, was emotional brittleness. The young John Lowell Jr. was self-confident to the point of arrogance, but the Jason Fairbanks trial followed by the death his father were severe blows from which he never fully recovered. Burdened by depression and anxiety he was no longer able to practice the law or assume the mantle of head of the family. Francis began well but his expulsion during his final year at Harvard shook him badly. Francis spent the rest of his life proving to himself and others that he was capable of great things. The youngest brother Charles was insecure, did poorly at Harvard, and failed in his law studies. He did not participate in the rivalry of his brothers and was fortunate to find his life's purpose while studying for the ministry in Edinburgh.[13]

The larger stage had little appeal to the Lowell brothers, who did not seek national office but remained in Boston nearly all of their lives. They were comfortable within their social class and generally associated with other Essex County families who settled in Boston. John Lowell was "unequal in talent and learning among the brilliant group of Federalists in Boston."[14] From his Roxbury home, John wrote long and scathing political treatises against the Louisiana Purchase, the Embargo of 1807 and the War of 1812. John supported the British side against France and strongly opposed the pro-French policies of the Jefferson administration. Charles published in book form his sermons railing against slavery, drunkenness, love of money and greed. Francis filled his head with calculations on the cost of goods, shipping, insurance, and the price of property. Unlike his brothers, Francis Cabot kept his opinions on religion and politics to himself and did not publish a single word on these topics. Francis was preoccupied with the notion that money was the prime indicator of success.

For all their differences, John, Francis and Charles Lowell willingly and eagerly helped each other. The same degree of filial affection continued with their children. Their eldest sons were born only months apart and grew to become the best of friends. John Amory Lowell married Susan Lowell, the only daughter of Francis Cabot Lowell. Each of the brothers also benefited hugely from the support of their wives, sisters and sisters-in-law. Francis Cabot Lowell was greatly aided by his brothers-in-law Samuel Pickering Gardner, Benjamin Gorham, Warren Dutton and by the capable Jackson brothers, Charles, James and Patrick Tracy. The brothers Lowell passed on their love of travel, especially extended tours of Great Britain and the Continent, to their children. From one generation to the next, members of the Lowell family sent their sons to be educated in Europe before attending Harvard, comfortably combining their love of the New World with a passion for the history, arts and languages of the Old World.

5

Francis and His Sisters

Write me all about yourself. Indeed my dear Susan, my employment, my plea-sure, so little varied that a sketch of a day would be to describe a month. In the wintry season I seldom quit the family fireside, except for church. Books, pen, and the needle vary my occupation; and though they would not shine with splendour on the page of history they make time pass pleasantly, and, I hope, not altogether without improvement.

From a letter dated January 3, 1805,
sent by Mary Wilder to her friend Susanna Lowell

The life of women in America at the close of the eighteenth century was one of unremitting drudgery and backbreaking work. Living on farms in drafty, poorly heated houses, acrid with wood ash and the smell of unwashed bodies, women were kept busy from dawn to dusk, sweeping, washing, scrubbing, cleaning, carrying, cooking, baking, tending the sick, nursing the babies, working in the fields and tending the animals. Water for drinking was carried bucket by bucket from well to house. Epidemics of smallpox, whooping cough and scarlet fever carried away the young and old alike. Large families were the rule, complicated by difficult preg-nancies and infant deaths. The women spun the wool and wove the cloth to make the clothes. They tanned the leather to make the shoes.

Relatively few women were spared this life of hard work. These came from wealthy families with live-in servants to do the chores in the home and garden. The Lowell sisters and their circle were among this rare cat-egory. They were taught to read and write, manage the servants, order the meals, keep the books, play a musical instrument and entertain the guests. They attended church, visited the sick, read the books in their fathers' libraries, wrote letters, kept diaries to jot down their daily thoughts, tried their hand at poetry and stories, enjoyed the company of worldly men, and offered emotional support to their fathers and their brothers. Upper-class girls, such as the Lowell daughters, were taught to embroider, paint, dress elegantly and be graceful and charming. These skills improved their chances of marrying a young man with good prospects. The Lowell women were as intelligent as their brothers but remained dependent for lack of opportunities for education or employment in order to advance in the world.

THE EDUCATION OF GIRLS

The Massachusetts Bay Colony required by law that children learn to read and write, but in practice this requirement applied far more to boys than girls. The Boston Latin School, America's first public high school, opened in 1635 but girls were only admitted on an equal basis to boys in 1826, nearly two hundred years later. Before then, girls were educated at home and learned enough to read the Bible, write letters and keep household accounts. New England mothers, teaching their own daughters, sometimes included the children of neighbors in the lessons. These became known as "dame schools." Starting early in the nineteenth century, some New England towns offered a rudimentary education to the girls who came to school at five in the morning and left at seven o'clock when the boys arrived. In early colonial times there was a wide gap between the literacy of girls and boys but by the end of the eighteenth century, girls in New England almost closed the gap, with over 90 percent able to read and write.

A few pioneering women were determined to improve the education for girls. In 1792, Sarah Pierce of Litchfield, Connecticut, put into practice her belief that women were the intellectual equals of men by opening the Litchfield Female Academy in her home. The academy at Litchfield was one of the first schools for girls in the United States. Sarah Pierce taught literature, history, geography and foreign languages, as well as poetry, embroidery, music and dancing, and soon attracted girls from far and wide.[1] The Litchfield Academy was followed by the Reverend Joseph Emerson's Academy for Young Women at Byfield and Saugus, Massachusetts; the Emma Willard School, in 1814, in the industrial town of Troy, New York; and the Salem Female Academy, Winston-Salem, North Carolina, established in 1802. Even for these fortunate girls, education stopped at the secondary school level, with very few women admitted to universities until a half-century later.

The best known of the academies for young women in Boston was established by Mrs. Susanna Rowson. Born in Portsmouth, England, the daughter of Lieutenant William Haswell of the British navy, Susanna came to colonial Boston, where her father served as a customs officer. At the start of the Revolutionary War her father was placed under house arrest and, in 1778, the family was sent back to England in a prisoner exchange. Susanna turned to acting and, with her husband William Rowson, came to the United States. She performed at the Federal Street Theatre, Boston, and in 1797, decided to leave the stage to start an academy for girls. Actress, poetess, playwright and authoress of the best-selling novel *Charlotte Temple*, Mrs. Rowson attracted schoolgirls from "the most refined and intelligent families" of Boston. In 1800, she moved her school into the Bigelow mansion on the eastern bank of the Mystic River in the nearby town of Medford. In addition to teaching writing and reading in English, she offered French, penmanship, piano and dance. Mrs. Rowson charged $30 a month for board and 75 cents for each lesson in dance and pianoforte. As the demand increased she moved her school to Newton and finally to a large facility on Washington Street on the Roxbury line.[2]

The five daughters of Judge John Lowell who lived into adult life were tutored at home, where they learned to read and write in English, speak elegantly, dress beautifully and keep house in preparation for their roles as wives of successful men and mothers of gifted children. Poetry and literature were their passions, especially books written by female authors. Like the men of their social class, the Lowell women had a profound sense of duty and a deep loyalty to the family. Despite their lack of a classical education the Lowell sisters and sisters-in-law were skillful writers, as their abundant letters and diaries show. They were well informed, sensitive, perceptive and thoughtful, especially on "women's subjects." They supported each other and offered encouragement to their husbands and brothers. The Lowell women learned to cope with separation, financial loss and sickness. They faced the perils of pregnancy and infectious diseases in an age of poor sanitation, contaminated water and ineffectual medical care.

The three wives of Judge John Lowell gave him six daughters. From his first marriage were born Anna Cabot Lowell (1768–1810), "a woman of talents," and Sarah Champney (1771–1851), both born in Newburyport. From the second marriage came Susanna Cabot (1776–1816), Francis' only biological sibling, who married Benjamin Gorham (1775–1855) of Charlestown, Massachusetts. From Judge John Lowell's third marriage came Rebecca Russell (1779–1853), who married the wealthy merchant Samuel Pickering Gardner, who became a business associate of Francis Cabot Lowell; Elizabeth Cutts (1784–1864), who married in 1806 to Warren Dutton; and lastly, Mary, born 1786 but, sadly, died three years later. To complicate matters more, Anna was known in the family as Nancy, Sarah as Sally, Susanna as Susan and Elizabeth as Eliza. Francis Cabot Lowell was especially close to Susanna, with whom he shared both a father and a mother. They were too young to remember their own mother. Their stepmother, Rebecca Russell Lowell, was the only mother they knew.

Rebecca Russell in 1797 was the first of the Lowell girls to marry. Elizabeth Cutts married in 1806, and Susanna Cabot in 1807. Anna and Sarah did not marry.

REBECCA RUSSELL LOWELL

The Honorable James Iredell of North Carolina was an associate justice of the U.S. Supreme Court. In June 1795 he was in Boston to try a man for manslaughter on the high seas. Writing to his wife on June 12, Justice Iredell left an account of his meeting with Judge John Lowell: "I went Saturday evening to Judge Lowell (three miles from town) and stayed in his house, which is delightfully situated, till Monday morning. He has a very agreeable family, and I always pass my time very agreeably with them. His third daughter, is shortly to marry to a young gentleman, who lodges in the same house with me, of the name Gardner, with whom I am much pleased, who is a merchant of a very respectable and amiable character."

Associate Justice Iredell was referring to Rebecca Russell, daughter of John Lowell by his third wife, and Samuel Pickering Gardner, born in Salem. Gardner graduated from Harvard College in 1786, the same class as Rebecca's half-brother John Lowell Jr. Upon graduation Gardner made his way to Charleston, South Carolina, to enter a mercantile business with his brother John. After his brother died at age thirty-two, Samuel moved to Boston, where he met Judge John Lowell and his family.

Judge John Lowell may have wondered why Mr. Samuel Gardner was so frequent a visitor to the house in Roxbury. Certainly he enjoyed the company of the wise judge or perhaps he was attracted to either Anna or Sarah. Judge John Lowell must have been bowled over by the letter dated June 13, 1794, that he received from the twenty-seven-year-old Samuel Pickering Gardner. "Such was the extreme improbability of even the existence of sentiments which I possess," explained Gardner, "that they were either not seen, or if seen at all, were probably misconstrued. To prevent any erroneous conclusions I determined (after considerable conflict with my feelings) to discover to you an attachment which (from the disparity of age), I have not dared to disclose to anyone; and I dread your disapprobation will be equal to your surprise, when I inform you the object of it is your daughter Rebecca. [She] is probably ignorant of the passion she has excited in me." Judge Lowell may have heard rumors, continued

Gardner, that "another lady was the object of my particular attachment" but these rumors were false and Rebecca alone captured his heart. Samuel Pickering Gardner asked Judge Lowell's approval to court the fifteen-year-old Rebecca despite their disparity in age. "Whatever your decision I beg you to return me an answer in writing." If the answer is no, Gardner asked that his letter "may forever remain a secret with yourself and Mrs. Lowell."

Judge John Lowell responded to Gardner on June 17: "I do not hesitate to say that your character has been such that I have long greatly esteemed & that my acquaintance with you has conformed & increased that esteem and that I should readily have approved & promoted your wishes to be tenderly connected with either of my children. The tender age of my child alone occasions a difficulty in saying to you what in another case I should readily agree." But the object of Gardner's desire was young Rebecca, not one of her older sisters. Judge and Mrs. Lowell, and we can assume the girl herself, readily agreed to the match, but required that the wedding would wait until after Rebecca's eighteenth birthday.

Over the two and a half years of their engagement the lovestruck Samuel P. Gardner wrote endearing letters to "My dear girl." On July 2, 1795, he wrote, "You know my feelings too well to doubt that every sentence [I write] that does not discover the warmest attachment is an unfaithful index of my heart." Gardner showed he was attentive to her family and "accompanied your sister Sally a few miles on horse back, she was gracefully mounted on my pony and I somewhat less so, on one of your father's coach horses. I have lent my chaise to your sister Nancy and Mrs. Lee who are intent to set out tomorrow on a kind of Knight's errand." Gardner also saw Francis Cabot Lowell (July 7), who was preparing to leave Boston as supercargo on a vessel carrying flour and rice to France: "There is not any material alteration in Frank's health which causes him to delay undertaking the voyage to France."

After their marriage on September 19, 1797, Rebecca was no longer "My dear girl," but Gardner addressed her in his letters as "Dear Rebecca." Samuel Pickering Gardner and his Harvard classmate John Lowell Jr. were now brothers-in-law. Gardner became a successful merchant with offices at 66 Long Wharf. He and Rebecca had three daughters and two sons who grew to adulthood. The sons, John Lowell Gardner and George Gardner, inherited from their Gardner grandmother "all her real estate in Salem consisting of about one hundred and eleven acres of pasture."[3] John Lowell Gardner became wealthy in the East India trade and retired to enjoy his farm in Wenham surrounded by his books and family. On his death, the bulk of his money went to his older son, also named John Lowell Gardner. In 1860, John Jr., known as Jack, married the flamboyant twenty-year-old Isabella Stewart of New York City. In Boston, Isabella became known as Mrs. Jack. Her portrait showing a low neckline and flattering curves, painted in 1888 by John Singer Sargent, scandalized Brahmin society. Her husband insisted that the painting not be shown in public again during his lifetime. After Jack died in 1898, Isabella immersed herself in Fenway Court, her museum-home modeled after a renaissance palace in Venice. She filled her museum with works of art and sculpture acquired by the hundred in Europe, with the help of Bernard Berenson. The Isabella Stewart Gardner Museum opened with her portrait by Sargent in 1903 on the Fenway, and remains to this day one of Boston's quintessential attractions. Alas, a number of the finest pieces at the Isabella Stewart Gardner Museum, including a Vermeer and three works by Rembrandt, were stolen from the museum in 1990.

ELIZABETH CUTTS LOWELL

The second of the Lowell daughters to marry was Elizabeth Cutts. Her brother John Lowell Jr. was in Paris when he received word of the planned marriage. Reverting briefly to the role of the wise leader of the family, John wrote to Francis on July 24, 1805, "I hear that [Warren] Dutton talks of marrying [their sister, Elizabeth] before I return. I am sorry because I fear he can ill afford it at present." John instructed Francis to tell the young couple of his concerns and "induce them to go into a small house or part of a house at first." He would help them with furniture only if they showed they could live within their means.

Warren Dutton was the son of Deacon Ebenezer Dutton of East Haddam, Connecticut. He graduated Yale College in 1797, and was a tutor at Williams College. He showed a flair for politics and moved to Boston to work on the *Massachusetts Gazette*, a right-wing Federalist paper established by the Reverend Jedediah Morse of Charlestown with the backing of wealthy merchants. Dutton decided to switch to the law and, in 1803, began his studies in the law office of John Lowell Jr. Emotionally crippled and ready to leave Boston to recuperate in Europe, Lowell handed over his lucrative practice to Warren Dutton. Elizabeth and Warren married on June 3, 1806, in a ceremony conducted by her brother, the Reverend Charles Lowell. With his law practice growing, Warren Dutton and Elizabeth had two sons, John Lowell and James Russell, named respectively for Elizabeth's father and her maternal grandfather. Warren Dutton was a supporter of Francis Cabot Lowell and was among the first to invest in the Boston Manufacturing Company. In his later years Warren Dutton became ill and, with his wife, traveled in Europe. On their return they settled in Brighton, where Warren Dutton died in his eighty-third year.[4]

A grandson, Warren Dutton Russell, born in 1840, was killed on August 30, 1862, during the Civil War. A bullet struck Lieutenant Russell in the neck and severed the jugular vein. Elizabeth Cutts, the last of the children of Judge John Lowell, died in 1864 in her eighty-first year.

ANNA CABOT AND SUSANNA CABOT

Born in 1768, Anna Cabot was the oldest of the children of Judge John Lowell. In her teens and twenties, she developed a large circle of friends, both women and men. She was a talented letter writer and left keen observations of the relationships between family members, friends and between men and women. Anna Cabot met the highly suitable young John Singleton Copley, the son of the famous painter of the same name, and visiting Boston from London, "but the society in New York and Philadelphia have charms so seductive, that, I fear it will be long before he returns to us." Copley returned to London to a distinguished career as lord chancellor of England, for which he received the title of Lord Lyndhurst. Following the departure of young Copley, Anna Lowell hoped against hope that Mr. Quincy would return her affections. Anna shared her dreams with Eliza Sarah Morton of New York, writing on January 2, 1797, when she was twenty-nine years old: "Indeed, of all his excellencies, I shall only at this time mention one; it is a just and delicate taste in the selection of his female friends. I am aware of the apparent vanity of the last remark, but it will be sufficient when I add that Mr. Quincy never distinguished me as a favorite until he knew me as a friend. By the ladies here he is charged with coldness and indifference, but certainly I sometimes touch a string which vibrates to sensations very opposite to those of apathy. Last evening he was unusually animated."

The Mr. Quincy of Anna's hopes was none other than Josiah Quincy III, born in 1772 and, like Anna's brother John Jr., a scholar at Phillips Andover and a graduate of Harvard. Josiah Quincy married Eliza Sarah Morton in 1797, and went on to a distinguished career in the U.S. House of Representatives (1808–1813), and serving as mayor of Boston (1823–1828) and president of Harvard University (1829–1845). Boston's Quincy Market is named for him. Despite Anna Cabot's disappointment, she and Eliza Quincy remained close friends. Josiah Quincy wrote to his wife that Anna Cabot was "the most excellent and justly beloved of all your friends." Josiah and Eliza Quincy named their last child Anna Cabot Lowell Quincy, born two years after the death of Anna Cabot Lowell. Anna Cabot Lowell Quincy kept a diary, which, in 2003, was published in book form as *A Woman's Wit and Whimsy*.[5]

Still living at Bromley Vale after Judge John Lowell died were his widow, Rebecca Russell Lowell, and two daughters, Anna Cabot and Sarah, from his first marriage, Susanna from his second marriage and Elizabeth from his third marriage. The grand manor house and all the land at Bromley Vale were inherited by John Lowell Jr., who made it known that he intended to live there upon his return from Europe. Rebecca Lowell resigned from the First Church of Roxbury to join the First Church of Charlestown; a church that was established in 1632 by the freshly arrived Englishmen living on the hills in huts and tents. On December 12, 1802, Rebecca Lowell, together with her daughters Anna, Sarah, Susanna and Elizabeth took communion at the First Church, Charlestown. Joining them that day was Sarah Russell (who years later became "deranged"). Soon after the Lowell ladies joined the church Jonathan Nicholls also took communion. He was described as a "negro" suggesting that the church in Charlestown was desegregated as early as 1803.[6] By 1804, the widow Rebecca and the Lowell daughters moved from Bromley Vale to Charlestown to live in the home of her father, Judge James Russell.

We can learn something about the personality and interests of the half-sisters Anna Cabot and Susanna Cabot, now living in Charlestown, from their exchange of letters with Mary Wilder, a beautiful and talented young woman and the widow of a French plantation owner in Guadeloupe, French West Indies. Mary Wilder was the only one of the six children of Dr. Josiah Wilder and his wife Mary to reach adulthood. After her husband died Mary returned to America to live with her family in Concord, Massachusetts, and soon after developed a friendship with Anna and Susanna. Mary Wilder was twenty-four when she began her friendship with thirty-six-year-old Anna and twenty-eight-year-old Susanna Lowell. Mary Wilder was delighted with her new friends, describing Anna as possessing a "a remarkable intelligence" and Susanna as having "refined and literary tastes." Like other of the Lowell children, however, Anna and Susanna were sensitive and delicate. In October 1804, Mary's plan for a trip from Charlestown to Newburyport was thwarted by the reaction of the Lowell ladies. "I fear the season will be too advanced to journey in an open chaise unattended," wrote Mary to a mutual friend. "Not that I apprehend any danger but I fear our friends, Anna included, would pronounce us afflicted with some mental disease."

INTELLECTUAL LIFE OF THE LOWELL LADIES

Improving their minds was the great desire of these women shut up in their homes, without the same opportunities for education and employment available to their brothers. The women corresponded about the books they were reading, poetry they were writing and their occasional trips to the theater. The novel *The Letters of a British Spy* written in 1803 by William Wirt, at one time U.S. attorney general, was a favorite. *A Tale of the Times* written 1797 by the English authoress Jane West spoke to the advancement of education for women. The Lowell women read the magazine *Lounger* sent from Edinburgh, sharing their opinions about the articles they read. Mary and her friends enjoyed Samuel Johnson's *Lives of the Poets* and Benjamin Martin's *Philosophical Grammar*. Benjamin Martin wrote his book in 1755 as an "entertainment of the youth of both sexes. And that it may delight and allure them, as to engage and to pursue true knowledge to the greater perfection."

In March 1806, Susanna saw the famous actor Thomas Abthorpe Cooper in a performance as Hamlet at the Federal Theatre, Boston. She wrote Mary about her disappointment in Cooper's performance, only to receive a good-natured rebuke. "Don't share your opinion about Cooper," wrote Mary on April 1. "Your reputation for taste could never survive such an avowal. If you are really so *outré*, conceal it, lest the *beau-monde*, which has hitherto imagined Susan to be a civilized being, should pronounce her a mere barbarian." The friendship between Mary Wilder and the Lowell ladies cooled after 1806 when Mary announced her engagement to Daniel Appleton White of Newburyport, and Susanna her engagement to Benjamin Gorham of Charlestown.

Anna Cabot Lowell limited her literary ambitions to letter writing but was keen to advance the careers of other women authors. Her brother the Reverend Charles Lowell, who had studied in Edinburgh and maintained "an enthusiastic affection for it," gave her a copy of the *Memoirs of an American Lady, with Sketches of Manners and Scenes in America as They Existed Previous to the Revolution*, written by Anne MacVicar Grant, and published in London in 1808. Previous to this book, Anne MacVicar Grant published her *Poems of Various Subjects* and *The Highlanders, and Other Poems*. The book *Memoirs of an American Lady* tells of the adventures of Anne MacVicar, who came from her native Scotland to America as a small child in 1758 to be with her father, "a plain, brave and pious man," who was an officer in the British army. Anne MacVicar returned to Scotland, married and raised her family. The death of her husband left her "in circumstances above absolute want." Now known as Mrs. Grant of Laggan, she turned to writing to support herself and her children.

So taken with the *Memoirs* was Anna Cabot Lowell that she undertook to have the book published by B. W. Wells in Boston. Anna Cabot was eager to publish Anne MacVicar Grant's book in America "as models of epistolary style and lessons of life for our sex." Anna Cabot Lowell next planned to publish *The Life of Elizabeth Smith*. Born in 1776, the daughter of a wealthy banker, Elizabeth Smith was a child prodigy who spoke

Spanish, French and Italian, taught herself Oriental languages and was a fine poet.

From 1809 until her death the following year, Anna Cabot Lowell kept up a lively correspondence with Mrs. Grant in Edinburgh, discussing her family, the arts and the character of the young American nation. Anna Cabot told her Edinburgh friend on March 30, 1809, that she had assembled over eight hundred subscribers to fund the publication of *Memoirs of an American Lady*, and raised £200 from the sale of the book, which she sent to the very grateful Anne MacVicar Grant. In a letter of November 8, 1809, Anna informed Mrs. Grant that New England was different from the American South and that "the slave trade has been prohibited under severe penalties by the laws of Massachusetts ever since it became an independent state." Unlike Europe, Anna Cabot Lowell wrote on July 23, 1810, the United States "has no order of men who have the fortune and the leisure to cultivate and encourage talents. All men must push their own way to fortune." Men in America of ability "are obliged to employ all their talents to save the important institutions of law and freedom from popular fury. They become politicians rather than poets." In America, "there is no room for genius to unfold its fairest bloom." As a result, talented Americans feel obliged to move to Europe. As examples of American-born artists who moved away she gave John Singleton Copley, John Trumbull, Benjamin West (who served as president of the Royal Academy) and Gilbert Stuart (who "was many years in England and celebrated there").

Anna Cabot Lowell respected the leaders of Massachusetts as men of intelligence, refinement and education. She was also an early American feminist who believed that "our sex" had an important task in steering the rough-hewn nation toward literature and the arts. Anna remained too reserved to seek for herself the printed page and limited her literary works to private letters.

CHARLESTOWN

The Russell and the Gorham families were among the most distinguished in Charlestown. In 1788, James Russell and Nathaniel Gorham served on a committee to select the next pastor for the First Parish of Charlestown. They chose Jedediah Morse, recently graduated from Yale, to the position, which paid him $11 a week, a furnished house and barn and enough firewood to last through the year. In 1799, his eight-year-old son, Samuel Finley Breese Morse, entered Phillips Academy, Andover, on scholarship. At first Samuel was homesick and ran away, but he settled to become a fine scholar. On August 2, he wrote to his "Dear Papa," sending his love to all the family and asking his father to "send me up some very good paper to write to you. I have as many blackberries as I want. I go and pick them myself." Samuel F. B. Morse began as an artist but his great contribution to the nineteenth century was as the inventor of the electric telegraph and Morse code.[7]

Nathaniel Gorham (1738–1796) served with distinction as a delegate to the Constitutional Convention of the United States, and in 1786 was president of the United States in Congress Assembled. Nathaniel speculated in land and bought several hundred thousand acres in western New York State but soon defaulted on his loans. His son Benjamin Gorham was more cautious. After graduating Harvard College, Benjamin studied the law and opened his practice in Boston. It is likely that he met Susanna Cabot Lowell at the First Parish church. He was thirty-two and she thirty-one years when they married. The couple had four children; Susanna lost both her daughters before she herself died on February 26, 1816, aged thirty-nine.

In the same year that Susanna died, 1816, Rebecca Russell Tyng Lowell, third wife of Judge John Lowell, also died. She left an estate of $18,849.70, mostly to her children. $4,500 went to the three young children of Susanna Gorham. Rebecca Lowell left money to her church. The Reverend Jedediah Morse of the First Church, Charlestown, wrote on December 19, 1817, to thank the Lowell family after "having received through legal channels the liberal legacy of three hundred dollars from the estate of the late worthy and respected Mrs. Rebecca Lowell."

Benjamin Gorham started his public career in 1814 as a member of the Massachusetts House. From 1821 to 1835 he served in the Congress of the United States. Benjamin and Susanna's oldest son, William Cabot Gorham, graduated from Harvard and was dead at age thirty. The youngest child, Benjamin Lowell Gorham, became insane, probably schizophrenia, when only fifteen years old. Before Benjamin Gorham the elder died in 1851, he set aside a trust fund for the care of his mentally ill son. The funds for the trust came from his grandmother, Rebecca Lowell, and his great uncle William Cabot, as well as from his father Benjamin Gorham and the deceased William Cabot Gorham, totaling $8,102.67. The money was invested with the Massachusetts Hospital Life Insurance Company, with Francis Cabot Lowell Jr. and Edwin A. Hills as trustees. Through deft investing the trust fund grew and was valued at $150,000 when the insane Benjamin Lowell Gorham died on June 2, 1889. Two hundred and twenty people, residuary legatees of Benjamin Gorham and others "scattered from Boston to India," claimed a share of these funds. The legal fight over the Benjamin Lowell Gorham trust fund reached the Supreme Court of Massachusetts (*Hills vs. Putnam*, March–June 1890). The court determined that the funds belonged exclusively to the estate of Benjamin

Lowell Gorham.[8] One-third of the money was eventually paid to the Lowell descendants and two-thirds to the Gorham side of the family.

THE DEATH OF SISTER ANNA CABOT LOWELL

While Francis and his family were enjoying their stay in Edinburgh he received a letter from Samuel Pickering Gardner, written October 20, 1810, telling him that his mother, Rebecca Russell Lowell, and her two unmarried daughters, Anna and Sarah, were eager to move into a place of their own, choosing a new house built by Davis & Welles on Common Street, Charlestown. Gardner and John Lowell were against the idea and tried to dissuade the women from going ahead with their plan, "but so great was the desire of your mother and sisters to have it that we finally consented to the purchase." The cost of the house was $6,500, which was taken from Rebecca's account with Francis Cabot Lowell, and managed during his absence abroad by Samuel P. Gardner.

Rebecca and her unmarried stepdaughters were busy packing their possessions for the move when Anna suddenly took ill. Samuel Gardner broke the sad news to Francis in a letter dated January 9, 1811: "Your sister Anna was taken sick in the night of Thursday the nineteenth of December. The next morning (as your mother had commenced to move her furniture to the new house) she was carried to Mr. [Benjamin] Gorham's where she continued to decline till the day of the eighteenth when she expired. I am inclined to think that her death was more due to the state of exhaustion of her constitution than the severity of the disorder. She had so often recovered in times past from severe bouts of sickness; until the day of her death we were not altogether without hope that she might again be restored to her former health."

Anna Cabot Lowell, known as Aunt Nancy, "wrote charming letters which often chronicled the pleasant gayeties of the family at home, of the looks and the manners of the people whom she met when away." As she lay dying, she penned a final letter to her literary soulmate Mrs. Anne MacVicar Grant of Edinburgh. "Perhaps the vicissitudes of life may, at a future period, lead some of your family to this part of the world," wrote Anna Cabot Lowell. "In such a case they would not find themselves in a land of strangers. Many hands would be stretched out to welcome them, and many hearts would offer them a friendly greeting. But should my intercourse with you soon terminate, there are others who shall long cherish your remembrance and who are worthy of your friendship." Aged forty-two years at her death, Anna showed her love of family by bequeathing two shares in the "river bridge company" to her younger sister Elizabeth Dutton, two shares to her friend Anne Bromfield, and five shares in the Marine Insurance Company to her sister Susanna Gorham. She left money to the Society to Aid Widows and Orphans, $500 to the Horticultural Society, and funds for elderly clergymen in Massachusetts. Her brother Francis and his family were among those deemed worthy to continue the friendship of Anne MacVicar Grant, the female writer from Edinburgh. Anna Cabot Lowell appointed her brothers John Jr. and Francis Cabot and her three brothers-in-law as the trustees of her small estate.

During her life, Anna Cabot Lowell was concerned that America lacked the wealth and the leisure to contemplate painting, literature, poetry and music. These talents appeared in the generation that followed hers. Her nephew James Russell Lowell became a distinguished man of letters. Her namesake Anna Cabot Lowell Quincy (1812–1899) was a prolific author who wrote children's stories and treatises on the education of girls. Anna Cabot Lowell would have been proud of them.

THE UNLIKELY FRIENDSHIP OF
SARAH CHAMPNEY LOWELL AND
HENRY WADSWORTH LONGFELLOW

After the death of her mother and her sister, Sarah Champney, known as Sally, lived alone in the house on Common Street. Around the year 1835, she moved from Charlestown to nearby Cambridge, to be closer to her half-brother, the Reverend Charles Lowell, renting rooms in a house at 105 Brattle Street. The elegant mansion with ninety acres on Tory Row was originally built in 1759 by the Loyalist John Vassall, who fled to England at the start of the Revolutionary War. Nearby living in grand style were the royalists Richard Lechmere and Jonathan Sewall, who also abandoned homes and fled to the British side. During the months of the siege of Boston, the Vassall House served as the headquarters of General George Washington. Soon after Washington left Cambridge in April 1776 the house and the lands were confiscated by the state of Massachusetts. Five years later, the property was bought for the sum of £4,263 by Nathaniel Tracy of Newburyport, then at the height of his wealth as a privateer and a partner in Jackson, Tracy & Tracy. Nathaniel Tracy entertained lavishly both in Cambridge and Newburyport but when the firm went bankrupt in 1786, he lost his properties. In 1786, the great house in Cambridge was bought by the merchant Thomas Russell, brother-in-law of Judge John Lowell.

In 1791, the house was bought by Andrew Craigie and became known as the Vassall-Craigie House. After Craigie died in 1815 his widow took in boarders, including Sarah Champney Lowell and Henry Wadsworth Longfellow, the newly appointed professor of modern languages at

Harvard. Sarah Champney probably did not know that the house was once owned by her uncle Thomas Russell. In 1837, Longfellow recorded (August 28) a frightening event when a fire started in the house, nearly destroying his rooms and his library. "Aunt Sally Lowell is quietly in possession of about 2/3rds of the house," wrote the poet. "Some malicious person has told her that I was so much offended with her coming into the house, as to be on the point of leaving. Funny folks—these Cambridge folks."

Longfellow's wife, Mary Potter, died in 1835, after a miscarriage. The following year, he came alone to Harvard to start his professorship. He was a keen observer of people and recorded his first impressions of Sarah Lowell, whom he came to call Aunt Sally. She was, Longfellow wrote, "a lady under the eaves of seventy but with the figure and vivacity of a girl of seventeen. She was full of the romance of youth and endowed with the most lively imagination; a great pressure of conversation. She is the sister of the clergyman, aunt of the poet. She was in high degree an aristocrat; and pride in birth and family was one of her ruling passions. She is extremely affable & ladylike."

For eighteen months Miss Lowell and Longfellow occupied adjacent suites on the second floor of the Craigie House. The young professor grew fond of Aunt Sally, nearly twice his age. "I have made a new arrangement about my board," wrote Longfellow to his father on September 11, 1836, "living with Miss Lowell in close communion. She is a good deal like a fly, brisk and buzzy. She is an excellent old lady; and does everything in the most genteel style. We breakfast at 8 and dine at 3, take tea at 7. I feel much more comfortable than when I had to shoot my dinner in the wing, as it were. The arrangement is a mutual blessing—a mutual life-insurance company." The friendship emboldened the elderly lady to share her concerns, telling Longfellow that her nephew, James Russell Lowell, was inattentive to his studies and had been sent down from Harvard.[9] Aunt Sally had three servants to take care of her needs; one of them was assigned the task of cooking for herself and Longfellow. With his meals prepared for him and help with his laundry and cleaning, Longfellow was able to concentrate on his teaching and his writing. In return, the lonely Aunt Sally was delighted to dine regularly with so pleasant and distinguished a man of letters.

Early in 1840, Aunt Sally told Longfellow that she would have to leave her spacious rooms in the Craigie House and move to one half of "a little one-story cottage nearby." To his mother, Longfellow wrote on February 27, 1840, "Miss Lowell is leaving today. I am very sorry for her. She has lost seven thousand dollars by her nephew's failure." Together with other members of the family, Sarah Champney Lowell had entrusted her funds to Charles P. Lowell, older son of the Reverend Charles Lowell.

"The misconduct of the nephew," reported Longfellow in a letter to his brother Stephen on March 13, "which appears worse and worse the more it is investigated, involving moral delinquencies." Because of her losses, Sarah's income was much reduced, and renting the cottage for $400 a year left her little money for luxuries. She let go of one of her three servants but insisted on leaving one of the two who remained to look after Longfellow at the Craigie house, taking only one servant with her to the cottage. Longfellow's sister assured Aunt Sally that her brother could take care of himself, but Henry Longfellow himself was quite pleased, as he wrote on February 27, that one servant "remains here to provide me with food."

Sarah Champney Lowell told Longfellow that the nephew's irresponsibility was "the first stain on the esscutechon of the Lowells." Longfellow was "very sorry for her. She is quite heroic about it now, but when there is no longer any glory attached to this heroism, and she finds herself alone in her cottage, I think she will suffer very much." Sarah Lowell moved to her "nice little place," reported Longfellow to his father on March 8. "She has a talent for giving every place an aura of elegance. She will be very comfortable, notwithstanding her loss, but in great affliction on her brother's account, whose loss is much greater, and also according to the disgrace." The Reverend Charles Lowell's loss was so great that he was forced to take in boarders to supplement his meager salary from the church.

Henry Longfellow's friends showed far less compassion than did he, believing that Sarah Lowell planned to make her home into a shrine to attract future generations "to visit her small cottage and gaze upon it with feelings of reference as having belonged to the friend of Longfellow." They accused Aunt Sally of jealousy and sniggered at her for placing his portrait on the wall of her parlor, calling it Hyperion, the title of the prose poem he wrote in 1839.

Henry Wadsworth Longfellow remained loyal to his aged friend, visiting her in her cottage and presenting her with a bunch of May-flowers. He found her, as he recorded on May 9, 1841, "sitting doleful and alone, with some dismal forebodings about her own end." But she quickly perked up when he gave her the flowers and "was much gratified." Writing to his brother Stephen on February 27, 1842, Longfellow reported that he "found Miss Lowell in great distress at the death of her cat; killed the day before by two ruffian dogs. She had the body put into a shroud and decently buried." Longfellow wrote to Sarah Lowell while on his trip to Europe in the summer of 1842. After he married Frances Appleton, he continued to visit his aged friend and invited her to a number of his literary evenings. On October 13, 1844, Sarah Champney Lowell was one of twenty guests invited by Henry Wadsworth Longfellow to a performance of Shakespeare at the Melodeon Theatre in Boston, followed by a reading soirée.[10]

Sarah's health and income were failing. At the close of 1844, she left her cottage "to take shelter in the nest of Mrs. [Harriot Hillard] Peck, who flows about the village collecting gossip to feed her withal." The unlikely friendship between the young poet and the elderly Brahmin lady lasted close to ten years. They first met as two lonely people, eager for company. Sharing meals grew into shared concern and shared respect. He listened respectfully to her tales particularly about her noble family. She spoke with pride about the Lowell family and the Lowell Institute but voiced disappointment that her nephew lost her money. As a child Sarah Champney Lowell knew wealth and the love of family, but at the close of her long life she was poor and abandoned. Sarah Champney Lowell died in Cambridge at eighty-six years, outliving all of her siblings save for the Reverend Charles Lowell and Elizabeth Dutton. Sarah Champney Lowell was buried alongside her beloved father in the Lowell tomb in Roxbury.

LONGFELLOW MARRIES AGAIN

The merchant Nathan Appleton in 1813 was one of the first to show faith in the vision of Francis Cabot Lowell by investing money in the Boston Manufacturing Company. It was Appleton who devised the marketing strategy for the new textile mill and it was Appleton who developed the great textile city along the banks of the Merrimack River, named Lowell, in honor of Francis Cabot Lowell. Henry Longfellow met the wealthy Boston merchant Nathan Appleton and his family in the small town of Thun, Switzerland. There he fell in love with Appleton's daughter Frances, known as Fanny, but it took several more years before the independent-minded Fanny was ready to marry. Writing from the elegant Appleton home at 33 Beacon Street, Boston, on May 10, 1843, Frances sent a note to Craigie House telling Longfellow she was ready to become his wife. That year Longfellow moved from lodger to owner after receiving Craigie House as a wedding gift from his father-in-law. When Longfellow retired from Harvard his professorship was given to Sarah Lowell's nephew, James Russell Lowell. Henry Wadsworth Longfellow wrote his epic poem *The Song of Hiawatha* in 1858 and *Paul Revere's Ride* on 1860. Tragedy struck Craigie House on July 9, 1861, when a fire consumed the library and Fanny Longfellow was burned to death. The Vassall-Craigie-Longfellow House in Cambridge was declared a national historic site in 1972.[11]

6

The Merchant King: 1803–1808

To be in the East India Trade is almost a liberal education in itself.

Henry Lee, who married Mary Jackson,
sister to Hannah Jackson Lowell

[The East India merchant] possessed social kudos *to which no cotton million-aire could present. [He] enjoyed a greater prestige than any branch of Boston commerce.*

Samuel Eliot Morison in
The Maritime History of Massachusetts; 1783–1860

At the start of the nineteenth century, the twenty-five-year-old Francis Cabot Lowell was already a well-established Boston merchant with a home on Cambridge Street, Boston, where he lived with his wife Hannah and their one-year-old son John Jr., named either for his grandfather Judge John Lowell or for his uncle John Lowell Jr. The Lowell home stood close to the grand Federal-style home built for Harrison Gray Otis in 1795, and designed by Charles Bulfinch. Three years later Bulfinch, the leading Boston architect of the day, completed the Massachusetts State House, a short but steep walk from Cambridge Street up Beacon Hill. Bulfinch left his indelible mark with his design of the Massachusetts Hospital, and Massachusetts Hall at Harvard University. Cambridge Street in Boston crossed the Charles River at the West Boston Bridge and on to Cambridge. The toll bridge completed in 1795 allowed stagecoaches to travel between the two towns, replacing the ferry. The South Boston Bridge, completed in 1805, linked the Shawmut peninsula to the mainland. In 1794, the twenty-seven-mile Middlesex Canal was completed, linking the Merrimack River with Boston, and permitting farm produce from New Hampshire to arrive fresh in Boston.

By 1800, Boston was a crowded town of 780 acres built on a peninsula only three miles long by a mile and a half at its widest point. The Aqueduct Company piped fresh water from the Jamaica Pond for the growing town. The streets of Boston were "narrow, crooked and disagreeable. The settlers appear to have built where they wished, where a vote permitted, or where danger or necessity forced them to build. The streets [were] mere passages from one neighborhood to another."[1] Long Wharf, Boston's gateway to the wider world, jutted a third of a mile into the bay to accommodate the largest sail ships. The twenty-five thousand inhabitants of the town followed all manner of occupation. Over one hundred merchants were listed in the Boston Directory in the year 1800, including Francis Cabot Lowell, Joseph Lee Jr., his brother Nathaniel Lee, and Uriah Cotting. The merchants were clustered close to the wharves and the warehouses. Francis Cabot Lowell had his offices at 25 Long Wharf, sharing with Nathaniel Lee. Joseph Lee was at No. 22, the flour merchant Joseph Baxter at No. 2, Uriah Cotting at No. 47, William Bordman at No. 29 and George Bartlett at No. 8 Long Wharf. The merchants, wharves, warehouses and ships were together the main economy of the town, sending out cargoes of dried fish, lumber and rum and bringing in manufactured goods, textiles, wines and spirits, sugar and molasses.

Among the physicians practicing in Boston in 1800 were John Fleet, Aaron Dexter, Nahum Fay and J. G. Coffin. The most prominent lawyers were Harrison Gray Otis, Rufus Amory, John Lowell Jr., Samuel Dexter Jr. and David Everett. The Catholic minister, the Reverend John Cheveres, lived on Quaker Lane. Boston had many schoolmistresses, tavern keepers, innkeepers, and boarding-house-keepers. Constable Noah Butts kept law and order, William Callender made musical instruments and John Bright had a lace manufactory on Marlborough Street. William Dyer ran his tobacconist on Marlborough Lane and Joshua Davis sold jewelry at 43 Marlborough Street. The town supported laborers, dockworkers, ship captains, rope-makers, sail-makers, house builders and every other occupation and profession needed for its smooth functioning. The Alms House, opened in the year 1800, was on Leverett Street with a pleasant view of the Charles River. With its population growing in number and diversity, Boston was expanding beyond the waterfront, to Cambridge Street, Beacon Hill and the West End.[2]

By 1800, Boston had seven free schools with nine hundred pupils, with a further five hundred attending private schools. The "degraded and neglected children" of the Boston poor had to wait until 1818 before city-wide, publically funded primary schooling was provided for them. Crime in Boston was on the increase. In 1803, Robert Pierpoint and Abiel R. Story were convicted of destroying the brig *Hannah* in an attempt to defraud the underwriters. They were sentenced to stand in the pillory for one hour and then serve three years in prison. The pillory post and the whipping post stood for years on State Street, opposite the Merchants Bank. These tools of torture and humiliation were used for the last time in 1805 to punish John Nichols, convicted of counterfeiting.

By the start of the nineteenth century the town that had emancipated its slaves was more willing to accept people of different backgrounds. With the arrival of French and Irish immigrants came the desire to erect a Roman Catholic church. Planning started in 1800 and Charles Bulfinch submitted a design. The Church of the Holy Cross on Franklin Street was officially consecrated on September 29, 1803.

For decades the wealth of Boston came from trade with Europe and the West Indian sugar islands. To expand trade, the adventurous merchants next sent their ships to the Orient. On September 30, 1787, *Columbia*, under Captain Robert Gray, left the port of Boston, sailed the globe, logged 41,899 miles and took on teas, silks, and crockery from China. After an absence of three years the ship returned to a thirteen-gun salute to Boston, carrying tales of wonder about the mysteries of China. Soon, other small ships, generally one hundred feet long by twenty-eight feet wide, made the perilous journey from Boston to the Orient. At the start of the nineteenth century, Thomas H. Perkins, Ebenezer Dorr and other Boston merchants opened agencies in Canton to handle the China trade. Many of the sailing ships were built in the boat yards of Haverhill and Newburyport along the banks of the Merrimack River. Intrinsically risky, these ventures to the Far East brought disaster to some merchants but great wealth to others, who built large Federal houses in Salem or Boston to celebrate their successes.[3]

Around 1805, Francis and Hannah Lowell moved from Cambridge Street to 34 Hanover Street, Boston. With their children—John, aged six; Susan, aged four; and Francis Cabot Jr., aged two—the Lowells needed the larger house. Hanover Street at that time ran northeast from Court and Sudbury Streets to Middle Street. It was both a commercial and a residential street. Pearce Gardner, a housewright, lived at No. 44 Hanover; Gregg & Hutchins, chair makers, were at No. 25; Abigail Hall, the milliner, at No. 5; Cyrus Holbrook, the druggist, at No. 58; and Thomas Kaft, physician, at No. 15 Hanover Street. Nearby were several boarding houses, a merchant and a tailor. William Blanchard's livery stable and Joseph Akeley's hairdressing shop were also on Hanover Street. Francis and Hannah's last child Edward was born in 1807 and the family moved once again, this time to Tremont Street.

The merchant brothers Samuel and Nathan Appleton were at No. 5 South Row. Samuel Cabot lived on High Street and George Cabot, president of the

Massachusetts branch of the Bank of the United States, lived in a splendid townhouse on Park Street. Francis Cabot Lowell's brother John Lowell Jr. had his office on State Street. Francis moved his office to No. 3 Somerset Building, near the office of his relative by marriage, Nathaniel Lee.

A network of coach services served Boston. Daggett's Inn at Haymarket Square was the departure place for the stagecoach and mail coach to New York, to Albany, as well as daily service to Salem, Taunton and other Massachusetts towns. The Newburyport coach left from Palmer's Inn, the Amherst coach from French's Inn, the Leominster coach from India Queen's Inn and the Concord coach from William's Inn. The Cambridge coach departed twice daily from the Old State House, crossing the Charles River at the West Boston Bridge into Cambridge.[4]

URIAH COTTING

The merchant and real estate developer Uriah Cotting is little remembered today, but during the first two decades of the nineteenth century he engaged in large-scale enterprises and was known as "the chief benefactor of Boston." Cotting saw that the marketplace around Faneuil Hall would soon be too small to handle the flow of goods to supply the fast growing population. Boston needed more wharves, warehouses and shops, and Cotting with his associates were ready to provide these facilities. Uriah Cotting was born on September 29, 1766, son of an innkeeper in the village of Waltham. His parents died when he was young and he was placed in the care of his uncle Dr. Amos Cotting in the town of Marlborough. "With no extraordinary advantage of wealth or education, he possessed buoyant spirits, invincible good-humor and mental endowments, rarely found united."[5] As an ambitious nineteen-year-old, Cotting came to Boston carrying his small bundle of clothes and only twenty-five cents in his pocket. He started as an errand boy in a West India goods store and later formed a partnership with John Amory, father of John Lowell Jr.'s wife Rebecca.

In 1800, Cotting lived at 58 Orange Street and then moved to a splendid home on Somerset Street. Cotting was older than Francis Cabot Lowell by nine years but they trusted each other and began a partnership that endured for the remainder of Lowell's life. Under the tutelage of Uriah Cotting, Francis extended his reach beyond the buying and selling of goods and rum distilling into wharves, warehouses and retail stores. In 1802, Francis Cabot Lowell and Uriah Cotting, with James Lloyd, Henry Jackson and Harrison Gray Otis, planned the construction of India Wharf to accommodate the growing trade with India, China and Java. James Lloyd (1769–1831), born in Boston and Harvard educated, became a merchant but maintained a lively interest in politics. In 1808, as a Federalist, he was selected to fill the vacancy in the U.S. Senate after the resignation of John Quincy Adams. Harrison Gray Otis (1765–1848) was another of the affluent and well-connected men associated with Francis Cabot Lowell. Otis owned one of the grandest homes in Boston, had a lucrative law practice, served as attorney general for Massachusetts, and as president of the state senate. Later in his career he was elected U.S. senator for Massachusetts and served as mayor of Boston.

INDIA WHARF AND BROAD STREET

Boston merchants were increasingly taking advantage of American neutrality in the Napoleonic Wars to trade with Calcutta, Bombay and Madras. Indian teas, cotton textiles and silks were loaded on American ships for sale on the Continent or carried to American ports for transshipment to other markets. To handle some of this trade Francis Cabot Lowell and Uriah Cotting decided to build the India Wharf in Boston Harbor. India Wharf was the first of several large-scale projects initiated early in the nineteenth century by Uriah Cotting, Francis Cabot Lowell and their associates that transformed Boston from a provincial town into a thriving metropolis. Lowell and Cotting contracted with the construction firm of Newcomb & Baxter of Quincy to "find a good and sufficient quantity of proper and fit stone for a wharf or sea wall, to substantially build or erect a strong and uniform stone wall south of Long Wharf, where Wendell's wharf once stood, for a wharf five feet wide or thick at the trench or bottom, three feet at the top and of such height and such length as said Lowell, Cotting and Jackson may direct. And to further that the said Newcomb & Baxter engage and agree to provide and deliver good clean upland stone, ballast for filling or backing of the wharf wall." The cost of the project was $2,500. On March 9, the contractors received a down payment of $1,000, followed by another $1,000 when the job was half completed, with the final $500 paid on October 1, 1803.[6] The plans for the new wharf were approved by the Boston Board of Selectmen, of which the architect Charles Bulfinch was chairman. Bulfinch was given the job of designing at India Wharf a large brick building, five stories tall, containing thirty-two warehouses each with cellar walls built of stone.

Completed in 1804, India Wharf jutted out into the harbor for 1,340 feet: "For fifty years it was the headquarters of the trade with the Orient and many valuable cargoes from Canton, Calcutta, Russia and the Mediterranean ports were discharged there."[7] The buildings on India Wharf, designed by Charles Bulfinch, were completed in 1807 and were "a splendid collection of stores, built and arranged with singular elegance, and

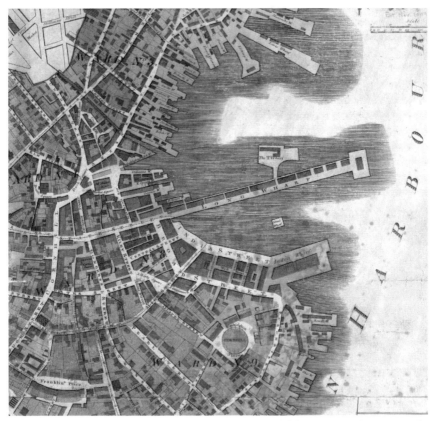

India Wharf, India Street and Broad Street, Boston. (Detail from "Map of Boston in the State of Massachusetts," by John G. Hales, 1814, image with permission of the Norman B. Leventhal Map Center at the Boston Public Library.)

far exceeding everything of the kind on this side of the Atlantic."[8] The ground floor of each warehouse provided easy access to the ships tied up at the wharf. On the second floor were the merchant's offices and counting houses, while the upper three floors were used to store the goods. The masonry work on the stores was done by John Vinton and Thomas Drayton and the carpentry by the firms of Partridge & Hartshorn and Nason & Eaton at a cost of $300 a store. The total cost of work on India Wharf and the warehouses was $84,779.98. Even before the project was completed these warehouses were sold to the leading East India merchants of Boston, including the firms of Stephen Higginson & Company, Andrew Cabot, Joseph Lee, Thomas H. Perkins, Israel Thorndike, Thomas Wigglesworth and Henry Oxnard. Francis Cabot Lowell and Uriah Cotting moved their businesses to India Wharf. By December 1807, nearly all the warehouses at India Wharf were sold at prices from $7,000 to $15,000. India Wharf and the warehouses were a success from the outset and helped move the East India trade away from Salem to Boston. To be an East India merchant in Boston at that time and to have an office and warehouse on India Wharf were signs of high social distinction. The East India trade goods consisting of tea, coffee, spices, textiles, chinaware, silks, scarves, handkerchiefs and bandannas were offloaded at India Wharf, for local sale or destined for ports along the eastern seaboard as well as the West Indies and South America.

Henry Jackson, the second of Jonathan Jackson's children, went to sea as a youth of fifteen and rose to captain. While on a voyage, Henry injured his right arm causing intense pain and paralysis. When he returned home, the arm was amputated but Henry continued his life at sea, traveling round the Cape of Good Hope to India and China. He "served always to the satisfaction of his employers, but not with any great financial profit to himself." In 1799, Henry married Harriet Swett of Marblehead, who bore him three children. Although still in his thirties, "he looked and felt like an old man" and wanted to settle on land to be with his family. No

Photograph taken in 1868 of the warehouses of India Wharf, Boston. The wharf was completed in 1804, and the buildings, designed by Charles Bulfinch, were ready for occupancy by 1807. India Wharf was "the headquarters of the trade with the orient." (Historic American Buildings Survey, 1868.)

longer having a livelihood, he turned to his brother-in-law Francis Cabot Lowell for a start in the commercial world. Eager to help a family member in need, Francis invited Henry to be a junior partner in his new venture.

Uriah Cotting, Francis Cabot Lowell and now Henry Jackson commissioned Charles Bulfinch to draw up plans for ten retail stores on Battery March Street. The crescent-shaped Battery March Street got its name in colonial times from the soldiers who marched along it on their way to the South Battery. Each store designed by Bulfinch measured seventy feet in front, narrowing to twenty feet in the rear and forty feet deep. The cellar walls were of stone and the floor boards timbered planks. Each store was offered for sale at $5,000, of which sum $500 was to be paid within six months and a further $500 at the end of twelve months, without added interest. During the following years, the buyer agreed to pay $400 annually in principal and interest until the outstanding debt was settled. These stores were quickly sold to John and William Sullivan, Cornelius Coolidge, Nathaniel F. Cunningham and others. As treasurer of the Battery March Street project, Francis Cabot Lowell negotiated the contracts for the sale of the stores.

Forming a consortium and selling wharf and store space from the architect's plans was the preferred financing method used by Uriah Cotting, Francis Cabot Lowell and their associates. These men, merchants, lawyers and ship owners, trusted each other and shared the profits and the risks of their bold ventures. Francis Cabot Lowell was associated with several other ventures initiated by Uriah Cotting, until 1812, when he took charge of his great venture making textiles in America.

The India Wharf was linked to India Street facing the harbor and to Broad Street running parallel one block inland. Beginning in 1804, Uriah Cotting, Francis Cabot Lowell and James Lloyd Jr. quietly bought the water rights and established the Broad Street Associates. Among the junior partners were Benjamin Bussey, Rufus Greene Amory, Joshua Loring, John Loring and Samuel D. Harris. In 1804, the syndicate submitted an act of incorporation to develop the area. On February 11, 1805, the General Court of the Commonwealth of Massachusetts approved the petition of the Broad Street Association to "lay out a spacious street near the harbour" and build shops for the retail trade. Broad Street linked State Street with Battery March Street and extended toward India Wharf. Francis Cabot Lowell was the treasurer of the Broad Street project in which he owned fifty of the four hundred shares. Charles Bulfinch was paid the paltry sum of $40 to design sixty retail stores built in a row on each side of the street. The dilapidated buildings along the street were torn down and, as befit its name, Broad Street was widened to seventy feet. Each four-story store was forty feet high, twenty feet wide and forty feet deep. The ground floor greeted the street with wide doors and windows. The second floor contained the offices for the merchant and his clerks, heated by a fireplace or stove. The third and fourth floors were for storage. When completed in 1808, the India Wharf, India Street and Broad Street projects together formed one of the most significant development projects undertaken by the young nation.[9]

Lowell, Cutting and their associates invested $211,168 on the landfill and the erection of the buildings along Broad Street. After selling the retail stores for a total of $328,460.65, the partners realized a nice profit of $117,292.35. In addition to twenty shares in India Wharf, Francis owned outright several of the warehouses as well as the retail buildings at 108-110, 112-114 and 116-118 Broad Street. Among the retail shops opening on Broad Street was William B. Bradford's, "offering a great variety of clothing, suitable for seamen and others." On May 4, 1809, Francis Cabot Lowell visited the store at 149 Broad Street and bought a jacket with two pairs of trousers, a waistcoat, shirts and a greatcoat for $37.50, less a discount of $2.00 for paying in cash. India Wharf, India Street, Broad Street and Battery March Street—all constructed by Cotting, Lowell and their associates, with plans by Charles Bulfinch—revitalized the area to the south of State Street and Long Wharf. Completed by 1808, the area was alive with ships and sailors, warehouses and workers and retail shops and shoppers.

Francis Cabot Lowell was involved in yet another project with the irrepressible Uriah Cotting—the Wheeler's Point Wharf Estate. Formerly known as Windmill Point, the land was bought by Jonathan Wheeler, and named in his honor. Another investor in the project was Isaac P. Davis, a wealthy merchant and businessman. Davis was an early patron to the artist Gilbert Stuart, and a friend of John Quincy Adams and Daniel Webster. The project to build a wharf at Wheeler's Point was launched in May 1807 and $23,000 paid by the investors. For reasons unknown the plan was aborted the following year.

Edward Cotton in his 1807 book *Boston Directory* describes the undertaking of Uriah Cotting, Francis Cabot Lowell and their associates in the construction of India Wharf and Broad and India streets. "Broad Street exhibits a flattering idea of the town," wrote Cotton. "Broad Street was seventy foot wide, had sixty elegant and large brick-built stores, each four stories high of uniform height and appearance. India Street, which is now building east of Broad Street, is considerably advanced, many stores are erecting and the street, when completed, will lead to India Wharf, recently finished, over which are built about 60 brick stores, 40 of them 5 stories high. All the stores on Broad Street have waterproof cellars, constructed at immense expense. These streets, wharf, and buildings, have been made and erected under the direction of a company, constructed for the purpose and form together, the most elegant and commodious seat of mercantile business on the United States."[10]

Francis Cabot Lowell, Uriah Cotting and Henry Jackson bought land on Chambers Street,[11] a street that ran into Cambridge Street, with a plan to subdivide and build houses. In 1805, Cotting, Lowell and Jackson received permission from the Board of Selectmen "to dig up Chambers Street and Belknap Street to their Distill-House for the purpose of laying pipes to convey the water to their works, provided that they put the streets into good order and repair the pavement." Their activities elicited a flurry of complaints. Charles Bulfinch, the president of the Boston Board of Selectmen, wrote to the developers that "a number of people residing in West Boston have attributed the loss of water in their wells to the great use made by you in Chambers Street." Cotting, Lowell and Jackson were ordered to reduce the flow of water to their rum distillery.

In October 1806 came the news that Henry Jackson had died. "It was not unexpected," wrote Francis. "I have no words to express how I feel." The merchant and property developer Isaac P. Davis bought Henry Jackson's shares in India Wharf and Broad Street to become a partner to Francis Cabot Lowell.

HELPING OTHERS

Francis Cabot Lowell took a keen interest in John Bromfield, born in 1779 in Newburyport. His family fell upon hard times and moved to Boston, where Mr. Bromfield "rented a house of his friend Judge Lowell." The family could not afford to send young John to Harvard and instead apprenticed him to the store of Larkin & Hurd in Charlestown. Francis Cabot Lowell arranged for John to serve as supercargo on ships to Europe and the Orient. John began his career "without patronage and without prospects" but by wit, sweet temper and hard work he advanced from a seafaring life to become a successful East India merchant. John Bromfield died in 1840, aged sixty-one. A bachelor, he left the bulk of his estate to various charities. The Massachusetts General Hospital received $15,000, Boston Female Asylum $10,000, the Asylum for the Blind $10,000, the Asylum for Indigent Boys $10,000, Seamen's Aid Society $10,000 and the Massachusetts Eye & Ear Infirmary $10,000. John Bromfield also left $10,000 to beautify his hometown Newburyport with trees.

Francis Cabot Lowell also helped launch the career of his brother-in-law, Patrick Tracy Jackson. In 1799, the nineteen-year-old Patrick Tracy began a 162-day journey from Boston to Calcutta as supercargo on board *Hannah*, captained by his brother Henry Jackson. The ship carried brandy, rum, claret, almonds, raisins, tobacco and hats, as well as a quantity of silver coin. These goods were the property of some thirty merchants including Moses Brown, Judge John Lowell and Samuel Pickering Gardner.

As supercargo, Patrick Tracy Jackson had the responsibility of selling the goods in Calcutta at a profit and using the money to purchase Indian cotton textiles, sugar and cow hides to take back to Boston. Writing from Calcutta to Francis Cabot Lowell on November 26, 1802, Patrick Tracy revealed his anxieties due to "my own inexperience & the number [of merchants] I have to please" and the hope of making a small profit for himself.

Patrick Tracy's second trip to Calcutta, on the *Pembroke*, began in 1804. From Calcutta he wrote to Francis on October 3, "Give my love to Hannah and all the little ones, from all accounts received, I expect to find a large brood when I arrive amongst you, which I hope will be very soon." Patrick Tracy next wrote to Francis on March 21, 1805, from the Cape of Good Hope that he had sold his Indian goods and his ship, and, with funds provided by Andrew Cabot, bought the larger 529-ton Dutch ship *Eliza*, "in very good repair," for $6,000, which he loaded with Cape wines and sugar. Patrick wrote that "there are a great number of American sailors & officers here that I could man her cheap."

World events delayed Patrick and his ship in Cape Town. The British government was convinced that the French and their Dutch allies would hinder shipping to India. In July 1805, Lord Castlereagh, the secretary of state for war and the colonies, authorized a force of 6,654 men under Major General Sir David Baird to retake the Cape from the Dutch. Conveyed in sixty-one ships under commodore Sir Home Popham, the British fleet arrived at the Cape of Good Hope on January 4, 1806, and the next day mounted an attack on the castle at Cape Town. The Dutch capitulated and the British stopped all shipping in and out of the harbor.

Stuck at the Cape of Good Hope, Patrick Tracy wrote to Ram Dololl Dey, his agent in Calcutta, "giving very favourable accounts of his cargo which has been disposed of in the above port." Patrick Tracy assured Ram Dololl that Francis Cabot Lowell would make good on the money loaned to him. In the era of sail, letters sent by businessmen reached their destination months later. Francis duly paid Ram Dololl the money owed to him.

Patrick Tracy Jackson with his American crew on board *Eliza* finally left the Cape of Good Hope on March 17, 1806, and sailed for the Orient, where he sold his wine at a profit and took on a cargo of saltpeter and nutmeg. After more trips between Asia and southern Africa buying and selling cargoes he at last returned to Boston on March 17, 1807, after an absence of three years. With this trip Patrick Tracy Jackson's nautical adventures were over.

Patrick Tracy Jackson had more than proved his worth buying and selling cargoes in Boston, Cape Town, Calcutta and ports in between. Still, he had a hard time establishing himself in Boston as a sedentary merchant specializing in the East India trade. He started as assistant to Francis Cabot Lowell minding the warehouse while Francis was away on business in New York and Philadelphia. Writing to Francis on May 10, 1807, Patrick reported that "Mr. Cotting says that the Broad Street lots sold yesterday at about the prices you expected." Hannah and the children had settled into the new house on Tremont Street "in spite of the bad weather." Patrick wrote from the heart to his sister Hannah on May 13, "I intend going to Newburyport in 2 or 3 days to see if I cannot obtain some business—for I begin to feel tired of doing nothing. I feel I am filling my letter with accounts of my own sweet self & my visionary projects, but what can I do, no great event has taken place to afford me a subject and my imagination is not sufficiently fertile to invent any."

Young Patrick told Francis on May 17 that "Mr. Cotting has bought the Cushing estate for $30,000. My author is Charles [Jackson]." The news that his partner Uriah Cotting had purchased a large estate raised the envy and competitive spirit in Francis, who immediately wrote to a source in Boston asking about Uriah Cotting's new home and inquiring after the cost of other estates then on the market. His source, signing his letter "Speculator," wrote back on May 20 confirming that Cotting was the buyer of the Cushing estate for $32,000. The larger Tilson estate was selling for $80,000. Instead of buying a grand country house, Francis decided to buy more income property.

Not all the efforts by Francis Cabot Lowell to help younger men get their start in business were successful. In 1804, Henry Lee married Mary Jackson, younger sister of Hannah Lowell. After the death of Nathaniel, Henry and his older brother Joseph Jr. formed H & J Lee and Company. The brothers came upon hard times during the Embargo of 1807 and turned to Francis for financial support. Henry bemoaned (December 13, 1810) that for the merchant "the only thought now is how to pay his notes, as they come round." By January 1811, H & J Lee and Company was on the verge of collapse and made desperate efforts to raise funds at high interest from moneylenders. In 1812, Henry Lee left his family in Boston and traveled to Calcutta in the hope of restoring his fortunes. Henry remained abroad four years.

Another ambitious Essex County young man, Andrew Thorndike, set up in Barcelona as an agent for the Mediterranean trade. Francis Cabot wrote to several American merchants vouching for Thorndike's ability and integrity. Andrew Thorndike, wrote Lowell on October 27, 1806, was "going to the Southern states to form connections who may give business to a house which he has established in Barcelona under the name Thorndike, Leonard & Company. Mr. Thorndike is esteemed as a man of good mercantile habits, principles and integrity. He is worth 20,000 dollars himself and his partner is worth considerably more; he has an uncle Israel

Thorndike of Beverly a man of a very large fortune. [Andrew] is a safe man for any amount of money and is in good credit here." In Barcelona, alas, Andrew Thorndike and John Leonard fell into dispute and entered a lengthy litigation against each other. When the courts decreed that Thorndike owed Leonard $50,000, he "somewhat suddenly" left the country.[12]

THE TRIAL OF THOMAS OLIVER SELFRIDGE

In 1806, Boston was transfixed by a high society murder trial that involved people in the circle of Francis Cabot Lowell. Thomas Oliver Selfridge, a graduate of Harvard University in 1797 and a well-known lawyer, became incensed over the writings of Benjamin Austin, who argued that lawyers should be banned from the courts of law. "The law and evidence are all the essentials required," argued Austin, "and are not the judges and the jury competent for these purposes?" Austin's pamphlet *Observations on the Pernicious Practice of the Law* incensed the law community. Selfridge, rising to defend his profession and responding to a personal disagreement, wrote a letter to the *Boston Gazette* of August 4 alleging that Benjamin Austin was a "coward, a liar and a scoundrel." The personal insults were aggravated by political differences; Selfridge was a member of the Federalist Party and Austin a Republican. Word spread that Austin had hired a bully to confront Selfridge and beat him up. Henry Cabot, the prominent Federalist, heard these rumors and alerted his friend Selfridge to be ready to defend himself against an attack. That very afternoon, Benjamin Austin's eighteen-year-old-son Charles, about to graduate from Harvard, confronted Selfridge on State Street in full view of the passers-by, and hit him about the head and arms with his walking cane. Selfridge pulled out his gun and shot Charles Austin through the heart, killing him instantly.

Much of the case for the prosecution centered on the question of whether young Austin had simply intended to frighten Selfridge rather than inflict serious bodily harm. Among the witnesses for the Commonwealth was the Reverend Charles Lowell, who by chance had met Charles Austin the morning of his death and declared him "a pleasant young man." Warren Dutton happened to be walking along State Street and glanced at the passing Thomas Selfridge. "I had hardly turned my eyes from him," testified Dutton, "when I heard the pistol." At six o'clock that evening Dr. James Jackson, another of Francis Cabot Lowell's brothers-in-law, examined Thomas Selfridge in prison. Dr. Jackson, who knew Selfridge as a patient of long standing, "observed a contusion on the forehead" measuring three inches long by two inches wide and elevated to one-half inch, and wounds on his arms. Selfridge was not a healthy man and was not physically able to fight off his young assailant.

The trial of Thomas Selfridge opened on December 23. The law fraternity of Boston rose as one to defend its reputation, giving Thomas Selfridge a brilliant team of attorneys to defend him against the charge of the murder of Charles Austin. His lead counselor was Christopher Gore, assisted by Harrison Gray Otis, Charles Jackson and Samuel Dexter, who had served as the U.S. secretary of war (1799–1800) and secretary of the treasury (1801). The jury debated only a half hour and found Thomas Selfridge not guilty of murder but guilty of the lesser charge of manslaughter. Thomas Oliver Selfridge escaped the gallows, and remained in Boston, where he died of natural causes on June 25, 1816.

BEFORE THE EMBARGO OF 1807

The years from 1803 to late 1807 were successful ones for Francis Cabot Lowell. The war on the Continent of Europe opened markets for flour, sugar, and dried fish. Francis kept busy importing cotton textiles from India, crockery from China and wines and brandy from France. He rented space on ships, hired captains and crews, and negotiated insurance on his cargoes. In addition he devoted time to his distillery and his Broad Street and India Wharf projects. Francis received a letter in August 1805 from his agents in Bordeaux informing him that the demand for "coffee has not been so good [but] cotton still keeps up," as was the demand for dry codfish. Potash was scarce, and beeswax and tortoise shells were in demand. From Grant Webb & Company, his agents in Leghorn, he learned (April 10, 1806) that "prime best India coffee continues to be a good article and finds a very ready sale." Too much sugar arriving from America depressed prices, but there was a good market for Indian nankeens and muslins. East India merchants like Francis Cabot Lowell acquired goods from all over the world and repackaged them in Boston for shipment to Europe on ships flying the flags of neutral countries. After suffering the disastrous loss at the Battle of Trafalgar, October 21, 1805, France restricted the transshipment of goods from American ports.

Relatively few men enjoyed continued success as a Boston merchant. Some, like Edward Bromfield of Newburyport and the Higginson brothers, John and George, set up in France as agents for American merchants. Harvard-educated Samuel Williams moved from Boston to London where he established a bank to service American commercial interests. With opportunities in New England limited, many thousands began the move to the interior of the fast-expanding nation. Francis Cabot Lowell had the ability, connections, family money and the luck to enjoy success as a Boston merchant. He entered the East India trade early in his career. He owned a rum distillery and invested much of the profits in property, the India Wharf and Broad Street projects, thus enjoying a steady stream of income even when the oversees trade was depressed. Like other successful men of his time, Francis Cabot benefitted from the continuous support of a bevy of intelligent and kind women. Hannah Lowell accompanied him on his business trips to New York and Philadelphia. His sisters Susanna and Anna wrote to him regularly when he was away, giving him news of the family especially the well-being of his children. His widowed mother Rebecca Lowell eased his anxieties with letters of support and praise. Francis was able to rest assured during his absences from Boston that his children, business and his property were in safe hands.

William Sullivan, for one, took a dim view of the benefits of the merchants in the economy of the New England: "The commercial part of the community who had the means (and some of them were wealthy from privateering), and all who had credit in England, engaged in importing English manufactures. This traffic drained the country of specie [hard currency], and introduced articles of luxury which the inhabitants needed not, and for which they contracted debts, which they could not pay."[13]

7

Mr. Jefferson's Embargo

At first the United States benefited greatly from the renewal of war between France and Great Britain and their allies. To raise money to fight his wars, Napoleon agreed to sell Louisiana to the United States, thus doubling the size of the new nation, at a bargain price. Goods from the French West Indies were offloaded in American ports, repackaged and sent on American ships to French ports. The custom revenues for the American treasury were considerable. Ship building intensified in Boston, Salem and Newport; American captains and crews were hired, ports were busy, and banking and insurance companies benefited from the increase in trade. The start of the continental wars in 1793 offered great opportunities for American merchants to ship flour and grains to feed the people and the armies of France. American merchants, as neutrals, were also doing a fast trade buying pepper from Sumatra, tea, silks and porcelain from China and homespun cotton textiles from India. Many of these goods were carried on American ships to American ports for re-export to the Continent or sold in the Caribbean or South America.

Since the seventeenth century, American merchants favored the French ports of Bordeaux on the Garonne River and Nantes on the Loire River, cities that had grown rich on the French slave trade. Francis Cabot Lowell, who arrived at Bordeaux in July 1795 on an American ship to deliver rice and flour, was one of many ambitious New Englanders willing to risk European waters during the times of war. From 1793 until the continental blockade of 1806, Bordeaux was a major port for neutral shipping: "United States ships and middlemen were extremely active in the colonial trade, inserting themselves more and more in the exchange network between Europe and the Americas."[1] Bordeaux dealers set up offices in Baltimore, Philadelphia and Boston, while American merchants had agents in the French city. Francis Cabot Lowell's cousin, John Bromfield of Newburyport, was the resident agent in Bordeaux for several of the Boston merchants. The "30 or 40" ships John Lowell saw together in September 1804 were some of the two hundred ships flying the American flag arriving that year in the port of Bordeaux, comprising one-quarter of the city's foreign sea trade. The ships carried back to Boston, New York and Philadelphia the French brandies and wines John Lowell and others so much enjoyed.

America's good fortune in times of war could not last. In 1805, British Admiralty courts decreed that any goods from French colonies could be seized "even though they had been landed and re-shipped in the United States."[2] The titanic struggle between France and Great Britain was played out on land and at sea. To maintain its hegemony over the sea routes, the British Navy "needed to recruit at least thirty thousand to forty thousand new seamen every year," many more than it could recruit in Britain. Because of the poor conditions onboard British ships, sailors frequently deserted to serve instead on American commercial vessels. Nine thousand of the twenty-four thousand seamen on American ships were British deserters.[3] In Britain's view these facts gave it the right to board American vessels on the high seas and impress any seaman considered to be a subject of the king. To enforce this ruling, British frigates regularly patrolled off American ports with orders to stop vessels coming in or out and search for contraband cargoes, as well as fugitive British sailors. When found onboard American ships these sailors were removed and impressed into British service. In 1804, British ships captured thirty-nine American vessels. The following year, 116 more American ships were seized and over one thousand seamen impressed. The British government decreed a blockade of the coast of Europe from the Elbe to Brest. Napoleon responded to his defeat at the Battle of Trafalgar by declaring a blockade of the British Isles, hindering British trade with ports on the Mediterranean and in the Baltic Sea. He decreed that any neutral ship that had previously been in British territory was forbidden to enter a French port. The intention was to cripple the flow of British manufactured goods abroad and to reduce the commerce of neutral countries, especially the United States. By these measures, neutral countries such as the United States were swept into the Napoleonic Wars. Between 1803 and 1807, the British seized 528 American ships and the French seized 389 more. American shipping into Bordeaux fell dramatically as the town ceased to be the leading portal into France for international trade.

THE *CHESAPEAKE* AFFAIR

Seamen Daniel Martin, John Strachan and William Ware deserted from the British brig *Melampus* and seaman Jenkins Ratford from the *Halifax* when these vessels entered the American port of Hampton Roads. These men then enlisted on the American naval frigate *Chesapeake*. The British demand for the return of these four seamen was refused. On June 22, 1807, *Chesapeake* under Commodore James Barron cleared Norfolk bound for service in the Mediterranean to fight the Barbary pirates. Waiting offshore was the fifty-gun HMS *Leopard* under the command of Captain Salisbury Pryce Humphreys, carrying a letter from Vice-Admiral George Cranfield Berkeley, commander of the king's fleet in Halifax, Nova Scotia, authorizing him to search the American vessel for the deserters. After Commodore Barron refused to allow the British to search his ship, *Leopard* fired its guns broadside, killing three sailors on *Chesapeake* and wounding eighteen others. Coming onboard the stricken *Chesapeake*, the British arrested the four deserters and carried them in chains to *Leopard*, which set sail for Halifax. The London-born former tailor Jenkins Ratford was found guilty of desertion and hanged. The other three deserters faced five hundred lashes each.

At the time of the attack on the *Chesapeake*, Francis Cabot Lowell, his wife Hannah and their children set out from Boston to visit the falls at Niagara. The coach trip westward took the family across Massachusetts to Albany in New York State and on to visit the village of Canandaigua, site of a former Seneca town. The Scotsman, John Melish, visited around the same time and in his *Travels through the United States of America*, he wrote glowingly of the village: "On entering Canandaigua I was really surprised at the beauty of the place, and the surrounding scenery. The lake at the south, and the scenery around it, forms one of the most beautiful landscapes to be seen anywhere; and to the north, on the brow of an elevated swelling country, stands the village; which for beauty of situation, and elegance of buildings, is decidedly the handsomest village I have ever seen." In 1786 people from New England settled the town. Its Main Street was 130 feet wide and ran north to south for a mile and a half. The village then had 150 houses with five hundred inhabitants, and "a handsome brick courthouse in the centre square, a jail and an elegant academy. The inhabitants are mostly from New England, and the young ladies, with whom the village abounds, exhibit the appearance of the Yankee ladies in a new and beautiful edition, with great improvement."[4]

From Canandaigua, the Lowell family traveled to Chippaway, a mile and a half upriver from the Niagara Falls. The Duke of Rochefoucauld-Liancourt, exiled by the French Revolution, visited the area late in the eighteenth century. "At Chippaway," he wrote, "the grand spectacle begins. The river, which has been constantly expanding from Fort Erie to this place, is here upwards of three miles wide, but, in a sudden it is narrowed, and the rapidity of the stream is redoubled by the declivity of the ground on which it flows, as well as the sudden contraction of its bed. The waters of the lakes Erie, Michigan, St. Claire, Huron and lake Superior, and of numerous rivers, emptying themselves" creates an awesome spectacle as the water cascades down the rocks one hundred and seventy feet below.[5] Leaving the cares of the world behind them, Francis Lowell and his family enjoyed the sight of the great falls, even though, as Hannah Lowell wrote to her mother-in-law on August 19, "we are very much fatigued by our visits to the falls." Hannah was especially worried about Francis (Mr. Lowell, as she called him), who drove himself relentlessly, even on vacation.

"Well, Mr. Lowell, have you settled the question of War or Peace?" wrote Dr. James Jackson to his brother-in-law on July 26. People like himself were "pacifically inclined, or rather dread so much the smell of gunpowder that after a little blustering, they will sit down quietly as lambs. For policy on either side, it appears to me, nothing would be more absurd than for England and America to be at loggerheads at the present time or to see which would do the other more harm."

Federalists, particularly in New England, sought to avoid widening the conflict and were even apologists for the British position. John Lowell Jr., in his pamphlet *Peace without Dishonour—War without Hope*, argued that the British action of boarding American ships to remove sailors considered to be British subjects was understandable and hardly a reason for war. By keeping France at bay, "Great Britain alone stood between us and slavery, which would be our portion if France should prevail." A war with Great Britain, John Lowell concluded, "will ruin 250,000 merchants, beggar all the mechanicks immediately dependent upon the merchants, and produce the failure of many at the banking institutions [and] thousands of honest creditors will be left to starve." Any threat to American shipping by seizure and confiscation would cause a great increase in the insurance rates. As a result the insurance companies would fail at a time when the government lacked the revenue to pay down the national debt. John Lowell may have had his uncle Stephen Higginson in mind when he wrote about the losses to the merchants. Stephen Higginson was a successful Boston merchant "until Jefferson's embargo deprived him of much of his wealth."

In other parts of the nation, particularly in Republican strongholds in the South, the *Chesapeake* affair caused outrage. The *Washington Federalist* declared there had seldom been "so great a degree of indignation, or such a thirst for revenge." President Thomas Jefferson exclaimed that "the English [were] equally tyrannical at sea as France is on land. . . . Down with England." But Jefferson was well aware that the United States lacked the sea power to take on the Royal Navy. Instead, he chose to impose sanctions against Britain and called for an embargo on "all ships and vessels in the ports and places within the limits or jurisdiction of the United States, cleared or not cleared, bound to any foreign port or place; and that no clearance be furnished to any ship or vessel bound to such foreign port or place." The Embargo Act was passed in the House by a vote of eighty-two to forty-four and in the Senate by twenty-two to six, and was signed into law on December 22, 1807.[6]

During the weeks before the Embargo Act became law, Francis Cabot Lowell shipped twenty hogshead of New England rum by the ship *Cybernia*, bound for the Italian port of Leghorn (now Livorno). Later, he received news that a French privateer captured the ship. The seizure of the *Cybernia* and other American ships disrupted trade into European ports, followed by the Jefferson embargo, deepened the gloom and despair among the merchants of Boston, New York and Philadelphia. In 1807, before the embargo, American exports reached $150.4 million. During the first year of the embargo, exports fell by 70 percent to only $45.4 million. Similarly, imports to the United States reached $144.7 million in 1807, falling 60 percent the following year to $58.1 million. At home, the price of cotton, tobacco, flour and rice fell sharply and farmland from the South to New York lost value.[7] The embargo that "crippled the commerce of all the states, wrought, of course, its greatest hardships in Massachusetts, where, before the passage of the Embargo, about one-third of all shipping in the country was owned." Ships in Boston Harbor were left to "rot at the wharves. Owners and sailors alike the sufferers." The Embargo of 1807 reduced the output of New England agriculture, shipbuilding and fishing. Hard money became scarce as the economy shriveled.

On April 24, 1808, Francis Cabot Lowell informed his foreign business associates, "I am closing my business." Other Boston merchants and ship owners attempted to circumvent the embargo and ordered their captains to stay out of American waters. A number even conspired with the British Admiralty to divert ships to Halifax, and continue to trade abroad.[8] Still, the embargo had a serious impact on trade and reduced the flow of money. During January 1808, a crowd of one hundred seamen carrying a flag at half-staff marched to the home of Governor James Sullivan to demand "work or bread." Soup kitchens opened in Boston to feed the hungry.

The situation in Salem was even more serious. Ralph D. Paine noted that before the embargo, the port of Salem had 152 ships engaged in foreign trade. "The Embargo fell with blighting effect upon this imposing fleet and the allied activities interwoven throughout the life and business of the town, and the square-riggers lay empty and idle at the wharves. The port indeed was full of ships but they were dismantled and laid up; their decks were cleared; their hatches fastened down; and scarcely a sailor was to be found aboard. Not a box, bail, cask, barrel or package was to be seen upon the wharves. Many of the counting houses were shut up or advertised to be let, and a few solitary merchants, clerks and porters and laborers that were to be seen, were walking about with their hands in their pockets."[9] The trade in and out of Boston and Salem harbors remained depressed until 1810, when once again "Yankee ships hastened to spread their white wings on every sea," carrying cargoes of rice, grain, tobacco and cotton.[10]

At first the Embargo Act met with the approval of people in New England. On February 8, 1808, the General Court of Massachusetts resolved that "we consider the imposing of embargo a wise and highly expedient measure, and from its impartial nature calculated to secure us the blessings of peace." However, the Embargo Act was a failure, as it hurt the New England merchants and the Southern farmers much more than it hurt the British or the French. With the ports of Boston, Salem, Newburyport and New Bedford now moribund, opposition to the embargo began to build.

Signing himself "a fellow sufferer," on October 10, 1808, John Park published the pamphlet *An Address to the Citizens of Massachusetts on the Causes and Remedy of Our National Distress*. The attack on *Chesapeake*, wrote John Park, evoked "a high sense of national honour, preferring even the risk of life to disgrace [but] it is not inexorable, and when falsely directed, it ceases to be a virtue, it becomes a crime." The federal government, Park argued, should accept the British apology and restore good relations rather than continue the embargo that will lead to "the ruin of the United States. It cannot be believed that the people of the country concur with the present administration in the pernicious, unjust and self-destructive hatred" toward Great Britain.

The villain, argued Park, was not Britain but France, which had "swindled our government in the sale of Louisiana, the boundaries of which remain undetermined." France had blocked its ports to American shipping, seized and confiscated American ships, obstructed American commerce and "made our citizens prisoners of war." At home there was a "deep-seated hostility of the present ruling party." The Embargo Act would impoverish America: "By the destruction of commerce the merchant and the mariner are the first sufferers; but the shock soon extends to every class of society." Park called for political action and the election to Congress of people who will vote to repeal the Embargo Act so that "our beloved country will again prosper, individual happiness will be restored; and our government once more merit and command the respect of foreign nations."

On October 16, 1807, four months after the *Leopard* fired on the *Chesapeake*, John Quincy Adams at the Suffolk Insurance office in Boston overheard John Lowell Jr. openly justifying the British action. Enraged, Adams had a heated argument with Lowell and afterward wrote that "this was the cause which alienated me from that day and forever from the councils of the Federal party." Wrapped in the patriotic mood, John Quincy Adams, the senator for Massachusetts, came out strongly in support of the Jefferson embargo and broke ranks with Timothy Pickering, George Cabot and other Massachusetts Federalists. He paid a stiff price for his action as his friends cut him loose and he was vilified by the local press. Massachusetts turned against Adams and the Democratic-Republican Party, and instead moved to support the Federalists in the fight against the embargo. John Quincy Adams resigned his seat in the Senate and was succeeded by the Federalist James Lloyd Jr., one of Francis Cabot Lowell's close business associates. Under intense pressure from the merchants of New England, President Thomas Jefferson agreed on March 1, 1809, two days before he left office, to repeal the Embargo Act and replace it with a Non-Intercourse Act that permitted trade with all nations except Great Britain and France. To reward him for his support, President James Madison in 1809 appointed John Quincy Adams ambassador to Russia.[11]

The divide over the Embargo Act reflected the different attitudes toward Great Britain and France. According to Adolphe Thiers (1857) the merchants and lawyers who led the Federalist Party in Boston, New York and Philadelphia were men who "were long engaged in the English trade [and] whose manners, tastes, and ideas were those of the great English commercial class of which they had once formed a portion." The Democratic-Republican Party, strong in the South, represented the cotton, tobacco, sugar and cereal farmers who wanted to trade with France.

VIOLATIONS OF THE EMBARGO

Both the Embargo Act of 1807 and the Non-Intercourse Act of 1809 were heavily violated. In September 1808, Governor Daniel Tompkins of New York called out the militia to patrol Lake Champlain to stop the smuggling of goods into Canada.[12] Clandestine roads opened in upstate New York to carry illegal goods to the St. Lawrence River and onward to Canada for shipment to Europe. During the winter months these goods were carried on sleighs. Violations of the law were so numerous that Jefferson declared the border region separating Canada and New York to be in a state of insurrection. The lack of naval surveillance allowed commercial ships to slip undetected out of New England ports and break the embargo. "Infractions of the Embargo Law were open and frequent all along the New England coast." Federalist opposition "made the Embargo Law as odious as possible" in order to punish the Republican Party.[13]

In December 1807, John Henry, an immigrant from Ireland, saw an opportunity to make money by suggesting there was a plot afoot to take New England out of the Union and join with Canada. He claimed that the leading men of Boston were opposed to a war against Great Britain and, if the embargo on trade continued, would be ready to withdraw from the Union. Henry wrote that Massachusetts, Rhode Island, Connecticut, New Hampshire, Vermont and even New York would opt for secession. Without naming names, and relying on hearsay, gossip and newspaper reports, John Henry offered to supply information to Sir James Henry Craig, governor of Canada, about the alleged insurrection. Fearing an invasion of Canada and eager to weaken America, Craig agreed to pay John Henry the princely sum of £32,000 for regular reports from New England. When President Madison learned about the alleged New England Federalists plot to break the Union, he authorized the payment to John Henry of $50,000 in return for copies of the complete set of letters sent to Sir James Craig. The John Henry affair, accusing leading New Englanders such as John Lowell Jr. of disloyalty to the Union, echoed the allegations made in 1800 that his father Judge John Lowell and his uncle, Stephen Higginson, had accepted bribes to side with the British. After the John Henry letters were made public there were loud accusations, based on gossip and innuendo, that leading New England Federalists were guilty of treason.

In Europe, the tide of battle began to turn in 1808, after Napoleon placed his brother Joseph upon the throne of Spain. The uprising of proud Spaniards gave Britain its opportunity to attack the French through the Iberian Peninsula. In August, a British expeditionary force fought a series of battles in Portugal and Spain that severely weakened the French armies. The Duke of Wellington made sure that his armies were well fed, permitting the skillful American merchants to deliver grain and wheat to the British army from ports in the Iberian Peninsula.

Napoleon was determined to stop the American trade and ordered the Prussian government to seize the cargoes of American vessels and deliver them to France. Between 1809 and 1810, fifty-one American ships were seized in French ports, forty-four in Spanish, twenty-eight in Naples and eleven in Holland. The value of the cargoes seized exceeded $10 million. Despite these losses to France and her allies, American shipping continued. Colluding with merchants in England, the American traders found ingenious ways to circumvent Napoleon's blockade. Protected by the Royal Navy, American ships crossed the Atlantic with food supplies for the British troops.[14] American exports of grain and flour reached 1,383,028 bushels in 1809. During the years 1809 and 1810, over 60 percent of American grain and flour exports went to feed the British army in the Iberian Peninsula.[15,16]

Before the Embargo of 1807, Massachusetts controlled 37 percent of all the foreign trade coming into the United States. The port of Boston was, after New York, the busiest in the nation. The Massachusetts fishing fleet weighed in at sixty-two thousand tons, 90 percent of the nation's total. In 1807, Massachusetts brought in over $15 million in freight money. The Embargo of 1807 did not completely stop this activity but reduced the trade by half. Boston stayed active but the ports of Salem and Newburyport did not recover.

The embargo, by weakening the economy of New England, helped the Federalist cause.[17] In his 160-page pamphlet, *The New England Patriot, Being a Candid Comparison of the Principles and Conduct of the Washington and Jefferson Administrations*, John Lowell issued a scathing attack on Jefferson's embargo, which "aimed a debilitating blow at our whole foreign trade to which we owe most of our material greatness and much of our private happiness." Jefferson's policies favored the South over New England, claimed John Lowell, and squandered the national treasury. Lowell accused Jefferson of the "hypocritical pretence of regard to the rights of the people" and filling the high offices of the land with his followers. "This debasement of the national character, the corruption in the public manners and morals" would lead to "the ruin of our commerce and the corruption of our morals." Jefferson and the South were in league with the French. "The people of New England," thundered John Lowell, "would not yield their necks to the French yoke without a desperate struggle."[18] John Lowell also increased his opposition to his nemesis the governor of Massachusetts, James Sullivan, who supported the Jefferson embargo on British trade. John Lowell was emerging as one of the firebrands of the Federalist agenda. His statement that "it is better to suffer the amputation of a limb than to take the whole body. We must prepare for the operation" was taken as proof that he advocated the secession of New England from the Union.

The embargo changed Francis Cabot Lowell's business from trade to property. In 1808, he tabulated his income from investments in the C & C Turnpike, Salem Turnpike, Boston Bank, Essex Bridge and the Salem Marina, and from property at India Wharf, Broad Street, his distill house and other ventures. These investments brought him $1,647 a year, enough to live comfortably on and he could sell properties to raise extra money. He also had $5,150 in ready cash. As a result of the embargo, Francis "judged it right to lessen his family's expenditures by nearly two thousand dollars per annum for those years; which included, of course, the sacrifice of luxuries and many pleasures for himself, wife and family, all of which cheerfully acquiesced in, while both husband and wife decided that not one cent should be withdrawn from the sum of six hundred dollars, which they have been in the habit of appropriating every year to charitable purposes."[19]

Penury is relative, as Francis Cabot Lowell continued to invest in goods and property and spend money on small luxuries. On November 22, 1809, Francis Lowell and Henry Lee entered a partnership "to invest in cotton in Charleston," South Carolina. Lee put up $3,000 and Lowell $5,000. That same month Francis paid $42 to register his wife, daughter, sister, Miss Higginson, Miss Cutler and Mrs. Sullivan at John Roulstone's Riding School at Haymarket Place. At the school both "ladies and gentlemen are taught the polite art of riding." Twelve lessons and the hire of a horse cost the ladies $12, and for men a set of sixteen lessons cost $16. "Military gentlemen are taught the horse exercise from the drill to the attack at speed," eighteen lessons for $30. During the years of the embargo Francis undertook to raise funds for Harvard to support scholars from poor homes, collecting $16,000 from Nathan Appleton, Theodore Hollis, Joseph Sewall, Dorothy Saltonstall, Edward Holyoke and other prominent Bostonians. The interest of $1,606.93 in 1809 went to support these scholarships.

The French government made adjustments to lessen the impact of the blockade on its economy. As sugar became scarce and more expensive Napoleon and his ministers looked for a substitute. Benjamin Delessert discovered an efficient method to produce white sugar from beets, hailed as one of the great wonders of the day. By 1812–1813, France produced two million kilograms of white sugar made from sugar beet, with the taste and consistency of cane sugar. The rise of French sugar reduced the importance of the West Indies, leading to a decline of business for American merchants.[20]

8

✝

A Proper Bostonian on a Grand Tour

[Francis and Hannah Lowell] are distinguished persons in their country, and are, from attachment to British manners and principles, come here two years with their children to give them a favourable impression of the constitution, manners and literature of this country.

From a letter by Anne MacVicar Grant,
Edinburgh, April 1, 1811

They appeared to be a wealthy American family on an extended tour of the Old World seeking Enlightenment. The plan was to undertake a leisurely visit to Scotland and England before crossing the channel into France. Francis Cabot Lowell, aged thirty-five years, his wife Hannah and their four children—John Jr., aged eleven; Susan, aged nine; Francis, aged seven; and Edward, aged three—left Boston on June 25, 1810, on the brig *Eliza*. Their thirty-day journey was smooth and uneventful and the captain flattered them by saying "we had made out better than any other he has sailed with." The children, wrote Hannah, "as can be expected did very well" during the long sea journey. The *Eliza* arrived in Liverpool on July 25.

Liverpool was the great port of the British slave trade. At the start of the nineteenth century Liverpool with eighty thousand people was still the second-largest port in Great Britain, handling one-quarter of the foreign trade. Some 4,500 ships with a total of 450,000 tons entered or left the port of Liverpool each year. The port catered especially to the American and the African trade, bringing in raw cotton and exporting finished cloth from the Lancashire mills. The American Hotel near the King's and

Queen's Wharves was "chiefly frequented by the masters of ships in the American trade." The Music Hall on Bold Street was completed in 1785. A few years later the Athenaeum opened with a library and a reading room with the latest newspapers as well as shipping and trade periodicals for the merchants. The Liverpool Athenaeum would serve as the model for the Boston Athenaeum.

Hannah set her hopes on staying in Liverpool at the Star and Garter Tavern on Paradise Street, "offering genteel accommodations," but Mr. Lowell found that it was fully booked. On the arrival day Hannah wrote her mother-in-law Rebecca Lowell the first letter she penned on stepping foot on English soil. Writing with much delight and excitement, she praised "the verdant fields and green trees of the English countryside."[1]

News of the Lowell family tour was already made known to some people of importance in Great Britain. In a letter to her Edinburgh friend, Anne MacVicar Grant (written from Boston, June 10, 1810), Anna Cabot Lowell gave the reasons for the trip on which her brother Francis and his family were about to embark. "Various motives induced them to travel at this time," Anna Cabot wrote.

> The health of Mr. Lowell, which has been for some time delicate; the hope of giving their children some advantages of education superior to those in our own country; and the pleasure and improvement they anticipate from seeing other countries, have all their influence. They are solid, rational people, accustomed to domestic life, possessed of competence but without either the wish or the power to move in the dazzling sphere of fashion. They seek for themselves useful information and the society of the good and agreeable when they can be obtained with propriety; and for their children such attainments as will make them useful and happy in life, fit them for honorable professions and enable them to mingle in high society. You will find Mrs. Lowell so lovely in her character; you will discover in her so much good sense, so much delicacy of sentiment, awareness of temper and purity of heart, that you will see when you have penetrated the veil, which humility and modesty may draw over her excellencies in the presence of strangers. I am sure you will become interested in giving her your aid and forming a plan for her children while she resides among you.

In particular, Mrs. Grant was asked to make sure that Francis' daughter, Susan Lowell, received a good education while in Edinburgh.

The Lowell trip abroad took place at a difficult time in the affairs of Great Britain, France and the United States. Napoleon's empire on the Continent extended from Spain and Holland to the west and the Duchy of Warsaw to the east, and included Catalonia, Italy and much of Germany. Britain exploited a rebellion against France in Spain by sending an army under the Duke of Wellington. The peninsular wars steadily sapped

French strength and weakened its hold over the conquered lands. The war between France and Britain extended to the West Indies and even along the American coastline, with French and British men-of-war battling each other and seizing American commercial vessels. The *Chesapeake* affair and the Embargo of 1807 rendered it impossible for an American family to travel to Great Britain from 1807 to the end of 1809. After the embargo was lifted, relations between Great Britain and United States improved. The middle of 1810 was a good time to begin a tour of Great Britain.

With his mind still on unfinished business, Francis wrote from Liverpool to his brother-in-law and business associate, Samuel Pickering Gardner in Boston, reminding him to pay Captain Winslow for delivering a shipment of gin. The family, wrote Francis, "had a very pleasant passage" and in Liverpool enjoyed meeting their English relatives. Francis took with him £900, enough, he thought, "to last me six months at least," but he quickly realized he would need more money since London was "very expensive." Francis was less taken with Liverpool than was his wife, finding the city "a dirty place. It rains all the time." The Lowell family had not yet "got our land legs" but was already planning to leave Liverpool and travel to Edinburgh.[2] Francis and his family planned to stay abroad for two years visiting the intriguing places and meeting the interesting people that his brothers, John Jr. and Charles, recommended based on their tours abroad several years earlier. Both John and Charles spoke highly of Edinburgh and Francis made it his destination after Liverpool.

The trip to Europe was long in the planning but pressure of business kept Francis fully occupied until days before departure. He paid a medical bill of $89.50 for services rendered to the Lowell family and their domestic servants for the year 1809. Dr. James Jackson, son of Jonathan Jackson and Hannah's brother, was the family physician. Dr. Jackson had recently returned from London where he received his medical training. By means of letters Francis Cabot Lowell continued his extensive business transactions with Uriah Cotting, William Cabot, Rufus Amory and his brothers-in-law Charles, James, Henry and Patrick Tracy Jackson, among many others. His business account with Uriah Cotting from the beginning of 1809 until June 1810 came to $29,522.65, involving the transfer of shares, sale of property, dividends and lumber for India Wharf, Boston. His account with Patrick Tracy Jackson for the same period came to $13,291.85; Henry Lee, $7,050.26; the property developer Royal Makepeace, $6,732.34; William Cabot, $6,781.37; and Charles Jackson, $7,779.93. Francis was busy, selling shares in his India Wharf project, and in 1810 Senator James Lloyd bought in at the cost of $9,987.50. On May 17, 1810—a month before his departure to Europe—Francis sent Henry Lee the sum of $4,050.25 for payment of goods received from Philadelphia. On the twenty-sixth of that month, Francis purchased an eighteen-acre property in Roxbury from the estate of Cornelius Fellowes, suggesting that he planned on his return to retire to the life of a country gentleman, much like his brother John. The property lay close to his late father's thirty-acre spread at Bromley Vale, now owned by John Jr.

Francis invited his lonely bachelor uncle William Cabot to write often and direct the letters to the Edinburgh post office. Francis recommended Benjamin Gorham to his uncle "as a man of integrity and good sense" to manage his investments. Gorham graduated from Harvard in 1795, had a law practice in Boston and was married to Francis' sister Susanna. The Francis Cabot Lowell papers for the period 1810–1812 include dozens of promissory notes and other transactions, meticulously written in his own hand, suggesting that Francis was active and mentally sharp, up to the day he left with his family for Liverpool.[3] While traveling abroad, Francis left his business affairs in Boston in the capable hands of his brothers-in-law Samuel Pickering Gardner and Patrick Tracy Jackson, writing to them regularly with instructions on what to buy and what to sell. The merchant Samuel Pickering Gardner was eight years older than Francis. Gardner graduated from Harvard in 1786, and was married to Rebecca Russell Lowell, half-sister to Francis. Patrick Tracy Jackson, youngest brother of Hannah Lowell, was five years younger than Francis. The vibrancy of his letters to Gardner and Jackson and his business acumen suggest that Francis was fully in command of his financial affairs and quite capable of making important decisions, even from a distance. The claim that Francis Cabot Lowell traveled abroad because of a serious decline in his health is not supported. His motive was pleasure but spending such large sums of money to take his family on an extended and grand tour of Europe troubled his conscience. Claiming delicacy of health and the need for a long period of recuperation were acceptable reasons.

In addition to his extensive business connections, Francis did the bookkeeping and assumed the responsibility for his father's estate and ensured that the widow, Rebecca Lowell, received her regular payments. For the period 1807 until his departure for Europe, Francis recorded payments to the widow of $13,771.06 (about $3,500 a year) in the form of cash, annuities and the payment of interest on loans. Rebecca used some of her money to support her son the Reverend Charles Lowell, minister of the West Church, Boston.

On August 1, the Lowell family departed Liverpool by coach and reached the town of Lancaster, a journey of forty miles, at three o'clock. Hannah enjoyed the lush green of the countryside and noted that the English use of "hedges instead of fences or stone, gives the scenery a great advantage over ours." In Lancaster they met the widow of Dr. Currie and enjoyed a tour of the botanical gardens. The family reached Edinburgh on August 9 and moved into a hotel.

EDINBURGH

By the eighteenth century the Old Town of Edinburgh was so congested that a competition was held to design a more spacious New Town. The winning architect, James Craig, gave the city wide avenues, parks and crescents. The North Bridge was completed in 1772 and Princes Street in 1806, by which time the population of Edinburgh exceeded one hundred thousand. Edinburgh remained a city of lawyers, bankers and intellectuals, while fast-growing Glasgow became the center of industry in Scotland. Edinburgh was the heart of the Scottish Enlightenment, with the works of such luminaries as James Boswell (author of *Life of Johnson*), the poet Robert Burns, the philosopher and historian David Hume, the writer Sir Walter Scott, the moral philosopher Dugald Stewart and Adam Smith, the author of *An Inquiry into the Nature and Causes of the Wealth of Nations*. Completed in 1776, *The Wealth of Nations* observes that each person works not "to promote the public interest [but] he intends only his own security; and by directing that industry as its produce may be the greatest value, he intends only his own gain." Adam Smith wrote that he had "never known much good done by those who affected to trade for the public good." His faith in enlightened self-interest as the "invisible hand" driving the economy suited Francis Cabot Lowell admirably. The Scottish city was also the home of the *Edinburgh Review*, founded in 1802 by Francis Jeffrey and Henry Brougham.

The beauty of Edinburgh and her great centers of education had a special appeal for Americans. Even before 1800, over one hundred Americans earned their medical degrees in Edinburgh, and many others came to study theology, literature or the law. Most of the medical instruction was by lecture with little contact with anatomy or patients. By 1820, Edinburgh became a popular center for the study of anatomy attracting students from all over the English-speaking world. One of the most famous of these private anatomy schools was run by Dr. Robert Knox at Surgeons Hall. Knox gained notoriety when it was discovered that he was buying bodies from William Burke and William Hare. From 1827 to 1828 these infamous body snatchers murdered between thirteen and thirty people and delivered their bodies for dissection to the unsuspecting anatomist.

Upon their arrival in this exciting city Mr. and Mrs. Francis Cabot Lowell went shopping at Stevenson & Thomson, Haberdashers to buy gifts to send home to the family. Hannah penned a cheerful letter on August 13 to her sister Mary, wife of Henry Lee, telling that she was sending "a little black net cap for baby." Francis added a note saying by the time they returned home the baby would be "the belle of Boston." He begged her to "tell Mr. Lee not to work too hard" and that he should spend more time with his family. Edinburgh, he reported with enthusiasm, was beautiful: "Altho' I had high expectations of the beauty of this place, they are far exceeded." Writing two weeks after their arrival to Uncle William Cabot, on August 27, he was ready to offer his considered opinion about the city and its people: "We have been here about a fortnight and begin to be a little settled. We find the people very sociable and friendly. This city is, I believe, the second in the Kingdom for beauty, being only surpassed by Bath. [The height of the buildings] is much greater than in Boston even though the buildings are upwards of 400 years old and are still in perfect preservation and would be considered very handsome houses in our country. [Some of the Edinburgh houses] were built before Columbus discovered our world." The letters written by Francis show his distinct preference for measurement and comparison, quite unlike the literary flourish of his brother John and his sister Anna Cabot.

Since his school days at Phillips Academy, Andover, Francis Lowell was an inveterate letter writer, entreating others to write back often. Frequent letters made him feel connected with his world. Reading and writing detailed letters during their tour abroad occupied Francis and Hannah for hours each week. To his associates Francis was all business, addressing each formally as "Dear Sir," but to his family he was warm and engaging, expressing sadness over loss and joy over good news. Hannah wrote warm, enthusiastic and thoughtful letters to her family in America, and to the Scottish writer Anne MacVicar Grant. Hannah was the better tourist who enjoyed the British countryside, the theater, opera and the shops. Hannah was delighted to be a friend of a well-known female authoress and to share ideas about literature and philosophy. Francis, however, showed little interest in Anne MacVicar Grant's poems and writings. Francis found the Scots warm and sociable, but the English cold and withdrawn. He was more impressed meeting important people than extolling the beauties of the countryside. Hannah and Francis wrote nearly all their letters separately, each with its own style and emphasis. Four closely written pages were standard, but some letters were eight pages in length (about two thousand words). During the twenty-four months the Lowells were abroad several hundred letters passed back and forth over the Atlantic, following the family to Liverpool, Edinburgh, Glasgow, London, Bristol and Cheltenham. It took two to three months from the time a letter left Edinburgh or London before a reply was received. Within Britain letters were speedily delivered on horseback by the efficient postal service.

Samuel P. Gardner wrote to Francis Lowell on July 10, 1810, that he had approached Timothy Pickering, former U.S. secretary of state, for a letter introducing Francis Cabot to people of influence in Edinburgh. Pickering "immediately replied that he would with great pleasure give you one to

Mr. Liston who resides in Edinburgh." Timothy Pickering was referring to Sir Robert Liston (1742–1838), the distinguished diplomat who served from 1796 to 1800 as the British ambassador to the United States, when Pickering was secretary of state. His mission was to weaken the French influence on America. Liston was born in Scotland and attended Edinburgh University. He is said to have spoken ten languages and served Great Britain as ambassador to Spain, Sweden, Denmark and the Ottoman Empire.

"I have loaned P. T. Jackson thirteen hundred dollars of your money for which I have received his note, payable on demand," wrote Gardner to Francis on August 11. A follow-up letter a week later told Francis that Patrick Tracy Jackson had increased his borrowings to two thousand dollars. Henry Lee was also in need of money and asked Francis (October 20) to guarantee a loan from Mr. Oliver for $6,000. There were other business expenses as well as another bill for medical services rendered by Dr. James Jackson. Over the course of his trip abroad Francis Lowell made several requests to Gardner to sell bonds and property in order to ship gold coins to Lowell's banker in London. Fortunately for Francis Lowell, there was a steady stream of money coming into his account. Gardner regularly let him know of deposits from India Wharf, Broad Street and other rental properties owned by Francis Lowell. When major decisions on behalf of Francis C. Lowell needed to be made, Samuel Gardner consulted with John Lowell Jr., Benjamin Gorham and Charles Jackson—men of great competence and all in the family. Despite spending many thousands of dollars on their tour, the Lowell account with Samuel Pickering Gardner at the end of their two years was still in the black by $3,803.27. Patrick Tracy Jackson repaid his debt before Francis returned home.

Hannah was not made aware of her brother Patrick's financial woes. On August 26, Hannah wrote to Patrick that "Uncle Patrick is mentioned among us at least as often as anyone else." Even nine-year-old daughter Susan was encouraged to put pen to paper. In a much-corrected letter to her aunt Susanna Lowell Gorham, Susan wrote on August 27, "I have begun a letter to you to ask you how all my little cousins are. I expect when I come home to see a fine crop of potatoes and corn."

A letter sent by Ann Bromfield of Newburyport on October 30 gives an idea of the mobility of the Lowell family and their cousinhood. Henry Jackson sailed from Boston for Madrid, Ann and Tracy spent four weeks in Boston and John Bromfield was in Canton. The cousinhood sent the older boys to college and the younger sons on trading missions to the Far East, Europe, the Caribbean and South America.

During her time in Great Britain, Hannah Lowell maintained a special correspondence with her youngest sister, Mary, who was married to Henry Lee. Born on October 3, 1783, Mary was twenty-six years old when

Francis and Hannah Lowell and their four children left the port of Boston bound for Liverpool. In her diary Mary bemoaned her lack of education, but she was clearly an intelligent and insightful woman who lived vicariously through the achievements of others. Hannah's trip abroad excited Mary who was eager for news about the people the Lowells were meeting. "I have read Walter Scott's last poem with much pleasure. From his writings and the character Mrs. Grant gives of him, I feel a strong desire to see him. You must put a little literary information into your letters to me that I may not be quite distanced from the *belles-lettres* world," wrote Mary on September 10, 1810. "I feel myself so much better suited to the cares of family that I do not sigh with envy when I think of your advantages." On November 19 Mary wrote, "You may be assured you are very important now you are absent and when you come home, you will, of course, continue so, a European voyage gives such *éclat*."

Mary was gradually absorbed into the social circle of the Lowells, Cabots, Higginsons and the other well-off Essex County families, now moved to Boston. The beginning of their social rise was awkward, especially for her husband Henry. Mary related on August 11 an invitation to take tea with Susanna Gorham, Francis Cabot's biological sister, at her home in Charlestown. "How glad I was," wrote Mary, "that my husband had conquered his feelings of embarrassment sufficiently to go there. It was evidently a great gratification to her, not so much, perhaps, from the value of our company, as from having gained the object, which she had taken much pains to achieve. I often smile on the value attributed to everything which is rare, and tell my husband that his whims make his society much more coveted than any agreeable qualities he may chance to possess. We have been to Becca Gardner's [Rebecca, half-sister to Francis Lowell] this week, and have had our baby christened; thus, you see, we advance."

Their brother Patrick Tracy Jackson announced his engagement to his cousin Lydia Cabot. "Indeed, I think, my dear sister," wrote Mary on August 13, "we may be quite satisfied with this addition to our family. [Lydia Cabot] has qualities which will be more durable and useful than shining ones might be," suggesting that Lydia was more capable than she was beautiful.

The deteriorating economy of Massachusetts became a regular topic of discussion. "We are all well and in as good spirits," wrote Mary to Hannah on February 27, 1811, "as the failures your husband so prophetically predicted and vessels on the coast at this tempestuous season will let us be. My husband promises me that he will never again enter so largely into business, and I hope he will be firm." The seas proved too rough for Henry & Joseph Lee & Company, and for their brother, Patrick Tracy Jackson. Hannah and Francis wrote home to console the Lees and offer help. Mary responded on May 15, "I hope your husband's anxieties on ours and Pat's account will not induce you to return."

Francis was alarmed by the high cost of travel for two adults and their four children. The Lowell family spent £50 in Liverpool, £60 traveling to Edinburgh and £140 during their first two weeks in the city. Despite these anxieties, the Lowell family rented "a furnished house, all very good" at 5 South St. Andrew Street, Edinburgh, owned by Mr. Francis Davison. South St. Andrew Street is a short street linking St. Andrew Square with Princes Street. Built in 1772, St. Andrew Square soon became the most fashionable address in the New Town. The Grand Restaurant was sited at 3 South St. Andrew. St. Giles, the High Kirk in the Old Town, built in 1635–1638, can be seen from the street. The rental Francis paid to Mr. Davison was twelve guineas a month, £17 annually for the services of the cook and the cleaning maid, and an extra £8 a year for the chambermaid. As befits a gentleman, Francis Lowell allowed himself the luxury of a manservant at the annual cost of forty-two guineas. He complained that the price of groceries for the family and staff was "very high" especially for sherry, eggs, coffee and bread.

Writing to Samuel P. Gardner on August 27, Francis reckoned that "I have money enough to last 4 or 5 months, longer probably 6 months" but would need more. He asked Gardner to send him gold coins "as this is the best remittance [with which] you can buy bills of Exchange at 7 per cent discount. If you send Gold, Joannas of Portugal or Doubloons of Spain are the best. Very important that the Gold should be full weight each piece, that it be fair and free of flaws." Lowell asked that the money be sent to Henry Higginson in London. Each of these gold coins had a value of £4, 7 shillings and 6 pence. Gardner's reply of November 2 informed Lowell that he sent on the ship *Lothian* £800, purchased with gold, at a 6.75 percent discount. A few weeks later, Gardner sent an additional £200 sterling.

On September 15, Francis wrote that his sons "Francis and Edward go to day school," costing five shillings each a month. "I have got a private tutor for John [to prepare him for high school] which will commence next Monday a week. I hope to have him fitted so as to return and enter college at Cambridge in three years." Remembering his loneliness as a schoolboy at the Phillips Academy boarding school in Andover, Francis kept his boys at home. They were day students in Boston and remained day students in Edinburgh. Daughter Susan was not considered in the plans for schooling and was tutored by her mother. Francis Lowell's older brother John Lowell wrote on January 17, 1811, that Francis "was perfectly right in educating your boys in Scotland. Was I to go over the same ground again I certainly would have done the same."

The well-heeled and well-connected Lowell family, living in their grand house with servants and with their boys in private schools, was now ready to entertain and meet people of Edinburgh of their class and income. In the space of a few weeks Hannah visited Mr. Mackay, "a blind gentleman whose wife my husband declares himself an admirer." She called on Miss Lewis, Mr. Jeffries and Miss Gardner, "a lively, pleasant and pretty girl." She met Dr. Brown, his mother and his sisters, Mrs. Allen and Mrs. Dickson, and also "a highly interesting young man." The social whirl in Edinburgh enveloped the young and rich American family. Hannah Lowell confessed to a friend, "I was at two private balls last week, besides another evening in company, and have to struggle hard not to have company all this week, I have begun it by refusing invitations." Social life included the Theatre Royal on Shakespeare Square, at the east end of Princes Street, offering a wide range of plays. During the time Francis and Hannah were in Edinburgh, this theater staged *The Tempest*, *Speed the Plough*, *Lock and Key*, *The Quaker* and other plays.

In Edinburgh, the Lowells at last met Anne MacVicar Grant. Born in Scotland in 1755, Anne MacVicar spent her childhood in America, where her father was a British army officer with the 27th Regiment of Foot fighting in the French and Indian War. After the British victory against the French, the MacVicar family settled near Albany, New York where Anne met the Schuyler family, one of the most respected families in New York State. The MacVicar family returned to Scotland in 1768, when Anne was thirteen. Anne wrote nostalgic verses of the Scottish Highlands that brought her some fame. After her husband, the Reverend Grant, died she published in 1808 her *Memoirs of an American Lady* recalling her happy childhood in pre-revolutionary America. Francis' sister Anna Cabot Lowell was so taken with the book that she arranged for it to be published in America. In 1810, Anne MacVicar Grant moved from Sterling to Edinburgh, where Sir Walter Scott befriended her and helped her obtain a pension of £100 a year. Not having sufficient money to support her family, Anne MacVicar Grant took in boarders, including the Lowell children when Francis and Hannah left Edinburgh to tour Scotland and England.

Many other Americans found their entry into Edinburgh society through Anne MacVicar Grant. Her attentions to American visitors, some of whom boarded in her house, were "very constant and of the kindest description." But some doubted her literary skills. Writing one of his "Letters from, Edinburgh" in the *North American Review*, July 1, 1815, Theodore Lyman (Harvard 1810) wrote that Anne MacVicar Grant's "literary reputation in particular is not brilliant and hardly corresponds with the esteem in which she is held in some parts of New England."

Francis was especially delighted to receive a famous visitor known to his brothers. On December 31 he wrote, "The celebrated Dugald Stewart called to see us a few days ago. He is rather a small man, has a very intelligent countenance. He stayed but a short while and unfortunately other visitors called while he was here so that we had little opportunity to see him. He promised to call again. It gives me great pleasure even to see a man so distinguished as Mr. Stewart, he asked after Charles and after brother John." Dugald Stewart was professor of moral philosophy at the University of Edinburgh and was one of the leading figures of the Scottish Enlightenment. He was just the sort of man Francis Lowell came to Edinburgh to meet. Francis had not read Professor Stewart's works but took pride in knowing a famous man. The death of Stewart's sixteen-year-old son the year before was a bitter blow to the professor, who soon after resigned his university chair.

Feeling settled in Edinburgh, a city four times as large as his Boston, Francis Lowell began to reflect on the events of the larger world. He wrote to Patrick Tracy Jackson about selling his shares in his project at the India Wharf, and asked about the mortgages on his properties and the price of cotton, tobacco and gold. He wrote December 11 to tell Samuel Gardner about the state of the British economy during the bitter war against France. Bankruptcies in Britain were on the rise and amounted to "several millions sterling [and] if the Bankruptcies continue at this rate they will exceed the number in 1809. [There were] great losses in speculation in Spain and South America and the decline of currencies and the fall of funds amounted to 90 million pounds sterling to the holders of the debt."

Francis wrote to his partner in the India Wharf project, Uriah Cotting, asking him to sell some of his real estate holdings. In reply Cotting expressed his pleasure "to hear that you and Mrs. Lowell are in good health." Putting pleasantries aside, Cotting related that as in Europe, there were many bankruptcies in Boston. Despite his best efforts he was unable "to sell anything of consequence because of the falling values of real estate in Boston." Fortunately, he was able to rent some of Francis' properties on Broad Street "to people who pay." Cotting ended his April 14, 1811, letter saying that the depressed state of the Boston economy made it impossible for him and his family to join the Lowells in Europe. Among the bankruptcies in Boston to which Cotting referred was one that hit the Lowells hard. In 1811, the trading firm of Henry & Joseph Lee, buying goods in India for sale in Europe, closed its doors. The Lee brothers owed Francis Lowell $7,300. Hearing this news, Francis wrote to Patrick Tracy Jackson that "the hazards of business are much greater now than they ever were in my days."

When Francis Cabot Lowell and his family were on their grand tour, Great Britain was experiencing profound changes due to its industrial revolution and its great war against Napoleon. Every year thousands upon thousands of people left the countryside to sell their labor in the factories.

The rapidly urbanized population no longer had a patch of earth on which to grow vegetables, and depended on money to go to the shops to buy their food. British harvests were insufficient to feed the growing population that had developed a taste for tea and sugar and other imported foods. In order to pay for these imports, the British needed to increase their exports of manufactured goods. Sanitation and the control of diseases became major problems in the fast-growing British cities. Under the assault of industrialization and population shift, the traditional British social patterns were rapidly changing. New men, inventors and entrepreneurs who developed the new machines and opened factories, were rising to the top while the landed gentry was struggling.

Lowell reflected on how best to marshal his resources in a period when legitimate American trade with Europe was in the doldrums and the smuggling of goods across the Canadian border reached epidemic proportions. Francis concluded that America would remain hostage to foreign powers unless she manufactured goods at home equal in quality to and cheaper in price than imports. To generate wealth, America needed to build the factories and the machinery to mass-produce consumer goods. Lowell envisioned that American factories would be built with American money, machines designed and built by Americans, and employing American workers. Lowell resolved to devote time during his tour to discover the secrets of the British industrial revolution and take this knowledge back to America. Lowell proposed beginning the American industrial revolution by making cotton textiles in factories powered by the flow of American rivers, and using the abundant cotton grown in the American South.

Francis Cabot Lowell had to proceed with stealth and caution. Great Britain was reluctant to share its great textile inventions with the rest of the world and since 1774 had enacted laws to forbid the export of its machines or even the plans. Perhaps the first person to learn of Lowell's bold plan was Nathan Appleton, a Boston merchant then on a tour of Europe. Both of these men had a deep commercial interest in textiles. Lowell was a leading importer of silks and cotton textiles handwoven in China and India, while Appleton specialized in high-end British manufactured goods. Born in 1779 in New Ipswich, New Hampshire, Nathan Appleton was the ninth of twelve children of the Deacon Isaac Appleton and his wife Mary. As an infant Nathan nearly died from lung fever. During his childhood he crushed the forefinger of his left hand when a window sash suddenly gave way; he bore the deformity to his finger for the rest of his life. Nathan attended the local school where he and Rebecca Barrett were the outstanding students. He hoped to attend Dartmouth College, but his family was too poor and instead decided that "I should become a merchant, rather than a scholar." At age fifteen years, Nathan set out for

Boston, carrying all his possessions wrapped up in a large handkerchief, to join his older brother Samuel, who owned a store. Nathan, with a good head for figures, worked hard, and at age twenty-one he and Samuel established the firm of S & N Appleton Company, importing luxury goods from Europe for their wealthy clients in Boston. Nathan regularly traveled to Europe to buy goods and the Appleton brothers went from strength to strength to be listed among the leading merchants of Boston. In 1810–1811 Nathan Appleton and his new wife came to Europe for reasons of her health. The couple visited the Lake District, wintered in Bath to take the waters and then traveled to Edinburgh, where Appleton called on Francis Cabot Lowell.

Nathan Appleton, in his *Introduction to the Power Loom and the Origin of Lowell*, gives a brief but poignant account of his meetings with Francis Cabot Lowell. "My connection with the Cotton Manufactory takes date from the year 1811, when I met my friend Mr. Francis C. Lowell at Edinburgh, where he had been staying for some time with his family," wrote Appleton. "We had frequent conversations on the subject of the Cotton Manufactory, and he informed me that he had determined before his return to America, to visit Manchester, for the purpose of obtaining all possible information on the subject, with a view to the introduction of the improved manufacture in the United States. I urged him to do so, and promised him my co-operation."[4]

A slightly different version of the famous encounter in Edinburgh between the two Boston men of business was published in 1861 after Appleton died: "Whilst in Edinburgh I saw a good deal of Francis C. Lowell Esq., who was there with his family. We had a good deal of conversation upon the subject of cotton manufacture: and he told me that he had determined before he returned to make himself fully acquainted with the subject, with the view of the introduction of it at home. I urged him to do so, with the understanding that I would be ready to co-operate with him in such an undertaking."[5]

Francis Cabot Lowell, wealthy from birth and sheltered from the roughness of life, believed that success comes to those who work hard and failure is a personal weakness. His vision of the American textile factory differed from what he saw in Great Britain. America did not have a domestic cotton textile industry but depended on cloth imported from Great Britain and India. The factory he planned to build near Boston would create new jobs rather than replace home spinners and weavers. Lowell had great faith in the people of New England as the source of his labor force and believed "that the character of our population, educated, moral and enterprising could not fail to secure success." His workers would be housed and fed by the company and remain employed only a few years rather than form a permanently downtrodden underclass.

If he could not buy machines from Britain, he would design and build them in America. Well acquainted with the price of commodities, Lowell planned to buy raw cotton from the South where it could be purchased more cheaply than for the British companies, which shipped the cotton over longer distances. Francis Lowell planned to use "the abundant water power in every part of New England" to supply his mills. This cheap and plentiful power would give him the advantage over the British factories on slow flowing rivers or going to the added expense of steam power.[6]

For decades New England merchants like Nathan Appleton and Francis Cabot Lowell imported to America the handwoven cotton bandannas, handkerchiefs and cloth from India, silk textiles from China and manufactured cloth from Great Britain. To create a viable cotton textile industry in America, Francis Cabot Lowell would need to compete in cost and quality against the centuries-old homespun industry of India, and China and the decades-long lead of Great Britain in machine-made goods. Coming from a country lacking the tradition of craftsmanship or manufacturing, Francis Cabot Lowell's plan was audacious to the point of grandiosity.

THE TEXTILE INDUSTRY OF GREAT BRITAIN

The industrial revolution had gathered momentum for thirty years before Francis Cabot Lowell arrived in Great Britain. Before the introduction of machinery, the dressing, carding, spinning and weaving of cotton was done by hand in the cottages of the workers. The wives and daughters spun the yarn and the men folk wove the yarn into cloth, bought up for sale in the market places of the towns. Hundreds of thousands in the villages and towns of England and Scotland earned their keep in the home-craft textile industry. These textile workers made a decent living, supplemented by the produce of their gardens and milk from their cows.

The traditional methods of home spinning changed after 1764 with James Hargreaves' invention of the spinning jenny. Born in the village of Stanhill, near Blackburn in Lancashire, Hargreaves worked as a weaver until he devised a machine that could spin several threads at the same time. Three years later, Richard Arkwright, a wig-maker by occupation, from Preston in Lancashire, improved on the jenny with his water-powered spinning throstle. The illiterate and humble James Hargreaves and the energetic Richard Arkwright were the men at the forefront of the British industrial revolution.

Richard Arkwright proved the better businessman. Despite the riots that followed the introduction of his spinning machine, Arkwright formed a company to build textile mills. The first Arkwright mill, powered by river water, opened in 1771. The next great technological advance in cotton spinning came from Samuel Crompton of Bolton in Lancashire with his mule, so called because it combined the functions of the spinning jenny and the throstle. Crompton's machine could spin a yarn so fine as to make muslin cloth. The machines devised by Hargreaves, Arkwright and Crompton were very heavy and required sturdily built factories to hold them. Manufacturers found it economical to build large factories with a single waterwheel, giving great impetus to the factory as the preferred system for spinning cotton. The manufacturer owned the mill, machinery and the raw materials. With the coming of the factory system the worker sold his labor for whatever price the marketplace offered.

In 1786, David Dale and Richard Arkwright founded the village of New Lanark, some thirty-five miles southwest of Edinburgh, where they built cotton mills using the power of the River Clyde. By the 1780s the British cotton spinning factories provided the quarter million weavers of the nation with an unlimited supply of yarn at reasonable prices. So pleased was the British government with the invention of the water frame that, in 1787, they awarded Richard Arkwright the majestic sum of £10,000. That year, there were already 143 textile mills in Great Britain.

The power to turn the machines in the factories came at first from horses moving in rotation. With the invention of the waterwheel, power came from the rivers and streams. In England, with slower rivers, the steam engine, first installed in 1785, rapidly became the preferred source of power.

Edmund Cartwright's power loom was the next great advance in textile machinery. His first machine functioned poorly and he made several improvements. The power loom was seen as a great threat to the livelihood of the quarter million men and women who made their living weaving cotton. Cartwright's machines were destroyed and his factory burned, events that delayed the introduction of the power loom, but the momentum was shifting from hand to machine weaving. Parliament in 1809 acknowledged Cartwright's ingenuity and "the good service he rendered the public by his invention of weaving" with an award of £10,000 sterling. He used the money to buy a farm where he quietly lived out his life writing poetry and inventing new machinery.

In his 1843 book *The Condition of the Working Class in England*, Friedrich Engels, the disciple of Karl Marx, analyzed the dramatic changes caused by the introduction of machines to replace hand spinning and weaving. The use of machinery in factories transformed the face of Lancashire, Lanarkshire and other parts of the United Kingdom. Prices of manufactured goods fell sharply, impoverishing the home spinners and weavers and driving people from their villages to seek work in the factories. The efficient machines required far fewer people than the work done by hand. Those without work gathered around the mills. Men workers were replaced by women and children who were paid less. The unemployed were reduced to begging or selling shoelaces, oranges and matches at street corners, or stealing. "Every new machine brings with it unemployment, want and suffering," wrote Engels. "In his despair the worker either revolts against the middle class or drowns his sorrows in drink or debauchery." Furthermore, Engels wrote, "The most oppressed workers are those who have to compete against a new machine which is in the process of replacing hand labour." The workers were forced to accept lower and lower wages: "Of all the workers who compete against machinery, the most oppressed are the hand loom weavers in the cotton industry."[7] While the workers were dragged down, the ruling classes benefited mightily from industrialization.

With the expansion of its colonial empire, Great Britain gained new sources for raw materials as well as new markets to sell its manufactured goods. Its command of the sea gave Britain the means to transport goods on a vast scale. At the start of the eighteenth century, exports of cotton goods from Great Britain amounted to a paltry £23,252 sterling. In 1701, Great Britain imported a little over one million pounds of raw cotton. By 1750, raw cotton imports reached three million pounds and by 1792, over thirty million pounds of cotton. In 1800, with the British industrial revolution in full blast, imports of raw cotton exceeded £56 million, and by 1802, over £60 million—much of it from the American South. Exports of finished cloth also increased. In the year 1793, when Francis Cabot Lowell gradated from Harvard, British cotton exports were valued at £1,733,807 and in 1810 cotton textile exports reached £18,931,900. This trade, greatly enhanced by machinery, led to a massive expansion of capital and increased the wealth of the British nation.

When Francis Cabot Lowell was visiting Great Britain, weaving was still largely done by hand. By the year 1820, the number of Cartwright-type power looms rose to four thousand, and by the year 1835, Great Britain had over one hundred thousand looms at work.[8] Manchester, Leeds, Glasgow and other textile towns grew large with the industrial revolution.

NOBLESSE OBLIGE

Over the decades historians have pondered the origin of Francis Cabot Lowell's paternalistic management of the workers in his Boston Manufacturing Company. Some linked Lowell's benevolence to the example set by a remarkable Welshman, Robert Owen. At age twenty-one, Owen was appointed the manager of the Bank Top Cotton Mill in Manchester. His success running the mill with five hundred workers led to an offer to manage the larger Chorlton Company. While meeting with customers in Scotland, Owen fell in love with and married Caroline Dale. At the close of the eighteenth century, David Dale gave the management of his New Lanark mills to his son-in-law. New Lanark was one of the first of the British cotton mills to use the power loom.

Robert Owen became a passionate critic of the British manufacturing system, which he believed was motivated by the pursuit of money over social justice for the workers. Robert Owen wrote in 1817, "In the manufacturing districts it is common for parents to send their children of both sexes at seven or eight years of age, in winter as well as in summer, at six o'clock in the morning, sometimes of course in the dark, and occasionally amidst frost and snow, to enter the manufactories [and to remain at work] till eight o'clock at night. Such a system of training cannot be expected to produce any other than a population weak in bodily and mental facilities, and with habits generally destructive to their own comforts, of the well being of those around them, and strongly calculated to subdue all the social affections."

It was at New Lanark that Robert Owen put into practice his ideas for a more humane industrial system. With many of his workers coming from the poorhouses of Glasgow and Edinburgh, Owen provided them with housing, schools for their children and cost-price food at the factory store. The mills and housing were sanitary, the water pure and the streets clean. Robert Owen claimed that six hundred children were attending the schools of his New Lanark colony. Discipline was maintained "without punishment or individual rewards." In this nurturing environment "the habits, disposition, and character [are superior to those] of the same class to be found elsewhere." Furthermore, Owen stated, the 1,600 people working at New Lamark "with the aid of scientific power" produced the same quantity of goods that forty years earlier required 160,000 working by hand. The bold experiment at New Lanark brought renown to Robert Owen as the inspiration for utopian socialism, showing that good wages and humane conditions benefited worker and owner alike.

Francis Cabot Lowell was in Edinburgh for ten months during the period of Robert Owen's great fame. As one who kept his eye on the business news, it is almost certain that Francis knew about the controversy surrounding New Lanark and formed his own opinions. Some writers detect the influence of Robert Owen in the way Francis Lowell treated the workers in his Waltham mill. Francis Cabot Lowell, however, came from a very different mindset and was raised to believe that individuals had the capacity to shape their own lives rather than being molded by outside forces. Furthermore, he lacked the social consciousness and reformist zeal of Robert Owen. There exists no evidence that Francis Lowell actually met Robert Owen or even visited New Lanark.[9]

A more likely explanation for the paternalistic capitalism practiced by Francis Lowell can be found among the correspondence of Anne MacVicar Grant, who was the great friend of his family while they were in Edinburgh. Known as Mrs. Grant of Laggan, Anne was a dedicated letter writer, a member of the leading literary circles of Edinburgh and an ardent supporter of noble causes. On February 2, 1811, Anne Grant wrote a letter to the Duke of Kent at St. James Palace, London. Prince Edward, the Duke of Kent, was the fourth son of King George III and father (in 1818) of the future Queen Victoria, his only legitimate child. Anne MacVicar Grant told Prince Edward that the town of Sterling, where she lived before coming to Edinburgh, was "formerly supported by a manufactory of tartan, which gradually diminished as the article grew less and less a product of Scottish industry." The factory was managed by Mr. Gilchrist and after he died his widow took over the responsibility. The benevolent Mrs. Gilchrist carried on the failing business "chiefly to give bread to a great number of families, who were so brought up and confined to the various branches of this employment that they really could not get their bread in any other way." Mrs. Gilchrist was now no longer able "to supply the usual employment to these poor people, many of whom have become dependent upon her bounty."

Anne MacVicar Grant assured Prince Edward that neither Mrs. Gilchrist nor the workers in her tartan factory were looking for charity. Since he was the commander of the regiment stationed at Sterling Castle, Mrs. Grant, as she liked to be called, asked Prince Edward to consider buying the regiment's tartans from Mrs. Gilchrist's factory, and so give employment to the workers. Within weeks Anne MacVicar Grant received the response that the Duke of Kent "would immediately give direction that Mrs. Gilchrist of Sterling furnish the supply of tartans for the Highland regiment."

A delighted Mrs. Grant wrote back to Prince Edward thanking him for his generosity. "I am anxious," she wrote April 1, "to show the letter to a family from America, the brother of my dear lamented Miss [Anna Cabot] Lowell. They are distinguished persons in their country, and have, from attachment to British manners and principles, come here for two years with their children, to give them favourable impressions of the constitution, manners and literature of this country. I wish earnestly to have the opportunity of showing them what would tend to confirm the impression we wish them to carry back of the beneficence and gentle virtues of our most exalted personages; the anarchists who disturb the peace and distract the minds of the populace in their country, making it an argument against our government, that our rulers despise and insult us."

Francis Cabot Lowell must have been thrilled that Prince Edward, son of George III, knew of him. Like his brother John, he admired the British and their royal family. Benevolence and the moral obligation of the wealthy to be charitable to the needy were his guiding principles. With the vision of his textile factory set firmly in his mind, Francis would follow the royal example of *noblesse oblige* by seeking profits while still taking care of his textile workers and treating them with respect.[10]

After Francis Cabot Lowell and his family left Edinburgh, Anne MacVicar Grant continued to act as a guide to Americans visiting Edinburgh. In 1919 young George Ticknor, later professor of foreign languages at Harvard, came to visit. Ticknor remembered her as an "extraordinary person [whose] conversation is more sought after than that of anyone else." He was a frequent visitor to her home, where he was introduced to Robert Owen, Henry Brougham and others of Edinburgh's intellectual luminaries.

THE LUDDITE REBELLION

Other mill owners in Great Britain lacked the compassion and vision of Robert Owen. The mills spoiled the countryside and polluted the rivers and streams. With the coming of steam power the air was thick with smoke, sickening the workers. The poet William Blake (1757–1827) in his *Jerusalem*, written in 1804, bemoaned the industrial revolution and "these dark Satanic Mills" that defaced "England's green & pleasant land." The power looms and other machines of the industrial revolution concentrated production in the factories at the expense of the spinners and the weavers in their cottages. The large mills built along the rivers of the kingdom attracted hordes of poor people looking for work and spawned unsanitary slums and spread disease. While the poor competed for jobs, reduced wages and child labor became the order of the day.

On March 11, 1811, riots broke out in Nottinghamshire as textile workers revenged themselves against the mill owners who had reduced their wages. These riots were the start of the Luddite rebellion in which the workers smashed their looms in protest against the ills of industrialization. The rebellion spread to Yorkshire and Lancashire. The Rawfolds mill was attacked by a mob that destroyed the machines. At the Dickerson factory in Leeds rioters cut up the bolts of finished cloth and smashed the machinery. In Manchester "thousands of half-starved men" roamed the streets. The government deployed twelve thousand armed troops to put down the rebellion. Fourteen of the leaders were hanged and others sent in exile to Australia. From newspaper accounts, Francis Cabot Lowell was aware of the riots that were disrupting production in the British textile mills.

FRANCIS, HANNAH AND JOHN JR.
TOUR SCOTLAND AND ENGLAND

The Lowell family belonged to a different world and continued their docile travels at a safe distance from the riots. Taking their older son John Jr., and leaving behind the younger three children with Anne MacVicar Grant and her daughter Mary, Francis Cabot Lowell and his wife left Edinburgh in early May 1811 for a trip through Scotland. Francis planned to flesh out his bold idea of bringing textile manufacturing to America, and see for himself the British experience with power machines. While visiting Glasgow, "William Smith was very good in showing us the town manufactories." Rich in coal and iron, Glasgow entered the industrial revolution late in the eighteenth century and showed spectacular growth to become the "Second City of the Empire." The cotton mills and foundries in Glasgow brought great wealth to the owners but hard times and discontent to their workers.

After Glasgow, the Lowells moved south into England, where they were put off "by the cold English manners after being used to the Scottish warmth" (May 30, 1811). They spent three weeks traveling through England before arriving in London. Francis wrote, "The country looks delightful at this season, particularly for us who are so unused to see a county in such high cultivation. We have been to several watering places," but for Francis none could compare with the Ballston Spa in Saratoga County, New York, that attracted the well-to-do in America seeking the curative effects of its effervescent mineral waters. In addition to taking the waters at spas along the way to London, Lowell looked in at some of the English factory towns. He did not like what he saw: "We find the manufacturing towns very dirty; the people much disposed to be jealous of strangers, particularly Americans" (letter to uncle William Cabot, written from London, May 29).

Francis, Hannah and their son John Jr. reached London on May 23, and settled in at Probatt's Hotel, 35 King Street, close to the fruit, vegetable and flower markets of Covent Gardens. The area around Covent Gardens was also the home of the Theatre Royal, two of London's leading hotels, the Grand and British Imperial, as well as an assortment of taverns, restaurants and coffeehouses. As they did in Edinburgh, the Lowells chose a very respectable part of the city, rubbing shoulders with the aristocracy in Piccadilly and Leicester Square. The premises of Probatt's hotel were originally the home of the Welsh comedian William Lewis. In 1831, long after Francis Cabot Lowell had left, Probatt's Hotel was converted into the Garrick Club, named for the famous actor David Garrick (1717–1779). This prominent gentlemen's club was a place where leading actors and writers could mingle at ease with men of the moneyed aristocracy. Charles Dickens, William Makepeace Thackeray and Anthony Trollope were members of the Garrick Club.

In 1804, John Lowell Jr. and his wife spent several months in London before crossing to France. Francis set his heart on following his brother's itinerary with visits to France and Italy. He wanted to show his family the beauties of Bordeaux, Paris and Tours, the towns he had visited in his youth. Also, like his brother, he hoped to catch a glimpse of Emperor Napoleon. While in London, Francis applied several times to the French government for permission to cross over to France but, because of the war, the Lowell family was denied passage.

The London the Lowell family saw was a glittering city of over one million people, one in ten of all the inhabitants of the kingdom, and the largest city in the world. London was the financial center of the British Empire. Raw sugar, leather, cotton and furs came into British ports to be processed in English factories into manufactured goods. The money from all the trade came to London. Lombard Street, in the city of London, was the center of finance and insurance. Nearby, on Leadenhall Street, stood the vast East India House, headquarters of the British East India Company. Parliament was in London as were the homes of the king, members of the House of Commons and the Lords. London in 1811 had eleven theaters, including Drury Lane, The Haymarket, Lyceum, Sadler's Wells and Covent Gardens Theatre. Shakespeare's King Lear and Hamlet regularly strutted about on the London stage.

In her letters from London to Anne MacVicar Grant in Edinburgh and to her family in Boston, Hannah Lowell wrote excitedly of the joys of visiting the "great city." She went to the Lyceum to hear John Braham, one of the leading opera tenors in Europe.[11] The London theater, however, did not much please her husband. He wrote, "Either I have grown old and lost the little friendship I had for the stage, or else the acting has greatly deteriorated." Nor did Francis enjoy the circus: "So these horses are taught to rear up on their hind legs and act like gay and unruly horses. But the poor beasts have no spirit in them." What did impress him were his visits to the House of Parliament and the House of Lords. Lowell was enthralled by the speeches of the Prime Minister Spencer Perceval and Member of Parliament Samuel Whitbread. They spoke fluently, without grammatical errors, and "nothing very silly was said. The only fault I observed was the low abuse which the opposition members used towards the ministry. It was very evident that they had grown very impatient from their expectation of coming into power."

Spencer Perceval was the seventh son of the Second Earl of Egmont by his second wife, Catharine. After attending Harrow and Trinity College, Cambridge, Percival studied the law. He served as member of Parliament for Northampton and opposed Catholic emancipation. In 1809, he became prime minister of Great Britain at a time when King George III was descending into madness. Perceval pushed through the House of Commons a law making it punishable by death for a worker to destroy his loom. On May 11, 1812, Perceval was shot dead by a mentally deranged man, the only British prime minister ever assassinated. A month later the War of 1812 between the United States and Great Britain officially began. Samuel Whitbread was a member of the Whitbread brewing family. Educated at Eton, Christ Church, Oxford and St. Johns College, Cambridge, Whitbread was elected member of Parliament, where, as a supporter of Napoleon, he advocated the British withdrawal from the war on the Continent. Possessing an elite education similar to theirs one can see how, in his 1811 visit to Parliament, Francis Lowell was drawn to these two men.

A major concern to Francis and Hannah during the rest of their stay in Britain was the fate of Henry and Mary Lee. After his business failed Henry planned to travel to Calcutta, hoping to restore his fortunes, leaving his family behind in Boston. Hannah wrote frequently to her sister Mary asking how she would cope while her husband was away in India. Francis considered several times returning early to Boston to help the Lee family as well as Patrick Tracy Jackson, whose own business was intertwined with the Lees. Fortunately for Francis, his own affairs, deftly managed in his absence by Samuel Pickering Gardner and Uriah Cotting, were in good order. Writing to Gardner on June 11, Francis happily concluded "from all your letters that my own affairs are well managed." The reason why the family had to stay longer in Europe, Francis explained, was to restore Hannah's health. "Hannah," Francis wrote, "certainly is better now than she was in America, and the climate is much better suited to her health than ours." Writing to Patrick Tracy Jackson on June 20, Lowell warned him of the "danger of too large speculations." Upon his return to Boston, Francis was planning to take Patrick under his wing and give him a share of the future cotton mill enterprise.

On June 21, Francis Cabot Lowell reassured himself by tabulating his assets and debts and estimating his net worth. He owned property in and around Boston worth $61,650, and he had made loans to business associates and friends totaling $46,000. Among those who owed him money were Royal Makepeace, B. Wild, Mr. Vaughan and the architect Charles Bulfinch. With a net worth of $107,650, Francis felt financially secure and entitled to spend lavishly during his Grand Tour. Francis, Hannah and son John Jr. left the hotel at Covent Gardens and moved first to Fitzroy Square and then to 44 Queen Square, Bloomsbury. It was in a house on Queen Square about that time that the British government secreted the increasingly insane King George III. The Regency Act of 1811 appointed the Prince of Wales as regent to continue the royal authority and also provided for the care of George III in the hope (alas, not fulfilled) that he would recover.

Francis Lowell again badgered his brother-in-law Samuel P. Gardner to send more money. From London on June 21, Francis wrote, "My money will be exhausted by the time I hear from you." He still had £600 sterling as well as forty guineas in gold, but at the rate he was spending, the money would not last long. To prove the point he gave Gardner a tally of his expenses. From July 23, 1810, the date of their arrival in Liverpool until May 23, 1811, the Lowell family had spent £1234, 17 shillings and 10 pence sterling. From May 23 to June 1, expenses totaled an additional £52, 12 shillings and 8 pence. And, from June 1 to June 24, their expenses came to £132, 13 shillings and 10 pence. The trip thus far cost £1428 sterling. Francis felt obliged to help Benjamin Lincoln who was stranded in Edinburgh "because his brother had failed to send him any money." Francis loaned Lincoln $100 for his trip back to Boston.

During his long tour of Great Britain, Francis Cabot Lowell employed the banking house of Welles & Williams, 13 Finsbury Square, London, as his forwarding address and as his bank. Finsbury Square is close by the home and chapel built by John Wesley, the founder of Methodism. The banker Samuel Williams was an American expatriate. Born in Salem, Massachusetts, and a graduate of Harvard College, Williams was a flour merchant in Boston before he set sail for England in 1796 and established himself in a banking house. Williams was widely respected for advancing the commercial interests of American merchants, offering credit and advice, arranging business ventures and permitting American visitors to Great Britain, such as Francis Cabot Lowell, to collect their mail at his office. Welles & Williams was part of the commercial network linking New England merchants with their counterparts in England. In Lowell's opinion, Samuel Williams was as "safe as the bank of England." Some years later his trusting nature proved to be his undoing as a number of the merchants failed to repay their loans, forcing the banking house of Welles & Williams into bankruptcy. Samuel Williams returned to the United States in 1828, where he died a poor man.

Despite the drain on his resources and his requests to sell property to raise money to continue their journey abroad, Francis and Hannah spent money lavishly. The Francis Cabot Lowell Papers contain dozens of merchant bills for jewelry, dresses, bonnets, shoes, lace, lodgings, wine and port. The Lowells spent £34, 10 shillings at Francis Lambert, Goldsmiths & Jewellers, 2 Coventry Street, with a discount of £2, 3 shillings for paying in cash and £28, 8 shillings and 11 pence at Park & Ker, Milliner & Fancy Dress Maker. While in London Francis bought a gold watch for £31, and a gold seconds watch for £21, 14 shillings and 6 pence. Their accommodation in London cost twelve guineas a week, four times as much as they paid in Edinburgh. With expenses mounting, it was time to leave London. In preparation for their trip through northwestern England, Hannah bought an assortment of morning and evening gowns, bonnets, lace and shoes at a cost of over £100.

TAKING THE WATERS

Leaving London in August 1811, Francis and Hannah made their way to the spa town of Cheltenham, Gloucestershire, on the edge of the Cotswolds. The town gained fame after 1738 when Henry Skillicone popularized the medicinal virtues of his spring. George III, suffering from severe abdominal cramps, visited the town in 1788, making it fashionable. By 1811, when the Lowells visited, the population of Cheltenham exceeded eight thousand, with over five thousand visitors attracted to the spa. The mile-long High Street already boasted several inns, shops, a lending library, assembly rooms and a theater. Francis, Hannah and their son John Jr. stayed at Hall's Boarding House, one of the several boarding houses in the town accepting fashionable clients. The stay gave Francis an opportunity to closely observe wealthy Englishmen at leisure. Writing to Samuel Gardner on August 9, he noted that "the English character is very different from the Scotch or ours. The English seem to like to confine themselves very much to their own circles and not to dislike solitude. This solitude comes from the fact that the aristocracy and gentry spend so much time in their country places, which makes them very unsocial." While more gregarious, the Lowell family from Boston still shared many habits and values in common with the British upper classes as they leisurely made their way from one English spa town to the next in search of pampering and entertainment.

At the start of the nineteenth century there were a number of spa towns in England, including Bath, Cheltenham, Harrogate and Tunbridge Wells, that attracted wealthy clients. Needing to offer more to do than drink the medicinal waters, these towns spawned fashionable shops, coffee houses, tea rooms, pleasure gardens, and theaters. The leisured classes came to see and be seen, attended balls, consulted physicians on illnesses real or imagined, and visited the historic sites in the vicinity. William Makepeace Thackeray, in his masterly book on English manners, *Vanity Fair* (published 1848), assembled some of his leading characters in Cheltenham. After her downfall and the failure of her marriage, Rebecca Sharp moves into "a boarding house at Cheltenham." At the same time the corpulent Jos Sedley arrived to take the waters and display his wealth: "Jos went on at the boarding-house in Cheltenham pretty much as before. He drove his curricle; he drank his claret, he played his rubber; he told his Indian stories, and the Irish widow consoled and flattered him as usual." In May 1816, the authoress Jane Austen, in poor health, followed her fictional characters in *Sense and Sensibility* and *Pride and Prejudice* to seek the cure at Cheltenham.

From Cheltenham, the Lowells moved on to Great Malvern, Worcestershire, a quiet and pretty spa town set among the hills. By 1811, the town already had stagecoaches arriving three days a week from London as well as a daily post to and from London. The three hotels in Great Malvern were the Abbey House, Crown and the Well House. The Lowells chose the Abbey House, paying £5, 8 shillings for a five-night stay (September 13–18). A bottle of sherry (September 13) cost them five shillings and a bottle of port (on September 16 and 18) also cost five shillings. The Lowells paid extra for tea, sugar, cakes, apples and the medicinal waters from the stream at Great Malvern, sold by the glass.

Meanwhile, the news was troubling. A Boston friend wrote that "the war with Great Britain cannot be prevented." In England, Francis observed, people "seem very apprehensive of a war with America from the proceedings of congress." Mary Lee shared her distress in frequent letters to her sister Hannah, telling her that Henry was on his way to Calcutta, leaving her with little money to care for her children.

After Great Malvern the Lowells visited the Shropshire town of Bridgnorth on the Severn River and home to several water-powered cotton mills. They stayed at Hand & Bottle Inn, owned by Mr. R. Dukes. From Bridgnorth, Francis moved on to Oswestry, and then Worcester, most probably to examine their mills. The Lowells crossed into Wales and journeyed to Bristol, the home town of his ancestors. They visited the street where Percival Lowle had his store before he left with his family for America in 1639. The cold weather was coming and Francis considered returning home by the spring of 1812. Having been refused permission to travel to Paris, Francis and Hannah Lowell and their older children John and Susan moved into Duncan House, Clifton, Bristol, leaving sons Francis Cabot Jr. and Edward with Mrs. Grant in Edinburgh. While they stayed in Bristol, Francis and Hannah sent their daughter Susan to Miss Garrat's School for Girls.

Despite his enjoyment in his tour and the pleasure of meeting American friends, Francis continued to fret about money. Writing to his uncle, William Cabot, on January 2, 1812, he complained that "the expenses of living are enormous only partly to the luxury and partly to the rise of every article of necessity." Their accommodations in Bristol cost £10 a week, with five shillings for fire and candles. The Lowells frequently enjoyed wine at dinner at five shillings a bottle. They ate well: one grocery bill was for three partridges (seven shillings), beef (fourteen shillings), lobster (three shillings) and truffles (six shillings).

In Bristol, Francis met Richard Lechmere, who was once the royal collector of taxes at the port of Boston. As a Loyalist, he departed Boston with the British troops in March 1776. Banished from Massachusetts, the Lechmere family lost all its property, including the Brattle Street mansion, land in Cambridge and a rum distillery that Francis Cabot Lowell bought in 1801.

Hannah fretted over her two younger children, who remained in Edinburgh. Edward, a precocious five-year-old, wrote on January 15, 1812, to thank his mother for sending him two shillings. He told her about his daily routine. He woke at seven in the morning, "when a fire is made in our room for us." After breakfast he played games with his brother Francis, sometimes going outside to slide on the ice. "We are learning the Latin verb and Latin vocabulary," and he was learning to speak and write French. Francis, age nine, sent his "love to our father, brother and sister." In another letter, dated February 22, Edward admitted that "we cannot speak many words of French. We get two lessons dancing every day that takes up a great deal of time that we used to have for other lessons." Francis Jr. reported, "The Bishop is again examining us in Catechisms."

Hannah Lowell was distressed by the letter sent March 4 by Janet Wilson, telling her that her son "Francis has a sore throat." The doctor was called and prescribed calamine and senna and advised the boy to "gargle his throat frequently, and get his feet bathed." The fever intensified and the doctor prescribed a gargle "made with the tea of scarlet rose leaves." Having difficulty eating solid foods, Francis was given soft eggs, jelly and water. His nose was stuffed and the exhausted boy slept a good deal. Mrs. Wilson assured Hannah that her son "is the best patient sick boy that can be. He never frets and does everything his nurse bids him do." Scarlet fever was diagnosed but the boy was soon "better in health and spirits." Now he was hungry but the doctor ordered "that he get a little at a time and often; bread and butter is his general fare, and beef tea twice a day with bread." No sooner was Francis Jr. on the mend than his younger brother Edward came down with scarlet fever. The doctor charged two guineas to treat the first child and one guinea for the second. The boys were soon back to their studies. The oldest son, John Jr., was traveling with his parents and being tutored in Bristol. John was studying his Latin and Greek and displayed his skills to his father "when he has the time."

Francis Cabot Lowell worried over Hannah's health, writing home to friends that she is "thin or thinner than when she left America." To restore her health, Hannah, with her two older children, was sent back to Cheltenham, where Francis hoped "the Cheltenham waters will be of service to her." While Hannah was receiving the cure, Francis took a brief trip to Dublin before traveling to Edinburgh to collect the younger boys and take them to Liverpool, where he arranged to meet Hannah and the older children for the trip back to America.

ESPIONAGE OR INNOVATION?

There are numerous references in scholarly journals and books regarding Francis Cabot Lowell's meanderings in Lancashire, visiting textile mills and memorizing the details of the spinning machines, the waterwheels and the power looms. His activities have been described as economic espionage—a one-man spy ring in the disguise of a rich, educated, mild-mannered and seemingly innocent Yankee. Ferris Greenslet, in 1946, writes that "on his journeys back and forth between Edinburgh, Bristol and London [Francis Cabot Lowell] spent several weeks in Lancashire, standing for hours completely absorbed before the machines in the cotton mills, and asking a thousand questions of owners and operatives."[12] He was especially captivated by the improved Cartwright power loom, the brightest jewel of the British textile industry crown, capable of mass-producing high quality textiles, yet simple to operate. The mills Lowell saw in Lancashire and Shropshire were staffed by children as young as ten years working with young women drawn from the orphanages and poor farms of Britain. They worked from sunrise to sunset, seventy hours a week for little pay. In his letters, Francis Lowell briefly described the industrial towns of Britain as dirty places but he had little to say about the human suffering and exploitation. The dozens of letters Lowell wrote while in Great Britain contain only fleeting references to industrial cities, and certainly no detailed account of the textile factories and the machinery. It is likely that Lowell remained especially tight-lipped about his bold plan to build an American textile industry and kept his knowledge of the British machines and factories off the written page—not an easy task for a man accustomed to writing down his thoughts and calculations.

FRANCIS CABOT LOWELL
CONTINUES HIS TOUR

Despite his preoccupation with the high cost of travel in a foreign land, Francis continued to spend lavishly, supporting his younger sons in Edinburgh, his wife and the two older children in Cheltenham and himself in Dublin, not forgetting the cost of travel between Scotland, England and Ireland. There were expenses for tuition, clothing, dancing lessons, amusements and luxury goods. Having recovered her health and in preparation for the trip back to Boston, Hannah and Francis went on a buying spree to furnish their home. The Lowells bought fancy counterpanes, tablecloths, chinaware, cut glass, crockery, knives and forks, carpeting, clothing, gloves and gifts to load on the ship for the journey back to Boston.

Also sent to Boston were the books the Lowell children acquired during their two years in Great Britain. John Jr. carried home books on French, Latin, Greek literature and mathematics, and was prepared for the examination for admission to Harvard. Susan had thirty books in her collection, including a Latin dictionary, English grammar, books on philosophy and agriculture and a collection of the poems of Robert Burns. Francis Cabot Jr. carried home thirty books, including a French dictionary, books in French and Latin, and *The Life of George Washington*. The precocious Edward, only seven years old, had fifty books to take back to Boston, including *Excerpta Latina*, English, French and Latin grammar, books on Scotland, Greece and Egypt, Alexander Pope's translation of Homer's *Iliad* and Cicero, as well as *Embassy to China*, the story of the 1793 voyage of George Macartney in the hope of opening trade between Great Britain and China. As Francis Cabot Lowell planned, his children had indeed benefited from their Scottish education.

At that time, the British upper classes (and wealthy American tourists) were spending freely on luxury foods, accommodations, education, clothes and gold watches while the plight of the working classes was worsening. A domestic servant or a factory worker in a British cotton mill was earning £10 a year, hardly enough to feed, clothe and house a family. Hunger and want in Great Britain were so widespread that the Association for the Relief of the Manufacturing and Labouring Poor was formed in London in May 1812, under the auspices of His Royal Highness, The Duke of York, with the support of the Dukes of Kent, Sussex and Cambridge. The committee reported that "there were numerous cases of distress [due to] scarcity and exorbitant prices of all necessities of life."

Francis Cabot Lowell reassured himself that the extended tour of Great Britain costing some $10,000 was money well spent. He still owned fifty-seven shares in India Wharf worth $32,480 and fifty-seven shares in the Broad Street project worth $7,980. His shares in other properties were worth $18,500. He had personal assets worth $37,264 and the firm of Henry & Joseph Lee owed him $7,370. His net worth was $109,793. During the two years abroad, Francis Lowell became anxious when his boys and Hannah fell ill and he was disappointed at not being allowed to travel to France. But the Lowell family had a splendid time in Great Britain and the children were enriched by their British education. The family gathered together at Liverpool burdened with their many purchases to take home to America. Francis, Hannah and their four children sailed early June 1812 on an American ship bound for Boston.

Francis and his family set out on their Grand Tour intending to follow the route taken by his brother John Jr. in 1803–1805. Both men loved Edinburgh, complained of the cost of living in London and visited the spa towns. Each kept detailed accounts of the expenses, spent much more than planned and wrote urgent letters home with instructions to sell property and assets to raise more funds to continue their luxurious travel. John relied on Francis to manage his affairs in Boston, but Francis used the services of his competent brothers-in-law. Both men visited in England with old family friends who, as Loyalists, had chosen the hard life of exile. John and Francis were Anglophiles, but also intrigued by Napoleon and eager to see his power. Both Francis and John were proud men of Massachusetts and proud to be American, yet they emulated the style of the British wealthy merchant class. Francis desperately wanted to travel to the Continent and follow his brother's trail to France, Italy and Greece. John recorded in lyrical letters the beauty, culture and history of Old Europe. Francis, by contrast, showed little interest in Europe's past or its arts. What most caught his attention was Great Britain's rapidly changing economy, especially the wealth created in the machine-powered textile industry. Part engineer and part entrepreneur, Francis considered whether the benefits of industrialization could come to America without destroying its social fabric.

9

American Textile Industry Before 1814

From the beginning of the colonial history to the early part of the present century, the hand-card, the spinning-wheel and the loom, operated by hand and foot, were almost as common in the farm-houses of this country as the churn or the cheese-press.

William R. Bagnall, 1893

All the fabrics made of cotton were worked on a common loom, in which the shuttle was thrown through the web with one hand, and caught with the other, and the operation repeated for every thread of the woof.

Samuel Batchelder, 1863

On May 13, 1640, the Massachusetts General Court met in Boston to decide how to provide cloth for the people of this remote British colony. "The Court taking into serious consideration the absolute necessity for the raising of the manufacture of linen cloth" decided to distribute flax seed to all the villages of Massachusetts Bay Colony. The court sought to identify men and women skilled in the spinning and weaving of linen, who had spinning wheels, and were willing to teach "the boys and girls in all towns the spinning of yarn." The town of Rowley, inhabited by Goodman Nutt, John Whitney and other spinners and hand weavers from England, became an early center of cloth-making, selling at twelve pence a yard. On September 28, 1720, a committee was formed in Boston "to consider about erecting a spinning school for the instruction of children in this town."

In August 1751 the Society for the Encouraging of Industries and Employing the Poor was formed in Boston. The Legislature of the Province of Massachusetts, two years later, erected Manufactory House on Longacre Street (now Tremont Street), where the poor were encouraged to set up their spinning wheels and handlooms, working with hemp, flax and wool.

From these small beginnings, cloth-making became part of the pattern of life of the settlers in the New World. The wool and flax grown on the farms was spun and woven at home. The wives and daughters cut and sewed the homespun into clothing for the family. Some folks in the eighteenth century made a business of spinning and weaving at home and selling the linen and woolen cloth to their neighbors. The boycott by the thirteen colonies of British textiles and other goods in response to the Townshend Act encouraged the expansion of homespun industries. By "the close of the colonial period homespun manufactures, except in a few plantations districts, were everywhere." Each of these household industries generally employed a few women to make homespun products that were sold to shopkeepers and merchants.

In Great Britain the methods of producing yarn changed dramatically after 1768, when the wig-maker Richard Arkwright invented his spinning frame, using three sets of rollers, and powered by the waterwheel. "At one end of Arkwright's machine," wrote a historian in 1834, "the cotton was put in, an enlarged and knotty mass; the fabrics lying in every direction. At the other end it came out an even and delicate film, with the fibers straightened and the film minutely compressed with a uniform and continuous sliver, ready for the spinner." James Hargreaves patented his spinning jenny and others in England invented ingenious machines, bringing homespun to an end and introducing mass production in the factory. Recognizing the advantage of these labor-saving devices powered by water, the British Parliament in 1774 passed an act forbidding the export of the cotton-spinning machinery. These efficient machines brought about a rapid expansion of textile mills, increasing the demand for raw cotton.

Some people in United States learned about the industrial revolution that was changing the face of Great Britain and sought ways to smuggle the machines across the Atlantic. Yet there were many opposed, including Thomas Jefferson, who wanted to preserve in America an agrarian society based on the small farmer, without manufacturing. It fell to Alexander Hamilton, the secretary of treasury, to convince his fellow Americans of the benefits of combining agriculture with industry. In his *Report on Manufactures*, submitted to the House of Representatives on December 5, 1791, Alexander Hamilton dwelt on the importance of the cotton mill on the British economy.

The cotton mill, he wrote, was the place where "all the different processes for spinning Cotton are performed by means of Machines, which are put into motion by water, and attended chiefly by women and Children: and by a smaller number of persons in the whole, than are requisite in the ordinary mode of spinning. And it is an advantage of great moment that the operations of this mill continue with convenience during the night as well as through the day. The prodigious effect of such a Machine is easily conceived. To this invention is to be attributed essentially the immense progress, which has been so suddenly made in Great Britain, in the various fabrics of cotton."[1]

The United States, argued Alexander Hamilton, should encourage both the "cultivation of the earth" and the manufacture of goods. Factories making cloth, shoes and farm equipment would free the farmer "to pursue exclusively the cultivation of his farm [without the need to devote] part of his labor to the fabrication of clothing and other articles." The addition of industry to agriculture would provide more opportunities for employment, encourage immigration, stimulate enterprise, offer greater scope for the exercise of talent and provide farmers with a domestic market for their cotton, tobacco, flax and wool. Manufacturing at home would render the United States independent, and no longer captive to the policies of other nations. To establish American industry, Hamilton advocated subsidies and the use of tariffs against imports. The imposition of tariffs would provide a major source of revenue for the nation. Hamilton was well aware of the fledgling cotton enterprises in Beverly, Massachusetts, and Pawtucket, Rhode Island, and wanted them to succeed and set an example for the coming industrial revolution.

After leaving Boston in the summer of 1794, the English visitor Henry Wansey made his leisurely way through Massachusetts to Connecticut, New York and New Jersey, shrewdly assessing the readiness of the United States to enter the industrial age. Waltham (the future home of the Boston Manufacturing Company) was then "a struggling village [in which] some home-spun American cloth [was] made, very stout, and large spun, but serviceable; they could fix no price to it per yard." In the town of Spencer he visited a clothier "who mills and dresses home-spun woolen cloth for housewives in the neighborhood." In Connecticut, he visited a woolen manufactory "much on the decay and hardly able to maintain itself. I saw two carding machines, working by water, of a very inferior construction." At Northford, thirty miles from Hartford, he visited a struggling silk factory and in New Haven he toured a mill with two spinning machines "of good and complete workmanship, but the cotton yarn, which was the spinning, was not better than candlestick yarn. The cards were very badly made." Similarly, the cotton mills in New York and Paterson, New Jersey, were primitive. America in 1794 was stuck in the age of craftsmanship such as homespun, while British manufacturing was transformed by the industrial revolution. Great Britain kept its lead by refusing "to sell us any of her new machines, and prohibited the exportation of parts, plans, or skilled artisans."[2]

From these observations, Henry Wansey concluded that "the ability of the United States to manufacture cannot keep pace, by any means, with her increasing population; at least for a century. It therefore follows, that she must increase in her demand for foreign manufactures, and the Americans generally acknowledge that no country can supply them as well as Great Britain."[3] For the year 1792, Great Britain sold goods to the United States worth $15,285,428, while the United States sold goods to Great Britain for $9,363,416. With her growing population and an economy based on farming, Wansey foresaw America's dependence on Great Britain for manufactured goods to continue for many years to come.

ELI WHITNEY AND HIS COTTON GIN

It fell to Francis Cabot Lowell to guide New England into the industrial age, and to Eli Whitney to shape the economy of the South with his invention of the cotton gin. Whitney was born in 1765 in the town of Westborough, some forty miles southwest of Newburyport, the son of a farmer. Eli worked as a laborer and schoolteacher before entering Yale University. Upon graduation in 1792 (the year before Lowell graduated from Harvard), Whitney set sail for South Carolina, where he met Catharine, the widow of the Revolutionary War hero General Nathanael Greene of Rhode Island, and mother of his five children. While visiting her plantation, Mulberry Grove, he learned of the difficulty in separating the cottonseed from the white cotton fiber. The countless hours spent by plantation slaves removing the seed from the fiber made the crop uneconomical. Whitney set to work to invent a machine to separate the seed from the cotton fiber. Each of his cotton gins generated fifty pounds of seedless cotton fiber per day, giving the South the highly profitable crop it was seeking.

Before 1784, America exported to England only eleven million pounds of cotton each year. Eli Whitney's cotton gin was as important to the cultivation of cotton as the Arkwright water frame was in the production of cotton thread. The growing of cotton spread from the Carolinas into Georgia, Alabama and Mississippi, greatly expanding the plantation system and the demand for slaves. In the year 1801, the American South exported twenty-one million pounds of cotton. By 1820, cotton exports reached 128 million pounds, and by 1860, cotton exports exceeded 1,800 million pounds. The economies of the American South and the British Midlands were intertwined and gave the South the confidence to fight a civil war

Eli Whitney (1765–1828) was born in Westborough, Massachusetts. After graduating from Yale he traveled to the South. There, in 1793, he invented the cotton gin, which revolutionized the cultivation of cotton and expanded slavery. Whitney's invention gave the South its great cash crop. ("The textile industries of the United States including sketches and notices of cotton, woolen, silk and linen manufactures in the colonial period," by William R. Bagnall, copyright 1893 by Sarah F. Bagnall [The Riverside Press, Cambridge, 1893], 198. The Riverside Press, Cambridge, MA. Electrotyped and printed by H. O. Houghton & Company.)

against the Union. The raw cotton from the South supplied most of the needs of the English and French mills. In Britain, one-fifth of the population was dependent on the textile industry, and half of all British exports were in finished cloth. In the South, the value of cotton lands increased steeply and cotton served as security for loans, bonds and mortgages.

THE BEVERLY COTTON MANUFACTORY

In 1785 Thomas Somers, a midshipman in the British navy, arrived in Massachusetts hoping to interest local capitalists in the manufacture of cotton textiles. He claimed to be "a perfect master of the weaving in the specialised manner" and expert in the production of muslins, calico, jeans and handkerchiefs. Somers claimed to have recently arrived from England with "the descriptions and models" of the remarkable machines that had revolutionized the British textile industry, and offered to "procure machines for carding and spinning cotton." Somers succeeded in interesting a number of the enterprising capitalists of Beverly, Massachusetts, including the brothers John, Andrew and George Cabot, Israel Thorndike, Isaac Chapman, Moses Brown (brother-in-law to Israel Thorndike) and Henry Higginson (a relative of the Cabots and the Lowells). George Cabot joined the venture, believing that the domestic manufacture of textiles would save the nation "large sums [that] are yearly sent out of the country" for imported cloth.

Before the Revolutionary War, the Cabot brothers, Israel Thorndike, Joseph Lee and other merchants of Beverly, Massachusetts, grew rich on the trade with Spain. During the war, these merchants converted a number of their merchant ships into privateers. Using Bilboa as their port in Europe their privateer ships *True American*, *Oliver Cromwell*, *Pilgrim* and others attacked British vessels and sold the booty. After the war, John and Andrew Cabot used some of their new wealth to buy the extensive farm in Wolfenborough, New Hampshire, confiscated from the royalist governor John Wentworth who had fled into exile. These merchants, and now country gentlemen, were ready to expand into new ventures.

In June 1786, the Cabot brothers and their associates petitioned the Massachusetts legislature to incorporate the Beverly Cotton Manufactory. Because of the high cost of the venture they asked the legislature for financial help but were awarded only £500. The Cabot brothers and their partners went ahead with the project using $14,000 of their own money to build the factory, buy the machinery and pay the workers.

For the sum of £80 and five shillings the company bought a six-acre lot outside the village of Beverly and on it built a large three-story brick mill. In January 1789, the Beverly Manufactory began converting raw cotton into yarn to be woven on hand-powered looms. The owners claimed that their products were "equal in quality to any made in Europe." The raw cotton came from the West Indies and South America in exchange for dried fish. Nine women were employed in the laborious task of picking off the black cottonseeds from the white fiber. The factory had two cylinder machines, capable of carding 159 pounds of cotton a day, and 636 spindles. It employed thirty-one other workers, capable of producing ten thousand yards of hand-loomed textiles a year. The power to the machines in the factory came from a pair of horses in the basement moving in circles to turn the upright shaft. When the horses went too fast, the supervisor Mr. Somers stuck his head out the window and yelled, "Hold it there. Not so fast."

In 1789, President George Washington was on a triumphal tour of New England. On Friday, October 30, he breakfasted with George Cabot and was invited to inspect the cotton factory. Washington showed a great interest in the Beverly cotton mill. His diary entry for that day notes that his party left Salem, a town of some ten thousand, and "after passing Beverly two miles we came to a cotton manufactory, which seems to be carrying on with spirit by the Cabbots (principally). In this manufactory they have the newly invented carding and spinning machines. The Cotton is prepared by these machines by being first (lightly) drawn to a thread on the common wheel; there is also another machine for doubling and twisting the threads for particular cloths, this also does many at a time. For winding the cotton from the Spindles and preparing it for the warp there is a Reel which expedites the work greatly. A number of looms (15 or 16) were at work with spring shuttles; which do more than double work. In short, the whole seems perfect and the cotton stuffs, which they turn out are excellent of their kind, warp and filling, both are now of cotton."[4] The thread and cloth produced in the factory were sold by the Beverly firm of Baker & Allen and by "Francis Cabot of Salem who sold corduroys, royal ribs, thicksett, stockinette and rib delures, wholesale and retail, and all made in Beverly."[5]

Less than three months after visiting the Beverly Cotton Manufactory, President Washington gave his first annual message to Congress on January 8, 1790, in which he spoke of the need to advance manufacturing "by the introduction of new and useful inventions from abroad [and] the exertions of skills and genius in producing them at home." Washington contended that the safety and interests of a free people requires "that they should promote such manufactories, as tend to render them independent of others for essentials, particularly for military supplies."[6]

There were problems at the Beverly mill from the beginning. The concept of the Beverly mill was only a small advance from the traditional homespun. The company was undercapitalized and a number of the owners withdrew their support. Thomas Somers proved less capable than he claimed. Working without proper design plans, the owners spent $1,100 on the construction of a carding machine but it functioned poorly. The factory lacked skilled workers and the power produced by the two horses moving in circles proved inefficient and slow. Output was meager, amounting to only 7,500 yards of cloth produced from May 1, 1788, to August 1, 1789, yielding only £775 sterling. Debts were piling up and the Beverly Cotton Manufactory was unable to compete in quality or price with the British and Indian imports.

Despite these failings George Cabot wrote proudly to his friend Alexander Hamilton, secretary of the treasury, claiming that his was the first cotton factory in America. On September 6, 1791, George Cabot wrote again, telling Hamilton of the progress made at the Beverly Cotton Manufactory: "Almost four years have expired since a number of gentlemen in this place associated for the purpose of establishing a manufactory of cotton goods, of the kind usually exported from Manchester, for men's wear." Due to the lack of skilled workers, the owners hired "a number of Europeans, chiefly Irish" to run the machines. But, Cabot insisted, "We must at last depend on the people of the country alone for a solid and permanent establishment." By 1792, nearly all forty of the workers "are natives of the vicinity." Cabot listed the machines at work in the manufactory. These included a carding engine, nine spinning jennies, one doubling and twisting machine, one stubbing machine, one warping mill and two cutting frames.[7]

The factory had more difficulties after George Cabot withdrew from manufacturing to focus on importing cheap cloth made in India. After dabbling in textiles, George Cabot entered the trade with St. Petersburg, Riga and other Baltic ports. By 1796 as many as fifty ships from Massachusetts and New York were regularly sailing to the Baltic, carrying pepper, sugar, coffee, cotton and tobacco. George Cabot became prominent in Federalist politics and was appointed by Alexander Hamilton as a director of the Bank of the United States. The last of the Cabot owners sold the Beverly Cotton Manufactory in 1798 to Samuel Blanchard for the paltry sum of $2,630.29. Blanchard had no more success than the Cabots and after a long struggle the Beverly Cotton Manufactory finally shut down in 1807. Six years later the building and land were sold.[8]

The Beverly Cotton Manufactory in 1788 was the first cotton textile mill incorporated in the Commonwealth of Massachusetts. The second was incorporated in 1807. After 1808 six more cotton mills were incorporated in the state before the incorporation in 1813 of the Boston Manufacturing Company in Waltham.

Francis Cabot Lowell was well aware that his relatives John, Andrew and George Cabot were partners in the Beverly Cotton Manufactory in a failed effort to manufacture cotton textiles in America. The company was underfunded, the owners lacked sufficient knowledge and experience, the source of power was feeble, the workers untrained and the machinery defective. Francis Cabot Lowell did not repeat their mistakes. His concept of cotton textile manufacture was a quantum leap ahead of existing methods. When he was ready to build his cotton factory at Waltham, Lowell made sure that he had a thorough business plan, sufficient capital, a reliable source of power, a capable workforce and, above all, good machinery.

THE BOSTON TOP-SAIL MANUFACTORY

The legislature of Massachusetts in 1780 noting that large sums of money were spent on the importation of sailcloth, decided to support a local industry by paying eight shillings "for every piece of Top-sail-Duck and other stouter sail-cloth, manufactured within the Commonwealth, being Thirty yards in length and Twenty-eight inches in breadth." This offer was incentive enough for a group of eight men, mostly merchants, to raise the money and set up factories on Essex Street and Nassau Street in Boston. Among these men were John and Jonathan Amory (father and uncle to Rebecca Amory, who in 1793 became Mrs. John Lowell Jr.) and Frederick William Geyer. The sailcloth factories offered employment "to a great number of persons, especially females, who now eat the bread of idleness, whereby they may gain an honest living." President George Washington visited the Boston Top-Sail Manufactory during his tour of Boston in 1789. He recorded the event in his diary October 28. There were "twenty-eight looms at work, and fourteen girls spinning with both hands. Children (girls) turn the wheels for them. They are the daughters of decayed families; none other are admitted." Sales of the domestic cloth were not brisk as local ship owners had a prejudice "against domestic manufacture." The Boston Top-Sail Manufactory closed in 1790 and the title of the building and land became the property of attorney John Lowell Jr.[9]

MOSES BROWN AND SAMUEL SLATER

Historians argue whether Beverly, Massachusetts, or Pawtucket, Rhode Island, was the site of America's first cotton manufactory. The Quaker Moses Brown of Providence, Rhode Island, with his brothers Nicholas, John and Joseph, made their fortunes on overseas trade, including the slave trade. The Brown Brothers—the fifth generation of Browns in Rhode Island—were the largest mercantile house in Providence and one of the largest in all of New England. It was now time to give something back to his community. Moses Brown endowed the Rhode Island College, later renamed Brown University. Still eager to make his contribution, he invited his son-in-law William Almy to join him in setting up a cotton manufactory. The two men constructed some crude devices, based upon their limited knowledge of Richard Arkwright's spinning machines. Making little progress, Brown invited Samuel Slater to come to Rhode Island and build a cotton mill on the Pawtucket River and "install machinery of the English type."

Moses Brown chose the right man for the job. Samuel Slater hailed from Derbyshire, where he worked for Jedediah Strutt, a partner to Richard Arkwright, and gained a full knowledge of the Arkwright water press. Slater saw an opportunity for himself in the New World, despite the British ban on the emigration of skilled artisans. Disguising himself as a farm laborer and not even telling his plan to his mother, he left home for London. On September 1, 1789, he boarded a ship for New York, arriving there sixty-six days later. Still in his early twenties, he hoped to use his knowledge of the Arkwright machine and accepted an invitation from Moses Brown to come to Pawtucket and run the crude mill Brown and Almy built. Slater arrived in the village on January 1, 1790, and finding that the machinery was useless, offered to build from scratch a copy of the Arkwright machine for installation in the factory. Slater's machine was "the simplest form of the Arkwright spinning frame driven by water power." Slater also built a drawing and roving frame and carding machines.

It took many anxious months before the machines were built and the factory was ready to spin yarn. The raw cotton came to Providence packed in bails and was taken into homes where children as young as four years removed the seeds and loosened the cotton by hand. The cotton fiber was spread out on a whipping machine and beaten with whipping sticks to shake out the dirt and leave the fibers fluffy and light. The picked cotton was then taken to the mill where small children spread out the fibers on the carding machines. The weaving was done on hand looms, producing coarse cloth. The factory started full-scale production late in 1791, with nine children as laborers. By 1801, Brown and Almy employed over one hundred children, aged four to ten years, and several adult supervisors. The Pawtucket factory had only seventy-two spindles, far fewer than the 636 spindles at the Beverly Cotton Manufactory. In the Pawtucket mill there were "many hand processes, but the principal steps of carding and spinning were performed by machines, and the machines worked successfully. The superiority of the machinery made the Providence firm for several years, the only successful machine spinners of cotton in the country."[10]

The Rhode Island merchant Moses Brown, with his son-in-law William Almy, established a cotton spinning mill in Pawtucket. ("The textile industries of the United States including sketches and notices of cotton, woolen, silk and linen manufactures in the colonial period," by William R. Bagnall, copyright 1893 by Sarah F. Bagnall [The Riverside Press, Cambridge, 1893], 146. The Riverside Press, Cambridge, MA. Electrotyped and printed by H. O. Houghton & Company.)

In Pawtucket, Samuel Slater boarded with the family of Oziel Wilkerson, where he met and married his daughter Hannah. She made him a devoted and useful wife and was the mother of his ten children. With his family and reputation growing Samuel Slater built several more cotton mills along the banks of the Pawtucket and Blackstone Rivers. A number of his workers left to set up their own mills. These early mills spun cotton

*The Englishman Samuel Slater (1768–1835) arrived in America in
1789 and offered his knowledge of the Arkwright spinning frame
to Brown and Almy. Slater introduced to the United States the skill
of spinning cotton by water power. ("The textile industries of the
United States including sketches and notices of cotton, woolen,
silk and linen manufactures in the colonial period," by William R.
Bagnall, copyright 1893 by Sarah F. Bagnall [The Riverside Press,
Cambridge, 1893], frontispiece. The Riverside Press, Cambridge,
MA. Electrotyped and printed by H. O. Houghton & Company.)*

yarn for sale to home weavers and hand loom operators. This combination of a small spinning factory and homespun cloth-making became
known as the Rhode Island system. Until 1815, these small mills lacked
power looms and depended on home weavers to complete the job of making textiles.

Others followed the example set by Samuel Slater. The Newburyport Manufactory opened in 1794, followed by the Warwick Spinning
Mill in Rhode Island and the Cecil Manufacturing Company in Elkton,
Maryland. Three English brothers—James, Arthur and John Scholfield—
opened their mill in Haverhill, Massachusetts. In nearby North Andover,

Nathaniel Stevens started his mill. In 1804, Charles Robbins, formerly in the employ of Samuel Slater, moved north to New Ipswich, New Hampshire, in response to an invitation from the town's leading citizen, Charles Barrett, to open the first textile mill in that state. The mill, powered by the Souhegan River, caught the attention of the town's lawyer Benjamin Champney and, in 1810, Samuel and Nathan Appleton, who bought shares in the company. The Appleton brothers were born in New Ipswich but had long since moved to Boston, where they had become wealthy merchants. Nathan Appleton in 1813 partnered with Francis Cabot Lowell in the Boston Manufacturing Company.

Inventors and entrepreneurs in the United States were aware of the profound changes in Great Britain and other European countries stemming from the industrial revolution. Like saplings, small factories sprung up to make yarn, shoes, carriages and wagons, saddles, nails, clocks, silverware, and all other manner of goods. From 1787 until 1807, dozens of small spinning mills opened along the rivers of New England, Pennsylvania and Maryland as merchants moved their capital into domestic manufacturing.

OTHER SPINNING MILLS

In 1789, William Pollard, an Englishman who had settled in Philadelphia, made some improvements on an Arkwright spinning machine and was later awarded one of America's first patents under the Patent Act of 1790. Pollard lacked the money to exploit his patent and turned to John Nicholson, a wealthy entrepreneur, who hatched the grandiose plan to build a manufacturing town at the falls on the Schuylkill River, a few miles from Philadelphia. Here Nicholson and Pollard installed the water-powered spinning machines, by which time Nicholson was deeply in debt, and the mill failed. In 1797, James Davenport opened the Globe Mill on Second Street, Philadelphia, for spinning and weaving flax. In 1805, John Lee of Byfield, Massachusetts, clandestinely shipped cotton machinery from England marked as "hardware" to his cotton mill. In 1810, the Union Manufactory Company opened near Baltimore with a capital of $1 million, and powered by the Patapsco River.

These early industrial experiments took place at a time of profound political change. After two terms, George Washington declined to continue as president. On March 4, 1797, John Adams was inaugurated as president in Congress Hall, Philadelphia, with Thomas Jefferson serving as vice president. Adams kept most members of George Washington's cabinet, including Timothy Pickering serving as secretary of state. The Adams administration was heavily Federalist, favoring close ties with

Great Britain and against revolutionary France. John Adams served only one term, and was defeated in 1801 by Thomas Jefferson, who had a vastly different view of America's place in the world.

ESSEX JUNTO

In April 1778 a group of prominent lawyers and merchants from Salem, Beverly and Newburyport met in Ipswich, Massachusetts to determine how to use their influence to shape national events. They were dubbed the Essex Junto and over the years this little band became a powerful force in the Federalist Party. Most prominent among them were Theophilus Parsons, Timothy Pickering, Stephen Higginson, Judge John Lowell, Jonathan Jackson and George Cabot. Later, John Lowell Jr., known as "The Rebel," joined this influential group. Their hero was Alexander Hamilton, who advocated a strong central government, a national bank, fiscal responsibility and the rule of the aristocracy. The Essex Junto supported close ties with Great Britain and viewed the Louisiana Purchase as a threat to the centrality of the "good old Thirteen States" and in particular to the influence of New England. The Essex Junto, through the Federalist Party, strongly opposed Jefferson's embargo of 1807 and Madison's declaration in 1812 of war against Great Britain.

EMBARGO SPURS DOMESTIC MANUFACTURING

At the start of the nineteenth century the cotton textile industry of America was limited to the slowly failing Beverly Cotton Manufactory, four spinning mills near Pawtucket, Rhode Island, and three in Connecticut. Expansion of the domestic industry was slow. The Embargo of 1807 dealt the American cotton textile industry a "stunning blow." With ships and goods banned from leaving the New England ports sales decreased, unsold textiles piled up at the factories, mills closed and workers laid off. The price of cloth fell, leaving mill owners in a state of despair. However, with overseas trade severely curtailed, a number of merchants were willing to risk their capital in opening cotton mills in the hope of developing a domestic market. In 1809, there were fifty-seven spinning mills in New England; increasing to 113 by 1810 and 165 by 1815.[11] Rhode Island, with thirty-three cotton mills and 30,663 spindles by 1812, was ahead of Massachusetts with its twenty mills and 17,371 spindles, and New Hampshire's twelve mills.[12] These small spinning mills were established in villages along the rivers, employing whole families, including their small children to make the yarn, which was then sold to hand weavers working out of their homes. In Philadelphia homespun with flax and wool were used to make coarse garments, while imported cotton cloth was reserved for finer clothing.

The nascent industry looked to the growing population of the West for fresh markets, not an easy choice before the coming of the canals and railroads. In wagons and on horseback, New England textiles slowly found their way to Buffalo and on to the Midwest. Writing in the *Kentucky Gazette*, April 10, 1810, Dorothy Distaff called for a concerted effort to replace imported cloth with homespun: "A hundred thousand spinning wheels put into motion by female hands," she wrote, "will do as much towards establishing our independence as a hundred thousand of the best militia men in America." Efforts to organize a large industry based on homespun cloth were not successful. The War of 1812 further disrupted international trade but with a growing market at home, more entrepreneurs were willing to put their money into the domestic textile industry.

The first generation of American cotton mills evolved but a short distance from the handicraft stage of development. These spinning mills still depended on the local supply of labor, employing families and their children. The spun thread was then sold to hand weavers working out of their homes.

Francis Cabot Lowell was hardly alone in his efforts to build a cotton textile industry in America. His system, however, differed markedly from Philadelphia homespun or the craft-factory model used in Rhode Island. Lowell's new industrial order "came to dominate the cotton industry [and] marked a radical departure from all that had gone before."[13] In his 1864 book, Samuel Batchelder contrasts Francis Cabot Lowell's system with Samuel Slater's Rhode Island system. Slater ran small spinning mills, using copies of the English machinery, while Lowell developed new machines for his large factory and did spinning and weaving under power all under one roof. Slater used the labor of local families while Lowell employed healthy young women, housed and fed at the company's expense and paid wages in cash. Slater adhered to the old craft system while Lowell built labor-saving machines that required only a few weeks of training to master the repetitive tasks. Slater built small mills with a small number of spindles, while the mill at Waltham contained thousands of spindles and several looms watched over by hundreds of workers. The conservative Slater clung to his tried-and-true methods of production while Lowell leaped ahead with his modern factory using the machines of mass production. At Lowell's mill raw cotton came in at one end, and finished cloth left at the other.

The superiority of the Waltham-Lowell system became obvious at the end of the War of 1812. The small Rhode Island–style mills failed without the help of high tariffs to stem the flow of Indian and English imports, while the Waltham-Lowell system expanded greatly. Efficiency of scale, and advanced technology ensured the success of the Waltham mill and later the giant mills built along the banks of the Merrimack River. The Waltham-Lowell system was the prototype for the American factory of the nineteenth century.[14]

10

Return to Boston

[Boston was] more beautiful than anything I had seen in my absence.

Hannah Lowell, August 1812

[Francis Cabot Lowell was] always studying some scheme of development to benefit his fellow men . . . risking his fortune and his credit.

Colonel Henry Lee, 1905

On June 18, 1812, President James Madison responded to the pressure of the "war hawks" Henry Clay and Richard M. Johnson of Kentucky and John C. Calhoun of South Carolina by declaring war on Great Britain. "Mr. Madison's War" was supported in the House of Representatives by seventy-nine to forty-nine votes. The South Atlantic and Western states together with Pennsylvania voted for a declaration of war while most of New England, together with New York, New Jersey and Delaware, voted against. National pride, resentment over the fall in value of grain and rice, and a planned land grab of Canada carried the day. The vote largely followed party lines, with most of the Republicans voting for war and the Federalists to a man voting against. America was poorly prepared for its war for honor, backed by an army of fewer than seven thousand regular troops and a navy of only a few dozen men-of-war, to take on Great Britain's 250,000 men under arms and the mighty Royal Navy of a thousand ships. A vote in the House to also declare war against France lost only by a narrow margin. One week after America declared war on Great Britain, Napoleon's *Grande Armee* attacked Russia.

Francis Cabot Lowell and his family left the port of Liverpool only days before the news of the American declaration of war reached London. The family cleared Liverpool without incident but their American ship *Minerva* was halted by a British squadron off Nova Scotia and taken to Halifax. The British twice searched their baggage in Halifax, convinced that Francis had hidden drawings of the remarkable power looms and spinning machines he had seen in Britain. But Francis had committed all to memory and no drawings or calculations were uncovered.[1]

Even though the family was well treated in Halifax, Francis and Hannah were determined to return to Boston as soon as possible. Francis "hired at great expense a small dirty vessel to take us from Halifax to Boston." The captain assured them that the journey would take only five days but, wrote Hannah, "the first thing the captain did was to run us aground at a place which he passed about twelve times a year. He lost all self-possession. Our confidence in him was entirely destroyed and I don't think we would have had the courage to proceed if we did not have our own captain that we set out from Liverpool. Mr. Lowell had exerted him in his favour to get liberty for him to return home. We endured many unpleasant circumstances [until] we had the pleasure of beholding our native land after a sail of ten days." After all the trials at sea, Hannah Lowell found the sight of Boston "more beautiful than anything I had seen in my absence. The joy of finding myself *at home* [her emphasis] was overwhelming."[2]

On September 4, 1812, Francis Cabot Lowell sent a letter to the Herculaneum Pottery Company, 3 Duke Street, Liverpool, telling them about some problems with the shipment sent to Boston. The pottery company sold to the Lowells a complete set of chinaware No. 809, together with twelve extra cups and twelve saucers. When Francis and Hannah unpacked the crates in Boston they found nothing broken "except one soup tureen and one plate, but a large part of the tea set had been omitted." Only seventeen teacups, twelve saucers, six coffee cups and one teapot had arrived. The set of dishes as well as the additional cups and saucers cost £5, 19 shillings and 6 pence. Francis asked the company to make whole the order.

Despite the war between Great Britain and the United States, ships still sailed and the mail was delivered. At the start of the war, the British government was lenient with New England in the hope that the region would not engage in hostilities and would even side with Britain and Canada in the conflict. Though Congress (on April 4, 1812) forbade all ships in American ports from trading with Britain, this law was repeatedly circumvented. Early in June, the Massachusetts House resolved by a two-thirds majority that the war against Britain was "in the highest degree impolitic, unnecessary and ominous, and that the great body of the people of this Commonwealth are decidedly opposed to the measure, which they do not believe to be demanded by the honor or interest of the nation." Massachusetts was determined "to do nothing in active support of the offensive war." The governor of the Commonwealth, Caleb Strong, went so far as to refuse to call up the militia to join the federal army against the British.

During the War of 1812 some trade and the passage of letters continued into and out of Boston. The *New Hazard* under Captain Endicott arrived in the port of Boston carrying barrels of molasses to be made into rum. The *Rambler* arrived from Canton carrying a cargo of silk textiles, hand-kerchiefs, ribbons, teas and six thousand walking sticks. The Russian vessel *Alexander* arrived after a fifty-one-day voyage from Lisbon carrying salt, iron and corkwood. The *Hannibal*, under Captain Burgess, brought two thousand letters from Great Britain. In this manner the merchant houses of Benjamin C. Ward, Phineas Foster, Israel Thorndike, Thomas Wigglesworth and Francis Cabot Lowell sent out dried fish and lumber and received manufactured goods, even from the declared enemies of their country.

Anne MacVicar Grant addressed a letter to Hannah Lowell dated August 12, 1812, not realizing that the Lowell family had already sailed for the United States. The letter was a mixture of literary gossip and social tidbits involving some of the people Hannah met during her stay in Edinburgh. Dropping names of famous personages was Anne MacVicar Grant's style. Now that she was no longer looking after the Lowell children, Anne MacVicar Grant had agreed "to have two young ladies placed in my care." The first was a fourteen-year-old lass, the granddaughter of Sir James Grant. The girl was "pretty, artless, and very engaging in her modest simplicity, though very little informed." The second girl was the daughter of a colonel now stationed in the West Indies. She was good-tempered, amiable and "I see she has heart." Mrs. Grant informed Hannah that Miss Apreece "is married to the celebrated Sir. Humphrey Davy, who is considered to be the first chemist in Europe." Anne liked him, finding him "very natural and very amusing." Mrs. Grant concluded her letter with a subtle comment about the war between the United States and Great Britain. Claiming that she was too poorly informed about the war, she decided "to say nothing of war and peace." However, she "was full of suspense about the rumoured victory [of the Duke of Wellington] in Spain."

Hannah Lowell regularly sent letters and received replies from friends in the United Kingdom. An anguished relative in England inquired about their incarceration in Halifax and the confiscation of some of their goods: "A most unfortunate event. I fear you will suffer the loss of lots of little things you had been collecting in Europe." Despite the war, the many letters sent in 1812–1813 to and from the Lowells were, by the standards of those times, promptly delivered, permitting the friends to share the pleasures and concerns of family life with only an occasional reference to the war that separated their nations.[3]

Hannah wrote on October 13, 1813, to Anne MacVicar Grant at 2 East Harriot's Row, Edinburgh, saying that Francis Cabot had again gone to the spa in New York: "He has greatly recovered his health by using these means, together with strict attention to his diet, and I trust he will yet be a hearty old man." Her health "is now better than for several years." Hannah's letter sent in October 1813 to Janet Wilson, also of Edinburgh, received a long delayed response. Janet explained, writing March 23, 1814, that she had been ill with a "melancholy disease I was threatened with. I had for years observed a small lump in my breast, which I very soon let my brother, who is a doctor, see. He told me if it increased fast and adhered to the skin to let him know. This continued gradually for four years and last year on February 7, I went to him and he performed an operation. It was best to submit patiently to what must be." The pain during the operation and after was severe and her arm became swollen. Putting her faith in God, the pain and swelling gradually lessened and Janet reported that she was optimistic for a full recovery.

After two years abroad and the harrowing experience of capture on the high seas and detention in Halifax, the Lowells were delighted to be home again. The Lowell family quickly resumed the style of living befitting their income and class. They spent the summer at their country home in Waltham, making it necessary for Francis to travel through Boston Neck, a journey of more than one hour each way on horseback. The Lowells were proud Americans but deeply troubled by the war against their beloved Britain. As Hannah wrote, "The political state of our own country makes us very somber."

The continuation of the war curtailed more and more the passage of trade. American merchant ships carrying sugar, coffee, molasses, rum, flour, onions, tobacco, cotton, gin or soap were increasingly captured on the high seas and escorted to Halifax, Nova Scotia. The goods were confiscated and the vessels released only on payment of costs. Among the twelve hundred American vessels captured by the British during the War of 1812 were the *Ambitious*, carrying a cargo of 804 barrels of flour; the *Black Swan*, carrying lumber and dry goods from Boston to Havana; and the *Bunker Hill*, out of Newburyport on its way to New York, carrying boxes of chocolate, eight barrels of pork, ten barrels of rum and one hundred handspikes. The 320-ton *Montezuma* left Boston for Cadiz with a cargo of codfish, candles, tobacco, beef and cloves and was captured by the British. On March 26, 1813, the 457-ton *Volant* from Boyone to Boston was stripped of its cargo of brandy, wine, silks and dry goods. The 181-

ton schooner *Two Brothers* was captured between Bar Harbor and Boston with its cargo of lumber. The sixty-nine-ton schooner *Sarah* sailing from St. Bartholomew to Boston was captured with its cargo of molasses. These and many other losses severely affected the New England merchants who had their fortunes tied up in the ships, cargoes and crews.

THE LOWELLS AND THEIR WORLD

The economic upheaval claimed the property of Stephen Higginson and in London his brother Henry Higginson was forced into bankruptcy. Henry Lee, brother-in-law to Francis Cabot Lowell, set out to London to borrow the funds to buy Indian cloth for sale in the United States. Francis and Hannah Lowell were not greatly affected by the war. "Many of us," she wrote in September 1812, "who possessed incomes equal to our wishes, are obliged to talk of and practice economy much more than we like. I do not think that our situation will be worse than it is at present and we hope for some change that will increase our income. In any event we are safe. Mr. Lowell's own brother has more than a competency." Francis Lowell wrote demanding letters to customers who were in arrears. To Daniel Luce he wrote on August 21, 1813, "I should have received some money from you by now. I know that times are hard. I have not therefore expected all my money from you. You had better have a settlement with me."

The five-year period from his return to Boston until his death (1812–1817) was one of intense activity for Francis Cabot Lowell. He continued his activities as a merchant, helped establish the New England Bank and the Mechanics Bank, and undertook the immense task of fulfilling his great vision of a profitable cotton textile industry in America. During these years, he suffered disappointments and losses and the decline of his health. Yet he persevered, filling his days with letter writing, keeping the books, negotiating, calculating, planning, experimenting and traveling until the very end of his life.

After two years abroad the Lowell children had difficulties adjusting to life in Boston. The oldest son John Jr. began his studies at Harvard in August 1812 but "got poisoned I suppose by ivy, when walking in the fields." With his arms, legs and face swollen, John left college and came home to be nursed by his mother, already burdened by her husband's declining health. Their daughter Susanna, entering adolescence, was already taller than her mother. Little Edward so worried his parents that they sent him to live with a tutor in Newburyport. While abroad, it was Francis who was anxious over the health of his wife. Soon after their return to Boston, Hannah had cause to worry about his. Francis, she wrote, was "quite out of health [and had] frequent attacks of indisposition." During these attacks he was generally able "to keep about the house but was sometimes confined for a day to bed." His suffered so badly from indigestion that her "attention to him occupied much of my time and about all of my thoughts." So severe was Francis' condition that they seriously considered going "to a more southern climate for the winter."

From 1810 onward, the town of Boston kept detailed records of the causes of death. Unspecified infantile diseases accounted for one-fifth of deaths, while, on average, consumption (tuberculosis) accounted for one in four of all deaths each year. Vaccination greatly reduced the mortality from small pox but epidemics of typhus, yellow fever, measles and whooping cough frightened the people, some of whom fled to the country. Mary Lee, Hannah's youngest sister, wrote in her journal on July 5, 1813, of her concerns over the health of her brother-in-law. Hannah and Francis, she recorded, "have just returned from Ballston. The water did not suit Mr. Lowell and he seems to me as sick as before he left home. He is indeed a very sick man and will, I fear, not continue long with us unless there is a great change produced. His loss would be a very great one to us all; a man of such sound judgment, good sense and friendly feelings; will be a prodigious loss to the circle in which he moves. No one who knows him can feel insensible to his merits; which are as sterling pure gold. It seems to me Hannah could not support such an event, but with this trial is also sent the ability to sustain it. I pray that she may not be called to it, for she as to myself, should hope that the termination of their lives might be at the same moment. Good night, my dear Hannah, good night."

Living so close to sisters, brothers, uncles, aunts, nieces and nephews, and many friends, the Lowell family received much support during times of sickness or loss. Hannah and her family moved into "an excellent house. The sun rises and sets in my drawing room. We have a snug little breakfasting room and very good bedchambers." During November, Hannah was busy preparing "for our yearly feast—Thanksgiving. I have seven children in the house and I have my friends continually coming to see me. . . . It is all very delightful to me." Hannah supervised her servants, took care of her home, worried about her four children and her husband, wrote letters to friends at home and abroad and entertained. Of great importance was her role in keeping harmony within their kinship. A frequent guest was William Cabot, an astute mentor to Francis during his early years as a merchant, but now "our old bachelor uncle." The Lowells participated in the close world of the Essex County elite, traveling between Beacon Hill, their offices at the wharves, the Merchant's Exchange building and their clubs. Though well educated and well traveled, the Lowells were most comfortable within their own circle. On weekends and holidays the families left the town for their country homes in Roxbury, Brookline, Waltham or Nahant.

Francis and Hannah Lowell occasionally attended the Boston Theatre (founded 1794) on Federal Street, the Haymarket Theatre (founded 1796) or the Music Hall. At the start of the nineteenth century a small group of trained musicians in Boston formed the Philo-harmonic Society. At the Trinity Church, the organist G. K. Jackson, "a man of Falstaffian proportions" both in girth and arrogance, gave concerts of cathedral music. The Handel and Haydn Society was founded in 1815 with the financial backing of a number of Boston merchants. Boston was the home of Julien's Restorator, the first restaurant in America, opened by the renowned chef Julien Baptiste Gilbert Payplat, who escaped the French Revolution. The restaurant was especially popular with Bostonians who had traveled in France and delighted in the French cuisine. The Lowells attended private balls and fancy cotillion parties, as well as formal dinners. Cornhill had evolved as the street for luxury shopping, especially goods imported from England. At No. 17 stood Martin Goldthwait's shop selling brocades, at No. 19 Tucker & Thayer selling English and Indian textiles and at No. 65 Richardson & Walker with its "large and extensive assortment of English goods, particularly lustrings, satins, modes and Chinese and broad cloths." Cornhill was home to a number of bookstores, including the London Book Store once owned by Henry Knox, Lincoln Edmund's Bookstore and, at No. 68, Bradford Read's Law Booksellers.

Comfortably surrounded by family, Hannah compared the Jacksons with the Lowells. "The most incorrigible members of the clan," she wrote in 1813, "are of my side of the house. Mr. Lowell's family have too much vivacity and good taste to confine themselves exclusively to it." After their "pleasant summer in the country" the Lowell family rented a house and moved into Boston for the winter. The family attended the West Church on Cambridge Street, where Charles Lowell, brother to Francis, was the minister. By living in the city it was easier for Francis during the cold and snowy winter days to attend to his various responsibilities. He was a member of the board of the New England Bank, managed his properties at India Wharf and Broad Street, and attended to his duties as a merchant. Also, Francis needed to be close to the merchants who had the wealth to finance his cotton-manufacturing project.[4]

Jonathan Jackson died in 1810, leaving $10,000 to each of his three surviving daughters—Hannah, Harriet and Mary. For Mary the money was most opportune, as her husband Henry Lee was bankrupt. Francis' beloved stepmother Rebecca Lowell, third wife to Judge John Lowell, died in 1816, leaving $1,500 each to John Lowell Jr., Francis Cabot Lowell and Rebecca Gardner. To her biological daughter Elizabeth she left $3,600. Other relatives were given smaller amounts of money.

In October 1812, Boston was transfixed by the trial of Samuel Tully, aged forty-two, and John Dalton, aged twenty-four, on the indictment of piracy and murder. Earlier that year the two men were part of the crew on the schooner *George Washington* under the command of Captain Uriah Phillips Levy. The ship was carrying casks of wine bound for New Bedford. Tully and Dalton allegedly threw Seaman George Cummings overboard and briefly took control of the vessel. The two men were brought to Boston for trial. A jury of their peers before the Circuit Court of the United States, sitting in Boston found both men guilty as charged. After the judge pronounced the awful sentence of death by hanging, the men were removed to the state prison in South Boston. On Sunday, November 29, the Reverend Charles Lowell came to the prison and gave a sermon calculated for further use in the prisons but "with a concluding address to the two condemned pirates, Tully and Dalton." On December 10, 1812, both men were taken to the gallows, bound and black hoods placed over their heads in preparation for a public hanging, watched by a crowd of ten thousand. Samuel Tully was hanged and Dr. Josiah Bartlett, surgeon of the state prison, pronounced him dead. As the noose was placed around the neck of John Dalton there came the dramatic news that he had been reprieved on the authority of James Madison, the president of the United States. So ended one of the last public hangings in Boston. A month later John Dalton received a full pardon and was released. Shaken by his experience, John Dalton became religious and took to the cloth.

During the early part of the War of 1812, "New England experienced very little actual war within its borders." Starting in the spring of 1813, British squadrons were "hovering alongside our coasts, threatening the destruction of our maritime cities and villages." Matters became worse the following June when the *Superb* and the *Nimrod* attacked coastal towns. The British occupation of Penobscot Bay and Castine brought the fear that the British were about to attack Boston. The governor of Massachusetts mobilized the militia and "large numbers of the citizens of all classes might be seen day after day, toiling like common laborers" as they erected coastal defenses. The alert continued even after the peace treaty was signed on December 24, 1814, because the British remained in Penobscot Bay until April 25, 1815.[5]

THE GROWTH OF BOSTON

When Judge John Lowell moved into Boston in 1777 the town was still in a shambles following the British evacuation and the loss of much of its population. It took until 1790 for Boston to regain the population it had before the War of Independence. In 1812, the year Francis and his family returned from their trip abroad, the population of Boston was over forty thousand people, spread throughout the Shawmut peninsula. Boston had the amenities of a small city. Francis read the *Columbian Centinel*, a Federalist newspaper that supported Dewitt Clinton for President and opposed James Madison. A second newspaper, the *New England Palladium*, was for a time edited by Warren Dutton, who married Elizabeth Lowell, daughter of Judge John Lowell and half-sister to Francis Cabot Lowell. These newspapers, together with the daily *Boston Daily Advertiser* (established 1813) gave the news from America and abroad and informed readers, many of them merchants, about the comings and goings of ships and cargoes.[6]

Completed in 1797, the seven-story Merchants' Exchange on Federal Street was planned to be the center of Boston's commercial life. The exterior of the Exchange was dressed in hammered granite, and the main floor was intended as an enormous trading hall eighty-three feet in height. However, this space was never used as an exchange as the merchants, from long habit, preferred to conduct their business outside on the street, even when the weather was bad. The building housed a large coffee shop, a reading room and a post office. There was also an elegant dining room, a ballroom and rooms for rent. The Merchants' Exchange cost $500,000 to build but was a financial disaster, bringing ruin to many of the investors as well as to the unpaid carpenters and masons. The Merchants' Exchange building burned to the ground in July 1818.

Francis Cabot Lowell regularly met with his fellow merchants during his visits to the Exchange and its coffee shop. Most of the merchants were self-made men without the advantages of a Harvard education. Thomas Handasyd Perkins (1764–1854) was one of ten children of James and Elizabeth Perkins, who owned a small shop selling home goods such as cheese, sugar, tea and wine. At age twenty-one Thomas left Boston to seek his fortune on the island of Saint Domingue, but his business there crashed to the ground during the slave rebellion of 1791. Not to be deterred, Thomas and his brother James were among the first Americans to enter the China Trade. Their ships traveled to the Pacific Northwest to gather animal furs to take to Canton in exchange for chinaware, silks, and teas. The Perkins brothers expanded their business to carry horses and dried fish to the Caribbean, Turkish opium to China and slaves to the American South. At home Thomas Handasyd Perkins was the model of respectability. He invested in the Monkton Iron Works of Vermont, speculated in land in Cambridge and was an early investor in the cotton mills of Lowell. The Perkins School for the Blind, where Helen Keller and her teacher Anne Sullivan later resided, is named for Thomas Handasyd Perkins.

In 1810, Timothy Dwight, the former president of Yale College, recorded his impressions of Boston and its people. "The Bostonians, almost without exception," he wrote, "are derived from a single country and a single stock. They are all descendants of Englishmen; and of course, are united by all the great bonds of society: language, government, manners and religion. . . . They speak the English language in the English manner; are protestants; hold the great principles of English liberty; are governed voluntarily by the English common law. Their education also differs very little in the school, the shop, the counting house, or the University. Every New Englander, with hardly an exception, is taught to read, write, and keep accounts." Because Boston is a small, compact city, everyone "is known and conscious that he is known. The wealth of Boston is great."[7]

Using the duties on imported goods as a measure, trade in Boston Harbor increased year by year from 1801 to 1806. With the Embargo Act, trade declined precipitously in 1808 and remained low until the end of the War of 1812. Trade accelerated after the war with 775 foreign vessels and 1,649 coastal vessels arriving in 1817. In that year, Boston Harbor counted eighty wharves and quays. Boston manufactories included soap, candles, chocolate, beer, cordage and brass. There were thirty distilleries, eight sugarhouses and two breweries.

By the close of the eighteenth century, travel by sea from Boston to New York or Philadelphia was long established, but overland journeys between the states were still something of a novelty. The first regular stage-coach between Boston and New York started in 1767 by the enterprising Thomas Sabin. His coach left from Fowler's tavern in New York on Saturday, reaching Hartford by Monday morning and Boston two days later. The turnpike era in New England began in 1792 when investors financed the roads, and charged fees at tollgates along the way. The forty-two-mile Boston to Worcester turnpike opened in 1810. The trip from Boston to Providence took eight hours and cost $2. In 1810, the toll cost for the four-day trip from New York to Boston was $11, with extra charges for the coach, meals and lodging. The expansion of manufacturing increased the demand for overland travel between the fast growing cities of Boston, Worcester, Springfield, Hartford, New York and Philadelphia.

THE BOSTON ATHENAEUM

Francis Cabot Lowell was among the original 150 subscribers to launch the Boston Athenaeum. This renowned Boston institution developed out of a literary club formed by fourteen men in 1804. Known at first as "The Society" and then "The Anthology Society," Dr. James Jackson and others planned to establish a library and a reading room where they could meet with like-minded people, read books and keep up with the latest magazines and newspapers from the United States and Europe. On January 1, 1807, they announced a plan to open an institution "similar to the Athenaeum, then recently established in Liverpool." The head of the planning committee was Theophilus Parsons, chief justice of the Massachusetts Supreme Court, with Francis' older brother, John Lowell, as its treasurer.

Shares in the Boston Athenaeum were bought mainly by the members of Boston's merchant community, as well as by physicians, lawyers and men in the retail trade. Each share sold for $300, one-third down on signing, one-third the following year and the final one-third the year after. Among the original subscribers to the Athenaeum fund were Harrison Gray Otis, Josiah Quincy, John Quincy Adams, Charles Bulfinch, Thomas Hanasyd Perkins, Uriah Cotting and James Lloyd, as well as John, Francis and Charles Lowell. Armed with $45,000, the treasurer John Lowell was instructed to buy the premises of Doyle & Boyen on Tremont Street for $9,000 as the first home of the Boston Athenaeum. A further $12,000 was spent on books and subscriptions to magazines and newspapers.

The years of the war were difficult for the Boston Athenaeum. Business was down, money scarce and the future looked "gloomy and discouraging, and no present prospect of increasing the funds of the institution appeared." John Lowell was elected president of the Boston Athenaeum, with Josiah Quincy as vice president and Nathan Appleton as treasurer.[8] Unlike his brothers, Francis Cabot was not a literary, political or a religious man. Rather, he was a man of business—skilled in the manipulation of numbers, understanding invoices, mortgages, balance sheets, interest rates, the value of currencies and gold coins, and the ratio between risk and benefit. He understood well the importance of the price of goods in the competitive marketplace. His mathematical calculations to develop efficient machinery coupled with a willing labor force, reduced the price of cloth and increased the share values of the Boston Manufacturing Company. It is doubtful that he spent many hours in the reading room of the Athenaeum perusing books and magazines on philosophy, the arts or politics. More likely, he joined the Athenaeum to enhance his standing among this elite community. At his death in 1817, his $300 share in the Athenaeum was valued at only $130.

TRADING WITH THE BRITISH

Despite the war against Great Britain, Francis Cabot Lowell continued to ship flour and rice to feed the British army in Portugal and Spain. He wrote to his banker Samuel Williams in London on November 29, 1812, "I have made three shipments of flour to Cadiz and Lisbon; the cost of which here was about 11,000 dollars." Lowell requested that the proceeds from the sale be sent to London in care of Mr. Williams. By 1813 the war seriously affected the economy of the United States. Lowell wrote to Samuel

Williams on October 6, 1814, "You have no doubt heard of the failure of all the banks in New York, Philadelphia and Baltimore and the refusal of all the merchants there to pay their debts except in the papers of the banks in those places, which has already depreciated by 10 per cent. The banks of Old Massachusetts are all solvent and continue to pay in specie, except possibly two banks that have loaned the government of the United States the greater part of their capital." Francis Cabot Lowell received a response from Williams dated January 15, 1814, informing him of the receipt of his payment of £1,000. The shipment of flour and rice to Cadiz and Lisbon, however, found few buyers. Other goods, sent on the *General Knox*, had been impounded in Bermuda but would only be released on payment of fines. The American-born banker Samuel Williams, now a British subject, could not resist a display of British pride. Commenting on the war against Napoleon, "all the movements of the allies are forward to Paris. The chances are now greatly on the side of peace in Europe. In the event of such a peace, your American politics must take a different turn." With money tight, Francis Cabot Lowell called in the loans he had made to others. To one debtor he wrote on November 12, 1814, "I cannot in these times when I have lost much of my property, afford to let the matter lay as it now does."

Francis Cabot Lowell explored ways to circumvent the British blockade of American ports. Writing to his English relative, James Russell of Bristol, on June 23, 1813, Lowell reminded him of his prior offer to "procure business for me." Lowell asked Russell to use his influence to obtain "two to six licenses to carry grain or provisions, particularly hogshead of butter & pork & beef to Havana or any neutral port in the West Indies and to bring back coffee, rum and molasses or British manufactures, but the license must not say British as that would be introduced to this country as Spanish." He also asked for licenses to carry potash and cotton, and licenses to send American flour to Spain and Portugal and return with Spanish wine. Lowell reasoned that the British would approve these special licenses, even in times of war, as a means to increase the sale of British goods on the American market. "It is important," continued Lowell, "for the vessels to proceed with the license from one port to another of the United States for the purpose of loading, as the vessels are generally owned in the northward and the cargoes are raised in the Southern States."

Not all of Francis Cabot Lowell's transactions were successful. Writing to her husband in Calcutta, Mary Lee noted on January 10, 1814, that the demand for commodities such as sugar and coffee was falling. "Mr. Lowell and Pat had bought a large quantity of indigo, presuming upon the continuance of the war and were hoping to make an immense profit upon it. But now they could not help looking a little sober." Mary hoped that Patrick's luck would turn and that "he be rewarded for his cheerful submission to such frequent disappointments as he has experienced."

In a letter dated November 1815, Lowell's agent in Calcutta informed him that a shipment of cloth and bandanas valued at £4,055, 15 shillings and 3 pence onboard the American brig *Pickering*, under the command of Charles L. Sargent, was on its way to Boston. Francis was still actively engaged in importing cotton textiles at the same time his power loom at the Boston Manufacturing Company was beginning to produce domestic cloth. Even as his vision was becoming a reality, Francis still hedged his bets on the success of domestic manufacture, making cloth at home while still importing textiles from India.

In 1814, Hannah Lowell's correspondence with her friends in Scotland lessened as the blockade intensified, and as she became increasingly ill, she no longer had the strength to look after her younger boys; early in 1815, Francis placed twelve-year-old Francis Jr. and eight-year-old Edward at Phillips Academy, Andover, the same preparatory school he had attended in his youth. Hannah Lowell died May 10, 1815. She was thirty-nine years and was married only seventeen years. The much-loved Hannah was kind and caring, sweet of nature and with a quiet demeanor that hid an intelligent mind. On learning of Hannah's death, Anne MacVicar Grant of Edinburgh wrote to a friend July 15, 1815, "I should have been for some days lately unusually depressed, since it is not long since I heard of the death of dear Mrs. Lowell of Boston—the human being of all I personally know that comes nearest to perfection, and who loved me with a sister's love."

Francis had hardly buried his wife when new problems arose with his oldest son, John Jr., now at Harvard. In a letter to Hannah's sister, Mrs. Mary Lee, Francis wrote July 30, "I have taken John from college. I found that he had been rather inattentive to his college studies, although not altogether idle and not at all dissipated. [John] had few or no acquaintances at Harvard." Rather than continue his studies, John wanted to go to sea. Francis debated whether John "will go to sea immediately or go into the store for a year first. But it is decided that he is to go to sea to qualify himself as a captain and to come forward in the world that way. It has, of course, given me much pain to be obliged to make this change in John's situation. It has been his fate hitherto from his birth to occasion a great deal of pain & trouble with very little to give pleasure."

Francis wrote to Kirk Boott of the firm Boott & Pratt Importers, asking whether he could find a position for John Jr. Mr. Boott replied on June 26 that "I should be happy to receive him. I regret that you should feel yourself under any embarrassment. I have granted no favour and believe the benefit to each will be reciprocal. . . . As youths generally require a short relaxation after their studies are finished, you will if you desire take a week or two for this purpose." Francis Cabot Lowell agreed to pay his son's expenses while he apprenticed at Boott & Pratt. Kirk Boott (1755–1817) was born in the town of Derby in the English Midlands, where his family owned a market garden supplying vegetables and fruits. He moved to London where he worked as a porter in a warehouse. Ambitious to make something of his life, in 1783 he boarded the *Rosamond* for Boston, hoping to open a shop selling British goods. There he married Mary Love, another emigrant from Derby. Kirk Boott brought to Boston his passion for growing fruits and vegetables and became known to Theodore Lyman, who owned an estate in Waltham. With Mr. Lyman's help he set himself up as a merchant in partnership with William Pratt, importing goods from England and India. Later, Kirk Boott formed a partnership with his sons in the firm of Boott & Sons. The firm suffered losses when double duties were imposed on British goods. At war's end these duties were repealed leaving Kirk & Sons burdened with goods too expensive to sell.

THE REBEL

The Federalist Party detested France and its revolution, believed that Jefferson and Madison were under French influence, felt a kinship with Great Britain and envied the increasing power of the southern and western states. Because of his emotional vulnerability, John Lowell did not take part in the rough-and-tumble of politics. Known as "The Rebel," he was instead the intellectual leader of the right wing of the party and chief propagandist of its doctrine. During the War of 1812, the Federalist Party, strongest in New England, faced a decline in popularity elsewhere as its leaders were accused of disloyalty to the Union. John Lowell published several powerful pamphlets including the seventy-eight-page *Perpetual War, The Policy of Mr. Madison,* and *Mr. Madison's War,* in which he sought to justify Britain's right to search foreign ships and arrest deserters. John Lowell criticized the president of the United States for declaring war over so minor a matter as the impressment of British sailors. Writing in vigorous prose, John Lowell accused Madison of "adopting a remedy for the wrongs of our seamen infinitely more injurious to them than the evils which they suffered. . . . He ordered out the militia, in contempt of that very Constitution of which he was one of the principal framers. In short, whatever he attempted to vindicate by arms, by arms he lost."

In his argument against Jefferson, Madison and their Southern supporters, John Lowell claimed, "Not one member of Congress from Maine to Delaware, will be in favour of the war. These northern and middle states, who are now united in opinion, possess 3,000,000 of inhabitants; considerably more than did the whole United States at the time of the Declaration of Independence. They are a body of freemen, distinguished for their industry and virtue. They are the owners of two third parts of all the tonnage of the United States, and furnish probably three fourths of all the native seaman. They are totally opposed to a war for the privilege of protecting British seamen against their own sovereign, that this subject of impressment is a mere instrument, used by men who are utterly indifferent about the sufferings of the sailors and the merchants." Little wonder that the pronounced Anglophile, John Lowell, belonged to the so-called British faction of the Federalist Party.

John Lowell had a wider agenda, calling for a union consisting only of the original thirteen states and casting off lands of the Louisiana Purchase. He advocated for the New England states and other like-minded states to vote to end the war against Great Britain and suspend the Constitution, making "the people of that state no longer beholden to the National authority. They cannot be traitors or rebels. They may be treated as rebels, like the citizens of any foreign state, if a wrecked and abandoned and desperate policy should induce the National rulers to declare war against such a state."[9]

In 1813, John Lowell published his *Thoughts in a Series of Letters, in Answer to the Question Respecting the Division of the States*. In his six letters, John Lowell departs from his earlier suggestion that New England redress its grievances by secession from the Union. He argues instead that, with the Louisiana Purchase, the United States is too large a nation, and it is the West that should separate, leaving a nation made up of the "good old thirteen states," guided by New England.

The Hartford Convention held December 1814–January 1815 at the Old State House in Hartford, Connecticut, brought together representatives from the five New England states to denounce President Madison and demand a speedy end to the trade embargo. George Cabot was elected president of the convention and took a hand in selecting a delegation to carry its demands to the federal government. By the time the delegation arrived in Washington, the city was abuzz with patriotic pride over the news of Andrew Jackson's victory in the Battle of New Orleans. The leaders of the Essex Junto—Timothy Pickering, George Cabot and John Lowell—lost all political authority. Rufus King (1755–1827), born in Massachusetts and educated at Harvard, moved to New York. He ran as a Federalist twice for vice president and once for president of the United States but lost each time. The Federalist Party, tainted with disloyalty, soon disappeared. With the demise of Federalism, the merchant class of New England lost its clout, making way for a new elite of domestic manufacturers.

BANKING

Massachusetts' banking began to be organized toward the close of the eighteenth century. In 1791, Alexander Hamilton, secretary of the treasury, established the Bank of the United States, based on the Bank of England. The following year, the national bank opened a branch in Boston with Judge John Lowell, Israel Thorndike and Christopher Gore among its directors. In 1810, George Cabot was appointed president of the Massachusetts branch of the national bank. The National Union, chartered in 1792, was among the first of the banks in Massachusetts, followed by the Boston Bank (1803), the State National Bank (1811) and the New England Bank (1813). Most of the stockholders and directors were drawn from the merchant class. At the start of the War of 1812, the General Court of Massachusetts issued its own treasury notes.

Among the original stockholders of the New England Bank were Francis Cabot Lowell, Samuel and Nathaniel Appleton, Samuel Cabot, Amos Lawrence and Patrick Tracy Jackson. Lowell was among the twelve founding directors of the bank. The New England Bank preferred to deal only with money issued in Boston and placed a discount of between three and five per cent on money printed in other states. Francis Lowell wrote to David Greenough on October 27, 1813, "I observe that one of the Connecticut banks makes its bills payable at a bank in New York City." Lowell inquired "whether we could make a similar one if we desired." Based on the advice of Greenough, the New England Bank, in a transaction worth $138,874, "sent bills on New York to be collected and exchanged as specie." These funds, carried on an ox wagon, were seized by order of the collector of New York and deposited in the vaults of the Manhattan Bank. The reason given for the seizure was the belief that Federalist-dominated Massachusetts was attempting to transfer money out of the country and into Canada.[10]

The directors of the New England Bank chose Francis Cabot Lowell to go to New York City to retrieve the money and return it to Boston. Lowell remained in New York from January to March 1814, working with bankers and lawyers, and receiving regular letters about his mercantile interests in Boston, and the progress made at the mill in Waltham. In New York he was advised by Peter Remsen, a well-established New York merchant and a director of the Merchant's Bank of New York. Over the years, Remsen and Lowell had conducted business together. Of Dutch origin, Peter Remsen came from a long line of merchants in New York and was a trusted friend of Francis Lowell and other Boston merchants.

Francis Cabot Lowell threatened to sue the collector of New York but withdrew after Peter Remsen and his lawyers had "at last given their opinion that the grounds for prosecution against the collector are small" and that the prospects for Massachusetts to recover the money was "doubtful."

It took the intervention of James Madison, the president of the United States, to recover the funds. Writing from Washington, DC, on March 3, Christopher Gore, the former governor of Massachusetts and now U.S. senator, informed Francis Cabot Lowell that "the President has told me that the government has directed the Collector of New York to restore the money belonging to the New England Bank, unless some grounds of suspicion other than have been communicated here exist of its illegal destination. I can therefore have no doubt that it will be delivered up."[11]

CENTRAL WHARF

Much involved with his Boston Manufacturing Company, Francis Cabot Lowell still found the time and money to take part in yet another of Uriah Cotting's grand projects. On April 17, 1815, work began on the construction of Central Wharf, lying between Long Wharf and India Wharf. Cotting bought 25 percent of the four hundred shares in Central Wharf, Harrison Gray Otis 22.5 percent, James Lloyd 20 percent and Francis Cabot Lowell 16.5 percent, with David Hinkley, Israel Thorndike and Ebenezer Francis purchasing the remaining shares. Ebenezer Francis was a new business partner for Francis Lowell. Born in Beverly, Massachusetts, in 1775, he started life in poverty. Ebenezer Francis came to Boston at age twelve and made his way from a clerk in a counting house to the chairman of the trustees of the Massachusetts General Hospital and president of Suffolk Bank. His marriage to Elizabeth, oldest daughter of Israel Thorndike, greatly helped advance his mercantile career. Ebenezer Francis was aged eighty-three at the time of his death, leaving one of the largest fortunes in New England, worth some $4 million.

Central Wharf, with fifty-four warehouses, each four stories tall, became the hub of the Mediterranean trade. The *Nautilus*, *Martha Washington*, *Griffin* and other ships returned regularly to Boston carrying oranges, lemons, figs and raisins from the ports of Smyrna, Messina, Genoa, Malaga and Marseilles. The merchants Perkins & Co., Bryant & Sturgis and William F. Weld & Company sold the goods locally or carried the fruit on to New York or Philadelphia. With India Wharf and Central Wharf, Francis Cabot Lowell and his partners dominated the trade between Boston and the Orient and now with the Mediterranean.

DOMESTIC CONCERNS

The death of his wife and having his sons away at school tested the strength of Francis Cabot Lowell, yet he continued to keep up the appearance of his

Boston home. On May 1, 1816, Mr. Daniel Bray submitted his bill for "work done on Mr. Lowell's house":

• Repairing the front steps	50 cents
• Making plank box for drain	50
• Setting 4 panes of glass	66
• Laying kitchen floor & putting up partition	$5.00
• Caulking 2 windows & hanging a shutter	$1.50
• Making seat & repairing outhouse	75
• Repairing gutters	75
• Parts for fireplace	62
• 4 pounds of nails	50

The total bill for $10.78 was paid in June 1816.

August 30, 1815, was unusually hot and sunny, and the day of the Harvard Commencement. Had he continued his studies, John Lowell Jr. would have graduated that year. Instead Francis Cabot Lowell came to Harvard Yard to celebrate the graduation of his nephew John Amory Lowell. One of the speakers was Elisha Fuller, who drew applause when he spoke about Napoleon, "the deposed imperial despot of France."

By 1815, a national economy was rapidly evolving in the United States based largely on the products of the land and the sea. Manufactured products accounted for less than 5 percent of exports.[12] Francis Cabot Lowell built his factory at the start of American industrialization. With the expansion of textile mills and other factories, the export of American manufactured goods would rise dramatically in the years to come.

11

The Boston
Manufacturing Company

[At Francis Cabot Lowell's cotton mill at Waltham] all the operations for converting raw cotton into finished cloth, were for the first time introduced in this country, and probably the world.

James Leander Bishop,
A History of American Manufacturing from 1608 to 1860,
published 1864

The Boston Manufacturing Company erected the first modern factory in America.

Victor Selden Clark, 1916

Wealthy Boston entrepreneurs . . . led Massachusetts's transition toward large-scale industrial society. The most important of these men was a merchant, a native of Newburyport, Francis Cabot Lowell.

Richard D. Brown and Jack Trager, 2000

[When Francis Cabot Lowell made known his intention to engage in the manufacture of textiles] many of his nearest connections used all their influence to dissuade him from the pursuit of what they deemed to be a visionary and dangerous scheme. They thought him mad.

Henry Lee, 1830

One girl attends to two looms after she has learned the business, which generally takes about a month.

From a letter written by
Francis Cabot Lowell, April 26, 1816

Francis Cabot Lowell understood that the war between the United States and Great Britain offered the unique opportunity he needed to manufacture textiles at home. Official trade between the two nations ground to a halt as his fellow merchants could not legally send their ships to British ports or receive British goods. Exports of raw cotton from the American South to Liverpool fell sharply as England turned to India for supplies. The Southern plantation owners were desperate to find markets in the North. Without imports of Indian and English cloth the price of textiles in America began to soar.

Before he was seized by the idea of manufacturing textiles at home, Francis Cabot Lowell led a conventional albeit privileged Boston life. He followed his brother John Jr. into Philips Academy and Harvard University. He apprenticed under his Cabot and Lee relatives as an East India merchant. He educated his children in his footsteps. During his tour of Great Britain he visited the places recommended by his brothers. In the India Wharf and Broad Street projects in Boston he played second fiddle to the energetic Uriah Cotting. The plan to make textiles in America, however, was entirely his own. Despite the opposition from his family and business circle, he pursued his vision with single-minded doggedness, backed by proven business skills, an excellent memory and outstanding mathematical abilities. Francis was determined to succeed in the mass production of cloth where his relatives, the Cabot brothers of the Beverly Cotton Manufactory, had years earlier so miserably failed. Francis Cabot Lowell was convinced that a well-capitalized, well-managed American cotton mill with American labor, using the latest power machinery, was bound to succeed.

By 1810, there were over three hundred corporations in America, nearly all of them providing public services such as the construction of turnpikes, canals, bridges, water supply, banks and insurance. Among these corporations only eight were manufacturing companies. In 1807 there were eight thousand spindles in Massachusetts, but with the expansion of spinning mills after the embargo, the consumption of raw cotton to feed the machines began to rise sharply.[1]

Massachusetts was among the earliest of the American states to encourage manufacturing by passing, in March 1809, an act defining the general powers and duties of manufacturing corporations. On February 23, 1813, in the midst of the war against Great Britain, the Senate and House of Representatives of the General Court of Massachusetts, responding to the petition submitted by Francis C. Lowell, Benjamin Gorham, Uriah Cotting and Patrick T. Jackson, passed an act to incorporate the Boston Manufacturing Company "for the purpose of manufacturing Cotton, Woolen & Linen goods, at Boston, in the County of Suffolk, or within fifteen miles thereof, or at any place, or places, not exceeding fours; and for this purpose shall have all the powers and privileges, and be subject to all the duties and requirements contained in an Act, passed the third day of

March, Eighteen hundred and nine, entitled 'An Act defining the general powers and duties of Manufacturing Corporations.'" The company was authorized to raise up to $400,000 to buy property, erect a factory, build the machines and hire the workers to make textiles. The act to establish Francis Cabot Lowell's bold venture in mass production was signed into law by Caleb Strong, governor of the Commonwealth of Massachusetts.[2]

The incorporation of the Boston Manufacturing Company and raising money through a syndicate of investors followed the pattern Francis Cabot Lowell successfully used with the Broad Street and the India Wharf projects several years earlier. Then, Lowell was concerned with importing goods from Europe, China and India for sale in America. With his Boston Manufacturing Company, Francis Cabot Lowell sought to make textiles at home for sale in the American market and perhaps to export abroad. Lowell's plan, nothing less, was to build the first fully integrated textile mill in the United States, starting with the picking and carding of raw cotton to the spinning of thread, dressing and the weaving of finished cloth, all under one roof.

While still in Great Britain, Francis loaned money to his brother-in-law Patrick Tracy Jackson to overcome financial reverses and to get him back on his feet. Now that Francis was back in Boston, the first recruits to his plan were the three Jackson brothers: Charles, James and Patrick Tracy (two other Jackson brothers, Robert and Henry, had died young). Not only was he married to their sister, Hannah, but the Jackson brothers had great faith in Francis' integrity and ability. "None of us," wrote Charles Jackson, "engaged in any business and took any important step without consulting him." With hardly a moment's reflection the Jackson brothers agreed to take part in his great venture of textile manufacture in America. Charles had a lucrative legal practice and was soon to be appointed a justice in the Massachusetts Supreme Court. James had his busy and fashionable medical practice, leaving young Patrick to offer himself as Francis' lieutenant.

The Jackson brothers greatly respected Francis Cabot Lowell. As James Jackson Putnum wrote, "It was not the intellect only, which was so great in Mr. F. C. Lowell; his moral character was most pure and most elevated. He was singularly devoid of selfishness. He had the greatest love of doing good. He was the most honest of friends. The establishment of the Cotton manufacture was the last great object which engaged Mr. Lowell's attention, and he pursued it with great zeal. Most of the early plans for the new business were furnished by Mr. F. Lowell. Mr. [Patrick Tracy] Jackson gave the most time and labour in conducting it [and] was the most valuable aide of the wise and excellent friend, Mr. Lowell."

Above average in height, with a strong body, sanguine, ardent yet sociable, the grateful Patrick Tracy took twenty shares in the Boston

Manufacturing Company. His brother Charles took ten and James took five. How did the Jackson brothers come up with the money to buy their shares? Over the years Francis Cabot Lowell had loaned money to Charles to start his law practice, James to travel to England to study medicine and Patrick Tracy Jackson to pay off his debts. It is probable that Francis Cabot Lowell himself advanced to the Jackson brothers much of the money for their thirty-five shares, valued at $35,000. Another brother-in-law, Benjamin Gorham, took three, and yet another brother-in-law, Warren Dutton, took two shares. Francis Cabot Lowell committed $15,000 for fifteen of the original one hundred shares. The money Francis Cabot Lowell committed to his great project was less than one-fifth of his net worth of some $110,000; but the funds committed by the Jackson brothers were certainly a far larger share of their total assets. The remarkable bond between Francis and his brothers-in-law endured for the rest of his short life. The Boston Manufacturing Company grew from his vision and determination but much of its success came from his talented brothers-in-law who supported him in his venture. Patrick Tracy Jackson began as an able assistant to Francis Lowell but his role grew in importance as Francis became increasingly ill.

With commitments in hand for $55,000 of the initial $100,000 needed, Francis was ready to approach Nathan Appleton, who promised, in Edinburgh in 1811, to back the project. Nathan Appleton tells that during 1813, Francis Lowell and Patrick Tracy Jackson came "to me one day on the Boston exchange, and stated they were determined to establish a Cotton manufactory. Mr. Jackson had agreed to give up all other business and take the management of the concern."

Francis Cabot Lowell calculated that the capital needed would be the huge sum of $400,000, "but it was only intended to raise one hundred thousand until the experiment should be fairly tried." With Lowell and the Jackson brothers "subscribing the greater part," Appleton was asked to take $10,000 of stock. "I told them," Appleton wrote in his autobiography, "theoretically I thought the business ought to succeed, but what I had seen of its practical operation was unfavorable." Appleton agreed only to $5,000 of stock "in order to see the experiment fairly tried."[3] The support of so prominent a merchant as Nathan Appleton made it relatively easy to raise the remaining $40,000. The wealthy Israel Thorndike, father and son, were each down for ten shares at $1,000 a share, leaving John Gore (ten shares), Senator James Lloyd (five shares), and Uriah Cotting, Lowell's partner in the India Wharf and Broad Street projects, to purchase the remaining five shares. Israel Thorndike and James Lloyd were seasoned traders in handspun and handwoven Indian fabrics and understood the advantages of a domestic cotton industry driven by machines. The stockowners were not required to pay all the money at one

The dapper Nathan Appleton was about thirty years old when he sat for his portrait by Gilbert Stuart, circa 1810. Already a successful merchant, he was the first outside the family to back Francis Cabot Lowell's Boston Manufacturing Company. Appleton doubted that cotton textile manufacturing in America would succeed but in 1812, he committed $5,000 "to see the experiment fairly tried." (Courtesy of the National Park Service, Longfellow National Historic Site.)

time but allowed to spread out payment over a ten- to twelve-month period. Francis Cabot Lowell owned shares, numbered 14–28, paying $1,500 a month for ten months.

Lowell proposed a joint-stock arrangement instead of the individual or partnership ownership. This method allowed a group of moderately wealthy men to pool their funds and raise enough capital for the venture, unlike Great Britain, where men of great wealth created their own companies. In Lowell's plan, if a shareholder died or sold his stake, the company could continue to function. If the company prospered and paid high dividends old and new shareholders would be tempted to increase their stake by buying more shares. Francis Cabot Lowell used a similar arrangement in financing his India Wharf and Broad Street projects. The prospering Boston Manufacturing Company had little difficulty raising the additional $300,000 needed for its expansion.

Brother-in-law Henry Lee recalled in 1839 how Lowell had tenaciously overcome all resistance to his plan: "Many of his nearest connections used all their influence to dissuade him from the pursuit of what they deemed a visionary and dangerous scheme. They, too, were among those who knew, or thought they knew, the full strength of his mind, the accuracy of his calm calculations, his industry, patience and perseverance, and, withal, his power and influence over others, which was essential for his success. They still thought him mad." Neither John Lowell Jr. nor any of the Cabot brothers (once owners of the defunct Beverly Cotton Manufactory) were among the initial investors of the Boston Manufacturing Company. However, as the enterprise showed success, his once skeptical relatives and other critics rushed to purchase "into the business of the visionary scheme at thirty, forty, fifty and even sixty per cent advance."[4]

Francis Cabot Lowell and Patrick Tracy Jackson were soon so absorbed in launching their mill that the family began to worry. Mary Lee, youngest sister to Hannah Lowell and Patrick Tracy Jackson, recorded her concerns to the privacy of her diary. On May 23, 1813, she visited Hannah and Francis Lowell at their country home in Waltham. "Hannah was not very bright," Mary noted, "but Mr. Lowell was unusually so and on the whole I enjoyed the day very much. Pat was there in the afternoon to fix their famous loom. It really makes me feel depressed to see Pat so engrossed in business as he is. He is not as sanguine as he once was but seems almost to exclude all other things—even his wife and child do not draw him from it. I most sincerely hope this manufactory in which he is engaged, may prove lucrative. They have now completed their company and are beginning to think of fixing up on a stream and commencing their establishment; and I found, much to my surprise that they really intended to live at the place—certainly Pat and perhaps Mr. Lowell. I had no idea that it was a thing that would decide their future destination." Pat Jackson married Lydia Cabot of Beverly, daughter of Andrew Cabot, in 1810, adding yet another family connection between the Lowells and the Jacksons. Lydia bore him nine children, a number of whom died young. Patrick Tracy Jackson held his obligation to Francis Lowell so high that he lived in Waltham, close to the factory, while Lydia and the growing family remained in Boston. Owning a pair of sturdy horses, Patrick regularly made the ten-mile trip between factory and home.

In the October 2, 1813, issue of the *Columbian Centinel*, Francis Cabot Lowell, Uriah Cotting and Patrick Tracy Jackson gave notice that "the proprietors of the Boston Manufacturing Company are hereby notified to meet at the counting room of Mr. Uriah Cotting, No. 72 Broad Street on Monday 18th" for the purpose of organizing the company and choosing officers to fulfill the duties of incorporation. Others who attended that meeting were Benjamin P. Gorham, John Gore, Israel Thorndike, his son Israel Thorndike Jr. and Nathan Appleton. The proprietors agreed to meet annually on the first Tuesday of each October at ten o'clock in the morning. A five-member board of directors was chosen, with James Lloyd as president, Patrick Tracy Jackson as treasurer and clerk to keep records, Francis Cabot Lowell, Nathan Appleton and Israel Thorndike Sr.

Francis Lowell chose the first group of investors with care. The merchants among them Lloyd, Thorndike, Cotting, Appleton and Gore, were well accustomed to making big decisions and risking large sums of money on cargoes sent as far away as China and India. James Lloyd (1769–1831) was born in Boston, where he attended the Boston Latin School and graduated from Harvard University in 1787. He was a merchant before entering politics as a Federalist. In 1808, he was sent to the U.S. Senate, replacing John Quincy Adams and served until May 1, 1813, when he returned to Boston to invest in the Boston Manufacturing Company. Israel Thorndike (1755–1832) went to sea as a boy to learn about ships, ports and trade, and then returned to his hometown of Beverly to set up as a merchant in the China trade. During the Revolutionary War, Thorndike was captain of the privateer *Warren*, credited with capturing several British vessels. In 1779, the *Warren* was one of forty-two ships that sailed from Boston to engage the British who had captured Castine in Penobscot Bay. On August 14, the British destroyed the *Warren* and most of the rest of the American fleet in the Battle of Penobscot Bay. Thorndike was an investor in the Beverly Cotton Manufactory together with Francis Lowell's relatives, John, George and Andrew Cabot. Despite the failure of the Beverly company, he accepted Francis Lowell's invitation to invest in the much larger Boston Manufacturing Company, to mass produce textiles, using the latest machinery and powered by the flow of the Charles River.

PAUL MOODY

Essential to the success of the Boston Manufacturing Company was to hire someone who understood well the machinery of a cotton mill. The man Francis Cabot Lowell wanted was Jacob Perkins, "the most competent person to fill the situation." Perkins invented a nail-making machine and came up with a new method to make bank notes. Finding no interest in the United States, Perkins was due to leave for England and was not available to take up work in Waltham. On October 12, 1813, Francis Cabot Lowell wrote to Paul Moody living in the town of Amesbury: "Dear Sir, We have advertised machine makers to apply by the 1st of Nov. We shall wish you to come up here at that time. The fall from the apron of the wheel at Boies's, now our dam, to the apron of the wheel is 15 feet 1 inch. I think we may venture to raise our dam, including flush boards, to 12 feet, say 10 feet dam and 2 feet flush boards. We have a very good opportunity to send to England to get any information we wish. Will you write to me word, whether you wish any information of any kind about the construction of any of the machinery, or the manner in which any part of the process is performed."

Lowell asked Moody to reply as soon as possible "as the gentleman will leave for England in a few days." Despite the state of war between the United States and Great Britain, Lowell was sending an unnamed gentleman on a mission of industrial espionage to secretly examine the latest machinery of the British textile industry and bring the information back to Boston.

At the inaugural meeting of the board of directors, Lowell, Appleton and Thorndike were elected to a committee to find a suitable site to erect a factory "for the purposes of commencing and prosecuting the business of the company." Lowell and Jackson were given the responsibility "to contract for the erection of such buildings, the making of such machinery" as needed to begin the manufacture of textiles. The board also voted "that Paul Moody be engaged by the Treasurer in behalf of the corporation as a superintendent of the works of the company at the rate of fifteen hundred dollars per annum."

Like Francis Cabot Lowell and Patrick Tracy Jackson, the machinist Paul Moody (1779–1831) was born in Newburyport. He was one of seven sons, two of whom attended Dartmouth College and three of whom were farmers. Paul's brother David was a mechanic of great ability who served for several years as superintendent of works on Uriah Cotting's milldam project. Paul was "more inclined to mechanical pursuits than to books." As a result he received little formal education, starting at age twelve to work in his father's water-powered wool mill, where he learned spinning and how to operate the machinery. The mill was purchased by the inventor Jacob Perkins (yet another Newburyport man), who modified the machinery to

Paul Moody (1779–1831), a gifted machinist, worked with Francis Cabot Lowell to build the power loom and other machinery for their mill at Waltham. (Official National Park Handbook— Lowell, U.S. National Park Service.)

cut and head nails in one operation. When Perkins moved his nail factory to nearby Amesbury, Paul Moody went with him. Later Moody, at age twenty, partnered with Ezra Worthen as cotton spinners, and remained there fourteen years. Moody was acquainted with all that was then generally known of cotton-spinning and weaving. In 1813, Francis Cabot Lowell heard about Moody's mechanical skills from Jacob Perkins and probably also from Cotting through David Moody, and hired him to build the machinery for the Boston Manufacturing Company.

FACTORY PLANS

With his core team—Lowell, Jackson and Moody—assembled, it was time to choose the exact site for the factory. Horse power for a large factory

was simply not practicable. At that time the United States lacked the technology for steam power, leaving water power as the obvious choice. One
possibility was to stay in Boston, where Uriah Cotting had chartered the
Boston & Roxbury Mill Dam. This fanciful project called for the building
of a dam a mile and a half long to impound the tidal flow of the Charles
River near its mouth. At high tide, the water would flow into the Back
Bay basin, be directed through raceways into the South Boston basin and
emptied into Boston Harbor at low tide. Cotting envisioned that up to
one hundred mills could be built alongside the dam, bringing industry,
including cotton manufacturing, to the city. His faith in the great value of
water power was shared by his superintendent David Moody. The project was delayed but finally completed at great expense in 1821, the year
Cotting died. The mill dam caused stagnation and pollution but did not
create the water power Cotting hoped for. No mills were built on top of
the dam wall; instead, the mill dam wall became Beacon Street, leading
from Beacon Hill into the suburbs.

On April 6, 1814, the board of directors of the Boston Manufacturing
Company at the bidding of Francis Lowell approved a far more suitable site
for their factory. Seven miles west of Boston is a fifteen-foot waterfall on the
Charles River in Waltham, more than enough power to turn the waterwheel
of the planned factory. Waltham was incorporated as a town in 1738 and
grew slowly. In 1785 Theodore Lyman bought a four-hundred-acre estate in
the town. The future governor of Massachusetts Christopher Gore and his
wife Rebecca built their grand brick house on forty acres facing the Charles
River. In 1790, John Boies built his paper factory on the Charles River, making white and brown paper, and was soon followed by two other paper-
making factories. The largest factory along the Charles in Waltham was
the Waltham Cotton and Wool Company built in 1812, with two thousand
spindles worked by two hundred workers.[5] The paper companies did not
thrive. Acting on behalf of the Boston Manufacturing Company, Patrick T.
Jackson bought the lands and water rights of the defunct Boies Paper Mill
for $1,000. The seventy-seven-acre site, bought by Jackson, bordered on the
properties belonging to George Stearns and Samuel Wellington.

The board of the Boston Manufacturing Company met monthly at one
or other of the Boston homes or offices of the directors or in Waltham at
the manufactory. By the end of 1814, the board had spent money on a dam
above the waterfall ($29,675), the brick factory ($16,435), spinning machinery ($12,917), loom and warping machinery ($6,706), and new blocks
of tenements to house the workers ($3,620), workers' wages, the company
store and other expenses for a total of $93,894. Patrick Tracy Jackson was
appointed superintendent of the company at a salary of $3,000 a year,
later increased to $5,000. By December 1817, the expenses of the Boston
Manufacturing Company reached $200,000.

TEXTILE MACHINERY

The process of converting raw cotton into finished cloth was a complicated one, requiring many machines that worked together. In an early nineteenth-century mill the raw cotton passed through the willow, the scrutching machine and the spreading machine to separate, clean and spread the cotton evenly. The cotton was next placed into the carding mill, where the fibers were combed and laid out parallel to each other and then fleeced and compressed into a sliver. The sliver was placed into the dressing frame, where it was repeatedly drawn and doubled to ensure that the fibers were straightened more perfectly. Next came the rolling frame worked by rollers and spindles to produce a coarse and loose thread. The throstle (or mule) was used to spin the yarn. To make the warp the twist was transferred by the winding machine from the cops onto the bobbins, and from the bobbins onto the warping mill. Next came the dressing machine, where the warp was dressed and wound upon the weaving frame. The cotton thread was now ready for the power loom to be woven into cloth. To establish a cotton mill, Francis Cabot Lowell and Paul Moody would of necessity need to know all these machines and how best to position them to make the factory work efficiently.

Carpenters and blacksmiths from New England to Pennsylvania were adept at building the simple hand-operated spinning wheels and looms for textile-making at home. Seeing opportunities to make the larger machines for carding, roving, spinning, warping, dressing and weaving used in factories, a number of these craftsmen invented and patented new devices. Between 1795 and 1815, at least forty-five American inventors took out patents for power looms. The complexity of these machines required knowledge of the advances made in Britain and the ability to design upgrades so that all the machines in the mill would work efficiently together.[6] Samuel Slater trained in England with the Arkwright spinning machine and came to Pawtucket, Rhode Island, late in the eighteenth century to build a copy. The Beverly Cotton Manufactory had horse-powered machinery by 1790.

The U.S. Patent Office granted a patent on November 17, 1796, to Amos Whittemore for his hand loom. From 1796 until 1815, at least thirty patents were awarded for variations of the hand loom. Francis Cabot Lowell and his star machinist Paul Moody contacted the local networks of machinists to find the best equipment for their Waltham mill, in which they planned to complete all aspects of manufacture from raw cotton to finished cloth under one roof. Shepherd Leech from his Easton foundry delivered to the Waltham mill a roller lathe, fluting lathe, cutting machines and forges. Luther Metcalf built ten carding machines (with sixty spindles each), and five throstle-spinning machines (with 192 spindles each). F. Stowell of

Worcester and J. Stimpson provided other machines. In Taunton, Cyrus Shepherd patented a spinning device.

Based on Lowell's mathematical calculations, Paul Moody devised a double-speeder roving frame for winding yarn onto the bobbins. Lowell and Moody built a device to create "a more slack spinning on the throstle spindles and the spinning of filling directly on the cops, without the process of winding." Francis Cabot Lowell, entering the fortieth year of his life, was determined to build a power loom similar to the machines he had seen in the British textile factories.

The idea of weaving by machine came out of a discussion in the town of Matlock, Derbyshire, England in the summer of 1784. Edmund Cartwright was born in 1743 in the village of Marnham in the county of Nottingham. He attended University College, Oxford, and studied for the ministry. At heart a poet, the Reverend Dr. Cartwright came to Matlock to see the spinning machines that brought great fame and fortune to its inventor Richard Arkwright. One of Cartwright's friends commented that when the Arkwright patent ran out, many spinning mills would be built and not enough hands would be found to weave the abundant thread. In that event, competitors on the Continent would take the lead at the expense of the British hand-weaving industry. Cartwright responded by saying that "the only remedy for such an evil would be to apply the power of machinery to the art of weaving as to that of spinning by contriving looms to take up the yarn as fast as it was procured by the spindle."

His friends were amused at Cartwright's naiveté, telling him that weaving was too complicated a skill to be done by a machine. Undeterred, Cartwright immediately set about to invent a power loom. Without any knowledge of the art of weaving or mechanical experience but possessing a sharp intellect, Cartwright reasoned that since in weaving "there could only be three movements, which were to follow each other in succession, there would be little difficulty in producing and repeating them." He employed a carpenter and a smith to construct the machine from his drawings. His first efforts to build a power loom were crude and clumsy, but after a few more months, he made enough progress and on April 4, 1785, took out a patent to protect his invention. In his early loom, "the warp was placed perpendicularly, and the shuttle was thrown by springs connected with a cylinder placed beneath the machine. The cylinder also gave motion to two levers, one of which reversed the threads of the warp and the other elevated the reed, which again descended by means of its own weight. The tension of the warp was produced by weights suspended from the beams, as in the common loom."

Cartwright was aware that his device lacked refinement and, over the course of the next years, he made changes, such as placing the warp horizontally and using a crank on the axis. He set up a small factory in

Edmund Cartwright (1743–1826) patented his power loom in 1785. Francis Cabot Lowell saw the great potential of the power loom during his tour of the British mills. (Edmund Cartwright [1743–1823], English inventor. After a portrait by Robert Fulton.)

Doncaster but after the workers smashed his power looms, Cartwright turned away from the textile production. In 1790, Mr. Grimshaw from Gorton, under license from Edmund Cartwright, opened a weaving mill in Manchester with the plan to install four hundred power looms, but the factory failed. A major problem with the Cartwright power loom was the need to stop the machine frequently to dress the warp as it unrolled from the beam. A man was needed to stand by the machine to perform this task, taking away the cost advantage of power. These difficulties set back the introduction of the power looms by a decade.

Others in Great Britain saw its great potential and set about to make improvements on Cartwright's design. Radcliffe and Ross of Stockport made an ingenious device to dress the warp. The next important modification came from H. Horrocks, also of Stockport. In 1803, Horrocks built his iron loom with so compact a design that several hundred could be placed side by side on a single floor of a factory. These improvements made the power loom four times as efficient as a skilled weaver working by hand using the fly shuttle. Mr. Horrocks, alas, shared the fate of many other inventors; his enterprise failed and he died in poverty. During the time Francis Cabot Lowell was touring Great Britain, the power loom was still a work in progress.

Although the British carefully guarded the secrets of the power loom, not permitting models or even drawings to leave their country, word reached America of its potential. In Providence, Rhode Island, Judge Daniel Lyman in 1813 was trying to build a power loom, as were John and Rozeanne Sizer of New London (October 23). Having seen, during his recent trip to the United Kingdom, the Cartwright- and Horrocks-type looms in motion, Francis Cabot Lowell had the advantage over his American competitors. Francis Cabot Lowell and Patrick Tracy Jackson received a patent for their power loom on February 23, 1815. James Thorp, and Cyrus Shepherd of Taunton, Massachusetts, received their loom patent on July 25, 1816.

The power loom was at the center of Francis Lowell's plan for his cotton mill. He wanted not merely to build a copy but also to improve on the British looms. Lowell spent months working in a room on Broad Street to complete the calculations and experiments needed to perfect his power loom. He employed "a man to turn the crank" while testing his machine. The loom was ready for a trial only after the mill building in Waltham was already built. Nathan Appleton recalled that "Mr. Lowell told me he did not wish me to see it until it was complete, of which he would give me notice. At length the time arrived. He invited me to see the loom operate. I well recollect the state of admiration and satisfaction with which we sat by the hour, watching the beautiful movement of this new and wonderful machine." Francis Cabot Lowell's loom was the first efficient American-built power loom. A friend asked Lowell why he was so engrossed in his machine; after all, others had already registered patents for their power looms. Lowell replied that while the present cost of cotton cloth was thirty-four cents a yard, his power loom would soon lower the cost to only four cents a yard. On February 23, 1815, Francis Lowell received a patent for his improved power loom.

Nathan Appleton recalled the achievements of Francis Cabot Lowell in a January 1838 speech before the Massachusetts House of Representatives: "Seldom has a mind of so much science being turned to this subject [cotton textile machinery] and never was a triumph more complete." It was the knowledge and the mathematical skills of Francis Cabot Lowell that gave shape to the machines on paper, but it was the skills of Paul Moody that transformed the plans into functioning machines. On May 10, 1816, Moody was awarded his first patent for his winding frame. On June 7, 1818, he was awarded a patent for a machine "by which the warp was dressed preparatory to weaving in the power loom." On April 8, 1819, he received a patent for his double-speeder with other inventions and patent to come.

Edmund Cartwright advanced on Richard Arkwright's work and now the American Francis Cabot Lowell—gifted amateurs all—had improved on Cartwright's loom. With his power loom Lowell showed his knowledge of the existing technology and his ability to move beyond the familiar to make his machine work even better. The freezing of the Charles River in winter causing chunks of ice to clog the waterwheel was yet another problem that Lowell and his team solved. Moving from inventor to manufacturer was another hurdle. Edmund Cartwright failed as a manufacturer, while Francis Cabot Lowell succeeded both as an inventor and as a businessman.

In his memoirs, published in 1861, Nathan Appleton detailed the inventiveness and determination of Francis Cabot Lowell in developing the power loom. Lowell's loom, wrote Appleton,

> was different in several particulars from the English loom, which was afterwards made public. The introduction of the power-loom made necessary many other changes in the process of weaving. The first was the dressing; for which Mr. Horrocks of Stockport [England], obtained a patent, and of which Mr. Lowell obtained a drawing. On putting it in operation, an essential improvement was made upon it, by which its efficiency was more than doubled. This Waltham dressing-machine continues in use with little change, from that time. The stop-motion of the machine for winding on the beams for dressing was original with this company. The greatest improvement was in the double speeder. The original fly-frame was made on no fixed principle for regulating the changing movements necessary in the process of filling a spool. Mr. Lowell undertook to make the numerous mathematical calculations necessary to perfect these complicated movements, which occupied

him constantly for more than a week. Mr. Moody carried them into effect by constructing the machinery in conformity. Several trials at law were made under the patent; involving the nice question, whether a mathematical calculation could be the subject of a patent. The last great improvement consisted in a more slack spinning on throttle spindles; and the spinning of filling directly on the cops, without the process of winding.

Nathan Appleton recalled the amusing tale of when Lowell and Moody went to Taunton to purchase a spinning device patented by Silas Shepherd. The haughty Mr. Shepherd refused to lower his price for a bulk order, claiming that Lowell could not proceed without his invention. Moody responded, "I am just thinking that I can spin the cops direct upon the bobbin." "You be hanged," said Mr. Shepherd. "Well, I accept your offer." "No," said Mr. Lowell, "it is too late." After leaving Shepherd, Moody confessed to Lowell that he was merely bluffing in the hope of getting a bargain price. "Mr. Lowell told him that since he had suggested the plan of spinning the filling on the bobbin, now he must accomplish it." When they returned to Waltham, Moody turned his mind to the problem, and invented and patented the filling frame.[7]

Other machine toolmakers were eager to sell their equipment to Francis Cabot Lowell. On May 18, 1814, he received a letter from William Blackburn of Providence, Rhode Island. Mr. Blackburn wrote, "I will undertake to establish your factory in the most improved manner, and give you all the information I am possessed of in the art of spinning and manufacturing for which I shall expect to receive 1/4 of a Dollar per spindle for all machinery now built or building and 1/2 a Dollar per spindle for all the machinery that may be built under my supervision. The terms of payment are 25 per cent in hand and the remainder when the job is completed. If you agree to my terms the sooner I hear from you the better."

With devices from different manufacturers, Paul Moody was hard at work making modifications and getting the machines to work smoothly together. He found that the wooden rollers used in the dressing frame became swollen and warped from the moisture. He tried coating the wood with pewter but, after consulting with his brother David, fashioned rollers from soapstone that "worked perfectly." Moody is credited also with the invention of the dead spindle, the throstle-filling frame, the regulator for the waterwheel, the double-speeder and the warping and dressing frame.

Amongst the papers of Francis Cabot Lowell for the year 1813 is an illustration of the waterwheel designed by Jacob Perkins, the prolific inventor, and mentor to Paul Moody. The Perkins waterwheel was installed at the Boston Manufacturing Company to power the looms and other machines inside the factory. The dam upriver stored the water to provide a constant flow over the waterfall and into the sluice gate to turn the wheel. In 1818, Jacob Perkins demanded the payment of $5,974.39 from the estate of Francis Cabot Lowell, claiming that he had assisted also in the development of the power loom. Perkins moved to England, where he opened a factory printing bank notes. His company in 1840 was the first to print the British penny postage stamps.

On January 30, 1814, Patrick Tracy Jackson sent a letter to Francis Cabot Lowell that must have delighted him: "Dear Frank, I have been at Waltham all the time since you left [on bank business in New York]. I have got our loom up & yesterday wove several yards—*by water*. The loom is excellent tho' still susceptible to improvements. Our shuttle caught twice; which was owing to our not fixing the stop motion properly, partly to the unequal motion of the wheel, which owing to ice or some other cause, one part of the revolution is about twice as fast as the other. Moody begins to be quite assured of its success." Patrick Tracy Jackson promised Lowell that he and Moody would continue to work on the loom, shuttle and the waterwheel to get the various parts to work smoothly together.

Another significant innovation by Francis Cabot Lowell and his team was the decision to take good care of their employees. "By the construction of boarding-houses at the expense and under the control of the factory," noted John Amory Lowell, "they gained the confidence of the rural population who were no longer afraid to entrust their daughters in a manufacturing town." These young women suffered no degradation of character and showed "no impediment to a reputable connection in marriage."[8]

John Amory Lowell recalled, in 1848, the many difficulties his uncle (and father-in-law) Francis Cabot Lowell, together with Patrick Tracy Jackson and Paul Moody, encountered with the machinery. "They faced, as might naturally be expected, many defects in their model loom, but these were gradually removed." The mill at Waltham was "the first one in the world that combined all the operations necessary for converting raw cotton into finished cloth." Working from memory and without the plans, tools or materials available to the English machinists, the American trio conceived and constructed new, and better, machinery. One example was the double spinner: "The motions of this machine were very complicated and required nice mathematical calculations [by Francis Cabot Lowell]. Without them, Mr. Moody's ingenuity, great as it was, would have been at fault." Not only did Lowell and Moody buy or make high-quality machines, but they also "adopted an entire new arrangement; in order to save labor by passing from one process to another; and in so arranging all the machinery that the entire product should be converted into cloth within the mill."

Before the coming of the Boston Manufacturing Company, the one hundred existing "cotton mills in the United States up to this time had been principally for spinning; the weaving being done on hand looms, and in England the power looms were used in a separate establishment." The Boston Manufacturing Company succeeded because it combined in one factory "the first efficient American power loom [and] all the operations of converting raw cotton into finished cloth."[9]

By the close of 1814, the Boston Manufacturing Company, with 1,700 spindles, was ready to produce cloth. Employing three hundred workers, the Boston Manufacturing Company was by far the largest textile mill in the nation. Facing the Charles River, from whence its power came, the red-brick building stood five stories high, ninety feet long, and forty-five feet wide. Its roof was double pitched, trussed and braced to withstand rain, snow and wind. The machine shop was located in the basement; cotton was carded on the first floor, spun on the second and woven into cloth on the third and fourth floors. At the start were three thousand spindles and one power loom, capable of producing four thousand yards of cloth a week. Southern cotton growers supplied the new mill at Waltham.[10] The Waltham mill produced plain, coarse, white sheeting, well suited to the needs of farmers, especially Western pioneers. With demand soaring for locally made cloth, the company soon was making profits of ten to eleven cents a yard.[11] During its first decade the Boston Manufacturing Company paid annual dividends of 8–13 percent, doubling the value of the investment. Total sales in 1815 were $412, rising to $51,203 in 1817. With business growing and profits soaring, Francis Cabot Lowell had little difficulty in raising the additional $300,000 of capital needed for his mill.

The machinery in the Waltham factory required continuous adjustments. Patrick Tracy Jackson wrote February 14, 1816, to Francis Lowell, then in Washington, DC, lobbying Southern congressmen to vote in favor of a tariff on imported textiles. "I have got the bobbin machine going," wrote Jackson. "It costs less & winds better than the others. I hope next week to turn out 2,000 yards. We shall put more looms into motion. As you return [to Boston] go to Paterson. If Stowell is there he can show you all that is worth seeing. See the looms in Baltimore if you can." The town of Paterson, New Jersey, used the waterpower of the Great Falls on the Passaic River to power a number of small textile mills, similar in scale to Samuel Slater's mills in Rhode Island. Later, Paterson became the center of the American silk industry. In and around Baltimore in 1816, there were eleven cotton mills, including the Baltimore Manufacturing Company, the Union Manufacturing Company and the Washington Manufacturing Company, with a total of eleven thousand spindles. Jackson wanted Lowell to see the advances being made elsewhere in the United States, and bring new ideas back to Waltham.

PATERNALISTIC CAPITALISM

In 1812, the town of Waltham, with barely one thousand people, lacked the surplus population to work in the Boston Manufacturing Company. In rural New England there "was a fund of labor, well-educated and virtuous" among the unmarried daughters of farmers. Lowell sent recruiters to the small communities of New England explaining the needs of the mill and assuring the parents that their daughters would be comfortably housed and protected in "boarding houses, at the cost to the company, under the charge of respectable women."

Francis Cabot Lowell had several reasons to treat his workers well. In Britain he had seen the slums that grew around the factories and was well aware of the Luddite rebellion wherein textile workers smashed the machines and burned the mills to vent their frustrations against the industrial revolution. Lowell did not want a permanently downtrodden workforce but expected the Yankee mill girls to stay not more than five years. Temporary and contented workers, Lowell reasoned, were far less likely to rebel. By offering good conditions of employment, Lowell hoped to overcome the prejudice of the farmers toward factory work. Lowell was also guided by his sense of moral obligation to look after his workers and treat them well.

THE WALTHAM MILL GIRLS

The farmwomen of New England had long engaged in the weaving of cloth to dress their families. This activity was done mainly during the winter months after the many other household and farm chores had been completed. By the middle of the eighteenth century weaving cloth at home had become a considerable cottage industry, earning the family much-needed cash. For decades after achieving its independence, the United States still remained dependent on India and Great Britain for its cloth. Unlike Britain, a large-scale homespun and home-weaving industry did not develop in America. The coming of the factory did not displace large numbers of home spinners and weavers. Instead the Boston Manufacturing Company sought its labor from the fund of "well educated and virtuous" daughters of New England farmers. The company sent agents to the remote farming communities in Massachusetts, New Hampshire and Vermont, offering payments in cash and accommodation in the company boardinghouses with good supervision. The *Boston Gazette* wrote an enthusiastic account of the Waltham factory, praising especially the boarding house system. Advertisements for workers informed applicants they "must be of good moral character and industrious [but] those in the habit of profanity and Sabbath breaking are not invited to make application."[12]

The Waltham factory offered employment for young women paid in cash rather than in the form of provisions. These country girls arrived at the factory dressed in "the plainest of homespuns cut in such an old-fashioned style that each young girl looked as if she had borrowed her grandmother's gown. [The girls] were a very curious sight, dressed in various outlandish fashions and with their arms brimful of hand-boxes containing all their worldly goods. On each of them was sewed a card on which one could read the old-fashioned New England names of the owners." Poverty did not drive them to the mills; rather it was the desire for some independence, to save for a dowry, support a brother at college, pay down the mortgage on the family farm or buy fancy clothes and, perhaps, save money to buy a small house. Nathan Appleton noted that "the daughters of respectable farmers were readily induced to come into these mills for a temporary period." Because Francis Cabot Lowell was so "devoted to arrangements for the moral character of the operatives he employed, [their parents] were not afraid to trust their daughters to work in the mill."[13] The machinery in the factory, set up by Paul Moody, worked so well that the farm girls needed only a month of training to become proficient at their repetitive tasks. These young women did not fill all the needs of the factory; a small number of workers were recruited at great expense from Britain for the most highly skilled jobs.

The mill girls, generally from sixteen to twenty-two years old, were housed in boarding houses under the care of mature matrons of good character. These women supervised the meals and living conditions, kept strangers out and made sure the girls attended church on Sundays. The young women signed contracts for one or two years and were given a bonus for completing the terms of the contract. Most of the women remained only for a few years before getting married or returning to their farms. They were paid monthly in cash, to spend in the company store and to save in the local banks. The Waltham mill offered these young women a means to escape the drudgery of the family farm for the relative independence of living in town, earning money, with opportunities for education and the chance to marry for love.

The company bell rang at 4:30 in the morning, followed by a second bell twenty minutes later. Work started at five o'clock and continued for two hours, when the girls rushed back to the boarding houses for breakfast. Work started again at 7:35 and went on until noon. After a forty-five-minute break for lunch the girls were back on the job at 12:45 and worked until 7:00 at night, when they returned for supper. During the evening hours the girls had time to read, write letters, do their washing and go to the store. Curfew was at ten o'clock. Standing on their feet all day and attending to the clanging machines, with pulleys, belting and wheels constantly vibrating, stiflingly hot in summer and cold in winter, the mill girls worked six days for a total of sixty-five to seventy hours a week. They were paid $2–$5 a week, less $1.25 for room and board. On Sundays the girls attended church and rested to prepare themselves for the next grueling week of work.

They were Yankee girls, of solid British stock, and descendants of the early settlers of the Massachusetts Bay Colony, who came from the same background as the mill owners. They were healthy and intelligent, responsible and moral. Lowell and Jackson made sure that the company kept its promise to the parents and took good care of their daughters. The girls had an easy transition from the long hours of family farm to the conditions at the mill. By modern standards, the mill girls were exploited, but in the context of the times, these young women considered themselves fortunate to have regular wages and the opportunity to live independently. By 1817, the department supervisors at the Boston Manufacturing Company were earning $12 weekly, machinists $6–$11, card room workers $2–$6, spinners $2–$3 and weavers $4–$5. The women and girls in the Waltham plant earned an average of $2.23 a week.[14] The paternalistic capitalism of the early years at Waltham suited the girls, their parents, the company and the town of Waltham.

SELLING THE CLOTH

Accustomed to buying fancy goods made in England or cheaper textiles imported from India, the good people of Boston were at first reluctant to buy locally made cloth. Nathan Appleton tells that in 1814 "when the Waltham Company first began to produce cloth there was but one place in Boston at which domestic goods were sold," the shop at No. 17 Cornhill owned by Mr. and Mrs. Isaac Bowers. The Bowers dry goods store specialized in cloth from Great Britain and India. With the Waltham cloth languishing in the Bowers store, Appleton sent samples to Benjamin C. Ward & Company, a company which Appleton half owned, and learned that the customers wanted unbleached heavy sheeting No. 14, thirty-seven inches wide and forty-four picks to the inch, running three yards to the pound; namely, the type of cheap cloth long imported from India. The Waltham Company was instructed to produce cloth of similar size and quality, and at a lower price. Francis Lowell saw a profit for the company at twenty-five cents a yard.

In early nineteenth-century Boston the sale of goods was commonly done by auction. The Board of Alderman licensed over sixty persons as auctioneers, a trade carefully regulated to prevent auctions being held in the open street and to ensure that stolen goods were not put up for sale. One of the prominent auctioneers in Boston at that time was David Forsaith, a shopkeeper and part-time auctioneer. Ward & Company, known for its high-priced British imports, decided to consign the lowly Waltham sheeting to David Forsaith who first sold it at auction in October 1815 at "something over thirty cents a yard," allowing a nice profit for the manufacturer, agent and the auctioneer.[15] With this success Benjamin C. Ward became the official selling agent for the Boston Manufacturing Company, earning 1 percent commission on sales. With its good management and integrated production methods the Boston Manufacturing Company dramatically reduced the cost of producing cloth per yard from thirty cents in 1815 to ten cents in 1820 and as low as seven cents a yard thereafter.[16] With sales increasing and in a burst of optimism, the board on November 6, 1815, authorized Patrick Tracy Jackson, the company treasurer, "to make the necessary contacts to build one Block of two Houses, similar to those already built, for workmen and eight smaller Houses, provided it can be done as cheap as usual." Boston Manufacturing opened a company store to serve its workers.

The treasurer, Patrick Tracy Jackson, kept meticulous records of the money flowing in and out of the Boston Manufacturing Company's account at the Boston Bank. For the first two years the survival of the company depended on the monthly payments made by the principal investors. Francis Cabot Lowell agreed to pay $1,000–$1,500 each month; Israel Thorndike and his son together, $2,000; Patrick Tracy Jackson, $1,000; Charles Jackson, $1,000; James Jackson, $500; Nathan Appleton, $500; John Gore, $500; James Lloyd, $500; Benjamin Gorham, $300; Uriah Cotting, $300; and Warren Dutton, $200. Monthly inflows of $7,800–$8,300 would be sufficient to pay for the construction of the factory, dam, machinery and the salaries of one hundred workers (earning $2 per worker per week). But the principal investors were not always timely in paying their monthly share, leading to serious cash flow problems.

Despite his declining health Francis Cabot Lowell regularly attended the board meetings and in November 1815 was elected chairman of the company. At the close of March 1816, the company had $3,955.30 in its cash account at the bank. On April 30, cash on hand had declined to $1,005.50, and on May 31 it was down to $219.80; it reached a low point on August 31, with a paltry $8.46 on hand. Late fees of 5 percent were charged in order to encourage the directors to pay on time. Realizing the perilous state of his company, in December 1816, Francis Cabot Lowell sent in a payment of $3,000. Patrick Tracy Jackson started borrowing $200–$300 a month from the bank to meet expenses. On February 26, 1817, the directors of the Boston Manufacturing Company met at the home of Nathan Appleton to discuss the cash flow crisis. Represented at the meeting were Nathan Appleton, the Thorndikes, Francis Cabot Lowell, Charles Jackson, Benjamin Gorham and Patrick Tracy Jackson. The mood of gloom was rapidly dispelled with the announcement that Francis Cabot Lowell had agreed to loan the company $20,000 and the "treasurer was hereby authorized to pay the said F. C. Lowell the interest as it becomes due or until otherwise authorized by the directors." To further boost capital the directors added an assessment of $200 on each share and authorized Appleton and Lowell to form a committee to examine "the best modes of raising money sufficient to finish the manufactory's new building and the same for the machinery." At the meeting of May 7, 1817, the directors agreed to raise more capital by issuing new shares at $1,000 per share. Francis Cabot Lowell took fifty shares; Patrick Tracy Jackson, thirty; Thorndike father and son, forty; Appleton, sixteen; Dutton, four; James Jackson, ten; and Paul Moody, eleven shares. Francis Cabot Lowell had committed $70,000 more of his own money to keep the Boston Manufacturing Company afloat. These funds together with the new shares bought by other directors kept the company liquid until it established a solid market for its cloth.

The first three years were critical and tested the management of the Boston Manufacturing Company. Fortunately, sales of cloth through Benjamin Ward & Company began to trickle in. During March 1816, the company sales agent sent in $250, with additional payments of $495 in January 1817, and $600 in December. Another source of revenue was the Waltham Machine Shop, making and selling spinning machines and power looms to other cotton mills.

On June 21, 1817, Francis Cabot Lowell purchased twenty shares that were previously allocated to John Gore, who had recently died. The last monthly payment from Francis Cabot Lowell was received on July 5, 1817. Francis Cabot Lowell missed the board meeting on July 21 and died on August 10, 1817, leaving his devoted friend and brother-in-law Patrick Tracy Jackson the task to carry forward the dream of American independence in textiles. After the death of its founder, the Boston Manufacturing Company sought new investors. J. J. Colburn, R. Fiske, Henry Lee and James Townsend joined the company and helped keep it solvent. After 1817, the Boston Manufacturing Company began to turn in profits from the rapidly increasing sales of its cloth.

THE WALTHAM-LOWELL SYSTEM

The mill established what became known as the Waltham-Lowell system. Before the Boston Manufacturing Company the processes of carding, spinning and weaving were carried out in separate mills owned by different proprietors, in which the workers were paid in provisions and clothing. In the Waltham mill of Francis Cabot Lowell all the processes of converting raw cotton to cloth were carried out in one factory under one ownership. The workers were accommodated in boarding houses and paid in cash. The Waltham-Lowell system was so successful that it was soon widely adopted and became the standard in American industrialization. The passage of the Tariff Act of 1816 encouraged the directors of the Boston Manufacturing Company to put up a second mill with 3,584 spindles. The three-story brick building, 150 feet in length and forty feet deep, was completed in 1818 and doubled the manufacturing capacity of the company. The second mill was built alongside the first, following the pattern Francis Lowell had seen in Great Britain.

During its first decade the "profits of manufacturing were great," with no other textile company doing as well. The town of Waltham was proud of its factory and the workforce. *The Waltham Mirror* noted that the mill girls saved "thousands of dollars which are annually deposited for safe-keeping in our banking institutions—such economy is praiseworthy. . . . They are well read and well educated, which shows they have improved some of the precious hours of life in mental culture. [The] odium, which formerly attached to a factory life, has been entirely neutralized by the intelligent and high-minded girls who have engaged in this type of employment. Intelligence and character always give dignity to a life of labor."[17]

At the end of the War of 1812, Francis Lowell invited Nathan Appleton to take a trip to the cotton mills of Rhode Island. "We saw several manufacturers, they were all sad and despairing." These small spinning mills depended on old machinery and could not match the flood of cheap imports coming from Britain and India. "By degrees," noted Appleton, "the manufacturers woke up to the fact that the power loom was the instrument which changed the whole character of manufacture." The desperate Rhode Island mill owners were demanding a 100 percent tariff on imported cloth. Lowell and Appleton were convinced that with upgraded machinery, American companies could still prosper with a much lower protective tariff. In 1814, Lowell's factory made a profit selling at thirty cents a yard, and by the close of 1817, was still profitable at six cents a yard.[18] The arrangement with Ward & Company continued for a number of years until Nathan Appleton switched, selling to James W. Paige & Company.

Conflicts arose between the Boston Manufacturing Company and the Waltham Cotton & Woolen Manufacturing Company over "damages from the backwater flowed upon our wheel by their dam." The case between the two companies was heard before the Supreme Judicial Court of Massachusetts in October 1815 and settled with Waltham Cotton & Wool paying a fine of $750 and agreeing to lower the height of its dam by eighteen inches. The Boston Manufacturing Company's second red-brick mill drew off even more waterpower and crippled the Waltham Cotton & Wool. In February 1819, the Boston Manufacturing Company bought out its local rival for $16,000. The wooden building was torn down and the Boston Manufacturing Company erected in its place a new red brick factory, for its third mill, with two thousand spindles, producing finer quality goods than the upper mills.

SUCCESS IN HIS LIFETIME

Even in Lowell's lifetime, the success of the Boston Manufacturing Company spread rapidly. Francis Cabot Lowell heard from Joshua and Thomas Gilpen, brothers from a prominent Quaker family in Philadelphia and owners of flour and papers mills who considered getting into the textile business. Lowell wrote them April 26, 1816, about the progress made by the Boston Manufacturing Company: "Our manufactory is a new one having begun about 15 months since. We had but a few looms at first. We now have twenty-eight at work. We have made in all our looms about 50,000 yards of plain cloth, 4/4 and 5/4 wide. One girl attends to two looms after she has learned the business, which generally takes about a month. Our best weavers generally weave from 250 to 300 yards on two looms 4/4 cloth, number 14 warp or number 15 filling, in one week or six working days of about 11 hours each, exclusive of meals, including all the time lost in shifting the beams. The whole manufactory averages about 100 yards a loom per week. The first machine is one of our own invention. The second is English. The first machine, which we call a warping machine, is important. . . . We are erecting 31 more looms but at present we are delayed by our spinning, which cannot quite supply 28 looms. We have only woven plain cloth on our looms."

Showing his grasp of the details of the operation, Lowell told the Gilpen brothers that the new looms being built at the company machine shop in Waltham were for sale at a cost of $2,050 each. The Poignand & Plant Cotton Company of Lancaster, Massachusetts; Crocker & Richmond of Taunton, Massachusetts; and the Dover Cotton Company of Dover, New Hampshire, were among the first customers to buy power looms from the Waltham machine shop. The power loom and the expansion of textile mills lead to a decline in the homespun industry. In a highly competitive market the price of manufactured textiles continued to fall, making time-consuming homespun even less competitive.[19]

The Boston Manufacturing Company was the principal source of wealth for the town of Waltham. The company opened the first store in the town (1816), and the first schoolhouse built on Elm Street (1817), in which one teacher took care of seventy children. Patrick Tracy Jackson served as both landlord and good town citizen. He was a member of the school committee and saw to it that the school was subsidized. In 1822, the company built a second schoolhouse for the growing town. The town bank and the town fire department, both supported by the company, were added.

The Boston Manufacturing Company increased the number of shares of stock from 100 to 571. Francis Cabot Lowell bought thirty-five more shares (numbers 108–23 and 151–65) on May 28, a further thirty shares (218–47) on July 5; and five more (169–74) on August 1, 1817, to become the largest shareholder with 115 shares, followed by Patrick Tracy Jackson with 90; Israel Thorndike Sr. with 60; Christopher Gore with 52; Nathan Appleton, Charles Jackson and Israel Thorndike Jr. with 50 each; James Jackson with 46; J .W. Booth with 30 and Paul Moody with 23. Lowell kept buying shares in his Boston Manufacturing Company until days before he died. After his death, his brother John Lowell Jr. attended company board meetings, representing the interests of Francis Cabot Jr. and Edward Lowell, the two younger sons. At the end of 1820 all the Francis Cabot Lowell shares in the Boston Manufacturing Company had been sold. Patrick Tracy Jackson and his brother Charles and James also reduced their shares in the Boston Manufacturing Company as the center of textile manufacturing shifted from Waltham to the new industrial city of Lowell, along the powerful Merrimack River.

Douglass Cecil North, winner of the 1993 Nobel Prize in Economic Sciences, captured the importance of Francis Cabot Lowell and his cotton mill:

> Introduction of the power loom and the performance of all the cloth-making operations with water power initiated the growing size, specialization, and localization of the industry. . . . The Boston Manufacturing Company at Waltham in 1813 was spectacularly successful. The early success of the Waltham mill was the result of pioneering a coarse cloth in growing demand in America, and which could be woven on the new power loom. This plain white "sheeting" lent itself to mass production, and met a wide variety of needs in a predominantly agricultural society. New England mills following in the footsteps of the Boston Manufacturing Company found they could compete with British textiles in this type of product, and had a market that grew with the developing regional interdependence.[20]

In his *History of the Manufactures in the United States, 1607–1860*, published in 1916, the eminent American economist Victor Selden Clark wrote, "The Boston Manufacturing Company erected the first modern factory in America, performing all operations of cloth-making by power at a central plant. Labor was specialized and the workers were organized into departments. Wages were paid in cash, output standardized, and buying and selling systematized. In a word, the commercial, technical and operative elements of the factory were brought together in accordance with an intelligent plan and so coordinated as 'to make a more efficient producing unit that had hitherto existed in this country.' For the first time in America manufacturing in a factory was fully separated from industry done in the household."[21]

In his *Account of the United States of America*, published in 1823, the Englishman Isaac Holmes wrote about the "factory at Waltham, near Boston." By then the Boston Manufacturing Company had five hundred throstle spinners and one hundred and fifty power looms. Other American textile mills averaged twenty power looms and none had more than fifty. "There is not in Great Britain a cotton factory with more complete machinery," wrote Holmes. "It is the largest concern in the Union."[22]

The Boston Manufacturing Company remained profitable for many years even after Patrick Tracy Jackson and Paul Moody left and the industry shifted away from the Charles to larger rivers. In 1827 the immensely capable John Amory Lowell replaced Patrick Tracy Jackson as manager of the Boston Manufacturing Company. For most of the nineteenth century and part of the twentieth, the Waltham mill was fairly profitable. In 1885, for want of orders, the company shut down, idling six hundred workers. In 1893, the company lowered wages to an average of $3.50 per week, forcing its seventeen hundred workers to strike demanding their old wages. In 1905, the workers again went on strike "to resist a change of method and the adoption of new machinery, which was deemed equivalent to a reduction of more than one-half of their earnings."[23] The Great Depression was the final blow and the Boston Manufacturing Company closed in 1930. The site was declared a national historic landmark in 1977.

12

The Tariff of 1816

All of the Southern States voted with South Carolina in support of the bill, while most of the New England members were opposed to the measure. It was a tariff of revenue, and not for protection.

John C. Calhoun, written in 1833

[The tariff of 1816] was a South Carolina tariff supported by South Carolina votes. If it depended on Massachusetts votes it would have been lost.

Daniel Webster

[The tariff act of 1816 marked] the beginning of a distinctly protective policy in this country.

F. W. Taussig, 1892

Thomas Jefferson once opposed large-scale manufacturing in America, saying "that it was better for our work-shops to remain in Europe." The War of 1812 led him to change his mind: "We must now place the manufacturer by the side of the agriculturalist." Domestic manufacture answered the question, wrote Jefferson, "whether we shall make our own comforts, or go without them at the will of a foreign nation [and was] consistent with our peace, and the preservation of our rights as an independent nation."[1]

In 1803, there were only four cotton mills in the whole of America. By 1809, there were sixty-two mills with a total of thirty-one thousand spindles. In 1811, there were eighty thousand spindles processing ten thousand bales of raw cotton. During the years of the war against Great

Britain, 1812–1815, many more capitalists in New England and the Middle Atlantic states put their money into the manufacture of textiles. The Pembroke Cotton & Woolen Manufactory, Neponset Cotton Factory, Walpole Cotton Manufacturing Company and the Hampden Cotton Manufactory were but a few of the dozens of newly incorporated cotton mills hoping to follow the success of Francis Lowell's Waltham mill. These companies had a capital base of $100,000–$150,000, far less than the Boston Manufacturing Company, and they also lacked efficient power looms. With foreign textiles kept out during the war years, the domestic manufacturers hoped for quick success. By 1815, there were five hundred thousand spindles at work in the United States processing ninety thousand bales of raw cotton. That year, there were one hundred thousand industrial workers in the United States, mostly women and children.

With the defeat of Napoleon at Waterloo in 1815, Great Britain emerged as the strongest country in Europe. Britain was eager to reestablish its profitable markets in the United States. Henry Brougham, an Edinburgh-born and -educated lawyer (and the future Baron Brougham, Lord Chancellor), bluntly stated the British policy in a speech before the House of Parliament. "It is worthwhile," Brougham said, "to incur a loss upon the first importation, in order by the glut, to stifle in the cradle those rising manufactures in the United States, which the War has forced into existence, contrary to the natural course of things." With the encouragement of the British Parliament, cheap hand-loomed cloth from India and high-end manufactured textiles from Britain once again flooded into the American market, threatening failure to the young American industries.

Nathan Appleton, writing in 1858, left a vivid picture of these times: "The effect of the peace of 1815 was ruinous. In June 1816, Mr. Lowell invited me to accompany him in making a visit to Rhode Island, with a view of seeing the actual state of the manufacture. We proceeded to Pawtucket. We called on Mr. [Oziel] Wilkinson, the maker of machinery. He took us into his establishment—a large one; all was silent, not a wheel in motion, not a man to be seen. He informed us that there was not a spindle running in Pawtucket, except a few in [Samuel] Slater's old mill, making yarn. All was dead and still. In reply to questions from Mr. Lowell, he stated, that during the war the profits of manufacturing were so great that the inquiry never was made whether any improvement could be made in machinery, but how soon it could be turned out. We saw several manufacturers; they were all sad and despairing." Oziel Wilkinson was father-in-law to Samuel Slater and in a good position to assess the downturn in Pawtucket, home of some of America's earliest spinning mills. Pawtucket waited too long to introduce power weaving and fell behind the Boston Manufacturing Company.

In 1814, total imports into the United States were valued at $12,967,659. After the peace the value in 1815 rose to $83,356,680 and shot up to $151,448,644 in 1816.[2] Much of the increase in imports was due to the flow of British manufactured goods and cheap cotton cloth and calicos from India. In New England upward of sixty thousand factory workers lost their jobs.

Politics in America took up the debate of protective tariffs or free trade. In his address to Congress on December 5, 1815, a few weeks before the war ended, President James Madison noted that the national debt had reached $120 million and proposed tariffs on imports as a source of revenue. "In adjusting the duties on imports," Madison said, "to the object of revenues, the influence of the tariff on manufactures will necessarily present itself for consideration." William Lowndes and John Calhoun carried Madison's message to secure the backing of the southern and western states and enact the Tariff of 1816. Henry Clay (1777–1852) from Kentucky was one of the most prominent politicians of his day. Motivated by nationalism, he advocated the American system to advance domestic industrialization by means of federal subsidies to build factories and roads, and high tariffs to keep imports down.

Writing in 1888, F. W. Taussig, the Henry Lee Professor of History at Harvard University, noted that during the war of 1812, "a knot of young men of the rising generation [were] strongly protectionist of the young industries." During the twenty years after the war of 1812, wrote Taussig, "the protective controversy was one of the more important features in the political life of the nation; and the young industries argument was the great rallying cry of the protectionists."[3]

The Tariff of 1816 had its strongest support among the southern states, which lacked manufacturing, but aspired soon to build factories. The chief supporters of tariffs were William Lowndes and John Calhoun of South Carolina, backed by Henry Clay. Calhoun believed that the young industries of America should be protected as a matter of national security, even if they could not compete against imports. The protected domestic textile industries would ensure supplies of cloth at times of war, and a tariff on imports could be used to reduce the national debt. In 1812, Henry Clay and John Calhoun were the leading war hawks, and in 1816, these men were leaders in the fight for American industrial independence.

The Massachusetts and Rhode Island manufacturers, representing 170 cotton mills, sent a petition to Washington, DC, demanding that the federal government save the domestic industry by imposing tariffs as high as 100 percent on imported cloth. The industry chose James Burrill Jr., the attorney general of Rhode Island, to go to Washington and lobby for the passage of a tariff on imported textiles.

Francis Cabot Lowell believed that with modern equipment and advanced business methods American companies could compete even with imports from low-wage countries. He calculated that American companies could produce textiles to sell at six cents a yard "and without loss to the manufacturer." He was swayed, however, to consider the plight of the less efficient mills, and agreed to travel to Washington, DC, with James Burrill to advocate for a tariff of 25 percent on imports, but not the 100 percent that Rhode Island was asking for. The shrewd Francis Cabot Lowell understood that with his power looms and efficient factory he stood to gain market share by selling his cloth more cheaply than the old-style Rhode Island mills.

Israel Thorndike Sr., as a major shareholder in the Boston Manufacturing Company, was concerned about the outcome of the tariff debate, but he had other irons in the fire, such as his rum distillery. Thorndike wrote to Lowell (February 11, 1816), in Washington, DC, asking, "Can the duty upon foreign spirits be continued at its present rate? Whiskey distillers are as much interested in this question as are New England rum distillers. It appears reasonable there should be some protecting duties to favour these other establishments."

During the war, the British army sacked Washington, DC, setting fire to the White House, Senate, House of Representatives and the Treasury building, leaving only the outer shells of the buildings standing. The reconstruction of the nation's capital began in 1815 and was far from complete by the time Lowell and Burrill reached the city. The two emissaries, who remained in Washington from February to April 1816, found a divided Congress. The support for open markets and opposition to tariffs was strongest in New England, long dependent on overseas trade. The middle states, led by Pennsylvania, favored tariffs, while the West was divided. The votes of the planting states, particularly South Carolina, were key to Francis Cabot Lowell's hopes for a majority in Congress in support of tariffs. He set about to persuade the South Carolina representatives that "by the establishment of the cotton manufacture in the United States, the Southern planter would greatly increase his market. He would furnish the raw material for all those American fabrics, which would take the place of manufactures imported from India, or partly made in England from Indian cloth. He would thus, out of his own produce, be enabled to pay for all the supplies which he requires from the North."[4] In particular, Lowell set out to convince the immensely able and influential South Carolinians William Lowndes and John Calhoun.

WILLIAM JONES LOWNDES

William Jones Lowndes (1782–1822) favored the protection of the domestic cotton and wool industries and shepherded the 1816 tariff bill through the House Committee on Ways and Means. He was born on the Horse-shoe plantation in the parish of St. Batholomew's, Colleton County, South Carolina, to the elderly Rawlins Lowndes, president of South Carolina during the Revolution, and his third wife, Sarah. The nine-hundred-acre plantation, with 124 slaves, grew rice. His mother was "much impaired by grief for the loss of her first two children," and, at the suggestion of the family doctor, decided on a long stay in England to recover her spirits. Sarah Lowndes and seven-year-old William set sail for London, where they remained three years. In London, young William displayed his "wonderful intellect" and astonishing ability to translate and recite pages of Latin verse. On his return to America he was tutored in Charleston before studying the law. He inherited the Horseshoe plantation, owned a summer residence near Charleston, married Elizabeth, daughter of the Federalist leader Thomas Pinckney, and served in the South Carolina House of Representatives.

At age twenty-nine Lowndes set out for Washington to represent South Carolina in the U.S. Congress. His rise was rapid and in 1815, he was appointed chairman of the Committee of Ways and Means, authorized to find the $25,369,000 needed to meet the government's obligations. On January 15, 1816, the Lowndes committee proposed "an act for imposing duties upon all goods, merchandise, wares imported from any foreign port or place."[5]

The gentlemanly yet forceful William Lowndes of South Carolina seemed destined for greatness and was considered a candidate for the presidency. He died at age forty on October 27, 1822, en route to England, and his remains were buried at sea. Lowndes County, Alabama, was named in his honor. This county became notorious for the practice of seizing blacks on the flimsiest of charges and sending them as convict slave labor to the mines and farms.[6]

JOHN CALDWELL CALHOUN

John Caldwell Calhoun (1782–1850) was another of the band of forceful young politicians born around the time of the Revolutionary War. The son of a Scots-Irish father and his second wife, in the South Carolina backcountry, John grew up on his father's 1,200-acre plantation, worked by thirty-one slaves. After his father died, John helped run the plantation at the neglect of his education. At age eighteen he returned to school to prepare for college. He enrolled at Yale University in October 1802, where, at six feet two inches, Calhoun excelled even in competition with the graduates of the finest academies in the North.

In the summer of 1804, John Calhoun visited Floride Bonneau, the widow of his cousin John, who, with her children, was summering at

Newport, Rhode Island. Calhoun was instantly drawn to the family but was determined to finish his studies at Yale and start a career in law. He traveled to Charleston to apprentice in the law office of Henry William De Saussure and then returned to Connecticut to study at the Litchfield law school. In December 1807, John C. Calhoun was admitted to the South Carolina bar, and four years later was elected by the state of South Carolina to serve in the U.S. House of Representatives. For years, the disciplined Calhoun had kept his eye on Floride's beautiful young daughter, also called Floride. Two months after his election to the House, Calhoun, at age twenty-eight, married the eighteen-year-old Floride, the daughter of Floride Bonneau Colhoun. The marriage gave John Calhoun the financial security he needed for a career in public service. John divided his time between Washington, DC, and his slave plantation Fort Hill, where he grew cotton.

In Washington, John Calhoun quickly made his mark as a gifted orator and a "war hawk," his hostility to Great Britain stemming from the blockade by British warships preventing South Carolina cotton from reaching European ports. In 1817, President James Monroe selected the thirty-five-year-old Calhoun as secretary of war. Calhoun served as vice president both to John Quincy Adams and Andrew Jackson. In 1844, he served as secretary of state.[7] With Daniel Webster and Henry Clay, he was among the great debaters of his time.

FRANCIS CABOT LOWELL
INFLUENCES THE TARIFF DEBATE

The negotiations for a tariff began in earnest. Henry Clay from Kentucky asked for a high tariff on a wide range of imports to provide the revenues needed to pay down the huge federal deficit and also "to strengthen the argument for a high tariff to protect manufacturers by dependence upon it also as a major source of revenue." Secretary of the Treasury Alexander Dallas recommended a 33.33 percent tariff on textiles. Henry Clay countered Dallas by arguing for 33.33 or at least 30 percent for three years and then lowered to 25 percent. Lowndes argued for 25 percent. Clay "encountered resistance from Daniel Webster, who was concerned about the adverse effect of protectionism on New England shipping. Webster got the better of him, and the final vote was 25 per cent for three years, then 20 per cent on cottons. Woolens received the same treatment."

Despite his declared opposition to protection, Daniel Webster was willing to respond to the wishes of the New England industrialists. While Francis Lowell was in Washington, DC, he met frequently with Webster to garner his support for the domestic industry and the imposition of tariffs. Webster recalled, "I was much with him & found him full of exact practical knowledge on many subjects," particularly low-cost cotton sheeting produced by the Boston Manufacturing Company and the fierce competition from imports. With Lowell's guidance, Webster added a provision to the tariff bill putting a minimum value of twenty-five cents on every square yard of cloth. The effect of this provision was to keep out Indian cloth—the main competition for the Waltham mills.[8] Francis Lowell rewarded Webster by inviting him to leave New Hampshire for Boston, where great financial opportunities awaited him. As a Boston lawyer, Webster defended the interests of the Boston Manufacturing Company and shifted his position from a free trader to become a supporter of tariffs.

On April 8, 1816, after a long and heated debate, the House recorded eighty-eight votes in favor of the tariff on imported cloth with fifty-four voting against. The decisive votes came from the South, with twenty-five Southern members of the House voting for the tariff. Almost all the New England representatives voted against tariffs showing that here the merchants and ship owners still held sway. The merchants-turned-manufacturers like Appleton and Lowell were then only a small part of the New England economy. Webster mysteriously did not attend to record his vote. The Tariff Act of 1816 was the first protectionist measure enacted by the government of the United States. The passage of the act divided the North and the South and opened the debate whether tariffs should be used to protect weak domestic industries. Others saw tariffs on imports as a convenient source of revenue for the federal government. The Tariff Act of 1816 imposed a 25 percent duty on imported woolen and cotton goods and thirty per cent on iron products. The great success of Francis Cabot Lowell and James Burrill Jr. as lobbying agents for the cotton textile manufacturer encouraged other industries to send lobbyists to Washington, DC—a practice that has grown exponentially over the years.

A mill owner in Wilmington, Delaware, wrote to Lowell (May 25, 1816) to congratulate him on his successful intervention on behalf of the Northern textile manufacturers. He wrote, "Soon after the happy conclusion of the Treaty of Peace with England, in consequence which it is likely to have over our cotton manufacturers, I conclude it would be useful and perhaps necessary to form some plan which would assist the cotton manufactures in our community." The writer suggested the cotton manufacturers in each state select delegates for a national meeting. A national association would become a powerful lobbying force for the industry, sharing information about advances in technology, buying machinery at lower prices and lobbying for barriers against imports.

With his pen dripping with malice, Karl Schriftgiesser, writing in the June 1927 issue of H. L. Mencken's *American Mercury* magazine, claimed that Francis Cabot Lowell's primary interest was to make "a great deal of money," and presented a Machiavellian account of the manner in which Lowell influenced the vote on the Tariff Act of 1816: "So Francis Cabot Lowell went down to Washington and there met a Southern gentleman by the name of John C. Calhoun. Into his courtly ear the cultured man of business poured out his tale, probably with a British accent, and not forgetting to add how much the Southern cotton planters would profit if his proposals were followed. Evidently Mr. Calhoun saw the point, for the outcome of Mr. Francis Cabot Lowell's year at the Capitol was a protective tariff, which quickly became a great help to the infant industry. Many a Boston and Cambridge family today blesses the name of John C. Calhoun. His statue should be placed in Harvard Yard."[9]

William Lowndes enjoyed an education and wealth every bit as privileged as that of Francis Cabot Lowell. Similarly, Yale-educated John C. Calhoun, married to the wealthy Floride Bonneau, had little reason to be awed by a visiting Bostonian with a strong Federalist pedigree. Plantation and slave owners both, the anti-Federalists Lowndes and Calhoun voted for the tariffs, not to placate Lowell, but to help American manufacturing industries, to encourage American industrial self reliance, and to advance the interests of South Carolina.

In the years to follow, John Calhoun sought to explain why he voted for the Tariff of 1816. He had nothing personally to gain from the tariff but it offered protection to the cotton and textile industries that were vital to the prosperity of the nation. America required a secure supply of goods produced at home. Manufacturing, Calhoun said, was a source of national pride, power and wealth as well as offering employment to many. "Revenue was the main object," he wrote. The tariffs were first and foremost the source of much-needed revenue for the federal government to reduce the huge debt "hanging over the country." He supported the Tariff of 1816 as beneficial to his native South Carolina. By curtailing foreign imports, South Carolina stood to gain with larger cotton sales. Hoping for an industrial future, the tariffs would encourage the building of cotton mills in the South. "In common with almost the entire South," Calhoun wrote, "I gave my support to the tariff of 1816 [as] a tariff of revenue, and not for protection. . . . Whatever support the State [of South Carolina] has given the bill, originated from the most disinterested motives." The interest of the South was "to buy cheap, and sell high." His interest in supporting the tariff came also "from a feeling of kindness, combined with a sense of justice," perhaps in response to the persuasive Francis Cabot Lowell. While he and other Southerners were eager to assist the textile industries of the North, Calhoun noted that "most of the New England members were opposed to the measure."[10] John Calhoun foresaw "clearly the benefit which the cotton planting states would derive from the introduction of the manufactures in this country." When he visited the Waltham mill in

1818 it was "with the apparent satisfaction of having himself contributed to its success." In later years, Calhoun turned against tariffs as detrimental to cotton interests.

The major opposition to tariffs on imports came from Francis Cabot Lowell's relatives and fellow merchants in Massachusetts, where for decades they made their fortunes from overseas trade and shipping. These self-same merchants were engaged in the business of importing the low-cost textiles from India and manufactured goods from Great Britain that were threatening the survival of the domestic industry. Manufacturing in New England was growing but, in 1816, was still only a small part of the economy. For most of his working life, Francis Cabot Lowell was a merchant, importing goods from the East Indies and China. He built India Wharf to berth the ships bringing in textiles from the Orient. Francis Cabot Lowell himself continued to import India cloth even as the tariff was about to take effect. By lobbying for a tariff on imported cloth, Lowell was opposing the interests of the Boston merchant community, his family, friends and his class. His courage came from his conviction that the growth and wealth of America lay with the manufacture of goods at home, using American workers, raw materials and American water power. He was determined to fight for the industry that had become the great passion of the remaining years of his life.

EFFECTS OF THE TARIFF OF 1816

The Tariff Act of 1816 helped replenish the U.S. treasury but did not slow the flow of British textiles or other goods. So important was the American market that the British cut their prices, rendering their goods cheap despite the added tariffs. Horace Greeley, editor of the *New York Tribune*, reported that "Great Britain poured her fabrics, far below cost, upon our markets in a perfect deluge." The port of Boston in 1816 welcomed 655 foreign vessels, rising to 755 the following year. The British government retaliated against the Tariff of 1816 by banning the import of American wheat and increasing imports of raw cotton from India. As a result the value of American cotton declined, leading to failures of farms and banks. Before the passage of the Tariff of 1816, Rhode Island, with ninety-nine mills and seventy-six thousand spindles, was ahead of Massachusetts, with only fifty-seven mills and forty-six thousand spindles. The power loom, introduced into America by Francis Cabot Lowell, was the key machine needed to lower costs and increase output. Helped by the sale of power looms, larger factories and the Waltham-Lowell system of production, Massachusetts soon eclipsed Rhode Island, with its smaller Slater-type mills, to become the nation's leading cotton textile state.

Rather than reducing costs through technological advances, the American manufacturers demanded increasingly high tariffs to protect their industries. In 1824, another tariff on imports was passed into law, followed by the Tariff of Abominations of 1828—all in the name of protecting the young domestic industries. Calhoun fought against these tariffs as harmful to South Carolina in particular and cotton interests in general. His nemesis Daniel Webster repeatedly reminded John Calhoun of his vote in 1816. "The tariff of 1816," fulminated Daniel Webster, "is, Sir, in truth, a South Carolina tariff supported by South Carolina votes. . . . But for those votes, it could not have passed in the form in which it did pass; whereas if it depended on Massachusetts votes, it would have been lost."[11]

In her 1930 book on the *Famous Families of Massachusetts*, Mary Caroline Crawford says that "the Lowells and the Appletons were the 'industrial radicals' in the stand they took against the imbedded conservatism of the great majority of their neighbors." At that time the livelihood of one in seven of all the people in New England came from shipping and trade. Backed by John Lowell and the Federalist Party, merchants wanted the sea lanes open, rather than imposing tariffs to support domestic industries.[12]

DANIEL WEBSTER

The role played by Daniel Webster in the debate on tariffs was murky. He was a Federalist and supporter of shipping and commercial interests who had opposed industrialization, saying, "I am not in haste to see Sheffields and Birminghams in America." Under the influence of Francis Cabot Lowell, Webster changed his views to become a strong supporter of domestic industry and of tariffs. Born in Salisbury, New Hampshire, in 1782, Daniel was the son of Ebenezer Webster and his second wife, Abigail. A shy boy, he was sent in 1796 to Phillips Academy, Exeter, but returned home after six months. Determined to overcome his fear of speaking in public he studied hard and was admitted to Dartmouth College where he spent four years. He chose to become a lawyer and moved to Boston where he apprenticed under Christopher Gore (who years earlier received his legal education from Judge John Lowell). Daniel Webster returned to New Hampshire to start a law practice. At the start of the War of 1812, he entered the U.S. Congress as a representative from New Hampshire. Even though he did not support tariffs he "succeeded in adjusting the tariff on cotton to suit the desires of the industrialist Francis Cabot Lowell."[13] He insisted that that the bill was a South Carolina tariff, yet he gave Francis Lowell the advice needed to gain the Boston Manufacturing Company a competitive edge against other domestic mills and also keep out cloth made in India. Daniel Webster served the interests of the Boston Manufacturing Company both as a congressman and as a lawyer.

Accepting the invitation of Francis Cabot Lowell to move to Boston, Daniel Webster resigned from Congress and, in August 1816, bought a house on Mt. Vernon Street and opened his practice on State Street. He was at the center of the thriving financial and commercial life of Boston and Francis Lowell made sure that business came his way. Soon Webster had a thriving practice earning him $20,000 a year. Webster rapidly adjusted to Boston ways, joined the Athenaeum and attended services at the Brattle Street church.[14] Daniel Webster was out of Congress from 1817 to 1823 and served the interests of the Boston wealthy. In addition to Francis Cabot Lowell, his list of clients included George Lee, John Jacob Astor, Nathan Appleton and the leading mercantile firms, shippers, insurance companies and manufacturers. Daniel Webster represented Paul Moody and the Boston Manufacturing Company in six patent infringement suits. Daniel Webster earned a lot, spent a lot and was usually in debt to his benefactors.[15]

Most of the New England merchants were ardent supporters of free trade and against protection. However, the mood shifted as the capitalists of Massachusetts followed Francis Cabot Lowell by moving their money from trade to manufacturing. The Boston textile manufacturers were Daniel Webster's clients and friends, and became his chief financial supporters when Webster reentered public life. These donations were used to finance his election campaigns as well as paying his personal expenses.

SUCCESS DESPITE INCREASED IMPORTS

The Boston Manufacturing Company of Waltham, with its power looms and efficient management structure, was one of the few American textile mills able to withstand the British deluge. In 1817, the owners of the Boston Manufacturing Company informed Congress "that they were making a profit of twenty-five per cent, and stood in no need for further protection."[16] James Lloyd, one of the first investors in the Boston Manufacturing Company and now representing Massachusetts in the U.S. Senate, opposed any increase in the tariff. "I am interested in manufacturing," James Lloyd said, addressing the Senate in 1822. "I own stock in one of the very few cotton mills now running in my state. That mill regularly pays good dividends, and is likely to do so indefinitely, if the Tariff is let alone. But should you pass the bill, hundreds of such factories will be erected till the market is glutted with their fabrics, while prices must fall, and our concern very probably may be broken down. I choose to let well alone, and entreat you not to pass this bill."[17]

OTHER TARIFFS

The Senate did not heed James Lloyd's warning and passed the Tariff of 1824. As Lloyd predicted, the Tariff of 1824 led to many more textile mills but the level of protection was still insufficient to hold back the flood of British imports. John Calhoun and the South voted strongly against the tariff, while Daniel Webster and New England voted in favor. The Tariff of 1828, known as the Tariff of Abominations, raising the duties on imported textiles by 50 percent of their value, passed in the House on a vote of 105 to 94 and in the Senate with a vote of 26 to 21. In the space of twelve years the North and the South changed sides on the tariff issue. The draconian Tariff of 1828 succeeded in restraining imports but led to a tremendous growth of domestic manufacturing, leading to cut-throat competition between American companies that continued for the rest of the nineteenth century and beyond.

THE LOWELL FAMILY ADJUSTS TO CHANGE

Francis Cabot Lowell was a leading force in the passage of the Tariff of 1816 at the time when his older brother John, the mouthpiece of the right wing of the Federalist Party, was a powerful advocate of free trade. After Francis Cabot Lowell died, John attended several meetings of the board of the Boston Manufacturing Company and bought shares in the company. Seeing the wealth to be made from textiles, John Lowell moved from agriculturalist to industrialist and in 1826 proclaimed that "we must be a manufacturing people. It is not to be supposed that I am unfriendly to manufactures, in which the fortunes of those most dear to me, and a large portion of my own are engaged." John Lowell saw the shift from farming and commerce to manufacturing as inevitable, and dropped his opposition to tariffs.[18] His son John Amory Lowell became one of the leading men in the American textile industry.

Before the Embargo of 1807, some fifty American ships each year entered Calcutta harbor, largely to buy hand-loomed cotton textiles for the growing American marketplace. The lucrative trade in India-made bandannas, handkerchiefs and shawls declined during the War of 1812. Tariffs and the dramatic rise in domestic manufacture further curtailed Indian textiles into American ports. In 1829, only sixteen American merchant ships entered Indian posts and the following year, nineteen. "The India trade dwindled as Americas learned to manufacture their own cotton." The trade picked up again in the 1840s with American ships carrying to India "lumber, cotton goods and Ice." In 1846, the American sailing vessel *Clio* arrived in Calcutta carrying a cargo of New England factory-made cotton textiles. No longer able to compete in textiles, the India trade shifted to indigo, saltpeter and animal hides.[19]

Henry Lee, brother-in-law to Francis Cabot Lowell, was one of the last of the Boston merchants who remained true to the India trade. Most of the Boston capitalists shifted away from the Federalist Party. Benjamin Gorham, brother-in-law to Francis Cabot Lowell, assumed Daniel Webster's seat in the 20th Congress. With the merchant class in decline, free trade was losing support in New England. In 1830, the protectionist Nathan Appleton defeated the free-trader Henry Lee for a seat in the U.S. House of Representatives.

13

Legacy

[Francis Cabot Lowell] reflected the highest honor on the character of the American merchant. He was distinguished by the originality of his views, the clearness of his perceptions, the variety and accuracy of his knowledge, and his power of bringing it to practical results, and perhaps still more, for the sterling purity and integrity of his character.

Edward Everett, 1839, governor of Massachusetts (1839–1840);
president of Harvard University (1848–1849);
U.S. secretary of state (1852–1853);
and U.S. senator for Massachusetts (1853–1854)

Many of the mills adopted the Waltham loom and most of the large establishments followed the Waltham plan in regard to other machinery, as well as the loom.

Samuel Batchelder, 1863

The younger and more far-sighted men put their money and brains into making Massachusetts a manufacturing state. . . . The center of interest in Massachusetts shifted from wharf to waterfall; by 1840 she had become predominantly a manufacturing state.

Samuel Eliot Morison in his book
*The Maritime History of Massachusetts;
1783–1860*, published 1921

Hannah Lowell, the wife of Francis Cabot Lowell, died on May 10, 1815, and was buried in the Central Burying Ground on Boston Common. Her sister Mary Lee felt pity for the four motherless Lowell children and took them under her care. She was especially worried over young Frank, whose "health is feeble and I sometimes think that the very sweetness we so much love is but a premature preparation for another country." (Francis Cabot Lowell Jr. far outlived his siblings and died an old man.) Susanna Gorham, sister to Francis Cabot Lowell Sr., died in 1816 and was also buried on Boston Common. Francis' mother Rebecca, another of his great supports, also died in 1816. After the deaths of his mother, wife and sister, Francis Cabot Lowell's own health declined rapidly. He again tried the waters at Ballston Spa but came out sicker than when he went in.

Despite his poor health, Francis Cabot Lowell drove himself relentlessly, even after his wife's death. He guided the Boston Manufacturing Company, the New England Bank, the Manufacturers and Mechanics Bank, and his properties at India Wharf and Broad Street, as well as his mercantile business. He was having difficulties collecting the interest on loans he made, and a number of people who rented his properties were late in their payments. Furthermore, he was worried about his sons, especially his eldest, John Jr. Francis continued trading until the close of his life. On March 3, 1817, he received a note from Henry Oxnard that the brig *Marcellus* was carrying for him 382 bags of coffee valued at $3,997.33. On May 31, his agents in Lisbon informed him that they were holding 3,785 gold Spanish dollars in his account. On May 22, his shipment of Java coffee reached Rotterdam.

Dr. James Jackson was so concerned about Francis's health that he sent a letter via John Lowell to Dr. Samuel Farr, a leading London physician, seeking a second medical opinion. On July 9 the London banker Samuel Williams wrote that he paid eight guineas from Lowell's account to Dr. Farr and was expecting his medical report, which he would send on to Boston. Francis Lowell was exhausted from the pressures of work, sick and lonely, and sensed that his life would soon end. To ease his gloom, Francis decided to retrace the memorable visit to Niagara Falls he had taken in 1807 with his wife and children.

Early in July 1817, Francis Lowell, in the company of his bereaved brother-in-law Benjamin Gorham, "set out on a long journey intended to the falls at Niagara." The five-hundred-mile trip from Boston to the Niagara Falls, by stagecoach over rutted roads, began along the Boston to Worcester Turnpike. Such long-distance travel started at two o'clock in the morning with frequent stops along the way. Lowell and Gorham refreshed themselves at Forbush's tavern in Westborough before crossing Lake Quinsigamond on the floating bridge to reach Worcester for an overnight stay. The stagecoach trip from Boston to Albany cost $8.75 and the complete one-way trip to Niagara Falls over $20, equal to six weeks' wages for a weaver in Francis Cabot Lowell's factory. Had Francis Cabot Lowell continued his trip to the falls, he possibly would have stopped at

Rome, New York, where on July 4 Governor DeWitt Clinton turned the first shovelful of earth to start the digging of the Erie Canal to link Lake Erie with the Hudson River.

James Monroe assumed the presidency of the United States of America on March 4, 1817. Proud of his Virginian roots and still chafing from his 1796 recall from France, Monroe decided on a trip of reconciliation to the North. On May 31, the president and his party set out for Baltimore and then New York and on to the New England states. In Massachusetts Federalists such as Harrison Gray Otis, Christopher Gore, James Lloyd and Timothy Pickering greeted him warmly. The parade in Boston extended for a mile to salute the elderly, amiable, long-limbed, and somewhat shy president. New England and the nation as a whole were eager for stability and to put the rancor and divisions of the past behind. Monroe reflected the national mood of "good feelings" by selecting John Quincy Adams as secretary of state, William Crawford as secretary of the treasury and John Calhoun as secretary of war.

The start of Francis Cabot Lowell's trip to Niagara coincided with the visit of James Monroe to Boston and its environs. Christopher Gore, former senator from Massachusetts in the U.S. Senate, accompanied the president on July 4, 1817, and left the following account of his punishing schedule. The president "rides hard, visits everything, and in so rapid a manner that it is utterly impossible he should burden his mind with any superfluous knowledge. This day he breakfasted with Commodore Bainbridge in Brookline, inspected the arsenal at Watertown, a cotton mill at Waltham, examined Mr. Lyman's villa, stopped at my house, ate a strawberry, bowed and shook hands cordially, returned to Boston to meet the Town Oration, the Governor's collation, and the Cincinnati address and dinner, take tea at Governor Gray's, etc. etc."

The president was especially interested in the "objects of public defense" he saw at the Watertown arsenal and in the "various manufacturing establishments." After touring the Boston Manufacturing Company, President Monroe mentioned that "a few establishments as he here saw would be sufficient to supply the United States with cotton fabrics." In all likelihood, Francis Cabot Lowell had already left town and therefore was not present on the afternoon of July 4, 1817, to show President Monroe his revolutionary water-powered mill that converted raw cotton into finished cloth, all under one roof.[1]

RAPID DECLINE IN FRANCIS CABOT LOWELL'S HEALTH

The decline in the health of Francis Cabot Lowell is described in an August 4, 1817, letter sent by his brother-in-law Samuel Pickering Gardner to Francis' older brother, John Lowell, then on a visit to London on behalf of the estate of the late Ward Nicholas Boylston. Gardner's letter told the story of Francis Cabot Lowell's last weeks of life.

> I write to give you an account of your brother Francis who is very low. A few days before they left Boston, your brother complained of not feeling quite so well, which he ascribed in some manner to his having had so much business to attend. On crossing the Chesterfield Mountains he took a severe cold, which produced an inflammation of his lungs, which, on his arrival at Saratoga, had increased to such a degree as to excite considerable alarm. But, by timely application of some remedies, he so far recovered that he thought he might venture to return home. They accordingly set out and in a few days reached Waltham without any evident aggravation of his disorder. He was then much emaciated, yet his face did not indicate a great deal of disease. He could walk the room without much apparent fatigue and sit up the greater part of the day.
>
> After staying two or three days at Waltham feeling that he had not much society as he wished and desirous of being near his physician he came to Boston. Soon after he began to be more sick and declined very rapidly till the day before yesterday, when he was apparently at the worst. At that time he kept in bed nearly all the time, took very little food, and though he liked to have his friends about him and hear them converse, did not incline to talk himself. . . . I was with him last night and he seemed to be comfortable and slept well.

THE DEATH OF FRANCIS CABOT LOWELL

Shortly before he died of pneumonia, Francis Cabot Lowell had one last look at his legacy, the Boston Manufacturing Company at Waltham. Samuel P. Gardner ended his letter early in order to send the latest news on Francis before the ship sailed for London. Francis died on August 10, 1817, aged forty-two years, several weeks before the letter reached his older brother in London. A notice of the death appeared in the *New England Palladium & Commercial Advertiser*, August 17, 1817.

Francis Cabot Lowell was laid to rest at the Central Burying Ground on Boston Common in Tomb 36, alongside Hannah his wife, Rebecca Lowell his stepmother, and five-year-old Sarah Cabot Lowell. The site of their tomb was rediscovered in 1894 during the construction of the streetcar subway under Tremont Street, which also unearthed the remains of some nine hundred others buried in that section of the cemetery. On April 24, 1895, the remains of Francis Cabot Lowell, his wife Hannah, his mother Rebecca, his sister Susanna Gorham, and Anna Cabot Lowell were re-interred at the Forest Hills Cemetery, Jamaica Plain, Boston. During the same period the remains of Judge John Lowell and his daughter Sarah Champney Lowell were removed from their Roxbury tomb and re-interred in the beautiful park-like cemetery at Forest Hills.[2] The remains of Judge John Lowell now lie with his third wife Rebecca Lowell.

LAST WILL AND TESTAMENT

Thomas Dawes, judge of the court of probate, Suffolk County, certified the final will and testament of Francis Cabot Lowell on August 25. The executors of the estate were his long-time business associates, best friends and brothers-in-law Patrick Tracy Jackson, Samuel P. Gardner, and Charles Jackson. The will declared, "I give all my Estate, real and personal, that is not herein otherwise disposed of, to my children John, Susan, Francis Cabot and Edward Jackson." His son John had already borrowed $2,000 and that amount was deducted from his share of the estate. Francis Cabot Lowell authorized the "executors to pay from time to time all the assessments, as they become due on my shares in the Boston Manufacturing Company [and] not to sell my said shares therein before the works are completed and in full operation; after which the shares may be divided among my four children, as may appear most for their benefit." Lowell also stipulated that he forgave the amount of $2,500 owed to him by his brother-in-law Warren Dutton, and the sum of $335.80 owed to him by another brother-in-law, Henry Lee. Lowell left $300 to Clarissa Gould, the devoted family domestic servant.

The will gives a detailed account of the property Lowell acquired during his short life. His real estate holdings included the following:

- The three story brick building at India Wharf $5,000
- The loft of rooms over the arch at India Wharf   4,500
- Building on Broad Street[3]   3,000
- Building 108-110 Broad Street   4,750
- Building 112-114 Broad Street   5,000
- Building 116-118 Broad Street   5,250
- Wood tenement on Nine Street   300
- Flats near Pleasant Street   1,000
- Twenty shares in India Wharf   8,000

At the time of his death Francis Cabot Lowell also owned thirty shares in the Boston Manufacturing Company, worth $33,000; one thousand shares in the Manufacturers & Mechanics Bank, $50,250; and one hundred shares in the New England Bank, $9,240. The value of cargoes onboard the *Suffolk*, *William* and *Camden*, carrying chinaware, Calcutta cloth and indigo were valued at $40,000. Lowell owned one share in the Boston Athenaeum valued at $130. His cash account in the New England Bank held $1,264.36. He owned five dozen bottles of Madeira wine, $49. He was owed $4,766.12 by Dr. James Jackson and $418.81 by Samuel Pickering Gardner. There was also an outstanding note owed by Wheeler & Foley.

The executors arranged for the contents of the Lowell home to be assessed. The inventory included a Kidderminster carpet (worth $40), twenty-four tablecloths ($72), thirty-nine sheets and twenty-two pillow cases ($50), one elegant table clock ($24), two chimney looking-glasses ($50), four dozen knives and forks ($16), a twelve-plate dinner set ($205.30), a mahogany bureau ($25), a mahogany dressing table ($22), four salt sellers, four large decanters, twenty tumblers, thirty-two wine glasses, thirty napkins and so on, for a total value of $1,014.42.

The value of the Francis Cabot Lowell estate before the deduction of obligations and expenses was $217,768.40. At the time of Lowell's death, his son John Jr. was eighteen years old and daughter Susan was sixteen, both old enough to receive their shares of the estate directly. The younger sons Francis Cabot Lowell Jr., fourteen years old, and Edward Jackson, only ten, being minors, were placed under the joint guardianship of Francis' older brother John Lowell and Patrick Tracy Jackson.

Francis Cabot Lowell still owed money on his Boston Manufacturing Company shares, which had a net value to his estate of $18,000. After selling all the property and paying off outstanding debts, the estate of Francis Cabot Lowell amounted to $109,714.78 in cash, plus the value of his shares in the Boston Manufacturing Company, giving each of the children $27,428.69 in cash and one-quarter of the company shares. The account books recorded all expenses for the minor children until they came of age, including the cost of their education, monthly allowances, French lessons, dancing lessons, clothing expenses and trips to Newburyport and elsewhere.

Francis Cabot took risks throughout his adult life. He loaned large sums that were sometimes left unpaid. He sent cargoes across the seas, speculated in land and property, and experimented with new methods to distill rum. Lowell was skilled in business and managed to keep his fortune even during the Napoleonic Wars, the Embargo of 1807 and the War of 1812. He is remembered especially for his great experiment with the manufacture of textiles in America. The estate of Francis Cabot Lowell was finalized in Boston on December 11, 1820. He died a wealthy man.[4]

Francis Cabot Lowell left no published account of his life or of his bold vision to bring textile manufacturing to the United States. His contribution to America endured through his children, his talented associates and especially the success of his Boston Manufacturing Company, which heralded in the American industrial revolution.

THE CHILDREN OF FRANCIS AND HANNAH LOWELL

Francis Cabot Lowell's oldest son, John Lowell Jr., was born in Boston on May 11, 1799, three months prematurely. Five months later, John was "a bright and healthy child" with sparkling blue eyes. As the first grandchild of Jonathan Jackson, John "was, of course, an object of great interest." At age eighteen months, John became very sickly and was near death. Dr. James Jackson, his uncle, diagnosed cholera infantum, caused by "dentition, the dogday-weather and the unpropritious diet." Dr. Jackson prescribed tepid baths at night "to sooth the whole system," alternating with cold sponging in the morning and for nourishment, boiled milk, lime water, crackers soaked in cold water and beef broth. With this treatment John gradually improved and grew into a tall and strong youth.

John Jr. had difficulties with his studies and at age eight was packed off to Bridgewater to the Reverend Zedekiah Sanger, the self-same tutor who helped Francis Cabot fifteen years earlier when he was sent down from Harvard. On October 6, 1807, Sanger sent Francis and Hannah a less than glowing report of their son's academic progress. John Jr. was studying Aesop's fables in the original Greek, "learning 5 or 6 lines a lesson, fore-noon and afternoon. [He also] reads in English for each part of the day and speaks. Such books as he will read he carries with him." Later, John Jr. benefited from his Scottish education and entered Harvard University in 1813, aged fourteen years. Harvard was a torment to the shy youngster. Because of his unhappiness and lack of attention to his studies, he dropped out after two years, and due to his father's connections, started working for Boott & Pratt, importers of goods from Britain and the East Indies. John Jr. sailed to Europe and India on the *Lascar* "to learn seamanship," returning home after his father died. Now well off from his inheritance, he followed commercial pursuits, learned to play the flute and he read vociferously. At twenty-five he fell in love with his cousin, Georgina M. Amory, and wrote her a letter proposing marriage. The eighteen-year-old Georgina replied that she "need not, I hope, assure you that the comments of your letter were totally unexpected to me; it is therefore, after mature deliberation, that I determined to hazard an answer. I have always felt for you the greatest esteem, founded on the deep principles which you possess." They married in 1825, and the gentle Georgina, who brought a large fortune into the marriage, made a fine wife to the high-strung and high-minded John Jr. He started a family, collected books and was active in the politics of Boston and Massachusetts. Mr. and Mrs. John Lowell Jr. moved into a grand house on Colonnade Row and kept a country house, with a fine library, in Belvidere in the new town of Lowell. It was said of John Lowell Jr. that he was "by nature a statesman, whom the caprice of fortune had made a merchant."

Tragedy struck in 1830–1831 when, over a brief period, he lost his wife and his two daughters, aged two and five, to scarlet fever. Heartbroken, John Lowell Jr. retired from business, sold all his properties and left his affairs in the very capable hands of his first cousin and brother-in-law John Amory Lowell, under whose deft management the fortune rapidly grew. Living off the interest, John Jr. traveled widely through Belgium, Italy and Greece, taking an apartment on the Rue de Rivoli in Paris for four months, followed by a long stay at the Clarendon Hotel, Bond Street. In London the wealthy widower "moved in the highest circles." After leaving the capital, John Jr. made visits to the cotton mills of Lancashire and the potteries of Derbyshire. From England he moved on to Edinburgh, where he had spent part of his youth, to renew his friendship with Mrs. Anne MacVicar Grant. He made his financial arrangements with Baring Brothers and received letters of introduction from Lord Glenelg, president of the Indian Board of Trade. In Rome, John Lowell Jr. approached Horace Vernet, director of the *Academie de Rome*, about hiring a companion and artistic recorder for his proposed tour of the Near East. On Vernet's recommendation John Lowell hired Marc-Charles Gabriel Gleyre, a talented but dirt-poor young Swiss watercolorist to accompany him on a trip. For a salary of $500 a year plus expenses, for nineteen months Charles Gleyre attended to the wealthy John Jr. as well as doing drawings in watercolor of the significant sights of their tour. John Jr. and his companion Gleyre conversed in French.

Traveling on foot, horseback, or by boat, John Lowell Jr. and his companion Charles Gleyre visited the sights in Rome, Athens and Istanbul before crossing the Mediterranean to Egypt. Gleyre completed over two hundred paintings as well as a portrait of John Lowell in Arab dress. Lowell and Gleyre visited the great pyramids and collected relics. Weakened by dysentery and inflammation of his eyes, Lowell barely managed to make his way to upper Nubia to visit the ruins. At Khartoum, following an argument over the ownership of the paintings, John Lowell broke with the exhausted Gleyre and took up instead with a young Englishman. John Lowell Jr. became seriously ill during a two-week camel ride across the blistering Egyptian desert to the coast. He barely managed to board a British steamship on its way to Bombay, where he died of dysentery on March 4, 1836, aged thirty-six years.[5]

After parting from John Lowell Jr., Charles Gleyre went to live in Paris, where he had an *atelier*. He would now be largely forgotten if it were not for his drawing classes where he taught aspiring painters. In the early 1860s a number of poor, original and highly talented artists came to study under Gleyre. Pierre Auguste Renoir, Claude Monet, Edouard Manet, Frederic Bazille, the American James Abbott McNeill Whistler and the Englishman Alfred Sisley met at the *atelier* Gleyre.

John Lowell Jr., son of Francis Cabot Lowell, in Arab dress, painted by Charles Gabriel Gleyre, the Swiss watercolorist, who accompanied John Jr. on his trip through the Middle East and Asia. (Harriet Knight Smith, The History of the Lowell Institute *[Boston: Lamson, Wolffe and Co., 1898], frontispiece.)*

Pierre Auguste Renoir tells that he started his career in art at the *atelier* Gleyre because it was "one of the most talked-of in the capital." The studio on the East Bank of Paris was "a big room crowded with young students working away at their easels."[6] French Impressionism had its roots in the *atelier* Gleyre.

JOHN LOWELL JR. AND HIS INSTITUTE

The Boston Manufacturing Company in Waltham was at the forefront in offering education opportunities to workers. In 1825 the Reverend Bernard Whitman "proposed to the families of his parish, who were connected with the Factories, to give a course of instruction by means of lectures on Grammar, Geography and other important but common branches of education." Whitman received permission from the Company to use "the school-houses connected with the upper and lower factories." On December 23, 1826, seventy gentlemen met together in the school house of the upper factory at Waltham to form "a society for the purpose of material instruction in the arts and sciences," to be called the Rumford Institute, named for Benjamin Thompson of Woburn, better known as Count Rumford. This was the earliest effort in the United States to set up an institution for adult education. The evening school proved so popular with the company workers that a larger space was needed. Whitman asked the Boston Manufacturing Company "for assistance in the erecting of a suitable building" for the Institute. Patrick Tracy Jackson, on behalf of the Boston Manufacturing Company, offered to "erect a building at their own expense and rented it to the Institute, with the condition that the rent should be expended in the purchase of books." The Rumford Institute, with three hundred students, had a reading room, a lending library with over one thousand books, and a large lecture hall.

The first speaker was the superintendent's brother, Dr. James Jackson, who spoke on the topic of staying healthy. The audience at these lectures was made up of the young workers at the Waltham cotton mills. Peer education methods were used and "more than half the lectures are given by our mechanics or manufacturers."[7] The Rumford Institute of Waltham was the model on which John Lowell Jr. established his Lowell Institute for adult education. In 1860, the Rumford Institute was designated the Waltham Public Library. With the growth of the textile industry the ideas of education for the workers was carried from Waltham to the new industrial town of Lowell. The young workers viewed education as a way to expand their minds. After an exhausting twelve-hour workday, many of these young women attended classes in literature, foreign languages, music and writing. The *Lowell Offering*, a remarkable monthly magazine written by the workers, showed their desire to expand their horizons well beyond the factory gates.

The sensitive, artistic and bookish John Lowell Jr. left an estate worth some $500,000, testament to the great increase in value of textile industry shares. Half of his fortune, nearly $250,000, went to a charitable trust for the "maintenance and support of public lectures, to be delivered in Boston, upon philosophy, natural history [and] the arts and sciences." This money was the largest single bequest by a private donor made to an American-based foundation until that time. The first course of lectures offered by the Lowell Institute was on the subject of chemistry and geology and given by Benjamin Silliman of Yale University. The first of the four lectures took place on December 31, 1839, when Professor Silliman was introduced by Edward Everett, Governor of the Commonwealth of Massachusetts. Silliman spoke for two hours before a "very great crowd." The Lowell Lectures became a major event in the Boston social life and for many years textile money was spent offering free lectures at the Lowell Institute presented by the likes of the naturalist Louis Agassiz, Oliver Wendell Holmes, Frederick Law Olmsted and the geologist Sir Charles Lyell. The subjects covered included electricity (1853), mental hygiene (1857) and public parks (1869). James Russell Lowell gave a series of twenty-four lectures on English poetry. In 1893, Henry Drummond lectured on evolution under the title of *The Ascent of Man*. In 1914, the eminent British philosopher Bertrand Russell delivered the Lowell Lectures on the scientific method in philosophy, later published in book form as *Our Knowledge of the External World*. The first series of lectures were given at the Odeon Theater, corner of Franklin and Federal Streets, Boston. Later sites included the Tremont Temple, the Boston Music Hall and the Rogers Building at the Massachusetts Institute of Technology.

Oliver Wendell Holmes said, "No nobler or more helpful institution exists in America than Boston's Lowell Institute," offering university-level lectures to lay-men and -women alike. The Lowell Institute was the inspiration for the "continuing education" movement in the United States. By the middle of the twentieth century, radio was attracting larger audiences. Seeing this medium as the wave of the future, the Lowell Institute took the bold step of establishing the signal WGBH, standing for Great Blue Hill. The lectures previously heard by a few hundred in the lecture hall could now be shared by thousands listening at home. The Lowell Institute's investment in radio was followed by its investment in television.

Another beneficiary of the estate of John Lowell Jr. was the writer Anne MacVicar Grant of Edinburgh. John and his siblings stayed with Mrs. Grant from 1810 to 1812, during the time their parents were touring Scotland and England. John Jr. "entertained for her the deepest veneration and affection and left her by his will a legacy of five thousand dollars."

SUSANNA CABOT LOWELL

Not much is recorded about the daughter of Francis Cabot Lowell, Susanna Cabot Lowell (born 1801). She preferred to be known as Susan. The Francis Cabot Lowell Papers at the Massachusetts Historical Society, in Box 5, for the year 1806, contains a lock of golden brown hair, still full of luster, that was cut from the head of Susanna Cabot Lowell when she was four years old.

She married her first cousin, John Amory Lowell, the son of Francis' older brother, John. The two grandsons of Judge John Lowell, John Jr. and John Amory, were born months apart and were close even as children. John Amory Lowell entered Harvard University at the tender age of twelve. At college he shared a room with John P. Bigelow, who served as the twelfth mayor of Boston (1849–1851). John Amory Lowell graduated in 1815 and became a merchant dealing in English goods. Susanna Cabot Lowell Amory died in childbirth, aged only twenty-six, leaving John Amory with two children, also named Susan Cabot and John. Their son became a prominent lawyer and judge.

After Susanna's death, John Amory married Elizabeth Cabot Putnam, who bore him four children. At age twenty-nine the immensely able John Amory Lowell was selected to replace Patrick Tracy Jackson as manager of the Boston Manufacturing Company. The company also had interests in Lowell, where John Amory opened the Boott Mill (1835) and the Massachusetts Mill (1839). John Amory Lowell agreed to run the Lowell Institute where he remained sole trustee for forty-two years, while continuing as a member of the board of the Merrimack Manufacturing Company, the Boott Cotton Mill and the Boston Manufacturing Company. The capital for the Lowell Institute yielded some $18,000 annually, providing ample funds to pay the lecturers and meet administrative costs. John Amory Lowell, one of the most successful of the Lowells, had his offices at 71 Milk Street and his home at 7 Pemberton Square, one of the most fashionable sections of Beacon Hill. John Amory Lowell was succeeded as director of the Lowell Institute by his son, Augustus Lowell. In 1900, Augustus passed the leadership on to his son Abbott Lawrence Lowell, who in 1909 became president of Harvard University.

FRANCIS CABOT LOWELL JR.

Francis Cabot Lowell Jr. (1803–1874) was the third of the children of Francis Cabot and Hannah Lowell, and the only one in the family who lived into old age. Francis Jr. graduated from Phillips Academy in 1817, and from Harvard University in 1821, in a class of fifty-eight men, which included his cousin John Lowell Gardner, the transcendentalist leader Ralph Waldo Emerson and George Washington Adams, the deeply troubled oldest son of John Quincy Adams, the sixth president of the United States. George Washington Adams became an alcoholic and died at the age of twenty-eight by drowning, probably an act of suicide. Francis Cabot Lowell Jr. managed the bleachery at Waltham and studied chemistry to master the process. Upon the death of Kirk Boott, Francis Jr. was appointed treasurer of the Merrimack Company in Lowell. He was also a director of the Columbian Bank, the Merchants Insurance Company, and the Provident Institute for Savings, and served as actuary to the Massachusetts General Hospital Life Insurance Company and as treasurer of the Amoskeag Mill in Manchester, New Hampshire.

On January 1, 1826, he married Mary Lowell Gardner, his first cousin and the second of the six children of Samuel Pickering Gardner and Rebecca Russell Lowell. Mr. and Mrs. Francis Cabot Lowell Jr. settled to an affluent life on Boston's Beacon Hill, meeting regularly with relatives on Pemberton Square or at the country estate of Bromley Vale. Francis Jr. was a conservative man, with the manners of a bygone age, having narrow and fixed views, which he generally kept to himself. His life was stable and orderly, without the brittleness and inner turmoil of his brother John Jr. In business he was scrupulously honest and was much respected by the men of his social class.

Over the winter of 1831–1832, Mary Lowell "set forth with my husband, little George and nurse (Lorenza Stevens) upon my travels." For six months from December 18, 1831, Mary kept an account of a journey that took the family to Havana and Matanzas in Cuba, as well as visits to American-owned slave plantations. Cuba had become the winter destination for wealthy Americans. After four months in Cuba, the family sailed for New Orleans and took a steamboat up the Mississippi and Ohio Rivers to Pittsburgh. From Pittsburgh, the Lowell family traveled by coach to Philadelphia before returning to Boston. The trip to Cuba and through the American South is recorded in a book *New Year in Cuba: Mary Gardner Lowell's Travel Diary, 1831–1832*, and offers a Boston Brahmin's view of a world much different from her own.[8]

In 1851 Francis Cabot Lowell Jr., his wife Mary and their daughters, eighteen-year-old Mary and fifteen-year-old Georgina, together with five-year-old son Edward and the ever-faithful Lorenza Stevens, went on a grand tour of Europe, staying at the finest hotels, much like the trip with his own father and mother forty years earlier. By the middle of the nineteenth century, however, steamships and steam-powered railroads made travel much quicker and much more comfortable. Travel abroad for wealthy American families had become the vogue.

On hearing of the passing of Francis Cabot Lowell Jr. in 1874, his Harvard classmate, the philosopher and transcendentalist Ralph Waldo Emerson, wrote a tribute: "The death of Francis Cabot Lowell is a great loss to me. . . . [Lowell was] fortunate in his birth and education, accustomed always to a connection of excellent society. He was conservative, often in the wayward politics of former years. [Lowell was] a man of a quiet inward life, silent and grave, but with opinions and purposes, which he quietly held and frankly stated. He was a friend in deed, silent but sure. On the next day after my house was burned, he came to Concord to express his sympathy in my misfortune, and a few days afterwards surprised me with a munificent donation from himself and his children which went far to rebuild it." Francis Cabot Lowell gave Emerson the sum of $5,000 "to rebuild his house more as he would like, or to use for any purpose he desired." Emerson was reluctant to accept so large a sum from one family. After Francis Cabot Lowell Jr. acknowledged that George Higginson, Henry Lee Higginson and others who preferred to donate quietly had contributed some of the funds, Emerson, with gratitude, accepted the money.[9]

EDWARD JACKSON LOWELL

Edward Jackson Lowell (1807–1830) was the last of the four children of Francis Cabot and Hannah Lowell. He was a precocious boy who read widely. He was only eight years old when his mother died and ten when his father died. The trustees of the estate were fearful that he was using his funds recklessly but it turned out that he was spending his money on books. Edward graduated from Harvard in 1822, at age fifteen. His class of fifty-nine contained the flower of the Boston Brahmins with an Adams, Ames, Endicott, Holmes, Lincoln, Tyng and a Wigglesworth. Edward received his law degree in 1825 and showed great promise, but was dead of consumption in 1830, only twenty-three years old. He left behind a large library, rich in literary and historical texts, the same topics he loved while a little boy at school in Edinburgh.

FASCINATION WITH FRANCE

The Lowell fascination with France and its language, history and culture passed down to the descendants of Francis Cabot Lowell. His sons John Jr. and Francis Cabot Lowell Jr. were frequent travelers to Europe. Edward Jackson Lowell (1845–1894) was the youngest son of Francis Cabot Lowell Jr., and named for his dead uncle. As a boy of ten, Edward traveled to

Europe to attend a French language school near Vevey, on the northeastern shore of Lake Geneva in Switzerland. After graduating from Harvard College he joined a business selling imported glassware. Dissatisfied with the career of a merchant, he attended Harvard Law School, passed the bar examination and joined Boston's leading law firm. Like his father and grandfather before him, Edward took his family on an extended trip of Europe, where he decided to give up the law and write history. His first book, *The Hessians and Other German Auxiliaries of Great Britain in the Revolutionary War*, was published in 1884. His major work, published in 1893, the year before his death, was *The Eve of the French Revolution*, which dealt with "the great events which astonished and horrified Europe and America . . . and changed the face of the civilized world."[10]

Another descendant and namesake was Judge Francis Cabot Lowell (1855–1911), who rose to the U.S. Court of Appeals of the First Circuit. Showing profound scholarship of events in the fifteenth century, together with knowledge of old and modern French, Judge Francis Cabot Lowell became interested in the life and times of Joan of Arc. In December 1895 he gave a series of four lectures on Joan of Arc at the Lowell Institute. In his 1898 book he wrote that in the middle of the fifteenth century "France was hardly a nation [and] the personality of Joan of Arc was so strong that her life takes its chief interest therefrom rather than from her surroundings."[11]

On September 27, 1905, Justice Francis Cabot Lowell sentenced James Francis Curley to two months in prison on the charge of defrauding the United States by completing an examination in someone else's name. Curley refused to apologize and claimed he was helping his friend. The prison sentence benefited rather than hindered Curley's career as he went on to serve as mayor of Boston, a member of the House of Representatives and also as governor of Massachusetts.

OTHER RELATIVES AND ASSOCIATES

The Lowell Institute was but one of the intellectual pursuits of the Lowell family. On a fine April day in 1857, a group of men met for dinner at the Parker House Hotel in Boston with a plan to publish a monthly journal on "literature, politics, science and the arts." Among those at the dinner were Ralph Waldo Emerson, Henry Wadsworth Longfellow, Oliver Wendell Holmes and James Russell Lowell. The bearded James Russell Lowell, a poet and a linguist, the son of the Reverend Charles Russell Lowell, was born two years after the death of his uncle, Francis Cabot Lowell. James Russell Lowell was appointed editor of the *Atlantic Monthly*, still published today.

In addition to a passion for politics, John Lowell, brother to Francis Cabot Lowell, showed a keen interest in the land. In 1792, he was among the founding members of the Massachusetts Society for Promoting Agriculture and served as its president from 1796 until 1803. The society published the *Massachusetts Agricultural Repository*, to which John Lowell made frequent contributions. In the winter of 1829, a group of prominent citizens established the Massachusetts Horticultural Society and invited "the Hon. John Lowell, who then stood at the head of the horticulturists of Massachusetts, to preside. His health was feeble, he had felt but a little hope that he should be able to be present. One of his neighbors at the Colonnade Row, Cheever Newhall, however, called on him that morning, with his sleigh and extra blankets, and induced him to wrap up and come down, to the great gratification of the company."[12] John Lowell served as a member of the corporation of Harvard University from 1810 to 1822.

Until the end of his life John Lowell delighted in inviting guests to his country seat in Roxbury and showing them around his greenhouses filled with rare and exotic plants. Among the specimens he cultivated were the *Pandanus* (or screw-pine), the *Araucaria* pine, the *Dracena*, the elastic gum plant and many types of orchids. John Lowell claimed to read every article of the *American Journal of Science*, and to understand it all, including the mathematical papers. John Lowell died in 1840, at age seventy-one. The youngest of the Lowell brothers, the Reverend Charles Lowell, died in 1861, at age seventy-nine. Francis Lowell's beloved uncle William Cabot remained a bachelor all his life and died in Cambridge in 1824, aged seventy-two.

Patrick Tracy Jackson, who for years carried forward the vision of Francis Cabot Lowell at Waltham, became an investor in ten textile-manufacturing companies as well as investing in the railroads. Patrick Tracy Jackson supervised the development of the Boston & Lowell, the twenty-six-mile railroad linking the textile city with Boston. The Boston & Lowell was incorporated in 1830 at a time when the Lowell Machine Shop, known for its textile machines, had little experience working with metals. The death of Paul Moody in 1831 added to the responsibilities of Patrick Tracy Jackson. With the coming of steam power, Patrick Tracy Jackson was among the first in New England to see the future of coal and, in 1828, invested in the remote central Pennsylvania Lycoming Coal Company. In 1832, Jackson imported from England two of the *Planet*-type locomotives constructed by Robert Stephenson. In April 1834, Jackson hired George Washington Whistler to come to Lowell to develop the locomotives for his railroad. Born in Fort Wayne, Indiana, Whistler graduated from the military academy at West Point and served as a civil engineer with the U.S. Army Corps of Engineers. In June 1835, Whistler delivered the first locomotive for the Boston & Lowell Railroad. The thirty-horsepower locomotive was aptly named *Patrick* in honor of Patrick Tracy Jackson. The *Patrick* was followed by the *Lowell*, *Boston*, *Merrimack* and other locomotives built at the Lowell Machine Shop, and similar in design to Stephenson's *Planet*. Whistler's son James Abbott McNeill Whistler was born in the Paul Moody House, 243 Worthen Street, Lowell, in 1834. Moving to Europe, young Whistler became an artist. His famous oil portrait *Arrangement in Grey and Black: The Artist's Mother*, better known as *Whistler's Mother*, painted in 1871, hangs in the Musée d'Orsay in Paris. Anna Mathilda McNeill was the daughter of Dr. Charles Donald McNeill of Wilmington, North Carolina. She was George Washington Whistler's second wife and met him through her brother William, who was a West Point classmate.

Patrick Tracy Jackson developed a taste for property speculation. In 1835 he purchased the Gardiner Greene estate in Boston for $160,000. To this land he added the abutting Phillips and Lloyd estates. Jackson hired Asa G. Sheldon to remove the hill and carry off the soil in order to level the land. Sheldon used sixty-three pairs of oxen hitched to wagons, "with Yankees for drivers and one hundred and ninety Irishmen as shovelers." Over five months one hundred thousand yards of gravel were removed, and the land subdivided into suitable lots and sold at auction. Patrick Tracy Jackson lost heavily on his venture.

Patrick Tracy Jackson died in 1847 at age sixty-seven having lost most of his money. His older brother Charles married Amelia Lee, daughter of Joseph Lee of Salem. She died childless and of consumption. In 1803 Charles Jackson moved to Boston where he practiced law. He married Frances Cabot of Beverly, a cousin of his first wife, in 1810. In 1813, he was appointed a judge in the Massachusetts Supreme Judicial Court. Judge Charles Jackson made wise investments in the textile factories of Lowell. The judge owned a lovely house on Bedford Street, Boston, where he kept his law library. During the summer months, he moved to his estate in Waltham. Charles Jackson died in 1855 at age eighty, leaving $200,000 to his large family. Dr. James Jackson, "the model of the good and wise physician," was, in 1807, one of the founding members of the Boston Medical Society and was one of the founders of the Massachusetts General Hospital. He was among the first in America to advocate vaccination against smallpox. In 1812, he was appointed the Hersey Professor of the Theory and Practice of Physic at Harvard Medical School and became the chief physician of the Massachusetts General Hospital. The good doctor, who was also a founding member of Harvard's medical school and the Boston Athenaeum, was a great believer in regular and vigorous exercise and counseled mothers to breastfeed their infants for at least twelve months. Dr. James Jackson died aged eighty-nine. The Jackson brothers remained forever grateful to their brother-in-law Francis Cabot Lowell.

Henry Lee (1782–1867), another brother-in-law to Francis Cabot Lowell, after the collapse in 1811 of his firm H & J Lee & Company, traveled to India as supercargo on the 284-ton *Reaper*, owned by his relative Andrew Cabot. He used his four years in Calcutta to advantage by establishing excellent contacts with the British East India Company as well as with Indian merchants. In 1816, with the help of Francis Cabot Lowell, he was back in Boston doing business at No. 39 India Wharf. As a large-scale importer of Indian cottons and silks subject to tariffs of 30 percent and higher, he competed against the domestic textiles produced by the Boston Manufacturing Company. An ardent Federalist and free trader, he opposed tariffs on imported goods. His support of free trade, however, did not prevent him in 1817 from buying shares in the Boston Manufacturing Company. With the India textile trade declining, Henry Lee turned instead to sugar, indigo and iron. In 1817, he sold two hundred thousand pounds of saltpeter to the Du Pont Company for the manufacture of explosives. Henry Lee found fresh markets in the West Indies and South America as well as Europe. Having lost to Nathan Appleton in the 1830 election for a seat in the U.S. Congress, Henry Lee ran in 1832 for vice president of the United States on the Independent Democratic ticket with John Floyd. The ticket received only the eleven South Carolina votes, losing to Andrew Jackson with 219 electoral votes. Henry Lee remained a merchant during most of his long life, even as others shifted their money away from trade to manufacturing, banking, mining, railroads and insurance. He and Mary Jackson Lee had six children. One of his sons, also called Henry, headed the Boston house of Lee, Higginson & Company, the bank that managed money for the Boston Brahmins. A descendant, Henry Lee Higginson (1834–1919), was the founder of the illustrious Boston Symphony Orchestra.

In 1813, Nathan Appleton agreed, with some reluctance, to risk $5,000 in Francis Cabot Lowell's bold plan to manufacture textiles in America "in order to see the experiment fairly tried." The spectacular returns on his investment converted Appleton into the leading advocate for local manufacture. After Francis Cabot Lowell died, it was Nathan Appleton, with Patrick Tracy Jackson, who developed the industrial city of Lowell. Appleton became wealthy from textile manufacturing and lived in a grand town house at 39-40 Beacon Street, overlooking Boston Common. In the 1830 election for the Congress of the United States, Nathan Appleton fought a spirited battle against the eloquent Henry Lee on the key issue of "free-trade or the protective principle." A strong advocate of protective tariffs, Nathan Appleton took his seat in the 22nd Congress, and, as a member of the Committee of Ways and Means, helped frame the Tariff of 1832, and later, the Tariff of 1842. In 1843, his daughter Fanny married the poet Henry Wadsworth Longfellow. As a wedding present to Fanny and Henry, Nathan Appleton bought for $10,000 the house on Brattle Street, Cambridge, that served in 1776 as the headquarters of General George Washington when he took command of the Continental Army. In addition, Appleton gave the couple $100,000 worth of stock in his textile mills, allowing Longfellow to enjoy the dual pleasures of living in great comfort and writing poetry when the creative spirit moved him. While living in the Brattle Street mansion, Longfellow wrote two of his most famous works, *The Song of Hiawatha* and *Paul Revere's Ride*.

Francis Cabot Lowell met Uriah Cotting at the close of the eighteenth century. The two men were the principal associates in the development of the grand India Wharf, the retail stores on Broad Street, and later Central Wharf. The historian Justin Winsor described Cotting as "the projector and guiding spirit of nearly every enterprise involving the development of the town for business during the first twenty years" of the nineteenth century.[13] In 1815 Uriah Cotting went ahead with his New Cornhill Corporation to develop twenty-three retail stores opening both on Cornhill and on Brattle Street, between Scollay Square and Adams Square. Over time Cornhill became Boston's street for used and antique books, as well as the home of several publishing houses. Best known among the Cornhill publishers was the ardent abolitionist William Lloyd Garrison, who published the magazine *Liberator*. Garrison attracted many like-minded people to 21 Cornhill, including Julia Ward Howe, who wrote *The Battle Hymn of the Republic*, and Harriet Beecher Stowe, who penned part of *Uncle Tom's Cabin* while working in the *Liberator* offices. During the Civil War, many runaway slaves found shelter in the basement of Garrison's office on the Cornhill.

Uriah Cotting became wealthy with his India Wharf, Broad Street, Cornhill, and other projects and lived in a splendid house on Somerset Street. His good fortune failed him near the end of his life. He heavily mortgaged his properties to finance the Boston & Roxbury Mill Dam project. With the project still unfinished, the frail Uriah Cotting died of tuberculosis on May 9, 1819, at age fifty-three. His death came during the Panic of 1819, America's first financial crisis, brought about by rampant speculation. The panic caused an "extreme depression of property" that rendered Uriah Cotting's estate insolvent. The properties he owned on Broad Street, India Wharf, Fort Hill and West Street carried combined mortgages in excess of $25,000. Among the holders of these mortgages were Israel Thorndike and Harrison Gray Otis. After Cotting was laid to rest in the Granary Burial Ground, his properties were put up for auction. John Amory emerged as the buyer of most of them paying bargain prices, one-third less than the outstanding mortgages.[14]

Israel Thorndike was born in Beverly in 1755 and attended only the public school in his town, but "possessed, in the vigor of his mind, a never-failing spring of self-advancement." He was a prominent merchant who, during the Revolutionary War, converted his ship into a privateer. After the war he was active in the China and India trade. Thorndike joined the Cabot brothers in forming the Beverly Cotton Manufactory. Despite the failure of the Beverly enterprise, Thorndike was willing to take a risk with Francis Cabot Lowell and invest in the Boston Manufacturing Company. His bet paid off and Thorndike became very rich from trade and from textile manufacture. In 1818, he purchased the library of Professor Christoph Daniel Ebeling of Hamburg for $6,500. The Ebeling collection of 3,500 books and 10,000 maps, many about the United States, is one of the most significant collections ever given to the Harvard University library. Israel Thorndike died in 1832, leaving an estate worth over $1 million.

In early nineteenth century the wealth of Boston was concentrated in a few hands. The family and associates of Francis Cabot Lowell became some of the wealthiest men in Massachusetts. Many of these men were merchants who shifted their money into cotton manufacturing. Each of the Appleton brothers—Nathan, Samuel and William—as well as each of the Lawrence brothers—Abbot, Amos and William—left estates in excess of $1,500,000. The Reverend Charles Lowell lost most of his money in speculation but at his death was still worth $150,000. Francis Cabot Lowell Jr. was worth $150,000; John Amory Lowell, $500,000; Judge Charles Jackson, $150,000; Dr. James Jackson, $200,000; and Benjamin Gorham, $200,000. The lawyer Harrison Gray Otis left $750,000. Known as the Boston Associates, by 1850, this small group of men owned 40 percent of the banking capital in Boston, forty percent of the insurance capital, 30 percent of the railroad mileage and 20 percent of all the cotton spindles in the United States. The Whitin brothers—James, Paul and John—and the Draper brothers—James, Ebenezer and George—became wealthy making the machinery for the cotton mills.[15] Had Francis Cabot Lowell lived seventy years instead of only forty-two, it is more than likely that his fortune would have equaled those of the Appletons and the Lawrences, who grew immensely rich after shifting to textile manufacture. The fortunes of the few were accumulated at a time when the average working man or woman earned less than $200 a year.

A number of these manufacturing moguls enjoyed the life of the country gentleman. Samuel Pickering Gardner and Dr. James Jackson delighted in the country life and experimented with various fruits and vegetables. Amos Lawrence owned an extensive estate in Brookline and the lawyer Daniel Webster invested money and energy in his Green Harbor estate with 1,400 acres of arable land. Others in Boston diversified away from textiles into railroads and mining. Quincy Adams Shaw, George Higginson and Horatio Hollis Hunnewell increased their fortunes with their Calumet and Hecla Copper Mining Company in the Upper Peninsula of Michigan. Quincy Shaw willed his collection of Italian sculptures and paintings by Jean-Francois Millet to the Museum of Fine Arts, Boston. Horatio H. Hunnewell named his town Wellesley in honor of his wife Isabella Pratt Welles, built the magnificent town hall and donated funds to Wellesley College. The success of the Waltham-Lowell system moved the wealthy of Boston from merchants to industrialists. Francis Cabot Lowell, Patrick Tracy Jackson and Nathan Appleton, together with their families and friends, comprised the elite families of nineteenth-century Boston. Their influence spread from the factories to politics, the arts and sciences, insurance, banking and academia. The little town of Boston, which they dominated, was fast changing by the influx of impoverished immigrants. In this changing world Oliver Wendell Holmes snobbishly designated the elite families as akin to the Brahmins, the highest class in the Indian caste system. Henceforth, the elite class with homes on Beacon Hill or Back Bay was known as the Boston Brahmins.

THE BOSTON MANUFACTURING COMPANY
AFTER THE DEATH OF FRANCIS CABOT LOWELL

Francis Cabot Lowell died too young to see the full success of his bold idea. Although his factory in Waltham was already successful during his brief lifetime, the impact on the nation of the Waltham-Lowell system of production became abundantly clear in the years to come as the Industrial Revolution took hold.

Under the able management of Patrick Tracy Jackson and the machinist Paul Moody, the mill at Waltham continued to flourish. In an address to the House on April 26, 1820, the Honorable Henry Clay of Kentucky, and speaker of the U.S. House of Representatives, laid out his ideas for an America benefiting both from agriculture and manufacturing. In his brilliant speech Clay described his 1819 visit to New England and especially to the Boston Manufacturing Company in Waltham.

New England was badly affected by the torrent of imports arriving at the end of the War of 1812. "In New England, in passing along the highways," said Clay, "one frequently sees large and spacious buildings with the glass broken out of the windows, the shutters hanging in ruinous disorder, without any appearance of activity and enveloped in solitary gloom. Upon inquiring what they are, you are almost always informed they were some cotton or other factory which their proprietors could no longer keep in motion against the overwhelming pressure of foreign competition."

How different matters were in 1818 at the Boston Manufacturing Company in Waltham. At this cotton mill "there is a very great benefit.

I witnessed the advantage in a visit which I lately made to the Waltham manufactory, near Boston. There, some several hundred girls and boys were occupied in separate apartments. The greatest order, neatness and apparent comfort reigned throughout the whole establishment. The daughters of respectable farmers were usually employed."

Patrick Tracy Jackson and Paul Moody showed Henry Clay around the mill. The Boston Manufacturing Company, Clay told the House of Representatives, "has the advantage of a fine water situation, a manager of excellent information, enthusiastically devoted to its success, a machinist of most innovative genius, who is constantly making some new improvement and who has carried the water loom to a degree of perfection which it has not attained in England—to such perfection as to reduce the cost of weaving a yard of cloth adapted to shirting to less than a cent—while it is abundantly supplied with capital by several capitalists in Boston. These gentlemen have the most extensive correspondence with all parts of the United States. Owing to this extraordinary combination of favorable circumstances the Waltham establishment is doing pretty well."

The Boston Manufacturing Company of Waltham was one of the few American textile mills to survive the onslaught of imported textiles from Great Britain and India. Sales in 1817 reached $51,205, in 1818 increased to $124,748 and in 1820 sales exceeded $260,000. According to Victor Selden Clark, writing in 1916, the success of the venture "convinced Boston capitalists that cotton goods could be made profitably in New England, and that the Waltham method best suited our conditions of production. Therefore, as soon as the business horizon cleared, measures were taken to start this system of manufacture at other places." The mills at Lowell, Massachusetts, were developed by the same group of industrialists of the Boston Manufacturing Company at Waltham. The mills at Dover in New Hampshire were developed by another group of Boston capitalists. Boston was emerging as the financial and commercial hub of New England, serving the factories located along the rivers.

THE COMPONENTS OF
THE WALTHAM-LOWELL SYSTEM

Francis Cabot Lowell's bold vision was to set up on home soil a factory capable of taking in raw cotton at one end and putting out finished cloth at the other. This vision was the outcome of many ideas and decisions merged into a single plan of action. Alexander Hamilton had issued the call for self-reliance by manufacturing at home. Lowell, too, saw the future of America in manufacturing goods on American soil rather than remaining dependent upon the skills of other nations. Lowell knew that his Cabot relatives thirty years earlier had set up a cotton mill at Beverly that had failed due to faulty machinery and the lack of skilled workers. The wars in Europe, the Embargo of 1807 and now the War of 1812 all conspired to add great risks to his career as a merchant. Furthermore, his tour of Great Britain from 1810 to 1812 had convinced Lowell of the great wealth to be generated from the new power machinery used in the cotton textile industry. With his Waltham factory, Francis Cabot Lowell hoped to make money for himself while doing his duty to his workers and to his country.

In particular, Francis Cabot Lowell was fascinated by the power loom recently introduced into British factories. The spinning machines invented by Richard Arkwright together with the weaving machines devised by Edmund Cartwright were capable of permanently shifting cloth-making from homespun to the factory. The challenge of building new machines appealed to the engineer in Francis Cabot Lowell. Fifteen years previously he had spent months tinkering with a new method to distill molasses into rum. In 1814, he applied the same determination in designing a power loom for textiles. New England's fast-flowing rivers would provide Lowell with the power needed to run his machines and New England ships would carry raw cotton from the South to the port of Boston at less cost than cotton carried to Liverpool.

The funding of the Boston Manufacturing Company followed the method used by Francis Cabot Lowell and Uriah Cotting to raise money for their Broad Street and India Wharf projects. They offered shares to a number of well-to-do and influential men. Lowell was much helped by his brothers-in-law, but it is probable that Francis Cabot Lowell loaned money to Patrick Tracy, Charles and James Jackson, enabling them to buy shares in his company. In 1816, when the company was fast running short of capital to build the factory and dam, buy the machines and pay the wages, it was Francis Cabot Lowell who personally advanced the huge sum of $50,000 and bought additional shares to keep his company afloat.

A key component of the Waltham-Lowell system was building the power machines for the Waltham mill. Francis Cabot Lowell established the Waltham Machine Shop with Paul Moody in charge. Most of the machinery, including the new looms, for the mill were "made in a shop attached to the mill." Francis Cabot Lowell supplied the ideas and the mathematical skills but it was Paul Moody who "had the remarkable facility of turning to practical account the suggestions of others." Already in 1816, the penultimate year of Lowell's life, the Waltham Machine Shop was making looms for sale to other cotton textile mills.

One of the first buildings in the new industrial town of Lowell was the Lowell Machine Shop. Much larger than that at Waltham, the Lowell Machine Shop employed some one thousand men making the machinery for the many mills at Lowell as well as for sale around the nation. The Proprietors of the Locks and Canals, the company that owned the water rights, bought the patents for the machines made in Waltham and transferred the work to Lowell, with Paul Moody in charge. In 1828, Moody invented the system of using leather belts, instead of iron gears, to transmit the power to the main shafting of the mill.

Several reasons can be advanced to explain why Francis Cabot Lowell built the boarding houses for his workers. Waltham in 1814 was a village of fewer than one thousand people and lacked a local pool of labor. To attract farm girls to work in the mills, Lowell needed to assure the parents that their daughters would be well looked after and protected. Lowell was determined to prevent the squalor and social unrest he had observed in the British factory towns. By offering the comforts of home he hoped to avoid a Luddite reaction with disgruntled workers going on strike and smashing the machinery. Lowell was also moved by the generosity of the Duke of Kent, who assisted the workers of Sterling, Scotland. The boarding houses in Waltham appealed to the paternalistic instincts of Francis Cabot Lowell, always eager to combine goodness with profit.

Friedrich Engels viewed capitalism as the enemy of the working classes and an economic system that served to enrich the few and degrade the many. Engels argued that the dignity of the masses could only be restored through revolution. Robert Owen, the founder of socialism in Great Britain, believed that the economic system could be peacefully reformed from within and that committed leaders like himself had the capacity and responsibility to lift up their workers through better pay, better conditions and schools for their children. Lord Brougham (1778–1868), the eminent British politician, who served as lord chancellor, saw the similarity between New Lanark and Lowell. In a speech given in October 1863, Brougham said that Robert Owen "in the great spinning mills of New Lanark made the workpeople partners of their profits by educating their children and giving them such instruction as not only fitting them for the work at the mills, but for any other employment. The communication of the workpeople at New Lanark and at Lowell of a share in the profits of their labor was affected in the large provision made for their education and their health, but this necessarily depended upon the employer, and on his charge, by death or other causes, the successor may not have the more enlightened view."[16]

The efforts of Robert Owen to improve the conditions of work in the British textile mills, especially the education of children, did not receive wide support in Great Britain. In 1843, the home secretary, Sir James Graham, proposed a law requiring compulsory education for children working in the factories. The law was strongly opposed and did not pass. Francis Cabot Lowell did not have the analytical powers of Friedrich Engels or the reformist zeal of Robert Owen. Nevertheless, his quiet paternalistic capitalism built the boarding houses, the company store and the schools at Waltham that offered benefits to the workers equal to those of New Lanark. The example set by Francis Cabot Lowell in Waltham was carried on in Lowell and in other mill towns across the United States.

Francis Cabot Lowell knew the importance of surrounding himself with capable and influential people. Among his investors were leading Boston merchants, politicians and lawyers. Patrick Tracy Jackson and Paul Moody were his lieutenants who worked tirelessly to launch the factory and carry forward his vision. Selling the cloth made in the Waltham factory was a challenge. Francis Cabot Lowell and Nathan Appleton had to overcome the prejudice against local goods and the belief that imported cloth was superior. Furthermore, Lowell and Appleton realized that they needed to manufacture what their customers most demanded: the coarse and cheap cloth for rough use. Using their long-established nationwide network of commission agents, Lowell and Appleton were soon able to establish markets for their cloth in Boston, New York, Philadelphia, Baltimore, and beyond.

Francis Cabot Lowell was lucky with his timing by starting his factory during the War of 1812, when British goods were excluded from the marketplace. Still, the key factors in Lowell's success were his personality, his business skills, and his dogged determination to carry out his vision to make cotton textiles at home and begin the transformation of America from a nation of farmers and merchants to a manufacturing people—a shift from the wharf to the waterfall. As Francis Cabot Lowell wrote in 1801, while working on his rum distilling equipment, his determination and perseverance came "as much from Pride as from any sanguine expectation of success."

LOWELL, THE MANCHESTER OF AMERICA

The Waltham mills gained steadily in efficiency and profitability. A yard of cloth that sold for thirty cents in 1816 fell to twenty-one cents in 1819, thirteen cents in 1826 and as low as 8.5 cents in 1829. In 1818, sales of cloth amounted to $124,728 and more than doubled in 1820 to $266,658. While Francis Cabot Lowell was alive the monthly earnings of his workers averaged $11. After his death, the wages rose slowly over the years. Productivity increased gradually, leading to a decline in the labor costs per yard.[17] The Honorable John Calhoun of South Carolina made the long trip to Waltham in 1818 to see the Boston Manufacturing Company. Francis Cabot Lowell would have been delighted to show him around. Instead Nathan Appleton conducted the tour of the mills protected by the Tariff of 1816. Calhoun toured the mill "with the apparent satisfaction of having himself contributed to its success."

By 1820, the existing mills at Waltham used all the power the small Charles River could provide. To keep its technological lead over its competitors, the company needed to expand elsewhere. In September 1821, Paul Moody's former partner Ezra Worthen told him, "I hear that Messrs. Jackson and Appleton are looking out for water power. Why don't they buy up the Pawtucket Canal? That would give them the whole water power of the Merrimack, with a fall of over thirty feet."[18]

The Pawtucket Canal project, incorporated in 1792, was an attempt to make the Merrimack River navigable from New Hampshire to Newburyport, bypassing the precarious Pawtucket Falls. The canal was one and a half miles long with four locks and allowed barges carrying wood and farm products from the interior to reach the coast. However, these objectives were soon defeated with the completion of the Middlesex Canal that led from the Merrimack River directly to Boston. The Middlesex Canal Company, incorporated in 1789, was one of the most ambitious undertakings in the United States of its time, costing $550,000. Along the twenty-seven-mile Middlesex Canal, cut to a width of twelve feet, were twenty-two locks. Barges pulled along the canal by horses carried fresh farm produce directly into Boston.

Paul Moody and Patrick Tracy Jackson learned from Thomas M. Clark of Newburyport, the agent for the struggling Pawtucket Canal, that the canal and the abutting lands could be bought cheaply. Since Jackson intended to remain in Waltham he recommended Kirk Boott Jr. as a man capable of taking on the vast enterprise of building a new textile city. Keeping their plans secret from outsiders, Appleton, Jackson and Moody used their own funds and employed surrogates to buy the lands and the water rights of the Pawtucket Canal. The first visit of the three gentlemen to the site was during a light snowfall in November 1821. Less than a dozen houses and scattered farms could be seen in the area known as East Chelmsford. To the amusement of Moody and Appleton, Patrick Tracy Jackson predicted that within their own lifetimes twenty thousand people would be living and working here. What should be the name of the new town? After only a few moments of thought the three men agreed to name their new manufacturing town Lowell in tribute to the late Francis Cabot Lowell.

Kirk Boott Jr. was born in Boston in 1790. Young Kirk benefited from his father's success and was sent to the prestigious Rugby School in England, and then served in the British army fighting Napoleon. Mechanically inclined, he toured the textile mills of England and studied the machinery to manufacture textiles. On hearing that his father had died, Kirk Boott Jr. returned to Boston in 1817 only to find that the business he hoped to inherit was near bankruptcy. He tried Harvard but dropped out before graduation. In 1821, Kirk Boott Jr. asked Patrick Tracy Jackson for a job with the Boston Manufacturing Company. He chose an excellent time to inquire, as Jackson and Nathan Appleton were beginning the company's expansion along the Merrimack River. Since Patrick Tracy Jackson was heavily committed to Waltham, the position of superintendent of works in the new town of Lowell was offered to Kirk Boott, at a salary of $3,000 annually.

Favoring the autocratic style of the British mill owners, Kirk Boott set himself up as the great potentate of Lowell, ruling the town while the owners stayed in Boston. He was highly effective but not popular. He built himself a magnificent house overlooking the Merrimack River. One July 4, he enraged the locals by flying both the British and the American flags, with the Stars and Stripes below the British colors. The Boott Mill, one of the largest in Lowell, was named for him. He built Lowell into the greatest industrial city in America. Kirk Boott died in 1837 and, as his late father had predicted, the help given to Francis Cabot Lowell in 1815 was more than adequately reciprocated.

On December 1, 1821, the Merrimack Manufacturing Company was established. Nathan Appleton and Patrick Tracy Jackson each took 180 shares, Paul Moody took 60, and Kirk Boott Jr. and his brother John Boott each took 90 shares. The act of incorporation was granted to the company on February 5, 1822. With a capital of $1,200,000 the Merrimack Manufacturing Company began to enlarge the Pawtucket Canal to a width of sixty feet and a depth of eight feet, giving enough water power to supply fifty mills. Using Waltham as a prototype, the Merrimack Company planned to build a series of mills along the river and canal and lease them to other textile companies. The machinery for the new mills would be made in the machine shops at Waltham. As in Waltham, boarding houses were constructed to house the mill girls. Paul Moody agreed to transfer from Waltham to the Merrimack Manufacturing Company and Patrick Tracy Jackson soon followed. Five shares of the Merrimack Company were allotted to Boston lawyer, and U.S. Congressman Daniel Webster, but since he did not pay for them, the shares were sold to someone else.[19] When completed, the large Merrimack Company alone had 67,965 spindles and 1,920 looms, operated by 2,050 hands.

It took several years to widen the canal, build the dams, erect the mills and install the machinery. The most impressive of the dams in Lowell was the 950-foot dam built at the head of the Pawtucket Falls. The quiet fields and farm land of East Chelmsford were transformed into a bustling town of large red-brick factories, waterwheels and boarding houses. In 1825, the Hamilton Manufacturing Company, with a capital of $1.2 million, took occupancy of its mill, with Samuel Batchelder as superintendent. Batchelder owned a small mill in New Ipswich and knew Nathan

Appleton, who recommended him for the senior position at the Hamilton Company. He is the same Samuel Batchelder who, in 1863, published his *Introduction and Early Progress of the Cotton Manufacture in the United States.*

According to *The Boston Newsletter and City Records* of October 14, 1826, five mills at Lowell were already in operation. Each ran four thousand spindles and each mill employed "200 men and 600 females, none are under the age of twelve." Workers' wages ranged from $2.25 to $3.25 a week with $1.25 deducted for board and lodging. The Merrimack Manufacturing Company opened "a large machine shop, where machinery for two mills is completed annually. In these, 200 first rate mechanics in iron, wood &c are constantly employed. The water power of Lowell is great and abundant."

In 1828, the Appleton Company and the Lowell Company were producing textiles, and in 1830, the Suffolk, Tremont and Lawrence Companies turned their waterwheels. The Boott Company opened in 1835 and the Massachusetts Company in 1839. All these mills followed the model of Francis Cabot Lowell as joint stock companies. With a combined capital of over $12 million, Lowell was much larger than Waltham. The Lowell Machine Shop, under the supervision of Paul Moody, expanded and employed upward of one thousand men, designing and making the machinery for Lowell and for sale to other mills. The traffic between the booming town of Lowell and Boston became so great that as early as 1830 there were plans to build a railroad. In 1835, the Boston & Lowell Railroad, the first in Massachusetts, was opened to carry freight and passengers, a journey of less than one hour each way. With over one mile of factories filled with machinery, Lowell far surpassed every industrial town in America. With the coming of steam power, the waterwheel and a location on the river became redundant. Instead, chimneys rose high over the mills to carry away the soot. The success of Lowell and its mills greatly encouraged the nationwide expansion of the cotton fabrics industry.

The astonishing growth of the city of Lowell led to the decline in the fortunes of the Boston Manufacturing Company at Waltham. In June 1823, the Merrimack Manufacturing Company bought all the patents of the Waltham Company and transferred the creative work to Lowell. With the departure of Paul Moody and Patrick Tracy Jackson, John Lowell Jr., eldest son of Francis Cabot Lowell, took over in Waltham as company agent and treasurer. John Jr. gave up these positions in 1831 after the death of his wife and two daughters.

Francis Cabot Lowell's original partners in the Boston Manufacturing Company were among the original subscribers to the mills in Lowell. Patrick Tracy Jackson bought shares in the Merrimack, Hamilton, Appleton and Lowell mills. Nathan Appleton was a major shareholder in the Merrimack and Appleton Companies. The brothers-in-law Charles and James

Jackson, Benjamin Gorham and Warren Dutton bought small numbers of shares in various other cotton mills.

CAPITALISM WITH A HUMAN FACE

The early mills of Lowell, Massachusetts, followed the employment practices that Francis Cabot Lowell first introduced in Waltham, recruiting farm girls and accommodating them in supervised boarding houses. Four-fifths of the mill workers were young women who stayed three or four years "and then return[ed] to fill their station in life as wives and mothers. The factory girl, whose intention it is to return in a short time to her native village, carries back the unsullied reputation with which she left her father's home." The remaining one-fifth of the new workers were young men, who stayed longer in the hopes of rising "to the situations of overseers, clerks or supervisors." According to James Sparks, writing in 1841, Lowell's employment practices left "no large dependent class of people hanging around our manufacturing villages, unfit for anything but factory work and subject therefore to the will of their employers, and in their helplessness and hopelessness growing more abandoned themselves, and tainting the whole neighborhood with their corruption." The boarding houses "are erected by the mill owners, and are let, at reduced rent to the families who keep them up." These supervisors had the responsibility of keeping the boarding houses neat and comfortable and ensuring that the workers were well housed, well fed and healthy. "There is no class of laborers in New England that is so well paid, clothed and fed as our factory operatives."[20]

The boarding house at 22 Dutton Street, Lowell, had four large bedrooms, each housing six mill girls, and two smaller bedrooms each for two girls. The young women shared a kitchen and a dining room. Supervising the twenty-eight young women was the matron and her family. "The design of the control of the boarding houses and their inmates was one of the characteristics of the Lowell factory system, early incorporated therein by Mr. Francis Cabot Lowell and his brother-in-law Patrick T. Tracy, who are entitled to all the credit of the acknowledged superiority of our early operatives," wrote Dr. John O. Green. The legacy of Francis Cabot Lowell was that corporations "should have souls and should exercise parental influence over the lives of their operatives." The mill girls of Lowell worked twelve hours a day, six days a week, and yet found companionship and independence. At night the girls read books, wrote poetry or stories, some of which were published in the *Lowell Offering* and *The Operatives' Magazine*. Lucy Larcom, who started working in the mills at age eleven, and Harriet Hanson Robinson went on to become famous writers, recalling their early lives among the looms and the spindles of Lowell.

Harriet Hanson Robinson was born in Boston, where her father worked as a carpenter and her mother managed a little shop. After the father died, his widow and her four young children moved to Lowell, where she found work as a matron in a company boarding house. Harriet "wanted to earn money like the other little girls, to go to work in the mills" and at age ten started work as a doffer in the spinning shop, speedily taking off the full bobbins and replacing them with empty ones. She earned two dollars a week and tells "how proud I was when my turn came to stand up on the bobbin-box, and write my name in the paymaster's book."

Like all the others, Harriet started work at five in the morning and remained until seven at night with only a half-hour for breakfast and a half hour for lunch. Despite her fourteen-hour workdays she had a pleasant life, with a warm home, three good meals a day, and plenty of friends. The children played games, told ghost stories and "we told each other of our little hopes and desires, and what we meant to do when we grew up. We had our aspirations." The Lowell children contrasted their good fortune with the children working in English factories, "who were treated so badly, and were even whipped by their cruel overseers." Harriet left the mill to marry, raise a family and establish herself as a gifted writer.

Cotton textile manufacture in America began to draw foreigners to learn the reasons for its success. In his great work *History of the Cotton Manufactures in Great Britain*, published 1835, Sir Edward Baines noted that "England had just lost her American colonies" as Richard Arkwright and others invented the ingenious power machines to create wealth from textiles. American manufacturers had the advantages of much cheaper freight rates for raw cotton and had abundant waterpower that was cheaper than steam power. The cost of spinning was equal in both countries but the cost of weaving in America was less "because a girl attends there to four power-looms, whereas in England a girl attends to two." The cost of machines and labor in America was higher than in Britain.

Michel Chavalier was a young Frenchman sent by his government to examine the industrial development of the New World. In 1835 he visited Lowell, where six thousand women were then employed making cotton fabrics. They were country girls living "far from their families, left to themselves." Their wages were higher than wages earned by French women in the textile industry and "a large number of workers in Lowell are able to save up to a dollar and a half each week. At the end of four years spent in manufacturing, their savings are able to accumulate to two hundred and fifty to three hundred dollars. They then have a dowry, quit the fabric industry and marry."

What most impressed Chevalier were the living conditions of the workers: "The manufacturing companies watch over these young girls with scrupulous care. Twelve years ago Lowell did not exist. When they constructed the factories, it was also necessary to build lodgings for the workers. The boardinghouses are under the supervision of matrons who are paid by the company a dollar and a quarter per week. These matrons, who are generally widows, answer for their boarders and are themselves under the control of the company for the administration of their small community." The rules were strict. Laziness, dishonesty, the violation of the Sabbath, and even playing cards were grounds for dismissal. In Chevalier's opinion, the proper and decent demeanor of the Yankee mill girls combined with the strict rules of conduct imposed by the textile companies gave Lowell "with its factories higher than steeples, the feel of a Spanish village with its nunneries."

Charles Dickens visited Lowell in 1842 during his first tour of America. Dickens had completed his novel *Oliver Twist* only three years earlier. Familiar as he was with the blighted state of the English mill towns, Dickens marveled at the orderliness of Lowell, the cleanliness and self-respect of its mill girls. Established only twenty years earlier, Lowell was "a large, populous, thriving place." The mill girls were "all well-dressed [and showed] extreme cleanliness. They had serviceable bonnets, good warm cloaks, and shawls, and were not above clogs and patterns. They were healthy in appearance, many of them remarkably so; and had the manner and deportment of young women, not of degraded brutes of burden."

Charles Dickens admired the working conditions in the mills. The workrooms were large, with many windows and green plants scattered about. The air was fresh and much attention was paid to cleanliness and comfort. The boarding houses where the girls lived were close to the mills, well managed and clean. There were pianos in the boarding houses, and the girls regularly used the lending library and deposited their money in the Lowell Savings Bank. By July 1841, the bank held the accounts of 978 mill workers, totaling over $100,000. Charles Dickens was particularly impressed by their writings, set down in the *Lowell Offering* that compared "advantageously with a great many English Annuals." The writing was as "wholesome as village air" and conveyed optimism and hope. How different it all was from the degrading conditions around the mills in England.

The English writer Anthony Trollope, during a visit in the 1840s, described the city of Lowell as "a commercial Utopia." What most surprised the English visitor on his visit to the Lowell mills was the personal appearance of the women who work there. "They are not only better dressed, cleaner and better mounted in every respect than the girls employed at the manufactories in England, but they are infinitely superior" in health, education and self-respect. The Lowell mill girls "are not sallow, not dirty, not ragged, or of low culture. They are taken in, as it were, to a philanthropic manufactory college and are then looked after and regulated more as girls and lads at a great seminary, than as hands by whom industry profit is to be made out of capital." The young women in Lowell earned about fourteen shillings a week, "fully a third more than women can earn in Manchester. This is all very nice and pretty at Lowell, but I am afraid it could not be done at Manchester."

Anthony Trollope quoted approvingly from the handbook of the city of Lowell: "Mr. F. C. Lowell had in his travels abroad observed the effect of large manufactory establishments on the character of the people, and in the establishment at Waltham the founders looked for a remedy for these defects. They thought that education and good morals would even enhance the profit, and that they could compete with Great Britain by introducing a more cultivated class of operatives. For this purpose they built boardinghouses, which were kept by discreet matrons, mostly widows, no boarders being allowed except operatives. At Lowell, the same policy has been adopted and extended, more spacious mills and elegant boarding houses have been erected." Mechanization had also advanced. The workers were trained to do specific and repetitive tasks leading to many different jobs, each with their own regulations and pay scales.

Francis Cabot Lowell admired famous people. He would have been delighted to read Harriet Hanson Robinson, Charles Dickens and Anthony Trollope's affirmation of his philosophy of doing good while doing well. However, not all observers of Lowell and its factories were as impressed as Dickens and Trollope. From nearby Concord, the American writer Henry David Thoreau in his great work *Walden*, written in 1854, observed that "the mass of men lead lives of quiet desperation." Furthermore, wrote Thoreau, "I cannot believe that our factory system is the best mode by which man may get clothing. The condition of the operatives is becoming every day more like that of the English. . . . The principal objective is not that mankind may be well and honestly clad, but, unquestionably, that the corporations may be enriched."

In the United Kingdom, home to Charles Dickens and Anthony Trollope, the Industrial Revolution surged forward. In 1771, Britain imported less than one million pounds of raw cotton. The industrial revolution greatly increased the demand for raw cotton and led to the expansion of the Southern plantation system and more slaves. By 1830, cotton had outstripped sugar as the world's most valuable commercial crop. Great Britain took two-thirds of the cotton of the American South amounting, in 1844, to over £600 million. By 1854, the populations of Liverpool and Manchester combined exceeded seven hundred thousand, and other textile centers also mushroomed in size. That year British cotton textile mills employed 220,000 workers, operating eight million mule spindles and 110,000 power looms. The United Kingdom exported over 550 million yards of cotton piece goods. Over one and a half million people, directly and indirectly, were employed in the British cotton textile industry. With one eye on Britain, the fledgling American textile industry absorbed an increasing amount of Southern cotton to produce 141 million yards of cloth in 1833, increasing to 857 million yards by the eve of the Civil War.

Karl Marx published the first volume of his monumental *Capital—A Critique of Political Economy* in Germany in 1867. After Marx died the work was completed by Friedrich Engels, who published the second volume in 1885 and the third in 1894. In volume 2, Karl Marx mocks "the capitalist attempts to elevate the working class." As an example of capitalist control under the guise of benevolence, Marx describes "the cotton goods manufacture in the Lowell and Lawrence Mills. The boarding and lodging houses for the factory girls belong to the company that owns the factories. The landladies of the houses are in the pay of the same company and act according to its instructions. The ten o'clock curfew is enforced by special police of the company." By these means, in Marx's view, the company seeks tight controls on its employees by increasing their hours of work and limiting their leisure time.[21]

THE GROWTH OF THE
AMERICAN TEXTILE INDUSTRY

The quick-flowing rivers of New England offered abundant water power for more textile mills. As fresh capital sought profits in textiles the establishment of the industrial town of Lowell was followed by Lawrence, Massachusetts; Saco, Maine; Manchester, New Hampshire; and the textile mill towns along the Connecticut River. The success of these large mills equipped with power machinery to convert raw cotton into finished cloth rapidly elbowed aside the smaller Pawtucket-style mills still tethered to their handcraft roots. The Boston lawyer Harrison Gray Otis, long associated with the Lowell family, was appointed president of the Chicopee textile company near Springfield, Massachusetts. The whaling towns of New Bedford and Fall River shifted to textile manufacturing. Along the Salmon Falls River near Dover, New Hampshire, a series of mills were built, all based on the Waltham-Lowell system. These five-story brick mills built on a foundation of granite followed "the Lowell plans in the form and arrangement of the mills as well as the style of their machinery." The Scottish-born James Montgomery, in his 1840 survey of American mills, considered Dover to be "one of the most beautiful manufacturing villages I have ever seen. . . . Along the outside of the Main Street are the boarding or dwelling houses for the mill workers; these are neat brick buildings, three stories in height, and each building containing four tenements; there are seven of these boarding houses which gives to the whole an appearance of neatness and uniformity. A great deal of money has been spent on this place." Montgomery was also impressed by the quality of the American machines. "With regard to the common power loom weaving," he wrote, "the Americans have attained as much perfection as the manufacturers of either Glasgow or Manchester." Neatness and expense notwithstanding, in 1828, at the Cocheco Mill in Dover, New Hampshire, "one of the Waltham-Lowell type firms," over five hundred women workers marched through the town in protest of low wages and restrictive rules. This was the first women's textile strike in the United States.

New Englanders carried the Waltham-Lowell system across the Mohawk Trail and into the Midwest, and to the South. By 1825, the American textile mills expanded beyond plain cloth and devised new techniques of calico printing. More and more people were moving from the country into the towns and cities and seeking clothing of better taste and refinement. Fine printed cottons with colorful patterns found their way into stores throughout the fast growing nation. Not only were the cotton mills of New England finding new markets across the America but were selling cloth abroad. After 1820, mechanized textile manufacture came to Philadelphia. Aided by a steady flow of immigrants from the United Kingdom and the waterpower of the Schuylkill River, textile mills were built in the village of Manayunk, which became known as "The Lowell of Philadelphia." By the 1820s American textiles were offered for sale in Rio de Janeiro, Buenos Aires and Montevideo. Americans competed with the British to sell cloth in Mexico, Chile and Cuba. Ships from Boston laden with cloth made in the mills of Lowell delivered their goods to Canton, China, and even competed with the vast Indian cotton industry. The dependence of Americans on homespun from the Orient and manufactures cotton textiles from Britain was broken as the United States produced its own cloth and competed for markets abroad. In 1855, the United States exported $31 million of manufactured goods, of which cotton textiles accounted for nearly $7 million.

By 1840, America boasted 1,025 cotton mills with 2,112,400 spindles. With a combined capital invested of $80 million the industry processed one hundred million pounds of cotton annually. Fully three-quarters of the industry was localized in the New England states. Lowell-type mills spread beyond New England and into Paterson, New Jersey, as well as New York, Philadelphia and Baltimore, but the city of "Lowell is decidedly the largest and most important in the United States."[22] Lowell; Paterson, New Jersey; and Mattawan, New York were the principal centers for the manufacture of machinery for the cotton mills. James Montgomery calculated that with the added cost of the boarding houses, the expense of labor in the United States was much greater than in Great Britain. American mills benefited, however, from lower costs of carrying raw cotton and lower costs of power. Thanks to its many powerful rivers, American cotton mills were "moved by water" well into the 1840s. Early in the second half of the nineteenth century, steam generated by burning coal became the principal source of power for American factories.

On June 27, 1843, President Andrew Jackson accompanied by Vice President Martin Van Buren and members of the Cabinet paid a visit to Lowell. The president was greeted on Jackson Street by 2,500 mill girls "dressed in the style of elegance and neatness" and by six hundred school children. The president visited the Merrimack Mill, No. 2, "where all the machinery had been put into operation," worked by the mill girls still dressed in their holiday attire, much to the delight of Andrew Jackson. Four months later, on October 25, the eminent Kentuckian Henry Clay visited the Lowell mills and the schools. A quarter-century earlier, Clay had paid a visit to the Waltham mill. The progress made at Lowell was confirmation to Henry Clay of the success of his American system of industrialization.

In the year 1822, Daniel Anthony of the village of Adams, in western Massachusetts, built a cotton mill with twenty-six water-powered looms. Anthony hired young women from Vermont to work in his mills. A number of these women were boarded in the mill owner's home and got to know his family. When she was eleven, Susan Brownell Anthony asked her father, "If Sally Ann knows more about weaving than Elijah, then why don't you make her overseer?" Her father Daniel Anthony responded, "It would never do to have a woman overseer in the mill." For years Susan pondered her father's reply. She became a teacher and learned that the male teachers earned more than she did for the same work. Susan B. Anthony determined that women deserved the same as men and devoted the rest of her life to the battle for women's rights and universal suffrage.

The mill girls of Lowell inspired a considerable literature dealing with such topics as devotion to family, hard work, independence and despair. The heroine of Harriet Farley's *Abby's Year in Lowell* covets the beautiful clothes her friends brought home after working in the mills. She decides, however, not to indulge herself but to improve her mind and save her earnings to buy gifts for her family on the farm. Another story tells of Cordelia Crane, who becomes pregnant, is disgraced and commits suicide by taking poison. In 1849, the play *Mill Girls of Lowell—A Drama of Innocence and Guilt* by William B. England, opened at the National Theatre, corner of Portland and Traverse Streets, Boston. The play begins with the girl traveling to Lowell. In the second act, the mill girl is working in the noisy factory.

> Did you ever go into Lowell; Oh, racket,
> Good Lord, what a buzzing it makes,
> Like fifty live crabs in a basket,
> And what a darned sight of cotton it takes.

In the third act two scoundrels plot to abduct and ruin the innocent mill girl, but in the final act, she is rescued and the kidnappers are captured.

WORKER DISSATISFACTION

After his death the paternalism of Francis Cabot Lowell steadily gave way to the cold demands of profits. Dissatisfaction and disgruntlement were creeping into the Waltham workplace. One machinist, Isaac Markham, writing to his brother on May 20, 1821, complained that the management of the Boston Manufacturing Company had "all the lordly & tyrannical feelings that were ever felt by the greatest despots in the world. . . . They were determined their word shall be law and shall be obeyed." The situation deteriorated and the workers went on strike. The management of the Waltham factory "cut down every man's wages that they employ without giving them the least notice, until the day came for payment. The same trick was played off the girls but they as one revolted and the works stopped 2 days in consequence." Markham hailed from Middlebury, Vermont, and came to Waltham to work in the nation's most advanced textile plant. Dissatisfied with the working conditions at Waltham he left, taking with him to Vermont drawings of the power loom.

Lucy Larcom was among the first to complain of the tyranny of the factory system. She compared the dressing frame on which she labored twelve hours a day to a "half live creature with its great growing joints and whizzing fan [that] was aware of my incapacity to manage it and had a fiendish spite against me."

Thomas Man of Pawtucket, in his 1833 poem *Picture of a Factory Village*, likened factory work to slavery:

> For Liberty our fathers fought
> Which with their blood, they dearly bought,
> The Fact'ry system sets at naught,
> A slave at morn, a slave at eve,
> It doth my inmost feelings grieve,
> The blood runs chilly from my heart,
> To see fair Liberty depart,
> And leave the wretched to their chains.

Other writers objected to the controlling sounds of the factory.

> The factory bell begins to ring,
> And we must all obey,
> And to our old employment go,
> Or else be turned away.

And,

> Hark! Don't you hear the fact'ry bell,
> Of wit and learning 'tis the knell,
> It rings them out it rings them in,
> Where girls they weave, and men they spin.

The themes of freedom and slavery were echoed during the Lowell Strike of October 1836, when hundreds of young women marched through the streets protesting the cut in their wages and an increase in the cost of lodgings.

> Oh, isn't it a pity, such a pretty girl as I,
> Should be sent to the factory, to pine away and die.
> Oh, I cannot be a slave,
> For I'm so fond of liberty,
> That I cannot be a slave.

In 1844 the mill girls formed the Lowell Female Labor Reform Association (LFLRA), campaigning for higher wages, fewer working hours and the dignity of labor. The first president of the association was Sarah Bagley. In her 1840 article in the *Lowell Offering*, Sarah Bagley wrote on the decidedly mixed "Pleasures of Factory Life." She was grateful for the opportunity "to earn money to assist aged parents who have become too infirm to provide for themselves, or perhaps to educate some orphan brother or sister." The factory also provided the opportunity to make new friends, to be educated and, in times of illness, to rely on the kindness of the supervisors. Factory life, continued Bagley, also brings "a constant clatter of machinery, that I could neither speak or be heard, nor think to be understood, even by myself."

For decades the British Parliament prohibited the emigration of skilled artisans. With mounting unemployment and overproduction of textiles these laws were changed. The British spinners and weavers who migrated to America after the War of 1812 found little work, as the country was flooded with cheap English goods. The migration of British workers picked up as the protective tariffs took effect and the American textile industry expanded. In 1824, the British government eased the restrictions on migration, starting the flow of British workers seeking employment in the American textile factories. Among these immigrants were William

Carnegie and his family from Dunfermline, a small weaving town in Fifeshire, Scotland. The Carnegie family settled in Allegheny City, Pennsylvania, in 1848, where William gave up hand-loom weaving for a job in a cotton factory owned by Mr. Blackstock, a fellow Scotsman. William's son, thirteen-year-old Andrew Carnegie, found his first job in the same factory as a bobbin-boy, changing spools of thread, earning $1.20 a week. "It was a hard life," recalled Andrew Carnegie. Working six days a week, he and his father arrived at the factory before sunrise and labored at their jobs until nightfall. A few months later, young Andrew found a job at $2 a week working for John Hay, another Scot, who owned a bobbin-making factory. Showing his legendary self-confidence and determination, Andrew Carnegie switched from textiles to railroads, to iron and then to steel to become the richest man in America.

THE RISING MERITOCRACY

The great contribution made by Paul Moody to the success of the Boston Manufacturing Company opened doors to many other gifted mechanics. Lacking privileged homes or university education these men used their intelligence and engineering skills to rise to top positions in the scientifically based textile industry. The mills were fast creating jobs for experts in designing, building and operating machinery, factory construction, fluid dynamics, finances marketing, and the management of workers. These jobs paid higher salaries and offered opportunities for social advancement. In Waltham, Paul Moody kept the machines running efficiently and worked on improvements. Between 1816 and 1821, Paul Moody was awarded ten U.S. patents for his cotton spinning frame, double-speeder, winding spool, cloth-dressing machine and other inventions. In 1823, he transferred to the industrial town of Lowell where he was appointed chief mechanic of the Lowell Machine Shop. Moody had neither the vision of Francis Cabot nor the organizational abilities of Patrick Tracy Jackson, but he was the "workhorse of the enterprise." In Lowell, he developed the system of leather belting and pulleys to power the machines throughout the factory, replacing the shaft and gear system imported from Britain. His mechanical wizardry is credited for the efficiency and profitability of the Waltham and Lowell factories. He married Susannah Morrill of Amesbury, who bore him five children. There is a Moody Street in Waltham and one in Lowell. Paul Moody stayed close to his roots. He believed in public education for boys and girls and was charitable to those less fortunate than himself. On the morning of July 5, 1831, he felt ill. By afternoon he was desperately sick and was dead the following day. He was fifty-four years old and was buried in the family tomb in Byfield.[23]

Before he accepted the offer from Francis Cabot Lowell to come to Waltham, Paul Moody was with Ezra Worthen a part owner of the Amesbury Wool & Cotton Company. After Moody left in 1814, the Amesbury Company enjoyed only a few years of success before it was close to failure under the onslaught of foreign textiles. Paul Moody suggested that he come to Lowell, and in 1822, Ezra Worthen was appointed the first superintendent of the great Merrimack Manufacturing Company. The pressure of work proved too great for him. In 1824, Worthen developed angina pectoris and died of a heart attack on June 18. His tombstone proudly reads, "He was the first superintendent of the great manufacturing establishment at Chelmsford, and in that capacity made full use of the great and rare talents which his Maker endowed him." His son William Ezra Worthen, only five years old when his father died, attended Harvard and became nationally known in dam construction. William Ezra Worthen served as president of the American Society of Civil Engineers.

Another youngster from a poor home who rose on his merits to great heights in the early textile industry was Warren Colburn. He trained as a machinist, studied at night and entered Harvard at age twenty-three. Colburn had a gift for mathematics and, while still at college, wrote a book titled *First Lesson in Intellectual Arithmetic*. His mathematical skills combined with a practical knowledge of machines brought Colburn to the attention of Francis Cabot Lowell Jr. In 1824, Warren Colburn was hired as superintendent of the Boston Manufacturing Company to replace Paul Moody, who had moved to the Lowell Machine Shop. Upon the death of Ezra Worthen, Colburn moved to Lowell as superintendent of the Merrimack Company. Warren Colburn greatly expanded educational opportunities for the workers in Lowell. In addition to his duties at the mill, he took on the job of superintendent of the Lowell school system and published further books on the teaching of mathematics.

After the War of 1812, Boston Harbor once again welcomed ships carrying manufactured goods from Europe, cotton textiles from India and pottery and silks from China. American ships, laden with dried fish, farm produce and lumber left Boston for distant ports. By the 1850s, the trade patterns were reversed. Ships carried in raw cotton, wool, leather and coal to supply the great factory towns and left the port carrying out manufactured goods.[24] By 1834 "seven-eighths of the Boston merchants were identified with the New England textile industry as stockholders, selling agents or directors."[25]

A great industry developed in New England to build the power machines for the mills. Ira Draper and Paul C. Whitin began early in the nineteenth century as cloth-makers before turning to the manufacture of power looms. On January 7, 1816, Ira Draper received a patent for his design of a fly shuttle hand loom. Following the example of the Boston

Manufacturing Company, his Draper Corporation making power looms was set up in the town of Hopedale, Massachusetts, and run by successive generations of the Draper family. Paul C. Whitin established his loom factory along the banks of the Mumford River. By the middle of the nineteenth century the Whitin Machine Works, in the town of Whitinsville, Massachusetts, had become one of the nation's leading makers of power machines for the textile industry. Both the Draper Corporation and the Whitin Machine Works followed the enlightened labor practices set by the Boston Manufacturing Company by providing housing, community services and subsidized food for their workers. In nearby Worcester, the Knowles Loom Works and the Crompton Loom Works (later merged as Crompton & Knowles Loom Works) entered the booming business of making power machines for the hundreds of textile mills in New England, the Mid-Atlantic states and the Midwest, as well as exporting machines to companies abroad.

THE WALTHAM-LOWELL SYSTEM
SPREADS ACROSS AMERICA

According to James Montgomery, by 1831 over $40 million had been invested in the American cotton manufacturing industry. Eight hundred and one mills were in operation, with two-thirds of them located along the rivers of New England. The mills contained 1,341,700 spindles and 33,483 looms and employed over fifty-seven thousand workers, two-thirds of them women. Rhode Island, still adhering to the small village mill, was the only state that still employed large numbers of children in its factories. In 1831, over 3,500 children under the age of twelve were working in Rhode Island cotton mills. The American mills in 1831 used 77,457,316 pounds of raw cotton to produced 56,514,926 pounds of finished cloth.

By 1848, the industry was beginning to spread to the South and the Midwest, with 122,000 employees and total wages exceeding $22 million. Started in Waltham only thirty-four years earlier, America was becoming a serious competitor to the mighty British textile industry. Hamilton Smith, of the Cannelton Coal Company of Indiana, posed in 1848 the question, "But is the manufacturing of cotton to be confined chiefly to the rugged hills of New England? To the minds of some of us, the day is coming when the valley of Ohio bears the same relation to New England that New England now does with Great Britain." The Cannelton Coal Company, developed with Boston money, was producing abundant coal for steam power, making it cheaper "than the cheapest water power for propelling machinery." With local coal and getting cotton from the coast by river steamers up the Ohio River, Hamilton Smith and his friends reckoned they could produce cotton textiles cheaper in Indiana than New England. Combining local capital with money and know-how from New England they built in 1849 the Cannelton Cotton Mills. The architect Thomas A. Tefft of Providence, Rhode Island, followed the design of one of the mills at Lowell, Massachusetts. Machinery was purchased from the Lowell machine shops and New England mechanics and mill girls were hired to move to Indiana on three-year contracts to work in the factory. The immigrant mill girls were paid "Lowell wages by the piece." The first cloth from Cannelton was woven in January 1851, and Hamilton Smith envisioned his enterprise as the future "Lowell of Ohio."

In his authoritative book, published in 1916, on the *History of Manufactures in the United States; 1607–1860,* Victor Selden Clark, one of the leading economists of his day, related how the Waltham-Lowell system reached down to the South. In 1844, William Gregg, a nephew of one of the earliest cotton spinners in Georgia, traveled north "to make a personal study of the Massachusetts system and became convinced that it could be transplanted successfully to the South." Under a pseudonym, Gregg wrote a series of articles in the *Charleston Courier* to dispel Southern prejudice against manufacturing and informed his readers "that Lowell mill-owners wore gloves and lived in fine residences." The following year, under his own name, Gregg published his *Essays on Domestic Industry,* reminding his readers that the cotton came from the South and arguing that the South was able to compete with the North in manufacturing. In 1846, with the aid of Charleston capitalists, William Gregg founded at Graniteville, South Carolina, the largest factory in the South, with nine thousand spindles and three hundred looms. His machines were powered by a turbine wheel of 116 horsepower to make the sheeting and heavy cotton fabrics that were then the staple fabrics of the South. Gregg hired skilled New Englanders as managers and as operatives he employed native whites, who were "housed, shepherded, and schooled in a comfortable village, with welfare institutions, on the Lowell plan." Graniteville had boarding houses for the single workers and cottages for families "all constructed and ornamented in the ancient Gothic style, and each house having its own gardens for vegetables and flowers." Gregg built a schoolhouse for children aged six to twelve and "furnished the teachers and books, and fined workers five cents a day, withheld from their wages, for every day their children were absent from classes."

In short order, Charleston, Mobile, New Orleans and Memphis opened large cotton mills, built on the Waltham-Lowell system. The Natchez cotton mill, with two thousand spindles and ten looms, was operated by men who came from Boston. In 1840, New England still controlled over 70 percent of the nation's spindles and cotton textile production. From 1848 until the Civil War, the South was a fast-growing cotton textile-producing region, sending its fabrics all over the United States. The Civil War disrupted manufacturing but by 1880 the South was again moving forward, soon to replace New England as the nation's leading cotton textile region. Much of the growth in the South was the result of northern companies opening branches in the South. In 1894, the Massachusetts Cotton Mills of Lowell opened its namesake in Georgia, equipped with machinery from the Lowell Machine Shop. The Charleston Manufacturing Company, 1882, bought three hundred looms made in Lowell, Massachusetts. The Merrimack Manufacturing Company, incorporated in Lowell in 1822, opened a branch mill in Huntsville, Alabama; and the Pacific Mills, incorporated in 1850, opened the Hampton Cotton Mills in Columbia, South Carolina. The Atlanta Cotton Factory Company ordered its machinery from the Lowell Machine Shop. The acorn that Francis Cabot Lowell planted in Waltham was growing into a mighty oak, with its branches extended over New England, the South and the Midwest.

From 1840 onward, immigrants such as the Carnegie family coming from Scotland, Ireland and England entered the United States in large numbers with many finding work making cotton fabrics. The industry was deeply affected by the financial panics that periodically swept across the nation. During the Panic of 1857, the Middlesex Mills in Lowell, and the Bay State and the Pemberton Mills in Lawrence were nearly wrecked after their selling agents went bankrupt. Shares in the Pacific Mills that stood at $1,000 a share fell to below $50. Other mills were forced to cut wages and lay off workers. The Civil War restored the fortunes of the northern mills and increased the demand for labor. After 1880 came French Canadians seeking work in the mills, followed by immigrants from the east and south of Europe. In 1840, there were in New England alone 46,834 workers in the cotton textile industry, jumping to 155,951 in 1905.

The eminent Harvard historian Samuel Eliot Morison published in 1921 the remarkable tale of *The Maritime History of Massachusetts*. Early in the nineteenth century, "the younger and more far-sighted men put their money and brains into making Massachusetts a manufacturing state," wrote Morison. "Two scions of shipping families, Francis C. Lowell and Patrick T. Jackson prepared against peace by setting up power looms at Waltham, in the first complete American cotton factory. Every country town with a good-sized brook or river set up a textile or paper mill or iron foundry; and similar expansion in shoemaking altered the economy of fishing villages. The center of interest in Massachusetts shifts from wharf to waterfall; by 1840 she had become predominantly a manufacturing state."[26] The shift was indeed dramatic. By the year 1845, the cotton mills of Massachusetts together had 817,483 spindles and employed 6,603 men and 14,407 women. These mills used fifty-seven million pounds of raw cotton to weave 175 million yards of cloth. The state was home to hundreds of other factories making shoes, hats, woolen goods, furniture, and iron goods.[27]

During the era of the Andrew Jackson administration the city of Lowell with its many cotton mills was viewed as proof that the industrialization of America would not lead to the degradation of the workers as had occurred in Great Britain. Henry Clay remained skeptical, saying "Lowell will tell whether the manufacturing system is compatible with the social virtues." During its early years as the showcase of American enterprise, the mill girls of Lowell gained more than they were harmed. However, widening cracks in the Waltham-Lowell system of paternalistic capitalism appeared with the increase in competition for jobs from impoverished immigrants. By January 1834, the young women textile workers across New England were earning around $2.95 a week; board cost $1.25, leaving them $1.70 a week to save or to spend. In February, the managers of the mills in Lowell introduced a new set of rules, including fines for tardiness and easier ways to discharge workers. Discussing these matters in their boarding houses, the women demanded changes to the rules under a threat of walking off the job and withdrawing their money from the banks. Eight hundred of the two thousand women in the Lowell factories went out on strike. The strike lasted only a few days and the workers returned to their jobs but the leaders of the strike were discharged. The Lowell strike of October 1836 was over the reduction of twelve and a half cents a week in pay and an increase of twenty-five cents a week for board. This time, many of the workers stayed out for months. The partial success of this strike encouraged militancy among the workers in other mills in their demands for higher wages and shorter hours of work.

By the year 1840, the U.S. mills used 106 million pounds of raw cotton, much less than the 722 million pounds of cotton used by British mills. The American South was by far the main provider of cotton to British and American mills.[28] Taken together, by 1860 the growing and harvesting of cotton, the cotton textile industry and the textile machinery business constituted the largest source of employment and enterprise in the United States.

The success of Francis Cabot Lowell's venture into textile manufacturing was the catalyst for the industrialization of America. The Waltham-Lowell system spread from cotton textiles to shoes, sewing machines, pianos and other goods. Many other nineteenth-century American companies followed the example set by Francis Cabot Lowell by offering subsidized housing, cheap foodstuffs and community services to their employees. In 1907, James W. Cannon established the town of Kannapolis, North Carolina, where he built his Cannon Mills to make bed sheets and towels. He built a modern mill town complete with housing for his workers, schools and a YMCA with a swimming pool, bowling alleys and sports facilities.

The dominance of the New England cotton textile industry based on the Waltham-Lowell system lasted less than fifty years. Broadus Mitchell in his 1921 book *The Rise of the Cotton Mills in the South* chronicles the shift of the textile industry from North to South. After the South began its recovery from the Civil War, the attraction of building mills close to the source of the raw cotton became compelling. The savings in freight, commissions, insurance and wages gave the South a clear advantage over New England. By 1870 a steady stream of young Southerners traveled north to gain "experience in the Lowell machine shops to be able to operate mills at home afterwards." Columbus became "a miniature Lowell" and Athens "the Lowell of the South." In 1870 Southern mills had only 6,296 looms and 32,871 spindles. Thirty years later, the South had 110,015 looms and 4,299,988 spindles. In June 1882, a single railroad transported twenty-two carloads of machinery from the Massachusetts machine shops to the South. By the start of the twentieth century the South had overtaken New England as the center of the American cotton fabric industry. When automatic machinery was introduced, fewer native-born Americans entered the industry as waves of immigrants took the low-wage jobs that were offered.

Less than one hundred years after Francis Cabot Lowell built the Boston Manufacturing Company in Waltham with its solitary power loom, the American cotton textile industry had grown enormously. According to the U.S. Bureau of Labor, in 1910 there were 1,082 mills. These large mills held 550,000 looms and over 27 million spindles and employed 310,000 workers. The South, especially North and South Carolina and Georgia, had surpassed New England to become the dominant cotton textile producer of the nation.

With mills in New England, Midwest and the South, the United States of America was, until well after World War II, the world's leading industrial nation. However, the seeds of decline had been sewn. Too many factories, too little innovation, too high salaries and benefits, and dependence on tariff protection left the American textile industry vulnerable to the low wages paid in other countries. By the close of the twentieth century the once-mighty American textile industry was moribund. The fall of American textiles was followed by the fall in the manufacture of textile machinery. Francis Cabot Lowell's Waltham Machine Shop lost its importance after 1824, when the Lowell Machine Shops were constructed to make the machines for the many mills of Lowell. The Lowell Machine Shops in 1911 were merged into the Saco-Lowell Works. Later, Platt

Brothers, Britain's largest manufacturer of textile machinery, purchased its American competitor.

Judge John Lowell and his children were alive during the early years of the American republic. The judge raised a privileged family but his sons were eager to play a role in forming the character of the new nation. The oldest son, John Jr., followed most closely in the footsteps of their illustrious father. John Jr. considered the privileges of birth and wealth to fall within the natural order of nature. "There will always be the lazy and the industrious," he wrote in 1799, "the drones and the worker bees, of necessity the poor and the rich, the ignorant and the well-informed." Yet, to use Francis Cabot Lowell's expression, each of the sons was expected to find his own way "to come forward in the world." The Lowell brothers—John Jr., Francis Cabot and Charles—were highly educated, honorable and dutiful gentlemen, scions of one of the oldest families that settled in the Massachusetts Bay Colony. Writing clever but verbose pamphlets, John Lowell fought against change and championed an America led by the New England elite who shared his values. During the War of 1812, John Lowell showed his bitter opposition to the policies of the government. In a letter to Timothy Pickering (December 3, 1814), Lowell recommended that New England defy the government by not collecting federal taxes, refusing to raise a militia to fight the British and even declaring its neutrality in the war. Late in his life John Lowell recognized that American society was changing and wrote in 1823, "I happen to have lived in a middle generation between the revolutionary patriots & the modern man." Likewise, the Reverend Charles Lowell diligently attended to his upper-class flock and campaigned softly against slavery and drunkenness. Both John and Charles were guided by their conservative ideologies, believed in a hierarchical society and sought to keep the privileges and the values of the past.

The leadership of America was moving away from the moneyed, well-educated, well-dressed and well-spoken gentlemen elite, and toward the rough-and-tumble of the aspiring classes motivated by enterprise and profits. Despite his entitled upbringing, Francis Cabot Lowell was a modern man, open to scientific advances and the belief that individuals should rise on the basis of merit. He loved his family and cared deeply for his friends. He was well traveled but his roots remained in Essex County. Unlike his brother John, he did not have strong political views, and unlike his brother Charles he did not have deep religious convictions. His brothers John and Charles sought to occupy the high moral ground, but Francis was a practical man of business who took the world as he saw it. He embraced change and looked for opportunities to grow the economy of an expanding America. He was a major manufacturer of rum and importer of wine, brandy, whiskey and gin at the same time his brother, the Reverend Charles Lowell, was active in the Massachusetts Society for the Suppression of Intemperance. As an ardent capitalist, Francis wanted to make money and enrich his family. Before his trip to Great Britain he was a merchant, owned a distillery, invested in lands and buildings, and engaged in the development of Broad Street and India Wharf. On his return to Boston in 1812, he used his mathematical skills and inquiring mind to develop labor-saving machines suited to the scientific age. He had planned to retire in comfort while still in his forties but risked it all to pursue his vision of introducing modern textile manufacturing to America. By the standards of the times, Francis Cabot Lowell treated his workers well. Capitalism with a soul reflected his core values. His brother John railed against the South but Francis Cabot Lowell bought Southern cotton, sold his textiles in the South and West and cooperated with Southern politicians to pass the Tariff of 1816. Through determination and the luck of timing, his Boston Manufacturing Company launched America into the industrial age. The mill at Waltham, producing goods at home to replace imports, served as the model for the factory system of the nineteenth century that gave America its economic independence. While John Lowell supported the merchant class and free trade, his brother Francis Cabot was creating jobs in American factories, protected by tariffs.

"The greatest of evils and the worst of crimes," extolled the great Irish playwright George Bernard Shaw, "is poverty. Our first duty is not to be poor. Money is the most important thing in the world. It represents health, strength, honor, generosity and beauty." In his masterful 1907 play *Major Barbara*, Bernard Shaw pits the hard-nosed views of the industrialist Andrew Undershaft against the moralistic stance of his daughter Barbara, who is a major in the Salvation Army. In their well-mannered argument, Undershaft tells his daughter, "In your Salvation shelter I saw poverty, misery, cold and hunger. You gave them bread and treacle and dreams of heaven. I gave from thirty shillings a week to twelve thousand a year. They find their own dreams; but I look after the drainage."[29] Francis Cabot Lowell was closer in spirit to Andrew Undershaft than to Major Barbara. He created products, profits and jobs. He housed and fed his workers but left them to take care of their own souls.

Writing in 1895 of the Lowell family, William Thomas Davis noted, "Perhaps no family in Massachusetts has for so many generations and in so many of its branches been more distinguished."[30] Among the distinguished Lowell politicians, writers, poets, architects, academics, lawyers, judges, historians, astronomers and entrepreneurs, Francis Cabot Lowell made the greatest contribution. He is indelibly connected with the industrialization of America. For his pioneering work, Francis Cabot Lowell was recognized in 1978 by the National Business Hall of Fame as one of the most important figures of American business over the past two centuries, placing him among the likes of such luminaries as Andrew Carnegie, John Deere, Cyrus McCormick, Cornelius Vanderbilt and Thomas A. Edison. Francis Cabot Lowell's vision of capitalism with a soul gave his workers the money, shelter and food to maintain their pride, while his factory still made a profit. Little interested in politics and religion, Francis was the "informing soul" who launched the American industrial revolution, which for a century and a half was the powerful magnet that drew millions upon millions of impoverished immigrants across the oceans to find work in the factories and share in the American dream of a better life.

Original Sources

The great bulk of the research on the life and times of Francis Cabot Lowell was done by reading the original letters and correspondence, written with ink and quill on rag papers some two centuries ago. The fading ink and free script was taxing to my weak eyes, especially the letters written by Francis Cabot Lowell himself. His long and bountiful letters in minute handwriting, with lists upon lists of calculations, were immensely rewarding to read. Included in his papers, especially during his family's travels through Great Britain, are many letters written by Hannah Lowell. The Francis Cabot Lowell Papers (MS N-1602) are kept at the Massachusetts Historical Society, Boston. The collection consists of nine boxes of letters and nine bound volumes. They cover his life from age ten until his death.

The Patrick Tracy Jackson Papers (MS N-408) (Tall), also at the Massachusetts Historical Society, contains the last will and testament of Francis Cabot Lowell, as well as much data on the Boston Manufacturing Company.

The Gardner Family Papers (MS N-1273), Box 1, containing letters sent by Samuel Pickering Gardner to the Lowell family, are housed at the Massachusetts Historical Society, Boston.

The John Lowell Papers (1743–1802) are at the Houghton Library, Harvard College, MS Am 1882, and contain a number of letters written by Francis Cabot Lowell to his father.

The Reverend Charles Lowell wrote brief notes about people and places, and the weather, on the blank pages of the *Massachusetts Register and United States Calendar*, published in Boston from 1814. The Harvard Divinity School at 45 Francis Avenue, Cambridge, Massachusetts, has seven of Lowell's annotated volumes. Frances E. O'Donnell, curator of manuscripts and archives, kindly gave me access to the registers, with Charles Lowell's faded and largely illegible notes (bms-00682).

Copies of the letters written by Henry Wadsworth Longfellow to and about Sarah Champney Lowell are kept at the Longfellow National Historic Site, 105 Brattle Street, Cambridge, Massachusetts. Sarah Lowell lived in the home from 1837 to 1840. Thanks to James M. Shea, museum curator, for showing me the living quarters of Sarah Lowell and Henry Longfellow.

Notes

INTRODUCTION:
THE NEW INDUSTRIAL SYSTEM

1. S. P. Waldo, *The Tour of James Monroe, President of the United States, through the Northern and Eastern States, 1817* (Hartford, CT: Silus Andrus, 1820), 160–61.

2. H. Clay and D. Malloy, *The Life and Speeches of the Hon. Henry Clay, Volume 1* (Hartford, CT: Silus Andrus & Son, 1856), 477.

3. Address by John Amory Lowell at the semi-centennial celebrations of incorporation the City of Lowell, March 1, 1876. Proceedings (Lowell, Massachusetts, 1876), 51–56.

4. E. Cartwright, *A Memoir of the Life, Writings and Mechanical Inventions of Edmund Cartwright, Inventor of the Power Loom* (London: Saunders & Otley, 1843).

CHAPTER 1:
OCCASIONEM COGNOSCE

1. The genealogy of the Lowell family is laid out in great detail by Delmar R. Lowell in *The Historic Genealogy of the Lowells from 1639 to 1899* (Rutland, VT: Tutler Company, 1899), by Ferris Greenslet, *The Lowells and Their Seven Worlds* (Boston: Houghton Mifflin, 1946), and by Margaret C. Crawford, *Famous Families of Massachusetts* (Boston: Little, Brown, 1930).

2. Details of the *Telltale* periodical and the Spy Club at Harvard College appear in the *Publications of the Colonial Society of Massachusetts*, Transactions 1908–1909 (Boston, 1911), 220–21.

3. There are several histories of Newbury and Newburyport, including John J. Currier's *History of Newbury, Mass., 1635–1902* (Boston: Darnell & Upham, 1902)

and the *History of Newburyport, Mass., 1764–1905,* by the same author (Newbury-port, MA: Self-published, 1906), Joshua Coffin's *A Sketch of the History of Newbury, Newburyport and West Newbury* (Boston: Samuel Drake, 1845), and the *History of Newburyport,* by Euphemia Vale Smith (Newburyport, 1854).

4. The book *Vital Records of Newburyport, Massachusetts to the Year of 1849,* is-sued by the Essex Institution, Salem, Massachusetts, 1911, lists the early births in the town.

5. Details about the Loyalist Daniel Bliss appear in D. Michael Ryan, *Concord and the Dawn of the Revolution: The Hidden Truths* (Charleston, SC: History Press, 2007), 30.

6. The relationship between Jonathan Jackson and John Lowell is told by James Jackson Putnam in *A Memoir of Dr. James Jackson* (Boston: Houghton Mif-flin, 1905). The best account of their closeness comes from *Hon. Jonathan Jackson, His Wife and Many Members of His Family* (Boston: Alfred Mudge, 1866), 7–9, by his son, James Jackson, MD. John Lowell's student life at Harvard from *The Lowells and Their Seven Worlds,* by Ferris Greenslet.

7. K. W. Porter, *The Jacksons and the Lees; Two Generations of Massachusetts Mer-chants; 1765–1844, Volume 1* (Cambridge, MA: Harvard University Press, 1937), 156.

8. Foster T. A., *Sex and the Eighteenth-Century Man: Massachusetts and the His-tory of Sexuality in America* (Boston: Beacon Press, 2006).

9. Carol Bundy in her book, *A Biography of Charles Russell Lowell Jr.* (New York: Farrar, Straus & Giroux, 2005), offers insights into the accumulation of wealth by John Lowell and Jonathan Jackson. Also, Caleb Cushing, *The History and Present State of the Town of Newburyport* (Newburyport, MA: 1826), 5–7. Also, Currier, *His-tory of Newburyport, Mass., 1764–1905, Volume 1,* 45–46.

10. Charles Francis Adams, *Familiar Letters of John Adams and his Wife Abigail during the Revolution* (New York: Hurd & Houghton, 1876), 4–5.

11. John Quincy Adams' diary references to Newburyport have been collected in *Life in a New England Village, 1787, 1788,* edited by Charles Francis Adams (Bos-ton: Little, Brown, 1903).

12. Frank W. Bayley, *A Sketch of the Life and a List of the Works of John Singleton Copley* (Boston: The Garden Press, 1910).

13. James H. Stark, *The Loyalists of Massachusetts and the Other Side of the Ameri-can Revolution* (Boston: Self-published, 1910), 125.

14. John Collins Bossidy (1860–1928), American poet, at a toast given at an alumni dinner, Holy Cross College, 1910.

15. Euphemia Vale Smith, *History of Newburyport: From the Earliest Settlement of the Country to the Present Time* (Newburyport, MA: Self-published, 1854).

16. Currier, *History of Newburyport, Mass., 1764–1905.*

17. Warren F. Kellog, *The New England Magazine, Volume 27* (Boston, March–August 1900).

18. Letter from John Adams to John Lowell (June 12, 1776), and response by John Lowell (August 14, 1776), PJAd4d271, Massachusetts Historical Society, Boston.

19. John Codman, *Arnold's Expedition to Quebec* (New York: Macmillan, 1901).

20. Joshua Coffin, *A Sketch of the History of Newbury, Newburyport and West Newbury from 1635 to 1845* (Boston, Samuel B. Drake, 1845).

21. Jacqueline Barbara Carr, *After the Siege: A Social History of Boston, 1775–1800* (Boston: Northeastern University Press, 2004).

22. Greenslet's *The Lowells and Their Seven Worlds* describes John Lowell's life in Boston.

23. Samuel Eliot Morison, *The Life and Letters of Harrison Gray Otis, Federalist, 1765–1848, Volume 1* (Boston: Houghton Mifflin, 1913).

24. Letter of John Lowell to John Adams, October 12, 1779, PJAo8d143; letter from Abigail Adams to John Lowell, November 29, 1779, AFCo3d184; letter from John Lowell to Abigail Adams, December 15, 1779, AFCo3d194 (Massachusetts Historical Society, Boston).

25. More than a half-century later, in 1856, the Reverend Charles Lowell wrote, "My father introduced into the Bill of Rights the clause by which slavery was abolished in Massachusetts. [He] suggested and urged on the Committee the introduction of the clause, taken from the Declaration of Independence a little varied, which virtually put an end to slavery here."

26. Gerard A. Magnone, *United States Admiralty Law* (The Hague, The Netherlands: Kluwer Law International, 1997), 31–32.

27. Francis Samuel Drake, *The Town of Roxbury and Memorable Persons and Places* (Boston: Self-published, 1878), and Greenslet's *The Lowells and Their Seven Worlds* describe the Lowell estate in Roxbury.

28. Maeva Marcus (Ed.), *The Documentary History of the Supreme Court of the United States, 1789–1800, Volume Five* (New York: Columbia University Press, 1995), details the case of *Vassall v. Massachusetts*.

29. Maeva Marcus and James R. Perry, *The Documentary History of the Supreme Court of the United States, 1789–1800, Volume One, Part 2* (New York, Columbia University Press, 1985), 642.

30. Marcus and Perry's *The Documentary History of the Supreme Court of the United States, 1780–1800, Volume One, Part 2*, gives details of the jockeying for positions in the first Supreme Court (627–45).

31. George Jones Varney, *A Gazetteer of the State of Maine* (Boston: B. B. Russell, 1881), 170, 198, 432, provides the details of the territories in Maine purchased by John Lowell, Benjamin Lincoln and Thomas Russell.

32. Thomas Wentworth Higginson, *Life and Times of Stephen Higginson: Member of the Continental Congress* (Boston: Houghton Mifflin, 1907), 247–48.

33. Benjamin Hichborn's accusations against John Lowell are recorded in *The Writings of Thomas Jefferson*, edited by H. A. Washington, Volume IX (Washington, DC: Taylor & Maury, 1854), 201–2, and *Dial Magazine* (Volume 14, 1893), 111. A rebuttal against the accusations of disloyalty can be found in William Sullivan's *The Public Men of the Revolution: Including Events from the Peace of 1783 to the Peace of 1815* (Philadelphia: Cary & Hart, 1847), 389.

34. Currier, *History of Newburyport, Mass., 1784–1905*.

35. Letter from Jonathan Jackson to Oliver Wendell, Philadelphia, August 2, 1782, University of Virginia electronic text center; Delegates to Congress, Volume 19, August 1, 1782, to March 1, 1793.

36. Kenneth Wiggins Porter, *The Jacksons and the Lees; Two Generations of Massachusetts Merchants, 1765–1844* (Cambridge, MA: Harvard University Press, 1937), 380–90.

37. The account of the rise, decline and rise in the fortunes of Jonathan Jackson and his family comes from *Hon. Jonathan Jackson, His Wife and Many Members of the Family.* (Boston: Alfred Mudge & So, 1866), by his son Dr. James Jackson.

38. Over the years this famous Harvard club has included among its members Theodore Roosevelt, the twenty-sixth president of the United States, Oliver Wendell Holmes Jr., justice of the Supreme Court, and the architect H. H. Richardson.

39. John Torrey Morse, *Memoir of Colonel Henry Lee: With Selections from His Writings and Speeches* (Boston, Little, Brown, 1905), 9–10.

CHAPTER 2:
A PRIVILEGED EDUCATION

1. Sarah Loring Bailey, *Historical Sketches of Andover (Comprising the Present Towns of North Andover and Andover), Massachusetts* (Boston: Houghton Mifflin, 1880). I am grateful to Ruth Quattlebaum, archivist at Phillips Academy, Andover, Massachusetts, who provided me with the early class lists and the history of the academy. Also, Claude Moore Fuess, *An Old New England School: A History of Phillips Academy Andover* (Boston: Houghton Mifflin, 1917).

2. During the early years at Harvard the study of Hebrew was required on the assumption that a scholar should be able to read the Old Testament in its original language. From 1727 to 1760, the language was taught by Judah Monis. In 1764 the wealthy merchant Thomas Hancock left funds in his will to establish at Harvard a permanent professorship in Hebrew and Oriental languages. The first recipient was Stephen Sewall (trained by Monis), followed by Eliphalet Pearson and then Sidney Willard. The bulk of Thomas Hancock's money went to his nephew John Hancock.

3. Gavin Weightman, *The Frozen Water Trade* (New York: Hyperion, 2005), 13–17.

4. The Massachusetts Historical Society has a comprehensive collection of the papers of Francis Cabot Lowell and his family from 1742 to 1894 (Call # Ms N-1602).

5. Josiah Quincy, *The History of Harvard University, Volume 2* (Cambridge, MA: John Owen, 1840).

6. *Catalogue of the Honorary and Immediate Members and of the Library of the Porcellian Club of Harvard University* (Cambridge, MA: Allen & Farnham, 1857).

7. *The Quinquennial Catalogue of the Officers Graduates, 1636–1915* (Cambridge, MA: Harvard University Press, 1915).

CHAPTER 3:
THE YOUNG MERCHANT: 1793–1802

1. George Francis Dow in *Every Day Life in the Massachusetts Bay Company* (Boston: Society for the Preservation of New England Antiquities, 1935) gives an account of trade in early America.

2. Henry Wansey, *An Excursion to the United States of North America in the Summer of 1794* (Salisbury, UK: J. Easton, 1798), 1–30.

3. Matthew Dennis, William Pencak and Simon Newman, *Riot and Revelry in Early America* (University Park: Pennsylvania State University Press, 2002), 233–34. Also, Charles Downer Hazen, *Contemporary American Opinion of the French Revolution* (Baltimore: John Hopkins University Press, 1897), 166.

4. Susan Bean, *Yankee India; American Commercial and Cultural Encounters with India in the Age of Sail, 1784–1860* (Salem, MA: Peabody Essex, 2001).

5. The Higginson family of Salem intermarried with the Cabot family. Their ancestor, the Reverend John Higginson, was involved in the Salem witch trials of 1692. The Bromfield family came from Newburyport.

6. Rudol Hesdin, *The Journey of a Spy in Paris during the Reign of Terror: January–July 1794* (London: John Murray, 1895).

7. Edward Bromfield was a member of an old Newburyport family. He established himself in Paris as a merchant, trading with New England companies. He died around 1801, a young man. His younger brother John Bromfield traveled the world on merchant ships until he retired in Boston, a bachelor who loved books. At his death John Bromfield left $10,000 to his hometown to plant and care for the trees and to keep the sidewalks in good condition.

8. Julian Winsor, *The Memorial History of Boston, including Suffolk County, Massachusetts* (Boston: James R. Osgood and Company, 1881), 361–63. Details about the Boston theater are offered in Don B. Wilmeth and C. W. E Bigsby, *The Cambridge History of American Theatre* (New York: Cambridge University Press, 1998).

9. William Stevens Perry, *The History of the American Episcopal Church; 1587–1883* (Boston: James R. Osgood and Company, 1885), 488.

10. Accounts from the early years of Francis Cabot Lowell as a merchant come from the papers of his father, Judge John Lowell (1743–1802), MS AM-1582, 362–67, Houghton Library, Harvard University.

11. Details of some of Francis Cabot Lowell's early business connections were gleaned from William Willis, *A History of the Law, the Courts and the Lawyers of Maine,* 1863 (Clark, NJ: Lawbook Exchange, reprinted 2006), 242–43, and references to John Balfour in K. C. Laurence, *Tobago in Wartime, 1793–1815* (Kingston, Jamaica: Press of the University of the West Indies, 1995), 53, 74–75.

12. James Jackson Putnam, *A Memoir on Dr. James Jackson* (Boston: Houghton Mifflin, 1906), 73–80.

13. Robert Ephraim Peabody, *Merchant Ventures of Old Salem* (Boston: Houghton Mifflin, 1912), 56.

14. Cyril Henry Philips, *The British East India Company, 1784–1834* (London: Routledge, 1998), 81.

15. *The East-India Marine Society of Salem* (Salem, MA: East-India Marine Society, 1821).

16. Chittabrata Palit and Panjal K. Bhattacharyya, *Business History of India* (New Delhi, India: Kalpaz Publications, 2006), 14.

17. Samuel Lorenzo Knapp, *The Life of Aaron Burr: Volume 4* (New York: Wiley & Long, 1835).

18. *The Acts and Resolves, Public and Private, of the Province of the Massachusetts Bay, Volume IV* (Boston: Wright & Potter, 1890), 239. Also, Samuel Adams Drake, *Old Boston Taverns and Tavern Clubs* (Boston: W. A. Butterfield, 1917).

19. Wayne Curtis, *And a Bottle of Rum: A History of the New World in Ten Cocktails* (New York: Random House, 2006).

20. John T. Morse, *Memoir of Colonel Henry Lee; with Selections from His Writings and Speeches* (Boston: Little, Brown, 1905), 340.

CHAPTER 4:
THE BROTHERS LOWELL

1. Worthington Chauncey Ford (Ed.), *Writings of John Quincy Adams, Volume 1* (New York: Macmillan, 1913), 89. Also, John Quincy Adams, *Life in a New England Town, 1787, 1788* (Boston: Little, Brown, 1908), 27.

2. John Lowell Jr., *An Oration Pronounced July 4, 1799, at the Request of the Inhabitants of the Town of Boston*. My sincere thanks to Michael E. Holland, university archivist, University of Missouri–Columbia, who sent me a copy of John Lowell's oration. The remarks of George Cabot can be found in Henry Cabot Lodge, *Life and Letters of George Cabot* (Boston: Little Brown, 1887), 233.

3. Greenslet, *The Lowells and Their Seven Worlds*.

4. *A Massachusetts Mystery; The 1801 Tragedy of Jason Fairbanks & Elizabeth Fales*. *Dedham Historical Society* (Carlisle, MA: Applewood Books, 2009). Reprinted from the 1801 report of the trial of Jason Fairbanks.

5. Theodore Corbett, *The Making of American Resorts: Saratoga Springs, Ballston Spa, Lake George* (Piscataway, NJ: Rutgers University Press, 2001), 27.

6. Robert Means Lawrence, *Old Park Street and Its Vicinity* (Boston: Houghton Mifflin, 1922).

7. Samuel Eliot Morison, *The Life and Letters of Harrison Gray Otis, Federalist, 1765–1848, Volume 1* (Boston: Houghton Mifflin, 1913).

8. Alexander Biddle, *Old Family Letters: Contains Letters of John Adams* (Philadelphia: Lippincott, 1892), 350–51.

9. Charles Lowell, *Sermons Chiefly Occasional* (Boston: Ticknor & Fields, 1855), 112–13.

10. Cyrus Augustus Bartol and Charles Lowell, *The West Church and Its Ministers: Fiftieth Anniversary of the Ordination of Charles Lowell D.D.* (Boston: Crosby, Nichols and Company, 1856).

11. Charles Lowell, *Sermons Chiefly Practical* (Boston: Ticknor & Fields, 1885), 269–76.

12. Horace E. Scudder, *James Russell Lowell: A Biography, Volume I* (Boston: Houghton Mifflin, 1901).

13. George Willis Cooke, *Unitarianism in America: A History of Its Origin and Development* (Boston: American Unitarian Association, 1902).

14. Albert Jeremiah Beveridge, *The Life of John Marshall, Volume 4* (Boston: Houghton Mifflin, 1919), 9–10.

CHAPTER 5:
FRANCIS AND HIS SISTERS

1. Jennifer Monaghan, *Learning to Read and Write in Colonial America* (Amherst: University of Massachusetts Press, 2005), 41–45; Linda Eisenmann, *Historical Direc-*

tory of Women's Education in the United States (Westport, CT: Greenwood Press 1998), and Porter Sargent, *The Handbook of Private Schools* (Boston: Sargent, 1919), 17.

2. Elias Nason, *A Memoir of Mrs. Susanna Rowson, with Elegant and Illustrative Extracts from Her Writings in Prose and Poetry* (Albany, NY: Joel Munsell, 1878).

3. *Essex Institute Historical Collections, Volume 39, 1901* (Salem, MA: Essex Institute, Salem, 1903), 169.

4. Franklin Bowditch Dexter, *Biographical Sketches of the Graduates of Yale College with Annals of the College History, Volume V, June 1792–September 1805* (New York: Henry Holt, 1911), 277–79.

5. Eliza Susan Quincy, *Memoir of the Life of Eliza S. M. Quincy* (Boston: John Wilson, 1861), and Beverly Wilson Palmer (Ed.), *A Woman's Wit and Whimsy: The 1833 Diary of Anna Cabot Lowell Quincy* (Boston: Northeastern University Press, 2003).

6. James F. Hunnewell, *A Century of Town Life: A History of Charlestown, Massachusetts, 1775–1887* (Boston: Little, Brown, 1888).

7. Edward Lind Morse, *Samuel F. B. Morse: His Letters and Journals* (Boston: Houghton Mifflin, 1914).

8. *Hills vs. Putnam* examined the case before the Massachusetts Supreme Court, March–June 1890, involving the funds owned by Benjamin Lowell Gorham, son of Susannah Lowell Gorham and nephew of Francis Cabot Lowell. See *Massachusetts Reports: Cases Argued and Determined in the Supreme Judicial Court of Massachusetts, Volume 152, June 1890–January 1891* (Boston: Little, Brown, 1891).

9. Lawrence Roger Thompson, *Young Longfellow, 1807–1843* (New York: Macmillan, 1938). Also, Andrew R. Hilen, *The Letters of Henry Wadsworth Longfellow, Volume III* (Cambridge, MA: Harvard University Press, 1972), 46.

10. The correspondence and friendship between Henry Wadsworth Longfellow and Sarah Champney Lowell is recorded in Andrew R. Hilen (Ed.), *The Letters of Henry Wadsworth Longfellow* (Cambridge, MA: Belknap Press of Harvard University Press, 1966). I would like to thank the staff at the Longfellow House in Cambridge for showing me the correspondence and allowing me to see where Longfellow and Lowell lived while at the Craigie House.

11. The story of the ownership of the house from John Vassall to 1900 is told by Samuel Swett Green, *The Craigie House, Cambridge* (Worcester, MA: Proceedings of the American Antiquarian Society, Worcester, Massachusetts, April 1900), 312–52.

CHAPTER 6:
THE MERCHANT KING: 1803–1808

1. Timothy Dwight, *Travels in New England and New York* (New Haven, CT: Converse, 1821), 489.

2. *Boston Business Directory* (1800).

3. Samuel Eliot Morison, *The Maritime History of Massachusetts; 1783–1860* (Boston: Houghton Mifflin, 1922).

4. *The Boston Directory for 1805* (Boston: Edward Cotton, 1805).

5. Thomas Bridgman, *The Pilgrims of Boston and Their Descendants* (New York: D. Appleton & Company, 1856), 47.

6. Nancy S. Seasholes, *Gaining Ground: A History of Landmaking in Boston* (Cambridge, MA: MIT Press. 2003), 32, 43–47.

7. Albert William Mann, *Walks & Talks about Historic Boston* (Boston: Mann Publishing Company, 1917), 85. The act of incorporation of the Broad Street Associates is detailed in *Acts and Resolves Passed by the General Court of Massachusetts* (Boston: Young & Mines, 1898), 66. A description of the incorporation of India Wharf by the Massachusetts legislature is from *Private and Special Statutes of the Commonwealth of Massachusetts from February 1806 to February 1819, Volume 4* (Boston: Wells & Lilly, Boston, 1823), 152.

8. Timothy Dwight, *Travels in New England and New York* (New Haven, CT: Converse, 1821).

9. J. Garrison Ritchie, *Two Carpenters: Architecture and Building in Early New England, 1799–1859* (Knoxville: University of Tennessee Press, 2006), 36.

10. Edward Cotton, *The Boston Directory* (Boston, 1807), 17–18.

11. Anne Haven Thwing, *The Crooked and Narrow Streets in the Town of Boston, 1630–1822* (Boston: Marshall Jones, 1920), 205.

12. James F. Hopkins and Robert Saeger (Eds.), *The Papers of Henry Clay, Volume 6* (Lexington: University of Kentucky Press, 1981), 80.

13. William Sullivan, *Familiar Letters on Public Characters, and Public Events from the Peace of 1783 to the Peace of 1815* (Boston: Russell, Odiorne & Metcalf, 1834), 2.

CHAPTER 7:
MR. JEFFERSON'S EMBARGO

1. Martyn Lyons, *Napoleon Bonaparte and the Legacy of the French Revolution* (New York: St. Martin's Press, 1994), 266.

2. Albert Bushnell Hart, *Formation of the Union; 1750–1829* (New York: Longmans, Green, 1893), 191.

3. Gordon S. Wood, *Empire of Liberty: A History of the Early Republic, 1789–1815* (New York: Oxford University Press, 2009), 642.

4. John Melish, *Travels through the United States of America in 1806 & 1807, and 1809, 1810 & 1811* (Belfast, Ireland: J. Smyth, 1818).

5. Francois Alexandre Frederic, duc de la Rochefoucauld-Liancourt, *Travels through the United States of North America: The Country of the Iroquois* (London: Carpenter & Co., 1800).

6. William Macdonald (Ed.), *Select Documents Illustrative of the History of the United States, 1776–1861* (New York: Macmillan, 1898), 176.

7. Jack Hirshleifer, Amichai Glazer and David Hirshleifer, *Price Theory and Application: Decisions, Markets and Information* (New York: Cambridge University Press, 2005, 413.

8. Bruce Humphries, *Boston Looks Seaward: The Story of the Port, 1630–1940* (Boston: Boston Port Authority, 1941).

9. Mark Anthony De Wolfe Howe, *Boston: The Place and the People* (New York: Macmillan, 1903), 148–49, and Ralph D. Paine, *The Ships and Sailors of Old Salem* (New York: Outing, 1908), 482.

10. Timothy Dwight, *Travels in New England and New York* (New Haven, CT: Converse, 1821).

11. Herman Vandenburg Ames, *State Documents on Federal Relations: The States and the United States, Issue 6* (Philadelphia: University of Pennsylvania Press,

1906), 26–36. Also, John Torrey Morse, *John Quincy Adams* (Boston: Houghton Mifflin, 1898), 66.

12. Daniel D. Tompkins, *Public Papers of Daniel D. Tompkins, Governor of New York, 1807–1817: Military—Volume I* (Albany, NY: Lyon, 1898), 207.

13. Benson John Lossing, *The Pictorial Field-book of the War of 1812* (New York: Harper & Brothers, 1869), 172.

14. Peter P. Hall, *Napoleon's Troublesome Americans: Franco-American Relations, 1804–1815* (Dulles, VA: Potomac Books, 2005).

15. Christopher David Hall, *British Strategy in the Napoleonic War; 1803–1815* (Manchester, UK: Manchester University Press, 1992), 32.

16. W. Freeman Galpin, *The American Grain Trade to the Spanish Peninsular 1810–1814* (American Historical Review, Volume 28, 1922), 24.

17. Samuel Eliot Morison, *The Maritime History of Massachusetts, 1783–1860* (Boston: Houghton Mifflin, 1921).

18. John Lowell, *The New-England Patriot: Being a Candid Comparison of the Principles and Conduct of the Washington and Jefferson Administrations* (Boston: Russell & Cutter, Boston, 1810).

19. Ann Bromfield Tracy, *Reminiscences of John Bromfield* (Salem, MA: Self-published, 1852). She refers to Francis Cabot Lowell at the time of the embargo of 1812, but she surely meant the embargo of 1807.

20. William McMurtrie, *Report on the Culture of the Sugar Beet and the Manufacture of Sugar* (Washington, DC: Government Printing Office, 1880), 13. See also Lewis Sharpe Ware, *The Sugar Beet: Including a History of the Beet Sugar Industry in Europe* (Philadelphia: Henry Carey Baird, 1880), 27–28.

CHAPTER 8:
A PROPER BOSTONIAN ON A GRAND TOUR

1. Letter from Hannah Lowell to her mother-in-law Rebecca Lowell dated from Liverpool, July 26, 1810. Massachusetts Historical Society, the Francis Cabot Lowell (1775–1817) Papers (Call # Ms N-1602). Information about Liverpool early in the nineteenth century comes from *The Picture of Liverpool, or, Stranger's Guide* (Liverpool, 1805).

2. Letters of Francis Cabot Lowell to Samuel P. Gardner in Boston dated July 25 and July 30, 1810. Samuel Gardner was married to Rebecca Russell Lowell, half-sister to Francis Cabot Lowell.

3. Letter from Francis Cabot Lowell to his uncle, William Cabot, written on June 27, 1810, on the eve of his departure for Europe. Many dozens of letters passed between Francis Cabot and Hannah Lowell in Europe and their family and friends in Massachusetts.

4. The 1811 meetings between Lowell and Nathan Appleton are briefly described in Nathan Appleton, *Introduction to the Power Loom and Origin of Lowell* (Lowell, MA: Penthallow, 1858), 7–8.

5. J. W. Winthrop, *Memoir of the Hon. Nathan Appleton, L.L.D.* (Boston: John Wilson, 1861).

6. John Amory Lowell, *Memoir of Patrick Tracy Jackson* (Hunt's Merchants' Magazine, 1848).

7. Paul Mantoux, *The Industrial Revolution in the Eighteenth Century: An Outline of the Beginnings of the Modern Factory System in England in 1844* (Abington, Oxon: Routledge, 2006), 238, and Frederick Engels, *The Condition of the Working Class in England* (Stanford, CA: Stanford University Press, reprinted 1958), 156.

8. Lillian C. Knowles, *The Industrial and Commercial Revolutions in Great Britain during the Nineteenth-Century* (London: George Routledge, 1921), and Howard Robinson, *The Development of the British Empire* (Boston: Houghton Mifflin, 1922).

9. Robert F. Dalzell, *Enterprising Elite: The Boston Associates and the World They Made* (Cambridge, MA: Harvard University Press, 1987), 14.

10. John Peter Grant, *Memoir and Correspondence of Mrs. Grant of Laggan* (London: Longman, 1845), 271, 278.

11. John Braham (1771–1856) was born John Abraham, and sang in the London synagogue before starting his opera career. He was one of the best-known English Jews of his time.

12. Greenslet, *The Lowells and Their Seven Worlds*, 127–28, 130.

CHAPTER 9:
AMERICAN TEXTILE INDUSTRY BEFORE 1814

1. Alexander Hamilton, *Report on Manufacturers*, delivered to the House of Representatives on December 5, 1791. The ideas he expressed in his three reports to Congress formed the basis of the American school of economics.

2. Malcolm Keir, *Manufacturing Industries in America* (New York: Ronald Press, 1920), 145–48.

3. Henry Wansey, *An Excursion to the United States of North America in the Summer of 1794* (Salisbury, UK: J. Easton, 1798).

4. George Washington, *The Diary of George Washington from 1789 to 1791*, entry for October 30, 1789 (New York: Charles B. Richardson, 1861). Also, James M. Burns and Susan Dunn, *George Washington* (New York: Harry Holt, 2004), 59.

5. Perry Walton, *The Story of Textiles* (Boston: John R. Lawrence, 1912), 154–58. Also, Henry Cabot Lodge, *Life and Letters of George Cabot* (Boston: Little, Brown, 1876). A good description of the Beverly Cotton Manufactory can be found in William R. Bagnall, *The Textile Industries of the United States* (Cambridge, MA: Riverside Press, 1893).

6. *First Annual Message to Congress*, President George Washington, January 8, 1790.

7. Henry Cabot Lodge, *Life and Letters of George Cabot*. See letter of September 6, 1791, from George Cabot to Alexander Hamilton (Boston: Little, Brown, 1879), 43–45.

8. Samuel Batchelder, *Introduction and Early Progress of the Cotton Manufacture in the United States* (Boston: Little, Brown, 1863), 26.

9. William R. Bagnall, *The Textile Industries of the United States* (Cambridge, MA: Riverside Press, 1893), 112–16.

10. Caroline F. Ware, *Early New England Cotton Manufacture: A Study in Industrial Beginnings* (New York: Russell & Russell, 1966), 21.

11. Ware, *Early New England Cotton Manufacture*, 56.

12. Robert H. Baird, *The American Cotton Spinner and Managers' and Carders' Guide* (Philadelphia: Henry Baird, 1863).

13. Ware, *Early New England Cotton Manufacture*, 60–78.

14. Batchelder, *Introduction and Early Progress of the Cotton Manufacture in the United States*, 74–77. Also, Howard M. Gittleson, *The Waltham System and the Coming of the Irish* (Labor History, 6: 227–53, 1967). Details of the growth of mills during the period 1800 to 1815 were taken from Victor S. Clark, *History of Manufactures in the United States, 1607–1860* (Washington, DC: Carnegie Institute of Washington, 1893).

CHAPTER 10:
RETURN TO BOSTON

1. Greenslet, *The Lowells and Their Seven Worlds.*

2. Letter of Hannah Lowell to Anne MacVicar Grant, written from Roxbury, Massachusetts, August 17, 1812.

3. William Thomas Davis, *The Professional and Industrial History of Suffolk Country, Massachusetts* (Boston: Boston History Company, 1871), 105.

4. The reports of the Lowell household from July to December 1812 come largely from letters sent by Hannah Lowell to Anne MacVicar Grant in Edinburgh. Some of these letters were hand-carried by friends visiting Britain. Communication between the enemy nations continued during the war (1812–1815). Hannah used her letters to Anne MacVicar Grant to air her joys and troubles. Anne MacVicar Grant's responses after May 1812 are not included in the papers of Francis Cabot Lowell, and are probably lost. Anne MacVicar Grant kept the letters sent to her by Hannah and gave them to the Lowell family years later. Hannah Lowell's correspondence with Anne MacVicar Grant offers an intimate look at the daily life of her well-off Boston family.

5. Gardner W. Pearson, *Records of the Massachusetts Volunteer Militia* (Boston: Wright & Porter, 1913).

6. Joseph Tinker Buckingham, *Specimens of Newspaper Literature* (Boston: Redding and Company, 1852).

7. Timothy Dwight, *Travels in New-England and New York* (New Haven, CT: Converse, 1821).

8. Josiah Quincy, *The History of the Boston Athenaeum* (Cambridge, MA: Metcalf & Company, 1851).

9. Samuel Eliot Morison, *The Life and Times of Harrison Gray Otis, Federalist, 1765–1848, Volume 2* (Boston: Houghton Mifflin, 1913), 120.

10. John F. Chown, *A History of Money* (New York: Routledge, 1994), 165. Details of Francis Cabot Lowell's involvement in the New England Bank come from William Thomas Davis, *The Professional and Industrial History of Suffolk County, Massachusetts* (Boston: Boston History Co., 1891), 241–42.

11. The March 3, 1814, letter from Christopher Gore to Francis Cabot Lowell is included in the Francis Cabot Lowell Papers at the Massachusetts Historical Society, Boston.

12. Curtis Putnam Nettels, *The Emergence of a National Economy: 1775–1815* (New York: Holt, Reinhart & Winston, 1962).

CHAPTER 11:
THE BOSTON MANUFACTURING COMPANY

1. Phillip I. Blumberg, *The Multinational Challenge to Corporation Law: The Search for a New Corporation Personality* (New York: Oxford University Press, 1993), 10.

2. Boston Manufacturing Company records, 1813–1930 (Volume 1 and 2; Mss 442, 1813–1930), Baker Library Historical Collection, Harvard Business School.

3. Nathan Appleton, *Introduction to the Power Loom and Origin of Lowell* (Lowell, MA: Penthallow, 1858), 7–8. Also, James Jackson Putnam's *A Memoir to Dr. James Jackson* (Boston: Houghton Mifflin, 1906), 74, 90, describes the remarkable bond between Francis Cabot Lowell and his three Jackson brothers-in-law, reminiscent of the relationship between their fathers.

4. Frederick William Coburn, *History of Lowell and Its People, Volume One* (New York: Lewis Historical Publishing Company, 1920), 139.

5. Theodore Steinberg, *Nature Incorporated* (Amherst, MA: University of Massachusetts Press, 1994), 41.

6. David R. Mayer, *Network Machinists* (Baltimore: Johns Hopkins University Press, 2006).

7. Batchelder, *Introduction and Early Progress of the Cotton Manufacture in the United States*, 67. Also, Robert C. Winthrop, *Memoir of the Hon. Nathan Appleton L.L.D.* (Boston: John Wilson, 1861), 20–23.

8. John Amory Lowell, *Memoir of Patrick Tracy Jackson* (New York: Merchants' Magazine and Commercial Review, 1848).

9. Cathy Matson, *The Economy of Early America* (University Park: Pennsylvania State University Press, 2006), 269.

10. John Leander Bishop, *A History of American Manufactures from 1608 to 1860* (Philadelphia: Edward Young, 1864), 83, 123, 143, 187.

11. Ware's *Early New England Cotton Manufacture* shows that the large profits made from 1815 to 1818 by the Boston Manufacturing Company were not sustained. After 1820, the profit per yard of cloth hovered between two and four cents a yard. The lower profits were offset by lower prices of raw cotton and lower labor costs due to increased mechanization, greater productivity and stable wages.

12. Ware, *Early New England Cotton Manufacture*, 202–3.

13. Perry Walton, *The Story of Textiles* (Boston: John R. Lawrence, 1912).

14. Victor Selden Clark, *History of Manufactures in the United States, 1607–1860* (Washington, DC: Carnegie Institute of Washington, 1916), 395.

15. Walton, *The Story of Textiles*, 196.

16. Ware, *Early New England Cotton Manufacture*. The profitability of the Boston Manufacturing Company after 1820, despite the falling price of cloth "rested upon the exploitation of labor."

17. *The Waltham Mirror*, August 3 and December 14, 1848.

18. Appleton, *Introduction to the Power Loom*.

19. Clark, *History of Manufactures in the United States*, 438.

20. Douglass Cecil North, *The Economic Growth of the United States, 1790–1860* (New York: W. W. Norton, 1968), 160–61.

21. Clark, *History of Manufactures in the United States*, 450.

22. Isaac Holmes, *An Account of the United States of America* (London: Caxton Press, 1823), 189–97.

23. *Annual Report of the State Board of Conciliation and Arbitration for the Year ending December 31, 1904* (Boston: Wright & Potter, 1905), 151.

CHAPTER 12:
THE TARIFF OF 1816

1. George Tucker, *The Life of Thomas Jefferson, Third President of the United States* (Philadelphia: Carey, Lee & Blanchard, 1837), 368–69.

2. Cathy Matson (Ed.), *The Economy of Early America* (University Park: Pennsylvania State University Press, 2006), 269.

3. F. W. Taussig, *The Tariff History of the United States* (New York: G. P. Putnam's Sons, 1892).

4. Frederick William Coburn, *History of Lowell and Its People, Volume 3* (New York: Lewis Historical Publishing Company, 1920), 193.

5. St. Julien Ravenel, *Life and Times of William Lowndes of South Carolina, 1782–1822* (Boston: Houghton Mifflin, 1901), 151–53.

6. Douglas A. Blackman, *Slavery by Another Name: The Enslavement of Black Americans from the Civil War to World War II* (New York: Anchor, 2009).

7. Irving H. Bartlett, *John C. Calhoun: A Biography* (New York: W. W. Norton, 1993).

8. Maurice G. Baxter, *Henry Clay and the American System* (Lexington: University of Kentucky Press, 2004), 20.

9. Karl Schriftgiesser, *Lowell* (American Mercury, June 1927), 234–40.

10. John Caldwell Calhoun, *Life of John C. Calhoun: Presenting a Condensed History of Political Events from 1811 to 1843* (New York: Harper, 1843), 32–33.

11. Daniel Webster, *Webster's Speeches* (Boston: Athenaeum Press, 1897), 36.

12. Mary Caroline Crawford, *Famous Families of Massachusetts* (Boston: Little, Brown, 1930), 118.

13. Craig R. Smith, *Daniel Webster and the Oratory of Civil Religion* (Columbia: University of Missouri Press, 2005).

14. Merrill Paterson, *The Great Triumvirate: Webster, Clay and Calhoun* (New York: Oxford University Press, 1989), 96.

15. Smith, *Daniel Webster and the Oratory of Civil Religion*, 37.

16. Bishop, *A History of American Manufactures from 1608 to 1860*, 213.

17. Horace Greely, *Essays Designed to Elucidate the Science of Political Economy* (Boston: James R. Osgood & Company, 1875), 87; quotes from a speech of James Lloyd before the U.S. Senate, in 1822.

18. Tamara Plakins Thornton, *Cultivating Gentlemen: The Meaning of Country Life among the Boston Elite, 1785–1860* (New Haven, CT: Yale University Press, 1989), 130, 136–37.

19. Tyler Dennett, *Americans in Eastern Asia: A Critical Study of the Policy of the United States with Reference to China, Japan and Korea in the 19th Century* (New York: Macmillan, 1922), 27–28. Also, Susan S. Bean, *Yankee India: American Commercial and Cultural Encounters with India in the Age of Sail, 1784–1860* (2001), 175–93.

CHAPTER 13:
LEGACY

1. Waldo, *The Tour of James Monroe*, 160.

2. Details of the burial of the Lowell family at the Central Burying Grounds, Boston Common, were obtained from the City of Boston Parks Department. Details of the removal of the remains to Forest Hill were obtained from Elise Madeleine Ciregna, curator of history, archives and collections, Forest Hills Cemetery, Boston.

3. Details of the Francis Cabot Lowell estate can be found in the papers of Patrick Tracy Jackson the Massachusetts Historical Society (Call # Ms N-408) (Tall), Estate Papers, Series VI, Box 1, Volumes 51–53, folders 19–21. Francis Cabot Lowell's will is among his papers, also at the Massachusetts Historical Society, Box 9, N-1602.

4. Jack Trager, *Boston Riots: Three Centuries of Social Violence* (Boston: Northeastern University Press, 2000), 104–7, 120–23.

5. Edward Weeks, *The Lowells and Their Institute* (Boston: Little Brown, 1966).

6. Jean Renoir, *Renoir: My Father* (New York: New York Review of Books, 1962), 92–98.

7. Jason Whitman, *Memoir of the Rev. Bernard Whitman* (Boston: Benjamin H. Greene, 1837), 134–37.

8. Mary Gardner Lowell, *New Year in Cuba: Mary Gardner Lowell's Travel Diary, 1831–1832*, edited by Karen Robert (Hanover, NH: University Press of New England, 2003).

9. Ralph Waldo Emerson, *Journals of Ralph Waldo Emerson, Volume X, 1820–1878* (Boston: Houghton Mifflin, 1914), 432–35.

10. Abbot Lawrence Lowell, *Memoir of Edward Jackson Lowell* (Cambridge, MA: John Wilson and Son. 1895).

11. Francis Cabot Lowell, *Joan of Arc* (Boston: Houghton Mifflin, 1898).

12. *History of the Massachusetts Horticultural Society: 1829–1878* (Boston: Massachusetts Horticultural Society, 1880), 59.

13. Winsor, *The Memorial History of Boston*, 156.

14. *The Sale of the Property of the Late Uriah Cotting, Authorized by Thomas Dawes* (Boston: Broadsides, November 20, 1820). In the collection of the Massachusetts Historical Society.

15. A. Forbes and J. W. Greene, *The Rich Men of Massachusetts: Containing a Statement of the Reputed Wealth of about Fifteen Hundred Persons* (Boston: W. V. Spencer, 1851).

16. Arthur John Booth, *Robert Owen: The Founder of Socialism in England* (London: Trubner & Company, 1869), 17.

17. Ware, *Early New England Cotton Manufacture*, 111–12, 114. For the expansion of mills beyond Waltham, see Clark, *History of Manufactures in the United States*, 545.

18. Appleton, *The Power Loom*.

19. Perry Walton, *The Story of Textiles* (1912), 203.

20. *The North American Review, Volume 220* (Boston: John Munroe & Company, 1841), 49–50, and Harriet Hanson Robinson, *Loom and Spindle or Life among the Early Mill-Girls* (Boston: Thomas H. Crowell, 1898).

21. Karl Marx, *Capital: A Critique of Political Economy, Volume 2* (Chicago: Charles H. Kerr & Company, 1907), 603.

22. John S. Garner, *The Company Town: Architecture and Society in the Early Industrial Age* (New York: Oxford University Press, 1992), and James Montgomery, *A Practical Detail of the Cotton Manufacture of the United States of America* (Glasgow, Scotland: John Niven, 1840).

23. Charles C. P. Moody, *Biographical Sketches of the Moody Family* (Boston: Samuel G. Drake, 1847), 145–57.

24. John Haywood, *The Gazetteer of the United States of America* (Philadelphia: John Hayward, 1854).

25. Frederic Cople Jaher, *The Urban Establishment: Upper Strata in Boston, New York, Charleston, Chicago and Los Angeles* (Champaign: University of Illinois Press, 1982), 45–50.

26. Samuel Eliot Morison, *The Maritime History of Massachusetts, 1783–1860* (1921), 214.

27. John Hayward, *A Gazetteer of Massachusetts* (Boston: John Jewett, 1846), 382–86.

28. Robert H. Baird, *The American Cotton Spinners and Managers' and Carders' Guide* (Philadelphia: Henry Baird, 1863).

29. Bernard Shaw, *Major Barbara* (New York: Brentano's, 1917).

30. William Thomas Davis, *Bench and Bar in the Commonwealth of Massachusetts, Volume 1* (Boston: Boston History Company, 1895), 577.

Bibliography

Ames, H. V. *State Documents on Federal Relations: The States and the United States, Issue 6.* Philadelphia: University of Pennsylvania, 1906.

Appleton, N. *Introduction to the Power Loom and Origin of Lowell.* Lowell, MA: H. H. Penthallow, 1858.

Bagnall, W. R. *The Textile Industries of the United States.* Cambridge, MA: Riverside Press, 1893.

Bailey, S. L. *Historical Sketches of Andover (Comprising the Present Towns of North Andover and Andover), Massachusetts.* Boston: Houghton Mifflin, 1880.

Baines, E. *History of the Cotton Manufacture in Great Britain.* London: Fisher, Fisher & Jackson, 1835.

Baird, R. H. *The American Cotton Spinners' and Managers' and Carders' Guide.* Philadelphia: Henry Baird, 1863.

Bartlett, I. H. *John C. Calhoun: A Biography.* New York: W.W. Norton, 1993.

Bartol, C. A., and C. Lowell. *The West Church and Its Ministers: Fiftieth Anniversary of the Ordination of Charles Lowell D.D.* Boston: Crosby, Nichols and Company, 1856.

Batchelder, S. *Introduction and Early Progress of the Cotton Manufacture in the United States.* Boston: Little, Brown, 1863.

Bean, S. S. *Yankee India: American Commercial and Cultural Encounters with India in the Age of Sail, 1784–1860.* Salem, MA: Peabody Essex Museum, 2001.

Beveridge, A. J. *The Life of John Marshall, Volume 4.* Boston: Houghton Mifflin, 1919.

Biddle, A. *Old Family Letters.* Philadelphia: J. B. Lippincott Company, 1892.

Bishop, J. L. *A History of American Manufactures from 1630 to 1860.* Philadelphia: Edward Young, 1864.

Blackman, D. A. *Slavery by Another Name: The Enslavement of Black Americans from the Civil War to World War II.* New York: Anchor, 2009.

Blumberg, P. I. *The Multinational Challenge to Corporation Law: The Search for a New Corporate Personality.* New York: Oxford University Press, 1993.

Booth, A. J. *Robert Owen: The Founder of Socialism in England.* London: Trubner & Co, 1869.

Bridgman, T. *The Pilgrims and Their Descendants.* New York: D. Appleton & Company, 1856.

Brown, C. R. *The Northern Confederacy, According to the Plans of the Essex Junto, 1796–1814.* Princeton, NJ: Princeton University Press, 1915.

Brown, R. D., and J. Trager. *Massachusetts: A Concise History.* Amherst: University of Massachusetts Press, 2000.

Buel, R., Jr. *America on the Brink: How the Political Struggle over the War of 1812 Almost Destroyed the Young Republic.* New York: Palgrave Macmillan, 2005.

Bundy, C. *A Biography of Charles Russell Lowell Jr., 1835–64.* New York: Farrar, Straus & Giroux, 2005.

Burke, E. *List of Patents for Inventions and Designs, Issued by the United States from 1790 to 1847.* Washington, DC: 1847.

Calhoun, J. C. *Life of John C. Calhoun: Presenting a Condensed History of Political Events from 1811 to 1843.* New York: Harper, 1843.

Carr, J. B. *After the Siege: A Social History of Boston, 1775–1800.* Boston: Northeastern University Press, 2004.

Chown, J. F. *A History of Money: From AD 800.* New York: Routledge, 1994.

Clark, V. S. *History of Manufactures in the United States, 1607–1860.* Washington, DC: Carnegie Institute of Washington, 1916.

Clay, H., and D. Mallory. *The Life and Speeches of the Hon. Henry Clay.* Hartford, CT: Silas Andrus & Son, 1856.

Coburn, F. W. *History of Lowell and Its People, Volumes One, Two & Three.* New York: Lewis Historical Publishing Company, 1920.

Cochrane, W. W. *The Development of American Agriculture: A Historical Analysis.* Minneapolis: University of Minnesota Press, 1993.

Codman, J. *Arnold's Expedition to Quebec.* New York: Macmillan, 1901.

Coffin, J. *A Sketch of the History of Newbury, Newburyport and West Newbury from 1636 to 1845.* Boston: Samuel B Drake, 1845.

Commons, J. R. *History of Labor in the United States.* New York: Macmillan, 1921.

Cooke, G. W. *Unitarianism in America: A History of its Origins and Development.* Boston: American Unitarian Association, 1902.

Corbett, T. *The Making of American Resorts: Saratoga Springs, Ballston Spa, Lake George.* Piscataway, NJ: Rutgers University Press, 2001.

Cotton, E. *The Boston Directory.* Boston: Munroe & Francis, 1807.

Crawford, M. C. *Famous Families of Massachusetts.* Boston: Little, Brown. 1930.

Cunningham, J. T. *Specimens of Newspaper Literature.* Boston: Redding and Company, 1852.

Currier, J. J. *History of Newbury, Mass., 1635–1902.* Boston: Damrell & Upham, 1902.

———. *History of Newburyport, Mass., 1784–1905.* Newburyport, MA: Self-published, 1906.

Curtis, W. *And a Bottle of Rum: A History of the New World in Ten Cocktails.* New York: Random House, 2006.

Dalzell, R. F. *Enterprising Elite: The Boston Associates and the World They Made*. Cambridge, MA: Harvard University Press, 1987.

Daniels, G. W., and G. Unwin. *The Early English Cotton Industry: With Some Unpublished Letters of Samuel Crompton*. London: Longmans, 1920.

Davis, W. T. *The Professional and Industrial History of Suffolk County, Massachusetts*. Boston: The Boston History Company, 1891.

Dennett, T. *American in Eastern Asia: A Critical Study of the Policy of the United States with Reference to China, Japan and Korea in the 19th Century*. New York: Macmillan, 1922.

Dennis, M., W. Pencak, and S. P. Newman. *Riot and Revelry in Early America*. University Park: Pennsylvania State University Press, 2002.

Dexter, F. B. *Biographical Sketches of the Graduates of the College with Annals of the College History, Volume V, June 1792–September 1805*. New York: Henry Holt and Company, 1911.

Dickens, C. *American Notes for General Circulation*. London: Chapman, 1842.

Dow, G. F. *Every Day Life in the Massachusetts Bay Colony*. Boston: Society for the Preservation of New England Antiquities, 1935.

Drake, F. S. *The Town of Roxbury and Memorable Persons and Places*. Boston: Self-published, 1878.

Drake, S. A. *Old Boston Taverns and Tavern Club*s. Boston: W. A. Butterfield, 1917.

Duffy, J. J., S. B. Hand, and R. H. Orth. *The Vermont Encyclopedia*. Dartmouth, NH: University Press of New England, 2003.

Dwight, E., and M. W. Tileston. *Memorials of Mary Wilder White: A Century Ago in New England*. Boston: Everett Press, 1903.

Dwight, T. *Travels in New-England and New York*. New Haven, CT: Converse, 1821.

Eisenmann, L. *Historical Dictionary of Women's Education in the United States*. Westport, CT: Greenwood Press, 1998.

Emerson, R. W. *Journals of Ralph Waldo Emerson, Volume X: 1820–1878*. Boston: Houghton Mifflin, 1914.

Engels, F. *The Condition of the Working Class in England*. Stanford, CA: Stanford University Press, 1958.

Fearon, H. *Sketches of America*. London: Longman, 1816.

Fichter, J. R. *So Great a Profit: How the East Indies Trade Transformed Anglo-American Capitalism*. Cambridge, MA: Harvard University Press, 2010.

Fischer, D. H. *The Revolution of American Conservatism: The Federalist Party in the Era of Jeffersonian Democracy*. New York: Harper & Row, 1965.

Forbes, A., and J. W. Greene. *The Rich Men of Massachusetts: Containing a Statement of the Reputed Wealth of about Fifteen Hundred Person*. Boston: W. V. Spencer Publishers, 1851.

Ford, W. C. *Writings of John Quincy Adams, Volume 1, 1779–1796*. New York: Macmillan, 1913.

Foster, T. A. *Sex and the Eighteenth-Century Man: Massachusetts and the History of Sexuality in America*. Boston: Beacon Press, 2006.

Fuess, C. M. *An Old New England School*. Boston: Houghton Mifflin, 1917.

Garner, J. S. *The Company Town: Architecture and Society in the Early Industrial Age*. New York: Oxford University Press, 1992.

Grant, A. M. *Memoirs of an American Lady: With Sketches of Manners and Scenes.* New York: Dodd, Mead & Company, 1901.

Grant, J. F. *Memoir and Correspondence of Mrs. Grant of Laggan.* London: Longman, Brown, Green & Longmans, 1845.

Greeley, H. *Essays Designed to Elucidate the Science of Political Economy.* Boston: James R. Osgood & Company, 1875.

Greenslet, F. *The Lowells and Their Seven Worlds.* Boston: Houghton Mifflin, 1946.

Hall, P. P. *Napoleon's Troublesome Americans: Franco-American Relations, 1804–1814.* Dulles, VA: Potomac Books, 2005.

Hart, A. B. *Formation of the Union: 1750–1829.* New York: Longmans, Green, 1893.

Hayward, J. *A Gazetteer of Massachusetts.* Boston: John Hayward, 1846.

———. *The Gazetteer of the United States of America.* Philadelphia, 1854.

Hazen, C. D. *Contemporary American Opinion of the French Revolution.* Baltimore: John Hopkins Press, 1897.

Hesdin, R. *The Journal of a Spy in Paris during the Reign of Terror: January–June 1794.* London: John Murray, 1895.

Higginson, T. W. *Life and Times of Stephen Higginson, Member of the Continental Congress.* Boston: Houghton Mifflin, 1907.

Hirshleifer, J., A. Glazer, and D. Hirshleifer. *Price Theory and Applications: Decisions, Markets and Information.* New York: Cambridge University Press, 2005.

Holmes, I. *An Account of the United States of America.* London: Caxton Press, 1823.

Hopkins, J. P., and R. Seager (Eds.). *The Papers of Henry Clay.* Lexington: University of Kentucky Press, 1981.

Howe, M. A. DeW. *Boston: The Place and the People.* New York: Macmillan, 1903.

Hunnewell, J. F. *A Century of Town Life: A History of Charlestown, Massachusetts; 1775–1887.* Boston: Little, Brown, 1888.

Inikori, J. C., and S. L. Engerman. *The Atlantic Slave Trade.* Durham, NC: Duke University Press, 1992.

Jackson, J. *Hon. Jonathan Jackson, His Wife and Many Members of His Family.* Boston: Alfred Mudge & Son, 1866.

Jaher, F. C. *The Urban Establishment: Upper Strata in Boston, New York, Charleston, Chicago and Los Angeles.* Champaign: University of Illinois Press, 1982.

Kerr, M. *Manufacturing Industries in America.* New York: Ronald Press, 1920.

Knapp, S. L. *The Life of Aaron Burr, Volume 4.* New York: Wiley & Long, 1835.

Knowles, L. C. A. *The Industrial and Commercial Revolutions in Great Britain during the Nineteenth-Century.* London: George Routledge & Sons, 1921.

Laurence, K. O. *Tobago in Wartime, 1793–1815.* Kingston, Jamaica: Press of the University of the West Indies, 1995.

Lawrence, R. M. *Old Park Street and Its Vicinity.* Boston: Houghton Mifflin, 1922.

Lodge, H. C. *Life and Letters of George Cabot.* Boston: Little, Brown, 1878.

Lossing, B. J. *The Pictorial Field-book of the War of 1812.* New York: Harper & Brothers, 1869.

Lowell, C. *Sermons Chiefly Occasional.* Boston: Ticknor & Fields, 1855.

———. *Sermons Chiefly Practical.* Boston: Ticknor & Fields, 1855.

Lowell, D. R. *The Historic Genealogy of the Lowells of America from 1639–1899.* Rutland, VT: Tuttle, 1899.

Lowell, E. J. *The Eve of the French Revolution.* Boston: Houghton Mifflin, 1893.

Lowell, F. C. *Joan of Arc.* Boston: Houghton Mifflin, 1898.

Lowell, J., Jr. *An Oration Pronounced July 4, 1799, at the Request of the Inhabitants of the Town of Boston.* Boston: Manning & Loring, 1799.

—— (A Yankee Farmer). *Peace without Dishonour—War without Hope.* Boston: G. Stebbins, 1807.

——. *The New England Patriot.* Boston: Russell and Cutler, 1810.

——. *Perpetual War: The Policy of Mr. Madison.* Boston: G. Stebbins, 1813.

Lowell, J. A. *Memoir of Patrick Tracy Jackson.* Press of Hunt's Merchants' Magazine, 1848.

Lowell, M. G. *New Year in Cuba: Mary Gardner Lowell's Travel Dairy, 1831–1832.* Edited by Karen Robert. Hanover, NH: University Press of New England, 2003.

Lyons, M. *Napoleon Bonaparte and the Legacy of the French Revolution.* New York: St. Martins Press, 1994.

Macdonald, W. (Ed.). *Select Documents Illustrative of the History of the United States, 1776–1861.* New York: Macmillan, 1898.

Magnone, G. J. *United States Admiralty Law.* The Hague, The Netherlands: Kluwer Law International, 1997.

Man, T. *Picture of a Factory Village.* Providence, RI: Self-published, 1833.

Mann, A. W. *Walks & Talks about Historic Boston.* Boston: Mann Publishing Company, 1917.

Manning, E. *A History of the United States: Federalists and Republicans, 1789–1815, Volume 4.* New York: Macmillan, 1917.

Mantoux, P. *The Industrial Revolution in the Eighteenth Century: An Outline of the Beginnings of the Modern Factory System in England.* Abingdon, Oxon: Routledge, 2006.

Marcus, M., and J. R. Perry. *The Documentary History of the Supreme Court of the United States, 1780–1800, Volume One, Part Two.* New York: Columbia University Press, 1985.

Marx, K. *Capital: A Critique of Political Economy, Volume 2.* Chicago: Charles H. Kerr and Company, 1907.

Matson, C. D. (Ed.). *The Economy of Early America.* University Park: Pennsylvania State Press, 2006.

Mayer, D. R. *Network Machinists.* Baltimore: Johns Hopkins University Press, 2006.

McMurtie, W. *Report on the Culture of the Sugar Beet and the Manufacture of Sugar therefrom in France and the United States,* Washington, DC: Government Printing Office, 1880.

Mencken, H. L. (Ed.). *American Mercury Magazine.* May–August 1927, Kessinger Publications, 2003.

Mitchell, B. *The Rise of the Cotton Mills in the South.* Baltimore: Johns Hopkins, 1921.

Monaghan, E. J. *Learning to Read and Write in Colonial America.* Amherst: University of Massachusetts Press, 2005.

Montgomery, J. *A Practical Detail of the Cotton Manufacture of the United States of America.* Glasgow, Scotland: John Niven, 1840.

Moody, C. C. P. *Biographical Sketches of the Moody Family.* Boston: Samuel G. Drake, 1847.

Morse, F. R. *Henry and Mary Lee: Letters and Journals with Other Family Letters, 1802–1860.* Boston: Privately published by their granddaughter, 1926.

Morse, J. T. *Memoir of Colonel Henry Lee with Selections from His Writings and Speeches.* Boston: Little, Brown, 1905.

———. *John Quincy Adams.* Boston: Houghton Mifflin, 1898.

Morison, S. E. *The Life and Letters of Harrison Gray Otis, Federalist, 1765–1848, Volumes 1 & 2.* Boston: Houghton Mifflin, 1913.

———. *The Maritime History of Massachusetts, 1783–1860.* Boston: Houghton Mifflin, 1922.

Morse, S. F. B. *Samuel F. B. Morse: His Letters and Journals.* Edited by E. L. Morse. Boston: Houghton Mifflin, 1914.

Nason, E. *A Memoir of Mrs. Susanna Rowson: With Elegant and Illustrative Extracts from Her Writings in Prose and Poetry.* Albany, NY: Joel Munsell, 1878.

Nelson, C. A. *Waltham, Past and Present, and Its Industries.* Cambridge, MA: Moses King, 1882.

North, D. C. *The Economic Growth of the United States, 1790–1860.* New York: Prentice Hall, 1961.

Paine R. D. *The Ships and Sailors of Old Salem.* New York: Cotting Publishing Co., 1908.

Palfrey, J. G. *History of New England.* Boston: Little, Brown, 1890.

Palmer, B. W., ed. *A Woman's Wit and Whimsy: The 1833 Diary of Anna Cabot Lowell Quincy.* Boston: Northeastern University Press, 2003.

Park, J. *An Address to the Citizens of Massachusetts: On the Causes and Remedy of Our National Distress.* Boston: Repertory Office, 1808.

Paterson, M. *The Great Triumvirate: Webster, Clay and Caljoun.* New York: Oxford University Press, 1989.

Peabody, R. E. *Merchant Ventures of Old Salem.* Boston: Houghton Mifflin, 1912.

Pearson, G. W. *Records of the Massachusetts Volunteer Militia.* Boston: Wright & Potter, 1913.

Perry, W. S. *The History of the American Episcopal Church, 1587–1883.* James R. Osgood & Company, 1885.

Phillips, C. H. *The East India Company; 1784–1834.* London: Routledge, 1998.

Porter, K. W. *The Jacksons and the Lees: Two Generations of Massachusetts' Merchants, 1765–1844.* Cambridge, MA: Harvard University Press, 1937.

Proceedings of the City of Lowell at the Semi-Centennial Celebration of the Incorporation of the City of Lowell. Lowell, MA: Penhallow Printing, 1876.

Putnam, J. J. *A Memoir of Dr. James Jackson.* Boston: Houghton Mifflin, 1906.

Quincy, J. *The History of Harvard University.* Cambridge, MA: John Owen, 1840.

———. *The History of the Boston Athenaeum.* Cambridge, MA: Metcalf and Company, 1851.

Ravenel, S. J. *Life and Times of William Lowndes of South Carolina, 1782–1822.* Boston: Houghton Mifflin, 1901.

Robinson, H. H. *Loom and Spindle or Life among the Early Mill-Girls.* Boston: Thomas Y. Crowell, 1898.

Rochefoucauld-Liancourt, F. A. F. *Travels through the United States of America: The Country of the Iroquois.* London: R. Phillips, 1800.

Records of the Vice Admiralty Court, Nova Scotia. American Vessels Captured by the British During the Revolutionary War and the War of 1812. Salem, MA: Essex Institute, 1911.

Remini, R. V. *Daniel Webster: The Man and His Time*. New York: W.W. Norton, 1997.

Renoir, J. *Renoir: My Father*. Boston: Little, Brown, 1962.

Ritchie, J. G. *Two Carpenters: Architecture and Building in Early New England, 1799–1859*. Knoxville: University of Tennessee Press, 2006.

Robinson, H., and J. T. Shotwell. *The Development of the British Empire*. Boston: Houghton Mifflin, 1922.

Ryan, D. M. *Concord and the Dawn of Revolution: The Hidden Truths*. Charleston, SC: The History Press, 2007.

Scudder, H. E. *James Russell Lowell: A Biography, Volume 1*. Boston: Houghton Mifflin, 1901.

Seasholes, N. *Gaining Ground: A History of Landmaking in Boston*. Cambridge, MA: MIT Press, 2003.

Shaw, B. *Major Barbara*. New York: Brentano's, 1917.

Smith, C. R. *Daniel Webster and the Oratory of Civil Religion*. Columbia: University of Missouri Press, 2005.

Smith, E. V. *The History of Newburyport from the Earliest Settlement of the Country to the Present Time*. Newburyport, MA: Self-published, 1854.

Smith, H. K. *The History of the Lowell Institute*. Boston: Lamsen, Wolffe and Company, 1898.

Stark, J. H. *The Loyalists of Massachusetts and the Others Side of the American Revolution*. Boston: Self-published, 1910.

Steinberg, T. *Nature Incorporated*. Amherst: University of Massachusetts Press, 1994.

Stone, E. M. *History of Beverly, Civil and Ecclesiastical from Its Settlement in 1630 till 1842*. Boston: James Munroe and Company, 1843.

Sullivan, W. *Familiar Letters on Public Characters, and Public Events, From the Peace of 1783 to the Peace of 1815*. Boston: Russell, Odiorne & Metcalf, 1834.

Taussig, F. W. *The Tariff History of the United States*. New York: G. P. Putnam's Sons, 1892.

Thackeray, W. M. *Vanity Fair*. London, 1848.

Thiers, A. *History of the Consulate and the Empire of France under Napoleon*. London: Willis & Sothern, 1857.

Thoreau, H. D. *Walden, or, Life in the Woods*. New York: Dutton, 1908.

Thornton, T. P. *Cultivating Gentlemen: The Meaning of Country Life among the Boston Elite, 1785–1860*. New Haven, CT: Yale University Press, 1989.

Thwing A. H. *The Crooked and Narrow Streets of the Town of Boston, 1630–1822*. Boston: Marshall Jones Company, 1925.

Tompkins, D. D. *Public Papers of Daniel D. Tompkins, Governor of New York, 1807–1817, Military—Volume 1*. New York: Wynkoop Hallenbeck Crawford Company, 1898.

Tracy, A. B. *Reminiscences of John Bromfield*. Salem, MA: Self-published, 1852.

Trager, J. *Boston Riots: Three Centuries of Social Violence*. Boston: Northeastern University Press, 2000.

Trollope, A. *North America*. New York: Harper & Brothers, 1862.

Tucker, G. *The Life of Thomas Jefferson, Third President of the United States*. Philadelphia: Carey, Lee & Blanchard, 1837.

Varney, G. J. *A Gazetteer of the State of Maine*. Boston: B. B. Russell, 1881.

Waldo, S. P. *The Tour of James Monroe, President of the United States though the Northern and Eastern States, 1817, Second Edition.* Hartford, CT: Silus Andrus, 1820.

Walton, P. *The Story of Textiles.* Boston: John R. Lawrence Publishers, 1912.

Wansey, H. *An Excursion to the United States of North America, in the Summer of 1794.* Salisbury, UK: J. Easton, 1798.

Ware, C. F. *The Early New England Cotton Manufacture: A Study in Industrial Beginnings.* New York: Russell & Russell, 1966.

Ware, L. S. *The Sugar Beet: Including the History of the Beet Sugar Industry in Europe.* Philadelphia: Henry Carey Baird, 1880.

Washington, G. *The Diary of George Washington, from 1789 to 1791.* Edited by Benson J. Lossing. Richmond, VA: Press of the Historical Society, 1861.

Webster, D. *Webster's Speeches.* Boston: Athenaeum Press, 1897.

Weeks, E. *The Lowells and Their Institute.* Boston: Little, Brown, 1966.

Whitman, J. *Memoir of the Rev. Bernard Whitman.* Boston: Benjamin H. Greene Publisher, 1837.

Willis, W. *A History of the Law, the Courts and the Lawyers of Maine.* Portland, ME: Bailey & Noyes, 1863.

Wimeth, D. B., and C. W. E. Bigsby. *The Cambridge History of American Theatre.* New York: Cambridge University Press, 1993.

Winsor, J. *The Memorial History of Boston, including Suffolk County, Massachusetts, 1630–1880.* Boston: James R. Osgood & Company, 1881.

Winthrop, R. C. *Memoir of the Hon. Nathan Appleton L.L.D.* Boston: John Wilson, 1861.

Wood, F. J. *The Turnpikes of New England.* Boston: Marshall Jones Company, 1919.

Wood, G. S. *Empire of Liberty: A History of the Early Republic, 1789–1815.* New York: Oxford University Press, 2009.

Zonderman, D. A. *Aspirations and Anxieties: New England Workers & the Mechanized Factory System.* New York: Oxford University Press, 1992.

Index